West Coast Australia

**Broome &
the Kimberley**
p205

**Ningaloo Coast
& the Pilbara**
p183

**Monkey Mia
& the
Central West**
p165

Around Perth
p96

Perth & Fremantle ◉
p50

**Margaret River & the
Southwest Coast**
p121

Southern WA
p147

FEB   2018

Brett Atkinson
Carolyn Bain, Steve Waters

PLAN YOUR TRIP

ON THE ROAD

BEN CLARK / 500PX ©

SPLENDID FAIRY WREN,
CAPE NATURALISTE, P129

PAUL MARSHALL / 500PX ©

WINDJANA GORGE, P223

Contents

Welcome to West Coast Australia

If you subscribe to the 'life's a beach' school of thought, you'll fall in love with Western Australia and its 12,500km of spectacular coastline.

An Immense, Sparsely Populated Land

If the huge expanses of Western Australia (WA) were a separate nation, it would be the world's 10th-largest country. Most of the state's population clings to the coast – yet you can wander along a beach for hours without seeing another footprint, or be one of a handful of campers stargazing in a national park.

The south is a playground of white-sand beaches, expanses of springtime wildflowers and lush green forests teeming with life. Up north in the Kimberley, you'll encounter wide open spaces that conceal striking gorges, waterfalls and ancient rock formations.

Action Stations

WA has plenty for the active traveller. Traverse the 963km Bibbulmun Track or focus on spectacular day walks including sections of the Cape to Cape Track around stunning Cape Naturaliste. Equally interesting walks include wandering amid the wildflowers of the Stirling Range National Park and negotiating Porongurup's granite formations. On two wheels, options include mountain biking through the forests of Margaret River or negotiating the 1000km Munda Biddi Trail. Dive and snorkel in marine parks and around shipwrecks, surf around Margaret River, or kitesurf and windsurf off Lancelin's expansive beaches.

All Creatures Great & Small

WA's fauna includes kangaroos, emus and colourful parrots, and there are also chances to get acquainted with lesser-known local critters such as quokkas, bilbies and potoroos. The WA coast's lengthy dalliance with the Indian and Southern Oceans means opportunities to spot marine wildlife are also extraordinary. Each year about 30,000 whales cruise the coast-hugging 'Humpback Hwy', and at Bremer Bay, there is the opportunity to see orcas. At Ningaloo Marine Park you can dive with the world's largest fish, the whale shark, while at Rockingham, Bunbury and Monkey Mia you can interact with wild dolphins.

The Finer Things in Life

Perth and neighbouring Fremantle are cosmopolitan cities, yet both retain a laid-back feel courtesy of their fantastic beaches and parks. Bold infrastructure projects are transforming central Perth, while the inner neighbourhoods of Northbridge and Leederville are oozing culinary confidence. Elsewhere, earlier boom times have left grand architectural legacies in Fremantle, Albany, Guildford and York.

Around Margaret River and the southwest, vignerons and brewers craft world-class wines and beers, complemented by the inventive menus of the region's restaurants. Truffles are grown down south, and WA's seafood is consistently sublime.

Why I Love West Coast Australia

By Brett Atkinson, Writer

Perth's pride at being the world's most remote capital is reflected in the verve and independence of the locals, and I love exploring the state's culinary scene, which combines great wine, excellent beer, farmers markets and local produce. Fremantle's historic townscape is worth multiple leisurely explorations, and it's just a short hop out to Rottnest Island. Edging the southern fringes of the cobalt Indian Ocean, the coastline around Cape Naturaliste and Margaret River offers spectacular walking opportunities, and the elemental red dirt and ocean landscapes to the far north are equally stunning.

For more about our writers, see p288

Above: Hellfire Bay, Cape Le Grand National Park (p164)

West Coast Australia

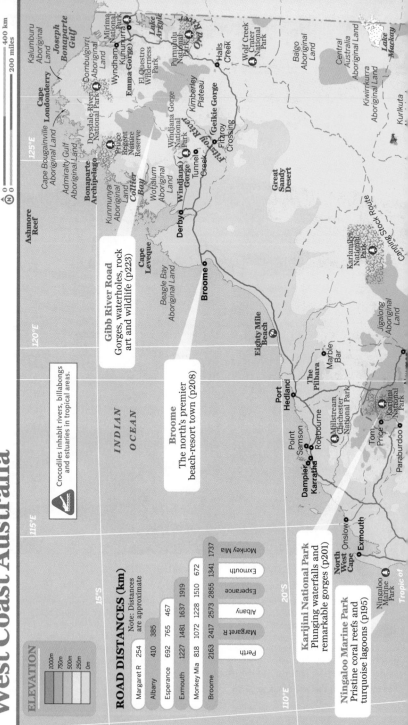

ELEVATION

1000m
750m
500m
250m
0m

ROAD DISTANCES (km)

Note: Distances are approximate

	Perth	Margaret R	Albany	Esperance	Exmouth	Monkey Mia
Margaret R	254					
Albany	410	385				
Esperance	692	765	467			
Exmouth	1227	1481	1637	1919		
Monkey Mia	818	1072	1228	1510	672	
Broome	2163	2417	2573	2855	1341	1737

Crocodiles inhabit rivers, billabongs and estuaries in tropical areas.

INDIAN OCEAN

Gibb River Road
Gorges, waterholes, rock art and wildlife (p223)

Broome
The north's premier beach-resort town (p208)

Karijini National Park
Plunging waterfalls and remarkable gorges (p201)

Ningaloo Marine Park
Pristine coral reefs and turquoise lagoons (p195)

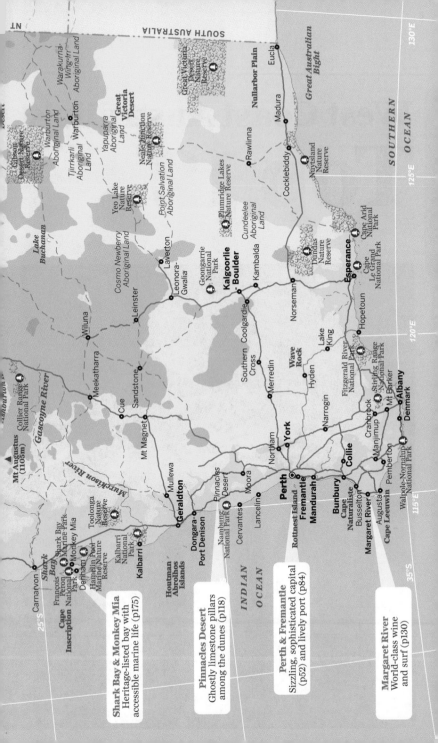

West Coast Australia's
Top 12

Ningaloo Marine Park

1 Swim beside 'gentle giant' whale sharks, snorkel among pristine coral, surf off seldom-visited reefs and dive at one of the world's premier locations at this World Heritage–listed marine park (p195), which sits off the North West Cape on the Coral Coast. Rivalling the Great Barrier Reef for beauty, Ningaloo has much more accessible wonders: shallow, turquoise lagoons are entered straight from the beach for excellent snorkelling. Development is very low-key, so be prepared to camp, or take day trips from the access towns of Exmouth and Coral Bay.

Margaret River Wine Region

2 The joy of drifting from winery to craft brewery along country roads shaded by tall gum trees is just one of the delights of Australia's most beautiful wine region (p130). Right on its doorstep are the white sands of Geographe Bay, and even closer to the vines are the world-famous surf breaks of Yallingup and Margaret River Mouth. And then there are the caves – magical subterranean palaces of limestone, scattered along the main wine-tasting route. Sup, swim, surf, descend – the only difficulty is picking the order.

MIGRATION MEDIA – UNDERWATER IMAGING / GETTY IMAGES ©

2

CATHERINE SUTHERLAND / LONELY PLANET ©

BLOCK 6 SAUV BLANC 1

Shark Bay & Monkey Mia

3 The aquamarine waters of World Heritage–listed Shark Bay (pictured; p175) teem with an incredible diversity of marine life, from the world-famous dolphins of Monkey Mia to the ancient stromatolites of Hamelin Pool. National parks provide simple coastal camping, and excellent Indigenous cultural tours explain how to care for and understand 'Country'. Explore remote, wind-blown Edel Land, Australia's westernmost tip, with towering limestone cliffs; cross over to historically rich Dirk Hartog Island; or relax, lie back and sail after the elusive, sea-grass-munching dugong.

Pinnacles Desert

4 It could be mistaken for the surface of Mars, but scattered among the dunes of Nambung National Park, thousands of ghostly limestone pillars rise from the surrounding plain like a vast, petrified alien army. One of Western Australia's most bizarre landscapes, the Pinnacles (p118) attract thousands of visitors each year. Although it's easily enjoyed as a day trip from Perth, staying overnight in nearby Cervantes allows for multiple visits to experience the full spectrum of colour changes at dawn, sunset and full moon, when most tourists are back in their hotels.

FRANCESCO RICCARDO IACOMINO / 500PX ©

SEAN FARROW / 500PX ©

Perth & Fremantle

5 Perth may be isolated, but it's far from being a backwater. Scattered across the city (p52) are sophisticated restaurants showcasing modern Australian cuisine, while chic cocktail bars bubble away in unlikely lanes and restored heritage buildings. In contrast to the flashy face that Perth presents to the river, charmingly grungy inner suburbs echo with the hum of guitars and turntables, and the sizzle of woks. Just downstream, the lively port of Fremantle has a pub on just about every corner, most pouring craft brews from around Western Australia and the world. Above: Standard bar, (p77), Perth

Broome

6 You can moan about the price of beer or how long your twice-cooked pork belly takes to arrive, but one thing is for certain: when that boiling crimson sun starts sinking slowly behind a conga-line of camels into a languid Indian Ocean at Cable Beach (pictured; p209), you'll realise there's no other place like it in the world. Broome (p208) is a melting pot of travellers, one of the world's great crossroads, and you'll find everything you need (though perhaps not everything you want) in the backstreets, bars and markets, and on the noticeboards.

Karijini National Park

7 Hidden deep in the heart of the Pilbara, the shady pools and plunging waterfalls of Karijini (p201) offer cool respite from the oppressive heat of the surrounding ironstone country. While most tourists are content to explore the open gorges, booking an adventure trip will take you beyond the public areas as you abseil, swim, dive, climb and paddle through deep water-worn passages. Up top, witness the amazing spring transformation as wildflowers carpet the plains, and get some altitude on the state's highest peaks, including the most excellent, Mt Bruce (Punurrunha; 1235m). Above: Hancock Gorge (p202)

DANITA DELIMONT / GETTY IMAGES ©

Water Adventures

8 If you can't catch a wave on WA's 12,000km of coastline, mate, you're doing it wrong. In which case, head straight to one of the many surf schools and leave Margaret River and Gnaraloo to the pros, where breaks with nicknames such as 'Suicides' and 'Tombstones' beckon the fearless. Diving and snorkelling are excellent in many spots, and WA is the place to swim with your favourite marine animal. Windsurfers breeze off to gusty Lancelin and Geraldton, while paddlers splash their way along the many rivers. Above: Kitesurfing on a beach just outside Fremantle (p84)

Bushwalking

9 WA has 96 national parks, not counting the dozens of other nature reserves and regional parks. These special places present oodles of opportunities to go walkabout on the many way-marked trails, and camp in isolated spots. The Bibbulmun Track (p155), the mother of them all, starts on the outskirts of Perth and heads nearly 1000km to Albany on the south coast, sheltered by the cooling giant eucalypts of the southern forests. At the Valley of the Giants you can walk through the canopy on the 40m-high Tree Top Walk (pictured, p149).

Gibb River Road

10 Launch yourself into Australia's last frontier on a wild drive down this old cattle road (p223) into the heart of the Kimberley. This is not for the faint-hearted; you'll need a serious 4WD, good planning and plenty of fuel, spares, food and water. Bring big doses of self-reliance, flexibility and humour. The rewards are fantastic gorges, hidden waterholes, incredible rock art and amazing wildlife, and you'll gain a first-hand insight into life in the outback. Did we mention there are also flies, dust and relentless heat?

Wildlife

11 Welcome to an idiosyncratic state-wide menagerie of wonderful species, many of which you may not have even heard of. Visit the endangered numbats, woylies, bilbies and boodies of the Dryandra Woodland, the quokkas of Rottnest Island or the freshwater crocodiles of Windjana Gorge National Park. Avian species include the migratory shorebirds of Parry Lagoons Nature Reserve, and the beautiful red-tailed tropic birds of WA's southwest coast. Oceanic attractions include migrating humpback whales and orcas, the dolphins of Monkey Mia and the awe-inspiring whale sharks of Ningaloo Reef.

Indigenous Art

12 From urban galleries showcasing contemporary artists to centuries-old rock carvings, the culture and spirit of Indigenous Western Australia potently infuses this land. In Perth and Fremantle, visit the excellent Indigenart and Japingka galleries, while in the far northern reaches of the Kimberley visit local art cooperatives such as Waringarri or Mowanjum before looking back across the aeons at the Wandjina and Gwion Gwion rock-art sites.

11

12

Need to Know

For more information, see Survival Guide (p259)

Currency
Australian dollar ($)

Language
English

Visas
All visitors require a visa, although New Zealanders receive one on arrival. Residents of Canada, the US, many European countries and some Asian countries can apply online (p268).

Money
Bank branches with 24-hour ATMs can be found statewide.

Mobile Phones
Australia's mobile networks (p14) service more than 90% of the population; Telstra has the best coverage, especially in the more remote north.

Time
Western Standard Time (GMT/UTC plus eight hours). Daylight saving does not operate in WA.

When to Go

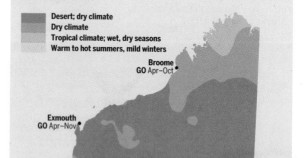

Desert; dry climate
Dry climate
Tropical climate; wet, dry seasons
Warm to hot summers, mild winters

Broome
GO Apr–Oct

Exmouth
GO Apr–Nov

Monkey Mia
GO Sep–Mar

Perth
GO Sep–Mar

Margaret River
GO Oct–Mar

High Season (Dec–Mar)

➡ In the south the weather is at its hottest and driest.

➡ The season peaks from Christmas until the end of the school holidays in January.

➡ In the north, this is the wet (low) season.

Shoulder (Apr, May & Sep–Nov)

➡ Wildflowers bloom from September.

➡ The best months to visit the north.

➡ Humpback whales from September to November, whale sharks from April to June. Monkey Mia's dolphins are seen throughout the year.

Low Season (Jun–Aug)

➡ Wettest and coolest time in Perth and the south.

➡ Lows in the south usually over 10°C.

➡ High season for the Coral Coast, the Pilbara, Broome and the Kimberley; dry and usually above 30°C.

Useful Websites

Department of Parks & Wildlife (www.parks.dpaw. wa.gov.au) Details on the state's national parks. Some camp sites can be prebooked.

Lonely Planet (www. lonelyplanet.com/australia) Destination information, traveller forum and more.

Tourism Australia (www. australia.com) Transport, event and destination information.

Tourism Western Australia (www.westernaustralia.com) Official tourism site.

West Australian (www.thewest. com.au) Online version of the newspaper.

Important Numbers

Drop the zero from the area code when calling from outside Australia (ie +61-8). If you're calling a WA number while in WA, you can drop the 08 prefix.

International access code	☑0011
Australia's country code	☑61
WA area code	☑08
Emergency (police, fire, ambulance)	☑000
Directory assistance	☑12455

Exchange Rates

Canada	C$1	$0.98
Euro	€1	$1.49
Japan	¥100	$1.21
New Zealand	NZ$1	$0.96
UK	£1	$1.72
USA	US$1	$1.33

For current exchange rates, see www.xe.com.

Daily Costs

Budget: Less than $150

➡ Camp site (two people): $25–30

➡ Dorm bed: $30–50

➡ Private double room in hostel: $80–120

Midrange: $150–300

➡ Double room in a midrange hotel: $150–220

➡ Lunch and dinner in cafes and pubs: $70

➡ Car hire: $40–50 per day

Top End: More than $300

➡ Main meal in top restaurants: over $35

➡ Double room in a top hotel: from $250

Opening Hours

Outside Perth, shops may not open on weekends. Vineyard and craft-brewery restaurants usually open only for lunch, while many cafes also open later for dinner. Most central-city stores in Perth and major shopping malls open seven days a week.

Banks 9.30am–4pm Monday to Thursday, 9.30am–5pm Friday, some open Saturday morning

Cafes 7am–4pm

Pubs 11am–midnight

Restaurants noon–midnight

Shops 9am–5.30pm Monday to Thursday, 9am–9pm Friday, 9am–5pm Saturday, 11am–5pm Sunday

Arriving in West Coast Australia

Perth Airport (p271) The Connect Shuttle runs every 50 minutes to five convenient and central locations in Perth ($15). A taxi is about $40 to $45 to central Perth and $60 to $70 to Fremantle. Buses run every 10 to 30 minutes to the city, hourly after 7pm; journey time is 44 minutes.

Getting Around

The distances between key WA towns are vast, especially in the north.

Rental Car Ideal for attraction-packed areas such as Margaret River. Where distances are huge, combine flying with local car rental.

Airlines Cover WA's huge distances quickly. Consider flying from Perth to Esperance, Exmouth or Broome, and then renting a car locally if your focus is these areas.

Train A good option for day trips from Perth to Mandurah and Rockingham. Regular trains make Fremantle a worthwhile base for exploring Perth.

Bus Relatively frequent between most traveller hot spots. Good links from Perth to Margaret River and the southwest, and north to Geraldton and Exmouth.

Public Transport Perth and Fremantle have excellent urban bus and train networks. Central Area Transit (CAT) bus services are free.

For much more on **getting around**, see p272

What's New

Elizabeth Quay
Perth's riverfront is enlivened with new public spaces, cafes, restaurants and hotels at this development linking the Swan River with the city centre. (p53)

Little Ferry Co
Explore the Swan River on this electric-powered ferry running between Perth's Elizabeth Quay and Claisebrook Cove. (p63)

State Buildings
An elegant makeover of this heritage precinct in central Perth houses stylish restaurants (p71) and bars (p75), and one of the world's finest new hotels (p68).

Humpback Whale Interaction at Ningaloo
In 2016, tour operators began offering visitors to Ningaloo Marine Park the opportunity to swim and interact with humpback whales. At the time of writing this trial was expected to continue into the 2017 visitor season. (p187)

Perth Stadium
From early 2018, Perth's new riverfront stadium will host AFL, international rugby and the city's biggest concerts. (p80)

Bathers Beach Art Precinct
Heritage cottages and warehouses in Fremantle are being repurposed as galleries and studios. (p87)

Margaret River Craft Beer
The region's beer scene continues to develop with new openings including the Beer Farm (p131), the Brewhouse (p139) and hoppy excursions with Margaret River Brewery Tours (p130).

Albany's Spectacular New Viewing Platform
Experience the incredible energy of the Southern Ocean from this vertiginous viewing platform in Torndirrup National Park near Albany. (p157)

Walk on the Ocean Floor at Busselton
At the end of Busselton's famed jetty, don special underwater breathing gear to walk on the ocean floor amid the 150-year-old timber piles of this 1841m heritage structure. (p126)

Orcas at Bremer Bay
From late January to mid-April take a tour with Bremer Canyon Killer Whale Expeditions to see orcas feeding amid the deep and nutrient-rich waters of the Bremer Canyon. (p160)

Adventure & Snorkelling at Jurien Bay
New options to enjoy this sleepy holiday settlement 2½ hours north of Perth include sandboarding and 4WD tours with Jurien Bay Adventure Tours (p119) and negotiating a well-marked underwater snorkelling trail (p119).

Kalbarri National Park
Improvements from late 2017 include a fully sealed road to Nature's Window and the Z-Bend, plus trails, a new 'Skywalk', and interpretive signage. (p174)

For more recommendations and reviews, see lonelyplanet.com/western-australia

If You Like...

Beaches

Western Australia (WA) has some of Australia's finest beaches, and you'll have many of them completely to yourself.

Cottesloe Perth's most iconic beach, with cafes and bars close at hand. (p57)

Bunker Bay Brilliant white sand edged by bushland; you'll have to look hard to spot the few houses scattered about. (p129)

Hellfire Bay Sand like talcum powder in the middle of Cape Le Grand National Park, which is precisely in the middle of nowhere. (p164)

Shark Bay Fifteen hundred kilometres of remote beaches and towering limestone cliffs. (p175)

Turquoise Bay A beautiful bay in Ningaloo Marine Park, with wonderful snorkelling. (p196)

William Bay National Park Sheltered swimming around the granite boulders of Greens Pool and Elephant Rocks. (p150)

Cable Beach Surely the most famous, camel-strewn, sunset-photographed beach in WA. (p209)

Cape Leveque Red cliffs and superlative sunsets on the Dampier Peninsula. (p219)

Diving & Snorkelling

Reefs and wrecks are plentiful around WA and the marine life is lush, providing a smorgasbord of options for geared-up diving pros or gung-ho first-time snorkellers.

Mettams Pool Excellent snorkelling within Perth's city limits. (p57)

Rottnest Island Over a dozen wrecks and two underwater snorkelling trails make this an excellent option. (p99)

Busselton Lots to see around the southern hemisphere's longest timber jetty, plus the wreck of a decommissioned navy destroyer not far away. (p126)

Albany Look for sea dragons among the coral reefs. (p155)

Houtman Abrolhos Islands Dive, snorkel, bushwalk or fish around these historic islands, which rarely see tourists. (p173)

Surfing & Windsurfing

Wax the board and fire up the Kombi van: WA's surfing is legendary.

Trigg Beach Perth's surfers come here straight from work to catch a few waves. (p57)

Lancelin A mecca for windsurfers and kitesurfers, and a great spot to learn. (p116)

Yallingup/Margaret River 'Yals' and 'Margs' are the hub of the WA surf scene – with a major pro competition held there every year. (p133)

Ocean Beach, Denmark You might find yourself sharing this beautiful bay with whales. (p150)

Geraldton The surrounding beaches are thrilling for both wind- and wave-powered surfers. (p168)

Gnaraloo Surfers flock here in winter to try their luck at the famous Tombstones break; in summer the windsurfers take their place. (p182)

Walking Trails

The state's dozens of national parks are crisscrossed with hundreds of walking tracks, heading along the coast, beneath forests, through gorges and up mountains.

Bibbulmun Track The big one – stretching nearly 1000km from the edge of Perth through the southern forests to Albany. (p155)

Cape to Cape Track Enjoy Indian Ocean views on this 135km trail from Cape Naturaliste to Cape Leeuwin. (p130)

Stirling Range National Park Climb every mountain...or maybe just one or two, in this luscious range, known for its flora and chameleon-like ability to change colour. (p159)

Punurrunha (Mt Bruce) In Karijini National Park tackle WA's second-highest peak and enjoy wonderful views along the ridge. (p202)

Mitchell Falls (Punamii-unpuu) The 8.6km track heads through spinifex, woodlands and gorges, passing Aboriginal rock art on the way. (p227)

Marine Mammals

It's extraordinarily easy to come close to the great creatures of the deep along WA's coast.

Perth & Fremantle Thirty thousand whales cruise past between mid-September and early December, and boat trips will take you out to cheer them on. (p61)

Rottnest Island The sharp-of-eye may spot New Zealand fur seals, dolphins and whales. (p98)

Rockingham Cruise out to swim with dolphins and spot seals. (p103)

Green Head Splash with sea lions in the shallows. (p120)

Dampier Peninsula Excellent whale-watching from a viewing platform. (p217)

Bunbury Wade next to the wild dolphins that regularly drop by, or take a boat trip to swim with them. (p123)

Albany Between July and mid-October the bay turns into a

Top: Seals at Rottnest Island (p98).
Bottom: Dessert, Cullen Wines (p136)

whale nursery, with mothers and calves easily spotted from the beach, while cruises take you a little closer. (p155)

Monkey Mia Watch dolphins feeding in the shallows and take a dugong-spotting cruise. (p179)

Beer, Wine & Food

WA's wine industry is now being complemented by innovative craft breweries, while vineyard restaurants and provedores also abound.

Swan Valley Within Perth's eastern reaches, this semi-rural area's cosy wineries and bustling microbreweries are packed with city folk on weekends. (p109)

Fremantle The traditional home of WA craft beer, from established Little Creatures to more recent players like The Monk. (p93)

Margaret River Known for its Bordeaux-style varietals, chardonnay and sauvignon blanc, as well as a growing number of craft breweries. (p130)

Pemberton Another esteemed wine area, producing extremely good pinot noir, chardonnay and sauvignon blanc. (p144)

Denmark Notable wineries and craft breweries dot this picturesque area of the cool-climate Great Southern wine region. (p150)

Mt Barker & Porongurup The most significant part of the Great Southern, with cool climes suiting riesling, pinot noir and cabernet sauvignon. (p157)

Aboriginal Art & Culture

Around 59,000 Aboriginal people call WA home, comprising many different Indigenous peoples, speaking many distinct languages.

Art Gallery of Western Australia A treasure trove of Indigenous art. (p53)

Wula Guda Nyinda Eco Adventures Offers bushwalks and kayak tours, and you'll learn some local Malgana language. (p179)

Dampier Peninsula Interact with remote communities and learn how to spear fish and catch mud crabs. (p217)

The Kimberley View artists' cooperatives, visit ancient rock art, and get to know 'Country' on a cultural tour. (p205)

Ngurrangga Tours Cultural and rock-art tours in Murujuga National Park in the Pilbara. (p198)

Uptuyu Personalised cultural tours taking in wetlands, rock art, fishing and Indigenous Kimberley communities. (p221)

Wundargoodie Aboriginal Safaris Offering a women-only Kimberley Spiritual Experience. (p223)

East Pilbara Arts Centre This striking new opening in Newman beautifully showcases the acclaimed works of the Martumili artists. (p257)

Getting off the Beaten Path

In a destination so varied and expansive, there are plenty of spectacular opportunities to craft your own journey of discovery.

Mornington Wilderness Camp The 95km stretch from the Gibb River Road to this riverside oasis is some of WA's most exquisite, lonely country. (p225)

Dryandra Woodland Less than two hours from Perth, but a world away, with endangered populations of endemic wildlife. (p106)

Gnaraloo Station Come for a night and stay for a month as your skills are put to work on this sustainable marvel. (p182)

Middle Lagoon Life doesn't get much more laid-back than at this Dampier Peninsula beachside camping ground far from anywhere. (p218)

Duncan Road A real outback adventure without the masses, Duncan Rd is both a destination itself and a 'long cut' to the Northern Territory. (p228)

Month by Month

January

The peak of the summer school holidays sees families head to the beach en masse. Days are hot and dry, except in the far north, where the wet season is in full force.

☆ Southbound Festival

This festival starts off the new year with three days of alternative music and camping in Busselton. Featuring big-name international artists, it's Western Australia's Glastonbury – but with less mud. (p127)

🕴 Lancelin Ocean Classic

In early January tiny Lancelin's renowned blustery conditions attract thousands for its world-famous windsurfing event. Held over four days, the event starts with wave sailing on the Thursday and Friday, followed by the marathon on Saturday and the Sunday slalom. (p117)

February

The kids head back to school, freeing up some room at the beach and taking some of the pressure off coastal accommodation. It's still hot and dry in the south, and soggy in the north.

☆ Laneway at Fremantle

Up-and-coming international bands with a boho indie vibe entice WA hipsters to Freo's West End at the annual Laneway festival. (p89)

⭐🎭 Perth International Arts Festival

Held over 25 days from mid-February, Perth's festival attracts an international line-up, spanning theatre, classical music, jazz, visual arts, dance, film, literature – the whole gamut. It's worth scheduling your trip around. (p65)

☆ Leeuwin Concert Series

Leeuwin Estate winery (www.leeuwinestate.com.au) in Margaret River hosts world-class performers of popular music, opera and the stage (James Taylor, Diana Krall, Sting) during its annual event in mid-February; other concerts run from January to April. (p141)

March

It's still beach weather, but it's not quite as swelteringly hot in the south. It's hot and steamy in the north, however, as the rain is still bucketing down. Prices shoot up at Easter.

☆ Nannup Music Festival

The sleepy forest town of Nannup comes alive with this festival, which hosts up to 30,000 fans of folk, blues and world music. (p142)

April

A pleasant month in Perth, with temperatures dropping to the mid-20s and a little more rainfall. Up north they're finally starting to dry out, and it's a great time for a Kimberley fly over.

🏄 Margaret River Surfing Pro

Officially called the Drug Aware Pro, this World Qualifying Series (WQS) event sees the world's best up-and-coming surfers battle it out in the epic surf at Margaret River. (p131)

May

Temperatures creep down and Broome and Exmouth both finally drop below the 30s, making them particularly appealing – especially now the box jellyfish have retreated. Autumn showers are more common in the south.

🎏 Ord Valley Muster

For 10 days Kununurra hits overdrive during the annual Ord Valley Muster, a collection of various sporting, charity and cultural events leading up to a large outdoor concert under the full moon on the banks of the Ord River. (p230)

June

Winter hits Perth with plenty of rain and possibly some snow on the Stirling Range further south. The warm, dry north, however, heads into peak season. Whale watching commences in Augusta.

☆ Denmark Festival of Voice

Rousing choruses blow away the cobwebs from the south-coast town of Denmark

during the Festival of Voice, held over the June long weekend. The town is flooded with soloists, duos, choristers and their admirers. It's accompanied by a workshop program. (p151)

July

It's wet and cold in the south and beautiful in the north – sparking a winter-break exodus from Perth. Whales congregate in the bays around Albany.

🎏 Derby Boab Festival

Derby goes off with concerts, mud footy, horse and mudcrab races, film festivals, poetry readings, art exhibitions, street parades and a dinner out on the mudflats (www.derbyboabfestival.org.au). (p222)

🎏 Indigenous Cultural Celebrations

Indigenous art exhibitions and performances take place throughout WA during National Aboriginal & Islander Day Observance Committee week (www.naidoc.org.au), which celebrates the history, culture and achievements of Indigenous people.

August

Lovely in the north, but still wet and cold in the south, though temperatures do start to edge up. Manjimup truffles come into season, to the delight of Perth's chefs and their customers; whales continue to hang out on the south coast.

🏄 Avon River Festivities

Northam and Toodyay both turn on festivals the day before the Avon Descent (www.avondescent.com.au), a gruelling 133km white-water-rafting event for powerboats, kayaks and canoes between the two towns. Northam hosts the Avon River Festival, while Toodyay has an International Food Festival.

☆ CinéfestOz

The sleepy southwest town of Busselton assumes a cinematic cosmopolitan sheen when this festival celebrating Australian and French cinema is held. Look forward to events and screenings in venues around town. (p127)

🏄 Broome Race Round

The local fillies and stallions frock up and get slaughtered as the Broome Race Round heads towards a frenzied climax with the Kimberley Cup, Ladies Day and the Broome Cup all held in early August. There's also some horse racing. (p214)

September

Spring brings a flurry of excitement, with wildflowers blooming and whales heading up the west coast. Broome pops back into the 30s and the tourists start to head south again.

☆ Rottofest

Make the journey from Perth or Fremantle across to Rottnest Island for this one-day festival (www.rottofest.com.au) of live music, DJs and comedy. (p101)

✹ Festival of the Pearl

Starting either in late August or in early September, Broome's Shinju Matsuri celebrates the town's pearl industry and multicultural heritage with a carnival of nations, a film festival, art exhibitions, food, concerts, fireworks and dragon-boat races. (p214)

✹ Kings Park Wildflower Festival

In September and early October, Kings Park and the Botanic Garden are filled with colourful wildflower displays in the annual Kings Park Festival (www.kingsparkfestival.com.au), which celebrates WA's unique and spectacular flora. Events include guided walks, talks and live music every Sunday. (p65)

✹ Pilbara Red Earth Arts Festival

Over 10 days, Karratha and the surrounding coastal Pilbara towns come alive for the Red Earth Arts Festival (www.reaf.com.au), an eclectic mix of live music (all genres), theatre, comedy, visual arts (including film, photography and sculpture) and storytelling. (p198)

✹ Perth Royal Show

The country comes to the city for the west's biggest agriculture, food and wine show (www.perthroyalshow.com.au). For Perth's kids it's a week of funfair rides, spun sugar and showbags full of plastic junk. (p65)

October

The last of the whales depart the south coast and hit the west-coast leg of the Humpback Hwy. The weather is noticeably warmer and drier, and the wildflowers are wonderful.

✹ Geraldton Sunshine Festival

It started in 1959 as a tomato festival, but now Geraldton's solar celebrations (www.sunshinefestival.com.au) include dragon-boat races, parades, sand sculptures and parties. It's held over a week in early October. Sunshine guaranteed. (p169)

November

A great time to be in Fremantle, with temperatures in the mid-20s, very little rain and a convoy of whales passing by. In the far north, it's the start of the box-jellyfish season.

✖ Margaret River Gourmet Escape

The culinary world's heavy hitters descend on Margaret River for four days of culinary inspiration (www.gourmetescape.com.au); Nigella Lawson and Rick Stein headlined the event in 2016. Australia's growing crew of celebrity chefs usually attend as well. (p131)

✹ Fremantle Festival

Ten days of parades, performances, music, dance, comedy, visual arts, street theatre and workshops. Founded in 1905, it's Australia's longest-running festival (www.fremantle.wa.gov.au). Highlights include the Kite Extravaganza on South Beach and the Wardarnji Indigenous Festival. (p90)

☆ Blues at Bridgetown

Now entering its third decade, one of Western Australia's longest-running music festivals fills the southwestern centre of Bridgetown with blues, folk and roots music annually on the second weekend of November (www.bluesatbridgetown.com.au). (p143)

✖ Broome Mango Festival

Broome celebrates the mango harvest with four days of mango-themed everything (www.facebook.com/BroomeMangoFestival). So how exactly do you celebrate mangos? With a quiz night, a fashion parade and a Great Chefs of Broome Cook-Off, apparently. If you don't come away with sweet, sticky fingers, you're doing it wrong.

Dancer at a corroboree, Derby

Itineraries

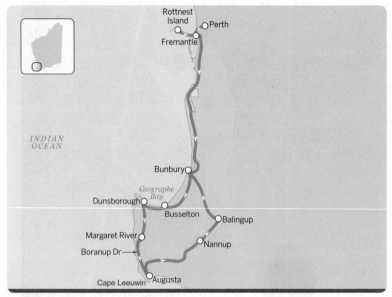

1 WEEK: A Southwest Short Circuit

If you've got limited time, this itinerary offers a taste of the best of the state – city life, colonial history, beaches, wildlife, wine, forests and rural roads.

Base yourself in either **Perth** or **Fremantle** and spend three days exploring the conjoined cities and one day on **Rottnest Island**. Hire a car and head south, stopping first at **Bunbury** for lunch and a visit to the Dolphin Discovery Centre. Continue on to **Geographe Bay**, basing yourself in either **Busselton** or **Dunsborough**, and use the rest of the day to explore the beaches. Pick up a wine-region map and spend day six checking out the wineries, surf beaches and caves, all of which are close by. Base yourself in the **Margaret River** township that night and visit Settler's Tavern, the local pub. The next morning, head to **Augusta** via Caves Rd and take the scenic detour through the karri forest along unsealed **Boranup Drive**. Visit **Cape Leeuwin**, where the Indian and Southern Oceans meet, before heading back to Bunbury on a picturesque rural drive through **Nannup** and **Balingup**. From here it's a two-hour drive back to Perth.

Above: Kangaroos, Margaret River (p130)

Right: Little Creatures brewery (p94), Fremantle

ORIEN HARVEY / GETTY IMAGES ©

DAVID STEELE / SHUTTERSTOCK ©

Above: Rottnest Island
(p98)

Left: Wave Rock
(p107)

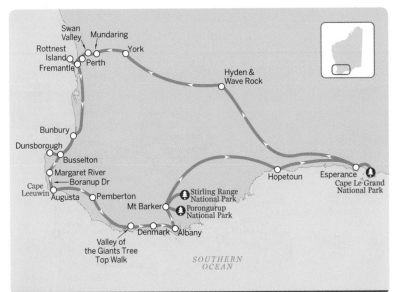

 The Southwest Uncut

Australia's southwest is a magical part of the continent and this itinerary covers its main highlights. Take another week to really relax into it.

Spend three days in **Perth** and **Fremantle** and a leisurely day on **Rottnest Island**. Head south to Geographe Bay – stopping at **Bunbury** first to visit the Dolphin Discovery Centre – before overnighting in **Busselton** or **Dunsborough**. Continue for two nights in **Margaret River** township to explore breweries, wineries, surf beaches and caves.

The following morning head to **Augusta** via Caves Rd and detour through the karri forest along scenic **Boranup Drive**. Visit **Cape Leeuwin**, where the Indian and Southern Oceans meet, and continue to sleepy **Pemberton**. Highlights include more wineries, three national parks and the Karri Forest Explorer scenic drive. The next day, visit the extraordinary **Valley of the Giants Tree Top Walk** near Walpole and overnight in **Denmark**. Check out beaches, wineries, breweries and good restaurants before continuing to **Albany**. Spend two days there swimming (in summer), whale watching (in winter), and exploring coastal national parks and the poignant National Anzac Centre.

Head north for more wineries at **Mt Barker** before tracking east to **Porongurup National Park**. Spend the next day (or two) tackling the mountainous tracks either here or at **Stirling Range National Park**.

From here the driving distances get longer. Continue to the South Coast Hwy and at Ravensthorpe hop down to **Hopetoun**. This takes three hours from the Stirling Range, so spend the afternoon at the beach. The following day, head back to the South Coast Hwy and continue east to **Esperance** (around 2½ hours). Base yourself there two days, spending one of them exploring **Cape Le Grand National Park**.

Head back on the South Coast Hwy and turn north just past Ravensthorpe for **Hyden** and extraordinary **Wave Rock** – around four hours.

The following day, head west to Brookton, turn north on the Great Southern Hwy, and follow the Avon Valley to quaintly colonial **York** – allow 3½ hours. For a leisurely final day back to Perth, travel via **Mundaring**, stopping at the **Swan Valley** en route for craft beer.

To make this itinerary shorter, head straight to Hyden from the Stirling Range, or take the Albany Hwy directly to Perth from Mt Barker.

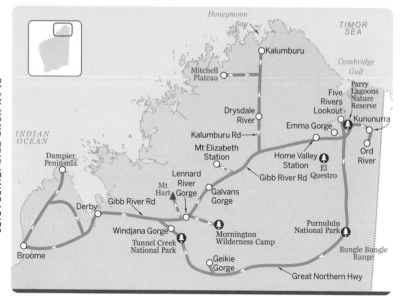

1 MONTH The Gibb River Road & Kimberley Outback

The biggest adventure in the west leaves **Broome** during the Dry and traverses the heart of the rugged Kimberley by 4WD.

First stop is the **Dampier Peninsula**, with its Aboriginal communities, beautiful beaches and mud crabs, and your last saltwater swim. Take the back road to **Derby** and its boabs, then on to the **Gibb River Road**, where **Lennard River** is the first of many inviting gorges. Explore wildlife and gorges at **Mt Hart** and remote **Mornington Wilderness Camp**, and look for examples of Wandjina art at **Galvans Gorge** and **Mt Elizabeth Station**. Turn off onto the **Kalumburu Road**, check the road conditions at **Drysdale River** and drive on to the **Mitchell Plateau**, with its forests of *livistona* and mind-blowing falls. Marvel at the area's rock art before hitting the northern coast and excellent fishing at **Honeymoon Bay**, just beyond the mission community of **Kalumburu**.

It's all downhill from here as you retrace your route back to the Gibb, then turn left for wonderful **Home Valley Station**, where someone else can do the cooking and the soft beds make a pleasant change from camping. Nearby **El Questro** has gorges aplenty, none more beautiful than **Emma Gorge**. Soon you're back on asphalt, but not for long as you take in the amazing bird life of **Parry Lagoons Nature Reserve**. Let Wyndham's **Five Rivers Lookout** blow your mind with its view of Cambridge Gulf, before heading for the civility of **Kununurra**, with its excellent food and supplies. You can look for fruit-picking work, ride a canoe down the mighty **Ord River**, or jump back behind the wheel for the wonders of **Purnululu National Park** and the orange-domed **Bungle Bungle Range**.

Darwin and the Northern Territory are beckoning, or you can follow the Great Northern Hwy back to Broome, stopping in at beautiful **Geikie Gorge** for a relaxing boat cruise where you might spot freshwater crocs. If you don't see any, don't worry, as nearby **Windjana Gorge** has loads sunning themselves on the river banks. Grab your torch and head for a cold wade through the icy waters of **Tunnel Creek**, with its bats and rock art, before planting the pedal back to Broome, where you won't care how much that beer costs any more.

Above: Windjana Gorge
(p223)
Right: Boab trees in
Derby (p220)

AUSTRALIAN SCENICS / GETTY IMAGES ©

LONEROC / SHUTTERSTOCK ©

Above: Hamersley
Gorge (p201), Karijini
National Park

Left: Dolphins,
Monkey Mia (p179)

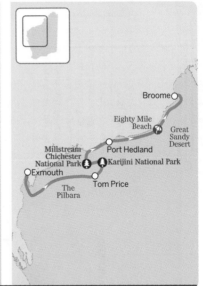

2 WEEKS Indian Ocean Dreaming

Beautiful beaches, spectacular sunsets and diverse wildlife are constants on this coastal cruise.

Take Indian Ocean Dr north from **Perth** to Cervantes for sunset on the otherwordly **Pinnacles Desert**. Cruise the wildflower-laden Kwongan back roads and marvel at the flora at **Lesueur National Park** before snorkelling with sea lions at **Green Head**. Follow the flowers out to **Perenjori**, then hit the cafes and museums of **Geraldton**. Go kitesurfing, then move on to the wonderful **Kalbarri** coastline. Enjoy a canoe in the gorges before sampling the outback on the long drive to World Heritage–listed **Shark Bay**. Watch dolphins at **Monkey Mia**, go sailing with dugongs, and learn about 'Country' on an Indigenous cultural tour. Check out the stromatolites of **Hamelin Pool**, before putting in more road time on the stretch north to **Carnarvon**. Drop into **Gnaraloo** for world-class waves before arriving at tiny **Coral Bay** and **Exmouth**, where whale sharks, humpback whales, manta rays and turtles inhabit the exquisite **Ningaloo Marine Park**. You can fly out of Exmouth, drive back to Perth in two days (overnighting in historic Greenough), or push on to the gorges of Karijini.

1 WEEK Pilbara Jewels

You'll camp most of the way on this link between Ningaloo and Broome, with long empty beaches, shady pools and surprisingly good food.

From **Exmouth**, take Burkett Rd back to the highway, and head north, turning off at Nanutarra for the long, scenic haul up to **Tom Price**. After stocking up, spend the next few days camped in **Karijini National Park**, exploring the sublime gorges and indulging in a spot of peak bagging among the state's highest mountains. Don't miss a swim at Hamersley Gorge en route to the relaxing, shady pools in **Millstream Chichester National Park**. Admire the mesas and breakaways of the Chichester Range before dropping down to the coast, checking out the petroglyphs at Murujuga, then onto lovely **Point Samson** for snorkelling. Take the North West Coastal Hwy directly to **Port Hedland**, and indulge in city treats before camping at remote **Eighty Mile Beach**, where you might spot nesting turtles. Your last leg is a long stretch of nothing as you skirt the Great Sandy Desert to arrive in tropical **Broome**.

Off the Beaten Track - West Coast Australia

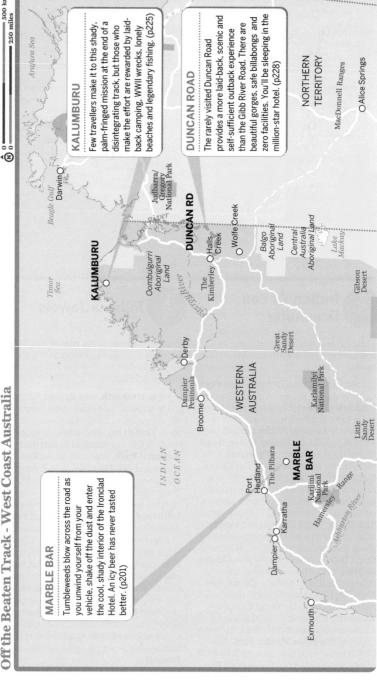

KALUMBURU

Few travellers make it to this shady, palm-fringed mission at the end of a disintegrating track, but those who make the effort are rewarded by laid-back camping, WWII wrecks, lonely beaches and legendary fishing. (p225)

DUNCAN ROAD

The rarely visited Duncan Road provides a more laid-back, scenic and self-sufficient outback experience than the Gibb River Road. There are beautiful gorges, safe billabongs and zero facilities. You'll be sleeping in the million-star hotel. (p228)

MARBLE BAR

Tumbleweeds blow across the road as you unwind yourself from your vehicle, shake off the dust and enter the cool, shady interior of the Ironclad Hotel. An icy beer has never tasted better. (p201)

STEEP POINT & DIRK HARTOG ISLAND

Sunsets from the mainland's most westerly point just don't come any better, nor does the fishing. Nearby, Dirk Hartog Island is replete with history, begging to be explored. Just getting here is an adventure. (p176)

DRYANDRA WOODLAND

Go marsupial crazy and get acquainted with bilbies, boodies and woylies at Dryandra's excellent Barna Mia Animal Sanctuary. Perth is just a couple of hours away from this protected stand of eucalypt forest. (p106)

Carnarvon

STEEP POINT & DIRK HARTOG ISLAND

Gascoyne River

Murchison River

Wiluna

Lake Buchanan

WESTERN AUSTRALIA

Cosmo Newberry Aboriginal Land

Gibson Desert Nature Reserve

Warakurna-Wing-Irr Aboriginal Land

Pitjantjatjara Aboriginal Land

Simpson Desert National Park

Simpson Desert

SOUTH AUSTRALIA

Flinders Ranges

Great Victoria Desert

Neale Junction Nature Reserve

Maralinga Tjarutja Aboriginal Land

Kalgoorlie - Boulder

Great Victoria Desert Nature Reserve

Nullabor Regional Reserve

Yellabinna Regional Reserve

Eyre Peninsula

Port Lincoln

Northam

DRYANDRA WOODLAND

Dundas Nature Reserve

Nullarbor Plain

Great Australian Bight

Perth
Fremantle
Mandurah
Bunbury
Busselton

Nuytsland Nature Reserve

Esperance

Denmark   Albany

SOUTHERN OCEAN

INDIAN OCEAN

Vineyard in the Margaret River wine region

Plan Your Trip
Discover Margaret River & the Southwest Coast

Margaret River features family-friendly beaches, brilliant surf-ing, labyrinthine caves studded with limestone formations, and a world-class gourmet scene – all in a relatively compact area. Vineyards producing excellent chardonnays and Bordeaux-style reds segue into rural back roads punctuated with craft breweries, provedores, cheese shops, chocolate shops and art galleries.

Best of the Region

Best Wineries

Vasse Felix (p136) Regional pioneer leading the way with its Heytesbury cabernet blend and Heytesbury chardonnay.

Cullen Wines (p136) Another Margaret River pioneer, with the 2009 Diana Madeline cabernet sauvignon merlot awarded Wine of the Year in the *Australian Wine Annual 2012*.

Leeuwin Estate (p141) Wonderful wines, especially its Art Series chardonnay and sauvignon blanc.

Watershed Premium Wines (p141) One of WA's best vineyard restaurants and renowned for its Awakening cabernet sauvignon.

Ashbrook (p136) Great quality, good value; try the cabernet merlot.

Four Things You Wouldn't Expect

➡ Artworks by Arthur Boyd and Sidney Nolan are hanging in the Bunbury Regional Art Gallery (p123).

➡ A highly rated French-Australian film festival, CinéfestOZ (p127), is held annually in beachy Busselton.

➡ A colony of **red-tailed tropicbirds** roosts off Cape Naturaliste (p129).

➡ Most of the best vineyard restaurants aren't open in the evenings.

Plan Your Attack

What's the Layout?

The sheltered white sands of Geographe Bay start south of Bunbury and arch along to Cape Naturaliste. Busselton and Dunsborough are the bay's main towns. At Cape Naturaliste the coastline pirouettes and runs nearly due south to Cape Leeuwin. The wine region runs parallel to this coast with the Margaret River itself cutting roughly east to west through the centre, passing through the town of the same name. Wineries are scattered all around, but the biggest concentration is found north of the river.

Where to Stay

➡ **For a beach holiday** Busselton or Dunsborough

➡ **For surfing** Yallingup, Prevelly or Margaret River

➡ **For wineries** Yallingup, Margaret River or anywhere in between

➡ **For caves** Anywhere between Yallingup and Augusta

➡ **For peace and quiet** Augusta

When to Go

➡ **For a beach holiday** December to March

➡ **For surfing** Any time, but the big surf pro is in March

➡ **For wineries, breweries and caves** All year

➡ **For whale watching** June to September from Augusta, September to December from Dunsborough

➡ **For French films** August

When to Avoid

➡ **Busselton in January** Unless you're going to the Southbound music festival or have booked well in advance.

➡ **Dunsborough in November** The place is overrun by end-of-school revellers.

➡ **Margaret River on weekends** Accommodation prices are higher and there are always loads of people – but at least everything will be open.

What to Do

Surfing the Wineries

The two main north–south routes are the Bussell Hwy (passing through Cowaramup, Margaret River and Augusta) and leafy Caves Rd (running south from Dunsborough). Numerous bucolic back roads link the two. Pick up one of the excellent free maps, squabble over who's going to be the nondrinking driver, and dive right in. The other alternative is to take a tour – public transport is not a workable option.

Most of the wineries offer tastings between 10am and 5pm daily. At busy times (this includes every weekend), consider booking ahead for lunch before you set out.

Above: Lake Cave
(p139)

Left: Chocolates from
the Margaret River
Chocolate Company
(p136)

LYNN GAIL / GETTY IMAGES ©

Tasting the Waves

Known to surfers as 'Yals' (around Yallingup) and 'Margs' (around the mouth of the Margaret River), the beaches between Capes Naturaliste and Leeuwin offer powerful reef breaks, mainly left-handers (the direction you take after catching a wave). The surf at Margs has been described by surfing supremo Nat Young as 'epic', and by world surfing champ Mark Richards as 'one of the world's finest'.

As is the way with such hot spots, surfers can be quite territorial, so respect the etiquette and defer to locals if you're unsure. If you're planning on spending a lot of time on the breaks, call in to the surf shops and get to know some locals.

Around Dunsborough, the better locations include Rocky Point (short left-hander) and the Farm and Bone Yards (right-handers), which are between Eagle and Bunker Bays. Near Yallingup there are the Three Bears (Papa, Mama and Baby, of course), Rabbits (a beach break towards the north of Yallingup Beach), Yallingup (reef with breaks left and right), and Injidup Car Park and Injidup Point (right-hand tube on a heavy swell; left-hander). You'll need a 4WD to access Guillotine/Gallows (right-hander), north of Gracetown. Also around Gracetown are Huzza's (an easy break within the beach), South Point (popular break) and Lefthanders (the name says it all). The annual surfer pro is held around Margaret River Mouth and Southside ('Suicides') in April.

Pick up a surfing map from one of the visitor centres.

Surfing is never without its risks. Three people have been killed by sharks in the vicinity of Gracetown in the last six years, and in 2014 a shark attacked an inflatable boat near Dunsborough.

Going Underground

The main cave complexes are spread, perhaps unsurprisingly, along Caves Rd. Ngilgi Cave (p133) sits by itself near Yallingup, but the other main complexes are between Margaret River township and Augusta. These are split between Calgardup Cave (p140) and Giants Cave (p140), which are run by the Department of Environment and Conservation, and Lake Cave (p139), Jewel Cave (p141) and Mammoth Cave (p139), which are more commercialised and are run by Caveworks. Caveworks offers a combined ticket for its caves.

Getting Crafty

The hoppy wave of craft beer that's sweeping many countries has also washed up on WA shores, and an innovative generation of brewers is proving there's more to beer than innocuous Euro lagers. Look forward to a global array of beer styles including India pale ales, Belgian ales and chocolate porters, and decide on a designated driver or join a tour.

Other Attractions

➡ **Beaches** And lots of them; they're particularly beautiful between Dunsborough and Cape Naturaliste.

➡ **Walking** There are excellent tracks around Cape Naturaliste and between the capes.

➡ **Diving** Trips leave from Busselton and Dunsborough to explore local wrecks and reefs.

➡ **Whale watching** Cruises leave from Augusta (starting in June) and Dunsborough (starting in September).

➡ **Lighthouses** Both capes have them and both can be visited. From Cape Leeuwin you can watch the Indian and Southern Oceans collide.

➡ **Adventure sports** From mountain biking to climbing and kayaking.

BEST FAMILY ACTIVITIES

➡ **Dolphin Discovery Centre, Bunbury** (p123)

➡ **Bunbury Wildlife Park** (p123)

➡ **Busselton Jetty** (p126)

➡ **Margaret River Chocolate Company** (p136)

➡ **Mountain biking at Wharncliffe Mill Bush Retreat** (p136)

Surfer at Yallingup Beach (p133)

Plan Your Trip

West Coast Australia Outdoors

With incredible landscapes and seascapes, intriguing wildlife and all that brilliant sunshine, Western Australia (WA) is the perfect playground for outdoor enthusiasts, with numerous tracks to follow, waves to surf and reefs to explore.

LYNN GAIL / GETTY IMAGES ©

Best Outdoors

Best for Daredevils

Scramble, abseil, slide and dive through the gorges of the Karijini National Park, or ride the surge in a speedboat on the Horizontal Waterfalls near Derby.

Best Whale Watching

Whale-watching boats leave from Perth, Fremantle, Bremer Bay, Dunsborough, Augusta, Albany, Coral Bay, Exmouth, Kalbarri, Broome and the Dampier Peninsula.

Best Wildlife Encounters on Water

Swim with whale sharks, manta rays and humpback whales in Ningaloo Marine Park. For dolphins head to Rockingham, Bunbury or Monkey Mia. Sea lions are best seen at Rockingham and Green Head, while seals can be spotted off Rottnest Island. Look out for dugongs at Monkey Mia.

Best Wildlife Encounters on Land

Seek out little marsupials on Rottnest Island or in the Dryandra Woodland, and huge lizards anywhere in the Kimberley. Emus are often spotted around Exmouth and Shark Bay, while kangaroos and parrots are everywhere!

Bushwalking

WA's excellent bushwalking terrain includes the southwest's cool forests, the expansive Bibbulmun Track and the north's rugged national parks.

See www.bushwalkingwa.org.au for details of local bushwalking clubs. To contact potential walking buddies, or to buy and sell gear, see the forums on www.bushwalk.com.

For tips on responsible bushwalking, see the camping and bushwalking guidelines online at www.parks.dpaw.wa.gov.au.

Perth & Surrounds

With hiking and camping facilities, John Forrest National Park (p108) has an easy 15km walk to waterfalls. The rugged **Walyunga National Park** (☑08-9290 6100; www.parks.dpaw.wa.gov.au; per car $12; ⊙8am-5pm) features a medium-to-hard 18km walk that fords the Avon River and has excellent wildlife viewing. Yanchep National Park (p116) has short strolls and challenging full-day walks. The **Yaberoo Budjara Heritage trail** (www.wanneroo.wa.gov.au) follows an Aboriginal walking trail.

Down South

Serious walkers gravitate to the ruggedly beautiful Stirling Range National Park (p159). Popular are the Bluff Knoll climb (6km, three to four hours), and the park's 1500 species of wildflower. Visit from September to November for the park's flowering glory, and be prepared for wind chill and rain (and sometimes snow) in winter.

North of Albany is the smaller Porongurup National Park (p158), with spectacular granite rocks and dense karri forest. Trails include the 10-minute Tree in the Rock stroll, the medium-grade Hayward and Nancy Peaks (three hours), and the challenging three-hour Marmabup Rock hike. Wildflowers and bird activity make springtime the peak season for Porongurup, but it can be visited year-round.

Spectacular coastal highlights are walks through Walpole-Nornalup, Fitzgerald River and Cape Le Grand National Parks. The Cape to Cape Track (p130) follows the coastline 135km from Cape Naturaliste to Cape Leeuwin, taking five to seven days, and features wild camp sites en-route.

Up North

Summer's no picnic in the sweltering, remote national parks of the north, so high season for many bushwalkers here is from April to October. The arid terrain can be treacherous, so research carefully, be prepared with water and supplies, and check in with rangers before setting out.

Kalbarri National Park (p174) showcases scenic gorges, thick bushland and rugged coastal cliffs. The popular six-hour loop features dramatic seascapes, including spectacular Nature's Window.

THE BIBBULMUN TRACK

Taking around eight weeks, the 963km Bibbulmun Track (p155) goes from Kalamunda, 20km east of Perth, through mainly natural environment to Walpole and Albany.

Terrain includes jarrah and marri forests, wildflowers, granite outcrops, coastal heath country and spectacular coastlines.

Comfortable camp sites are spaced regularly along the track. The best time to do it is from August to October.

Rugged, sometimes hazardous treks can be taken into the dramatic gorges of Karijini National Park (p201). The walk to the Mt Bruce (Punurrunha) summit (9km, five hours) is popular with experienced bushwalkers.

Visitors to the Kimberley's Purnululu National Park (p232) come to see the striped beehive-shaped domes of the World Heritage–listed Bungle Bungles. Walks include the easy Cathedral Gorge walk, and the more difficult overnight trek to Piccaninny Gorge. The park is only open from April to November.

Surfing & Windsurfing

Beginners, intermediates, wannabe pros and adventure surfers will all find excellent conditions to suit their skill levels. WA gets huge swells (often over 3m), so it's critical to align the surf and the location with your ability. Look out for strong currents, sharks and territorial local surfers.

WA's traditional surfing home is the southwest, particularly from Yallingup (p133) to Margaret River (p136). This stretch has many different breaks to explore.

Around Perth the surf is smaller, but there are often good conditions at bodyboard-infested Trigg (p57) and Scarborough (p57). If the waves are small, head to Rottnest Island (p99) for (usually) bigger and better waves. Check out Strickland Bay.

Heading north, there are countless reef breaks waiting to be discovered (hint:

take a 4WD). Best known are the left-hand point breaks of Jakes Bay (p172) near Kalbarri; Gnaraloo Station (p182), 150km north of Carnarvon; and **Surfers Beach** (Dunes Beach; Mildura Wreck Rd) at Exmouth. Buy the locals a beer and they might share a few secret world-class locations.

Windsurfers and kitesurfers have plenty of choice with excellent flat-water and wave sailing. Kitesurfers appreciate the long, empty beaches and offshore reefs.

After Perth's city beaches, head to Lancelin (p116), home to a large summer population of surfers. Flat-water and wave sailing are excellent here. Further north, Geraldton (p168) has the renowned Coronation Beach. The Shark Bay (p175) area has excellent flat-water sailing and Gnaraloo Station is also a world-renowned wave-sailing spot.

Wildlife Watching

Whales

Because so many southern right and humpback whales (upwards of 30,000) cruise along the WA coast, it has become known as the Humpback Hwy. From June onwards their annual pilgrimage begins from Antarctica to the warm tropical waters of the northwest coast; mothers with calves seek out the shallower bays and coves of King George Sound in Albany (p155) from July to October. In whale-watching season, whales can be spotted from coastal clifftops, and often from the beach as well. Tour operators at Ningaloo are trialling interactive tours with humpback whales in which it may be possible to swim with them.

Dolphins

Dolphins can be seen up close at the Dolphin Discovery Centre (p123) in Bunbury, around Rockingham, and at Monkey Mia (p179). Monkey Mia also has 10% of the world's dugong population.

Birds

The Broome Bird Observatory (p213) attracts a staggering 800,000 birds each year, and the **Yalgorup National Park** near Mandurah is another important waterbird habitat. The Lesueur National

Bluff Knoll, Stirling Range National Park (p159)

Park (p118) is home to the endangered Carnaby's cockatoo, while migratory shorebirds flock to Parry Lagoons Nature Reserve (p234) in the Kimberley. At the Mornington Wilderness Camp (p225), purple-crowned fairywrens and the endangered Gouldian finch are regular visitors.

BEST WILDFLOWER SPOTS

➡ **Kings Park and Botanic Garden** (p56), Perth.

➡ **Fitzgerald River National Park** (p159), between Albany and Esperance.

➡ **Porongurup National Park** (p158), north of Albany.

➡ **Stirling Range National Park** (p159), north of Albany.

➡ **Mullewa**, in the central midlands, especially at August's annual flower show.

➡ **Kalbarri National Park** (p174), on the Batavia Coast.

➡ **Wongan Hills and Morawa** in the central midlands.

Cycling

WA's southwest is good for cycle touring, and while there are thousands of kilometres of flat, virtually traffic-free roads elsewhere in the state, the distances between towns makes it difficult to plan.

Perth is a relatively bike-friendly city, with good recreational bike paths, including routes that run along the Swan River to Fremantle, and paths overlooking the city through Kings Park.

Cyclists rule on mostly car-free Rottnest Island (p103), with long stretches of empty roads circumnavigating the island and its beaches. Geraldton (p168) also has great cycle paths.

The most exciting route for mountain bikers is the **Munda Biddi Trail** (www.mundabiddi.org.au), meaning 'path through the forest' in the Noongar Aboriginal language. The 1000km mountain-biking equivalent of the Bibbulmun Track runs all the way from Mundaring on Perth's outskirts to Albany on the south coast. Camp sites are situated a day's easy ride apart, and maps are available online and at visitor centres.

Diving & Snorkelling

WA's fascinating diving and snorkelling locations include stunning marine parks and shipwrecks.

Close to Perth, divers can explore wrecks and marine life off the beaches of Rottnest Island (p99), or explore the submerged reefs and historic shipwrecks of the West Coast Dive Park (p103) within Shoalwater Islands Marine Park, near Rockingham. You can take a dive course in Geographe Bay with companies based in Dunsborough (p128) or Busselton (p126); the bay offers excellent dives under Busselton Jetty (p126), on Four Mile Reef (a 40km limestone ledge about 6.5km off the coast) and around the scuttled HMAS *Swan*.

Other wrecks include the HMAS *Perth* (at 36m), deliberately sunk in 2001 in King George Sound near Albany; and the *Sanko Harvest*, near Esperance (p162). Both teem with marine life on the wrecks' artificial reefs.

Divers seeking warmer waters should head north. Staggering marine life can be found just 100m offshore within the Ningaloo Marine Park (p195), fantastic for both diving and snorkelling. In Turquoise Bay, underwater action is equally accessible, and one of the planet's most amazing underwater experiences is diving or snorkelling alongside the incredible whale shark, the world's largest fish. Tours leave from Exmouth (p188) and Coral Bay (p186).

There's also excellent diving and snorkelling around the Houtman Abrolhos Islands (p173).

Fishing

From sailfish in the north to trout in the south, all types of fishing are on offer along WA's immense coastline. Fishing is the state's largest recreational activity, with many locals catching dinner nearly every time.

Close to Perth, Rottnest Island has plentiful schools of wrasse and Western Australian dhufish (previously called jewfish).

South of Perth, popular fishing hot spots include Mandurah (p104), with options for deep-sea fishing, catching tailor from

---

REDUCING THE RISK OF SHARK ATTACK

This list of shark safety guidelines is from WA's Department of Fisheries. See www.sharksmart.com.au for more information.

➡ Swim between the flags at patrolled beaches.

➡ Swim close to shore.

➡ Swim, dive or surf with other people.

➡ Avoid areas close to bird rookeries or where there are large schools of fish, dolphins, seals or sea lions.

➡ Avoid areas where animal, human or fish waste enters the water.

➡ Avoid deep channels or areas with deep drop-offs nearby.

➡ Do not remain in the water with bleeding wounds.

➡ Look carefully before jumping into the water from a boat or jetty.

➡ If spearing fish, don't carry dead or bleeding fish attached to you and remove all speared fish from the water as quickly as possible.

➡ If schooling fish or other wildlife start to behave erratically or congregate in large numbers, leave the water.

➡ If you see a shark, leave the water as quickly and calmly as possible – avoid excessive splashing or noise.

Above: The waters off Rottnest Island (p98)

Right: Melaleuca flowers, Lesueur National Park (p118)

STEVE WATERS / GETTY IMAGES ©

Cathedral Gorge (p233), Purnululu National Park

the beach or nabbing Mandurah's famed blue manna crabs and king prawns in the estuaries. In Augusta (p141) you can chase salmon in the Blackwood River or whiting in the bay, or drop a line from Busselton Jetty (p126).

Popular spots at sunny Geraldton (p168) include Sunset Beach and Drummond Cove, and fishing charters go to the nearby Houtman Abrolhos Islands (p173). There's great fishing all along the coast, and lots of charters in the hotter, steamier northwest. There's a good chance to hook a monster fish at Exmouth (p188), the Dampier Archipelago (p199) and the game-fishing nirvana of Broome (p208). The northern Kimberley is good for barramundi.

Buy a recreational fishing licence (RFL; $40) if you intend to catch marron (freshwater crayfish) or rock lobsters; if you use a fishing net; or if you're freshwater angling in the southwest. If you're fishing from a motorised boat, someone on the boat will need to have a Recreational Fishing from Boat Licence (RFBL; $30). Licences can be obtained online (www.fish.wa.gov.au) or from Australia Post offices. Note that there are strict licence, bag and size limits – see the Fisheries website for specific details.

NATIONAL PARK PASSES

Thirty of WA's 100 national parks charge vehicle entry fees (per car/motorcycle $12/6), which are valid for any park visited that day. If you're camping within the park, the entry fee is only payable on the first day (camping fees are additional). If you plan to visit more than three WA parks with entry fees – quite likely if you're travelling outside Perth – get the four-week Holiday Pass ($44). All Department of Parks & Wildlife offices (www.parks.dpaw.wa.gov.au) sell them, and if you've already paid a day-entry fee in the last week (and have the voucher to prove it), you can subtract it from the cost of the pass.

Travel With Children

With lots of sunshine, beaches and big open spaces, Western Australia (WA) is a wonderful destination for children of all ages. Australians are famously laid-back and their generally tolerant, 'no worries' attitude extends to children having a good time and perhaps being a little bit raucous.

West Coast Australia for Kids

Interacting with Australia's native fauna, either in the wild or in wildlife parks, will create lifetime memories for your kids. Australia's wildlife can be dangerous, but in reality you're extremely unlikely to strike any problems if you take sensible precautions.

The sun's harshness is more of a concern. Don't underestimate how quickly you and your kids can get sunburnt, even on overcast days. A standard routine for most Australian parents is to lather their kids in high-protection sunscreen (SPF 30-plus) before heading outside for the day. It's a habit worth adopting. Avoid going to the beach in the middle of the day. Head out in the morning or mid-afternoon instead.

On really hot days, dehydration can be a problem, especially for small children. Carry fluids with you, especially on long car journeys.

Many motels and larger caravan parks have playgrounds and swimming pools, and can supply cots and baby baths. Motels in touristy areas may have in-house children's videos and child-minding services. Top-end and midrange hotels usually welcome families with children, but some B&Bs market themselves as child-free havens.

Best Regions for Kids

Broome & the Kimberley
While there's wildlife interaction like camel rides and crocodile-park tours, it's the camping, gorge swimming and Indigenous culture that kids will remember, particularly in the Dampier Peninsula and along the Gibb River Road.

Ningaloo Coast & the Pilbara
Coral Bay has plenty of safe-water options and like-minded families.

Margaret River & the Southwest Coast
Geographe Bay features family-friendly beaches, Yallingup has a surf school and Bunbury has the Dolphin Discovery Centre and Bunbury Wildlife Park. The region also features whale watching.

Monkey Mia & the Central West
Visit the world-famous dolphins of Monkey Mia, feed the pelicans at Kalbarri or learn about Indigenous culture and 'Country' on a guided tour.

Perth & Fremantle
Open spaces, beaches, kid-friendly museums, bike paths, playgrounds and festivals. Many major attractions – including the Aquarium of Western Australia, Perth Zoo, the Art Gallery of Western Australia and the Maritime Museum – have hands-on, kid-friendly exhibits.

Babies & Toddlers

Perth and most major towns have public rooms where parents can nurse their baby or change nappies; check with the local visitor centre. While many Australians are relaxed about public breastfeeding or nappy changing, some aren't.

Many eateries lack a specialised children's menu, but others do have kids' meals or will provide smaller servings. Some supply high chairs.

Medical services and facilities are of a high standard, and baby food, formula and disposable nappies are widely available. Major car-hire companies will supply and fit booster seats for a fee.

School-Age Kids

The biggest challenge is a sudden attack of the 'are-we-there-yets?'. Adults – let alone kids – find the long drives tedious. Bring along books, computer games, iPads and child-friendly CDs. Consider hiring a car with a back-seat screen for playing DVDs.

Snacks are essential for journeys where shops might be 200km or further apart, and toilet paper is also a blessing.

Have a word to the kids about insects, snakes and spiders, stressing the need to keep their distance. This is particularly important for kids who like to prod things with sticks. While bushwalking, make sure they wear socks with shoes or boots.

Children's Highlights

Beaches

Beaches are a big part of the WA experience. Ensure the kids swim between the flags, and ask the locals about the safer beaches.

Wildlife Parks & Zoos

There are wildlife parks throughout WA, especially in tourist areas. Many have walk-in aviaries, so prepare for a freak-out when an over-friendly parrot lands on little Jimmy's shoulder. Watch out for emus: those beady eyes and pointy beaks are even more intimidating when they're attached to something that's double their height.

Whale Watching

➡ If you're on the right part of the coast at the right time of year, you'll definitely see whales from the shore.

➡ Organised whale-watching boat trips depart from Perth, Fremantle, Dunsborough, Augusta, Albany, Bremer Bay, Coral Bay, Broome, Kalbarri, Exmouth and the Dampier Peninsula.

Other Marine Mammals

➡ **Rockingham Wild Encounters** (p103) An opportunity for the over-fives to swim with wild dolphins.

➡ **Dolphin Discovery Centre** (p123) Wade into the shallows alongside the dolphins in Bunbury.

➡ **Monkey Mia** (p179) Watch dolphins being fed in the bay or head out on a cruise to spot dolphins and dugongs.

➡ **Sea Lion Charters** (p120) Splash about with sea lions in the shallows.

Surfing

➡ **Surfschool** (p61) Lessons in Perth for kids aged 11 and over.

➡ **Yallingup Surf School** (p134) 'Microgrom' lessons for the under-10s.

Amusement Parks & Rides

➡ **Adventure World** (p57) White-knuckle rides such as 'Bounty's Revenge', pools and water rides at this Perth amusement park.

➡ **Perth Royal Show** (p65) Funfair rides, show bags and farm animals.

Planning

➡ When booking accommodation and hire cars in advance, specify whether you need equipment such as cots, high chairs and car booster seats.

➡ If you're travelling with an infant, bring a mosquito net to drape over the cot.

➡ Bring rash shirts for the beach and warm clothes if you're travelling south in winter.

➡ Anything you forget can be easily purchased when you arrive.

Regions at a Glance

Perth & Fremantle

Beaches
Culture
Architecture

Beaches
They may not offer the solitude and pristine natural surroundings of elsewhere in Western Australia, but Perth and Fremantle's long beaches are popular playgrounds for city dwellers. Surfers, snorkellers and swimmers can all find a stretch of sand to suit.

Museums & Galleries
Perth's public institutions include the Art Gallery of Western Australia, housing traditional and contemporary art; the edgy Perth Institute of Contemporary Arts; and the Western Australian Museum. Fremantle boasts the superb Maritime Museum and Shipwreck Galleries.

Historic Buildings
Relics of the colonial era and early gold rushes abound. Fremantle has a frozen-in-time streetscape with a wonderful historic ambience. The big drawcard is the old convict-built prison, its murky stories brought to life through fascinating guided tours.

p50

Around Perth

Beaches
Wildlife
Day Trips

Beaches
Rottnest Island is ringed by gorgeous beaches that are often deserted midweek. Mandurah, Rockingham and Yanchep are built-up beach 'burbs bustling with cafes and marinas. Guilderton sits on a picturesque lagoon, while Lancelin is windsurfing heaven.

Wildlife
Whales, dolphins, sea lions, seals, penguins, kangaroos, possums, quokkas, bilbies, boodies, woylies – it's quite amazing how much wildlife lives in such close proximity to the city.

Heritage Towns
The quaint townships in the forests, hills and river valleys surrounding Perth make perfect day trips. York has contiguous rows of historic buildings, preserving a gold-rush atmosphere.

p96

Margaret River & the Southwest Coast

Beaches
Food & Wine
Nature

Geographe Bay
The sandy beaches of Geographe Bay are perfect for a bucket-and-spade family holiday. The most beautiful spots are near Cape Naturaliste. The state's primo surf breaks also roll ashore to the south.

Margaret River Wine Region
Australia's most beautiful wine region also produces some of the country's best wine. The cool-climate vineyards around Pemberton are worth exploring too.

Towering Forests
Studded with tuart and karri, WA's forests of tall trees are an impressive sight. Some of the larger specimens are rigged with spikes, allowing the fit and fearless to climb up to 68m into the canopy.

p121

Southern WA

Beaches
Wineries
National Parks

Isolated Beaches

Glorious, isolated bays of powdery white sand are spread all along this stretch of coast. On many you'll be more likely to spot a whale than another person.

Great Southern Wine Region

The wineries of the Great Southern region are growing in stature. Sup your way from Denmark to Mt Barker and on to Porongurup.

National Parks

This region's parks encompass the dramatic Tree Top Walk in Walpole-Nornalup and the silky sands of Cape Arid. Don't miss the rugged Porongurup and Stirling Range National Parks, or the vast wild heath of Fitzgerald River.

p147

Monkey Mia & the Central West

Beaches
Adventure
History

Epic Coastline

The white-shell beaches of Shark Bay – with the famous Monkey Mia dolphins – are just part of a turquoise coastline stretching from family-friendly Port Denison to the wilds of Gnaraloo Station.

Outdoor Adventures

Surfers and windsurfers flock to Geraldton and Gnaraloo for winter swells and summer winds, while fisherfolk and explorers head west to Edel Land. Bushwalkers prefer Kalbarri in winter.

Shipwrecks & Settlements

Historic artefacts, shipwrecks and 19th-century buildings stud this rugged coastline. Highlights include Greenough's pioneer settlement and the 1629 wreck of the *Batavia* off the Houtman Abrolhos Islands.

p165

Ningaloo Coast & the Pilbara

Beaches
Adventure
Wildlife

Ningaloo Marine Park

Superb, isolated beaches lead down to shallow lagoons hemmed by World Heritage–listed Ningaloo Marine Park. World-class snorkelling and diving are only a short wade from shore, and camping is right behind the dunes.

Karijini National Park

Karijini National Park is the Pilbara's adventure playground, with deep, narrow gorges inviting exploration, and the state's highest peaks begging to be climbed.

Native Wildlife

Whale sharks, manta rays, turtles and migrating whales all visit Ningaloo, while inland birds flock to the oasis pools of Millstream Chichester National Park, and pythons and rock wallabies hide in the shadows of Karijini.

p183

Broome & the Kimberley

Beaches
Culture
Adventure

Iconic Beaches

Don't miss the sunset camel trains of Cable Beach. A rising full moon creates the optical illusion of a golden stairway to the sky. Equally spectacular are the seldom-visited beaches of the Dampier Peninsula.

Indigenous Culture

Learn traditional practices from the Aboriginal communities of the Dampier Peninsula. Follow Broome's Lurujarri Dreaming Trail, before exploring the Kimberley's amazing Wandjina and Gwion Gwion images.

Gibb River Road

Drive the bone-shaking Gibb River Road, detouring to Mitchell Falls and remote Kalumburu. Zip along on a speedboat to the Horizontal Waterfalls, or negotiate a canoe down the mighty Ord River.

p205

On the Road

Perth & Fremantle

Why Go?

Basking under a near-permanent canopy of blue sky, Perth is a modern-day boom town, stoking Australia's economy from its glitzy central business district. Anchored by the broad Swan River flowing past skyscrapers and out to the Indian Ocean, the city boasts recent developments like Elizabeth Quay and Perth Stadium, which have added a more cosmopolitan sheen to this traditionally laid-back town.

But Perth's heart is still down at the beach, tossing in clear surf and relaxing on the sand. The city's beaches trace the western edge of Australia for around 40km, and on any given day you can often have one all to yourself.

Perth has sprawled to enfold Fremantle within in its suburbs, but the raffish port town with a great food and arts scene maintains its own distinct personality – immensely proud of its nautical ties, working-class roots and bohemian reputation.

Best Places to Eat

➡ Long Chim (p71)
➡ Brika (p72)
➡ Wildflower (p71)
➡ Bread in Common (p91)
➡ Manuka Woodfire Kitchen (p92)

Best Places to Sleep

➡ Como The Treasury (p68)
➡ Durack House (p69)
➡ Nest on Newcastle (p68)
➡ Sage Hotel (p69)
➡ Fremantle Apartment (p90)
➡ Fothergills of Fremantle (p91)

When to Go
Perth

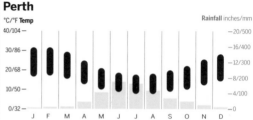

Feb Perth's Art Festival is on and school starts, so the beaches are less crowded.

Mar Warm and dry, so great weather for the beach and not as swelteringly hot.

Sep Kings Park wildflowers, the Perth Royal Show and the Listen Out festival.

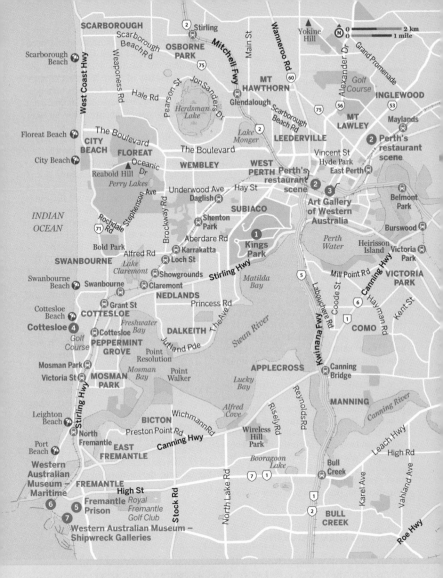

Perth & Fremantle Highlights

① Stretching out on the lawn in **Kings Park** (p56) with the glittering river and city spread out below you.

② Experiencing **Perth's restaurant scene** (p70) in the eateries of Mt Lawley, Northbridge and the city centre.

③ Exploring a wealth of local art, including a significant

Indigenous collection in the **Art Gallery of Western Australia** (p53).

④ Enjoying the sunset with a sundowner after a hard day's beaching at **Cottesloe** (p57).

⑤ Doing time with the ghosts of convicts past in World Heritage–listed **Fremantle Prison** (p85).

⑥ Exploring Freo's seafaring past in the spectacular ocean-front **Western Australian Museum – Maritime** (p85).

⑦ Learning about the fascinating 1629 wreck of the *Batavia* at the **Western Australian Museum – Shipwreck Galleries** (p85).

PERTH

POP 2.02 MILLION / ♪ 08

Laid-back, liveable Perth has wonderful weather, beautiful beaches and an easygoing character. About as close to Bali as to some of Australia's eastern state capitals, Perth combines big-city attractions and relaxed, informal surrounds, providing an appealing lifestyle for locals and lots to do for visitors. It's a sophisticated, cosmopolitan city, with myriad bars, restaurants and cultural activities all vying for attention. When you want to chill out, it's easy to do so. Perth's pristine parkland, nearby bush, and river and ocean beaches – along with a good public-transport system – allow its inhabitants to spread out and enjoy what's on offer.

History

The discovery of stone implements near the Swan River suggests that Mooro, the site on which the city of Perth now stands, has been occupied for around 40,000 years. The indigenous Wadjuk people, a subgroup of the Noongar, believed that the Swan River (Derbal Yaragan) and the landforms surrounding it were shaped by two Wargal (giant serpentlike creatures), which lived under present-day Kings Park.

In December 1696 three ships in the Dutch fleet commanded by Willem de Vlamingh anchored off Rottnest Island. On 5 January 1697 a well-armed party landed near present-day Cottesloe Beach. They tried to make contact with the local people to enquire about survivors of the *Ridderschap van Hollant,* lost in 1694, but were unsuccessful, so they sailed north. It was de Vlamingh who bestowed the name Swan on the river.

Modern Perth was founded in 1829 when Captain James Stirling established the Swan River Colony, and named the main settlement after the Scottish home town of the British Secretary of State for the Colonies. The original settlers paid for their own passage and that of their servants, and received 200 acres for every labourer they brought with them.

At the time Mooro belonged to a Wadjuk leader called Yellagonga and his people. Relations were friendly at first, the Noongar believing the British to be the returned spirits of their dead, but competition for resources led to conflict. Yellagonga moved his camp first to Lake Monger, but by the time he died in 1843 his people had been dispossessed of all of their lands and were forced to camp around swamps and lakes to the north.

Midgegooroo, an elder from south of the Swan River, along with his son Yagan, led resistance to the British settlement. In 1833 Midgegooroo was caught and executed by firing squad, while Yagan was shot a few months later by teenage settlers whom he had befriended. Yagan's head was removed, smoked and sent to London, where it was publicly displayed as an anthropological curiosity.

Life for the settlers was much harder than they had expected. The early settlement grew very slowly until 1850, when convicts alleviated the labour shortage and boosted the population. Convicts constructed the city's substantial buildings, including Government House and the Town Hall. Yet Perth's development lagged behind that of the cities in the eastern colonies until the discovery of gold inland in the 1890s. Perth's

---

PERTH & FREMANTLE IN...

Two Days

Have a leisurely breakfast in **Mt Lawley** or the **City Centre** and then spend your first morning exploring the art galleries of the **Perth Cultural Centre**. Grab lunch and go shopping in the hip **Leederville** neighbourhood before exploring verdant and view-friendly **Kings Park**. The following day, discover the lustrous riches of the **Perth Mint** before catching the **Little Ferry Co** from **Elizabeth Quay** to **Claisebrook Cove** to enjoy riverside eating and drinking.

Four Days

Follow the two-day itinerary and also make time to take excursions to the best of Perth's beaches – maybe pick up provisions for a picnic at **Cottesloe** or **City Beach.** Take a trip north to the **Aquarium of Western Australia** and spend the evenings hunting out hidden bars and good eating around **Northbridge**.

population increased by 400% within a decade and a building bonanza commenced.

The mineral wealth of WA has continued to drive Perth's growth. In the 1980s and '90s, though, the city's clean-cut, nouveau-riche image was tainted by a series of financial and political scandals.

Western Australia's 21st-century mining boom has cooled slightly in recent years, but there are still plenty of Aussie dollars awash in the state's economy, and Perth continues to blossom like WA's wildflowers in spring. Major civic works include a new football stadium, and visitors to Perth can witness ongoing work on two major reboots of the central city's urban landscape.

The City Link project will transform the area between Northbridge and the CBD. At the opposite end of the CBD, the Elizabeth Quay development is adding parks and retail and hospitality precincts to the riverfront land between Barrack and William Sts. Having turned its back on the river for many decades, downtown Perth will once again link with the silvery waters of the Swan. See www.getthebiggerpicture.com.au for information on these developments.

Largely excluded from this race to riches have been the Noongar people. In 2006 the Perth Federal Court recognised native title over the city of Perth and its surrounds, but this finding was appealed by the WA and Commonwealth governments. In December 2009 an agreement was signed in WA's parliament, setting out a time frame for negotiating settlement of native-title claims across the southwest. In mid-2015, a $1.3-billion native-title deal was settled by the WA government recognising the Noongar people as the traditional owners of the southwest. Covering over 200,000 sq km, the settlement region stretches from Jurien Bay to Ravensthorpe, and includes the Perth metropolitan area.

◎ Sights

Many of Perth's main attractions are within walking distance of the inner city, and several are in the Perth Cultural Centre precinct past the railway station in Northbridge. Easy day trips include the Swan Valley.

◎ City Centre

Elizabeth Quay   AREA
(www.elizabethquay.com.au) A vital part of the city's urban development is the Elizabeth Quay area taking shape at the bottom of Bar-

rack St. Luxury hotels and apartments are under construction, joining recently opened waterfront restaurants. With a busport, train station and ferry terminal, the area is also developing as a transport hub. Current highlights include the spectacular Elizabeth Quay pedestrian bridge.

Bell Tower   LANDMARK
(☑08-6210 0444; www.thebelltower.com.au; Barrack Sq; adult/child $18/9; ◎10am-4pm, ringing noon-1pm Sat-Mon & Thu) This pointy glass spire fronted by copper sails contains the royal bells of London's St Martin-in-the-Fields, the oldest of which dates to 1550. The bells were given to WA by the British government in 1988, and are the only set known to have left England. Clamber to the top for 360-degree views of Perth by the river.

The tower sits on land that was reclaimed in the 1920s and 1930s and now forms a green strip between the river and the city. Long, thin Langley Park is still occasionally used as an airstrip for light-aircraft demonstrations. Nearby Stirling Gardens and Supreme Court Gardens have lawns and formal gardens that fill up with city workers at lunchtime.

Perth Mint   HISTORIC BUILDING
(☑08-9421 7222; www.perthmint.com.au; 310 Hay St; adult/child $19/8; ◎9am-5pm) Dating from 1899, the compelling Mint displays a collection of coins, nuggets and gold bars. You can caress a bar worth over $200,000, mint your own coins and watch gold pours (on the half-hour, from 9.30am to 3.30pm). The Mint's Gold Exhibition features a massive 1 tonne gold coin worth a staggering $50 million.

◎ Northbridge

★ Art Gallery of
Western Australia   GALLERY
(☑08-9492 6622; www.artgallery.wa.gov.au; Perth Cultural Centre; ◎10am-5pm Wed-Mon) FREE Founded in 1895, this excellent gallery houses the state's pre-eminent art collection. It contains important post-WWII works by Australian luminaries such as Arthur Boyd, Albert Tucker, Grace Cossington Smith, Russell Drysdale, Arthur Streeton and Sidney Nolan. The Indigenous-art galleries are also very well regarded: work ranges from canvases to bark paintings and sculpture, and artists include Rover Thomas, Angilya

Perth

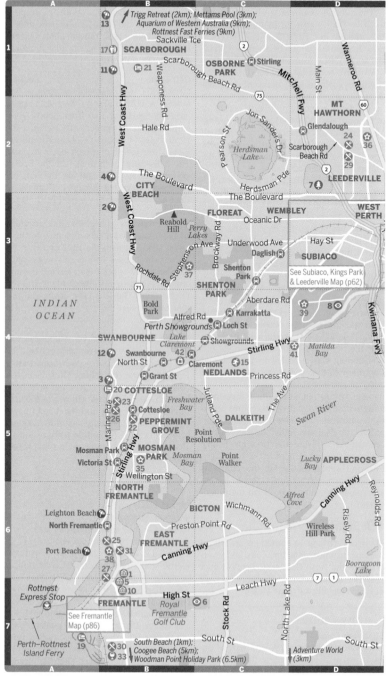

Trigg Retreat (2km); Mettams Pool (3km);
Aquarium of Western Australia (9km);
Rottnest Fast Ferries (9km)

13

17

11

21

SCARBOROUGH

Sackville Tce

OSBORNE PARK

Stirling

West Coast Hwy

Scarborough Beach Rd

Weaponess Rd

Mitchell Fwy

Main St

Wannaroo Rd

MT HAWTHORN

60

Hale Rd

Pearson St

Jon Sanders Dr

Herdsman Lake

Glendalough

24
36

Scarborough Beach Rd

29

4

2

West Coast Hwy

CITY BEACH

Reabold Hill

Perry Lakes

Herdsman Pde

The Boulevard

7

LEEDERVILLE

WEST PERTH

FLOREAT

WEMBLEY

Oceanic Dr

Brockway Rd

Stephenson Ave

The Boulevard

Underwood Ave

Daglish

Hay St

SUBIACO

See Subiaco, Kings Park
& Leederville Map (p62)

Rochdale Rd

71

37

SHENTON PARK

Shenton Park

INDIAN OCEAN

Bold Park

Perth Showgrounds

Alfred Rd

Loch St

Karrakatta

Aberdare Rd

39

8

Kwinana Fwy

SWANBOURNE

12

Swanbourne

North St

Lake Claremont

42

Claremont

Showgrounds

Stirling Hwy

15

NEDLANDS

Princess Rd

41

Matilda Bay

3

20

Grant St

COTTESLOE

23

Cottesloe

26

22

PEPPERMINT GROVE

Freshwater Bay

Jutland Pde

DALKEITH

Point Resolution

Swan River

The Ave

Mosman Park

Victoria St

35

MOSMAN PARK

Wellington St

Mosman Bay

Point Walker

Lucky Bay

APPLECROSS

NORTH FREMANTLE

BICTON

Wichmann Rd

Alfred Cove

Canning Hwy

Reynolds Rd

Leighton Beach

North Fremantle

EAST FREMANTLE

Preston Point Rd

Wireless Hill Park

Risely Rd

Port Beach

25

38

31

Canning Hwy

27

1

5

10

High St

6

Leach Hwy

7

1

Booragoon Lake

North Lake Rd

Rottnest Express Stop

See Fremantle Map (p86)

FREMANTLE

Royal Fremantle Golf Club

Stock Rd

Perth–Rottnest Island Ferry

19

30

33

South Beach (1km);
Coogee Beach (5km);
Woodman Point Holiday Park (6.5km)

South St

Adventure World (3km)

South St

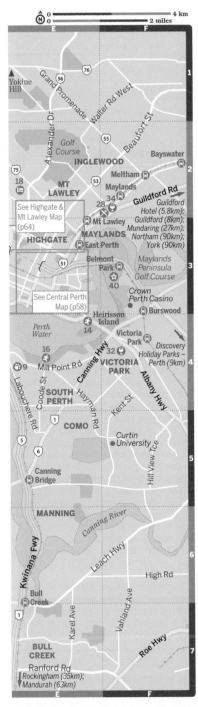

Mitchell, Christopher Pease and Phyllis Thomas. Check the website for info on free tours running most days at 11am and 1pm.

The annual WA Indigenous Art Awards entries are displayed here from August to December.

Western Australian Museum – Perth
MUSEUM

(☎08-6552 7800; www.museum.wa.gov.au; Perth Cultural Centre; ⊙9.30am-5pm) **FREE**
The state's museum is a six-headed beast, with branches in Albany, Geraldton and Kalgoorlie as well as two in Fremantle. This main branch in Northbridge is closed for renovation and is due to reopen as the renamed New Museum for WA in 2020. See online for details of the project, including concept plans. While the museum is closed, key exhibits are being displayed as pop-ups at other venues around town – see 'Museum Offsite' on the website.

Perth Institute of Contemporary Arts
GALLERY

(PICA; ☎08-9228 6300; www.pica.org.au; Perth Cultural Centre; ⊙10am-5pm Tue-Sun) **FREE**
PICA (*pee*-kah) may look traditional – it's housed in an elegant 1896 red-brick former school – but inside it's one of Australia's principal platforms for contemporary art, including installations, performance, sculpture and video. PICA actively promotes new and experimental art, and it exhibits graduate works annually. From 10am Tuesday to Sunday, the PICA Bar is a top spot for a coffee or cocktail, and has occasional live music.

Nostalgia Box
MUSEUM

(☎08-9227 7377; www.thenostalgiabox.com.au; 16 Aberdeen St; adult/child/family $15/10/45; ⊙10.30am-5pm) Ease into poignant low-pixel childhood memories of Atari, Nintendo and Super Mario at this surprisingly interesting collection of retro 1970s and 1980s gaming consoles and arcade games. Along the way, you'll learn about the history of gaming, and there are plenty of consoles to jump onto and see if the old skills are still there from a few decades back.

Hyde Park
PARK

(William St) One of Perth's most beautiful parks, suburban Hyde Park is a top spot for a picnic or lazy book-reading session on the lawn. A path traces the small lake, and mature palms, firs and Moreton Bay figs provide plenty of shade. It's within walking

Perth

distance of Northbridge; continue northeast along William St.

◎ Subiaco & Kings Park

★ **Kings Park & Botanic Garden** PARK (☎08-9480 3600; www.bgpa.wa.gov.au; ◎guided walks 10am, noon & 2pm) **FREE** Rising above the Swan River on the city's western flank, the 400-hectare, bush-filled expanse of Kings Park is Perth's pride and joy. At the park's heart is the 17-hectare Botanic Garden, containing over 2000 plant species indigenous to WA. In spring there's an impressive display of the state's famed wildflowers. A year-round highlight is the **Lotterywest Federation Walkway** (◎9am-5pm), a 620m path including a 222m-long glass-and-steel bridge that passes through the canopy of a stand of eucalypts.

The main road leading into the park, Fraser Ave, is lined with towering lemon-scented gums that are dramatically lit at night. At its culmination are the State War Memorial, a cafe, a gift shop, **Fraser's restaurant** (☎08-9481 7100; www. frasersrestaurant.com.au; Fraser Ave; mains $28-

45; ◎noon-late) and the Kings Park Visitor Centre. Free guided walks leave from here.

It's a good spot for a picnic or to let the kids off the leash in one of the playgrounds. Its numerous tracks are popular with walkers and joggers all year round, with an ascent of the steep stairs from the river rewarded with wonderful views from the top.

The Noongar people knew this area as Kaarta Gar-up and used it for thousands of years for hunting, food gathering, ceremonies, teaching and toolmaking. A freshwater spring at the base of the escarpment, now known as Kennedy Fountain but before that as Goonininup, was a home of the Wargal, mystical snakelike creatures that created the Swan River and other waterways.

To get here take bus 935 from St Georges Tce to near the visitor centre. You can also walk up (steep) Mount St from the city or climb Jacob's Ladder from Mounts Bay Rd, near the Adelphi Hotel.

◎ Beaches

Run by the Surf Life Saving Club of WA, the website www.mybeach.com.au has a profile of all the city beaches, including weather forecasts and information about buses, amenities and beach patrolling. Note that many beaches can be rough, with strong undertows and rips – swim between the flags.

Port Beach and **Leighton Beach** are popular for surfing. The Port (south) end is slightly better for swimming and has some eateries. Leighton Beach is a short walk from North Fremantle train station.

Hamersley Pool, North, Watermans and **Sorrento Beaches** are excellent for swimming and have picnic areas, BBQs and a bike path through scrub.

Cottesloe Beach   BEACH
(Marine Pde) The safest swimming beach, Cottesloe has cafes, pubs, pine trees and fantastic sunsets. From Cottesloe train station (on the Fremantle line) it's 1km to the beach. Bus 102 ($4.60) from Elizabeth Quay Busport goes straight to the beach.

Swanbourne Beach   BEACH
(Marine Pde) Safe swimming, and an unofficial nude and gay beach. From Grant St train station it's a 1.5km walk to the beach (2km from Swanbourne station). Catch bus 102 from Wellington St station and get off at Marine Pde. The recently opened Shorehouse restaurant has excellent ocean views.

City Beach   BEACH
(Challenger Pde) Swimming, surfing, lawn and amenities. Several new cafes and restaurants have opened here recently. Take bus 82 from Perth Busport.

Floreat Beach   BEACH
(West Coast Hwy) A generally uncrowded beach, but it can sometimes be windy. There's good swimming, surfing, cafes and a playground. Catch bus 82 from Perth Busport to City Beach and walk north 800m.

Scarborough Beach   BEACH
(The Esplanade) This is a popular young surfers' spot, so be sure to swim between the flags, as it can be dangerous. There are lots of shops and eateries, and the beachfront is being developed to make it more pedestrian- and bike-friendly, with new restaurants and cafes. Catch a Joondalup-line train from Esplanade to Stirling, and then bus 421 to the beach.

Trigg Beach   BEACH
(West Coast Hwy) Good surf, with a hardcore group of locals who come out when the surf's up; dangerous when rough and prone to rips – always swim between the flags.

Mettams Pool   BEACH
(West Coast Dr) Like a turquoise paddling pool with good snorkelling.

◉ Other Areas

Aquarium of Western Australia   AQUARIUM
(AQWA; ☑08-9447 7500; www.aqwa.com.au; Hillarys Boat Harbour, 91 Southside Dr; adult/child $30/18; ☺10am-5pm) Dividing WA's vast coastline into five distinct zones (Far North, Coral Coast, Shipwreck Coast, Perth and Great Southern), AQWA features a 98m underwater tunnel showcasing stingrays, turtles, fish and sharks. (The daring can

---

PERTH FOR CHILDREN

With a usually clement climate and plenty of open spaces and beaches to run around in, Perth is a great place to bring children. Of the beaches, **Cottesloe** is the safest and a family favourite. With older kids, arrange two-wheeled family expeditions along Perth's riverside and coastal bike paths. **Kings Park** has playgrounds and walking tracks.

The **Perth Royal Show** (p65), held late September, is an ever-popular family outing, with sideshow rides, show bags and proudly displayed poultry. Many of Perth's big attractions cater well for young audiences, especially the **Aquarium of Western Australia**, **Perth Zoo** (p59) and the **Art Gallery of Western Australia** (p53).

Scitech (☑08-9215 0700; www.scitech.org.au; City West Centre, Sutherland St; adult/child $19/12; ☺9.30am-4pm Mon-Fri, 10am-5pm Sat & Sun) is a good rainy-day option, with more than 160 hands-on, large-scale science and technology exhibits.

Adventure World (☑08-9417 9666; www.adventureworld.net.au; 351 Progress Dr; adult/child/family $58/48/180; ☺10am-5pm Thu-Mon late Sep-early May, daily school holidays & Dec) has exciting rides such as the G-force-defying 'Black Widow' and the 'Abyss' roller coaster, as well as pools, water slides and a castle.

Central Perth

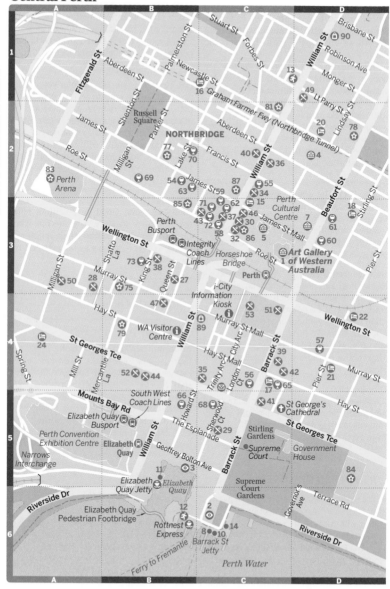

snorkel or dive with the sharks with the aquarium's in-house dive master.) By public transport, take the Joondalup train to Warwick station and then transfer to bus 423. By car, take the Mitchell Fwy north and exit at Hepburn Ave.

Diving costs $159 with your own gear (to hire snorkel/dive gear add $20/40). Behind-the-scenes tours (per person $95) run at 11am Thursday and Saturday. Bookings are essential.

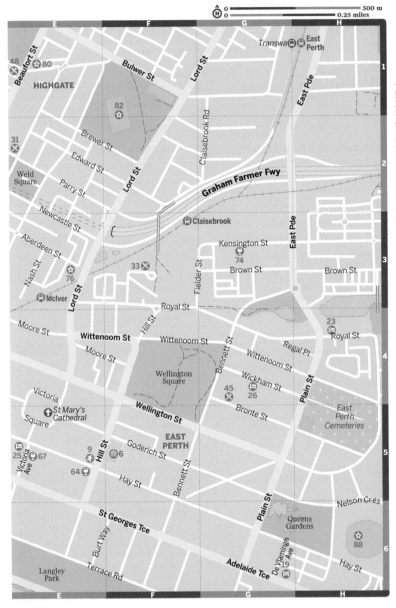

Perth Zoo ZOO
([📞08-9474 0444](); www.perthzoo.wa.gov.au; 20 Labouchere Rd; adult/child $29/14; ☺9am-5pm) Part of the fun of a day at the zoo is getting there – taking the ferry across the Swan River from Elizabeth Quay Jetty to Mends Street Jetty (every half-hour) and walking up the hill. Zones include Reptile Encounter, African Savannah (rhinos, cheetahs, zebras, giraffes and lions), Asian Rainforest (elephants, tigers, sun bears, orangutans) and Australian Bushwalk (kangaroos,

Central Perth

emus, koalas, dingos). Another transport option is bus 30 or 31 from Elizabeth Quay Busport.

Lake Monger PARK
(Lake Monger Dr) In spring black swans and their cygnets waddle about the grounds – something of a meeting place for local bird

life – nonplussed by the joggers circling the lake on the flat 3.5km path. There's plenty of grass for cricket, football and picnics. The lake's walking distance from Leederville train station; exit on the side opposite the shops, turn right onto Southport St and veer left onto Lake Monger Dr.

🏃 Activities

Whale Watching

Mills Charters WHALE WATCHING
(☎08-9246 5334; www.millscharters.com.au; adult/child $80/65; ☺9am & 1.30pm Sat & Sun mid-Sep–Nov) Informative three- to four-hour trips departing from Hillarys Boat Harbour.

Oceanic Cruises WHALE WATCHING
(☎08-9325 1191; www.oceaniccruises.com.au; adult/child $75/29) Departs Perth's Barrack Street Jetty or Fremantle's B Shed.

Cycling

Cycling is an excellent way to explore Perth. Kings Park has some good bike tracks and there are cycling routes along the Swan River, running all the way to Fremantle, and along the coast. Bikes can be taken free of charge on ferries at any time and on trains outside of weekday peak hours (7am to 9am and 4pm to 6.30pm) – with a bit of planning you can pedal as far as you like in one direction and return via public transport. Bikes can't be taken on buses at any time, except some regional coaches (for a small charge). For route maps, see www.transport.wa.gov.au/cycling/ or call into a bike shop.

Spinway WA CYCLING
(www.spinwaywa.bike/; from $11 per hour) Spinway WA has 17 self-serve bicycle-hire kiosks in city hot spots. Bikes, costing $11 for one hour, $22 for four hours, or $33 for 24 hours, can be rented in central Perth, Kings Park, South Perth, Scarborough and Fremantle.

Helmets are compulsory in WA, so Spinway WA includes one and a lock in your hire, collectable from the hotels the bike racks are connected to, or at Kings Park there's an automated helmet-dispensing cabinet. All 84 bikes are fitted with a smartphone holder, ideal if you've downloaded the free Spinway WA app. It can tell you where the nearest kiosk is, and certain rides you can do in the area. Wherever possible, its map will send you on bike paths rather than the road and it also provides information on the distance of each ride and the time it takes.

Gecko Bike Hire CYCLING
(☎08-9227 1400; www.geckobikehire.com.au; Emperor's Crown hostel, 85 Stirling St; per four hours/day $22/33) Located at the central Emperors' Crown hostel, at Ocean Beach Backpackers (p69) in Cottesloe, and further south in Bunbury, Busselton and Denmark. See the website for route maps.

Cycle Centre CYCLING
(☎08-9325 1176; www.cyclecentre.com.au; 326 Hay St; per day/week $25/65; ☺9am-5.30pm Mon-Fri, 9am-4pm Sat, 1-4pm Sun) See the website for recommended rides.

About Bike Hire CYCLING
(☎08-9221 2665; www.aboutbikehire.com.au; Causeway Car Park, 1-7 Riverside Dr; per hour/day/week from $10/24/64; ☺9am-5pm) Also hires kayaks (per hour/four hours $16/45) and paddleboards.

Other Activities

Australasian Diving Academy DIVING
(☎08-9389 5018; www.ausdiving.com.au; 142 Stirling Hwy) Hires diving gear (full set per day/week $75/200) and offers diving courses (four-day open-water $495). There are a variety of sites in the vicinity, including several around Rottnest Island, and four wrecks.

Funcats BOATING
(☎0408 926 003; www.funcats.com.au; Coode St Jetty; per hour $40; ☺10am-5.30pm Oct-Apr) These easy-to-sail catamarans are for hire on the South Perth foreshore. Each boat holds up to three people. Paddleboards and kayaks are also available. Cash only.

Surfschool SURFING
(☎08-9447 5637; www.surfschool.com; Scarborough Beach; from $60; ☺Oct-May) Two-hour lessons at Scarborough Beach (p57) (at the end of Manning St), including boards and wetsuits. Bookings essential. From June to September the operation moves to Leighton Beach just north of Fremantle.

Beatty Park Leisure Centre SWIMMING
(☎08-9273 6080; www.beattypark.com.au; 220 Vincent St; swimming adult/child $7/5; ☺5.30am-9pm Mon-Fri, 6.30am-6pm Sat & Sun) This complex has indoor and outdoor pools, water slides and a gym. Turn left at the top of

Subiaco, Kings Park & Leederville

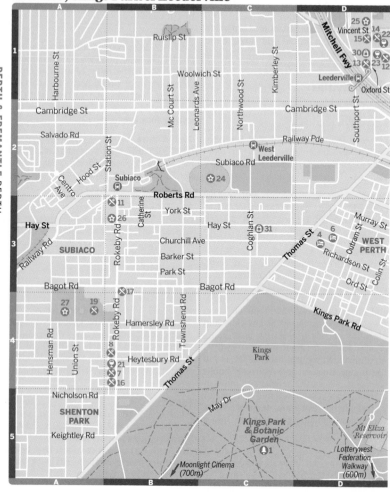

William St and continue on Vincent St to just past Charles St.

WA Skydiving Academy ADVENTURE SPORTS
(☑1300 137 855; www.waskydiving.com.au) Tandem jumps from 6000/8000/10,000/12,000ft from $260/300/340/380. Drop-zone options include Perth, Mandurah and Pinjarra.

Rottnest Air Taxi SCENIC FLIGHTS
(☑1300 895 538; www.rottnest.aero) Thirty-minute joy flights over the city, Kings Park and Fremantle (per person $149), leaving from Jandakot airport.

Tours

Food Loose Tours FOOD & DRINK
(www.foodloosetours.com.au; ⊘from $42) Fun and informative walking tours negotiating flavour-packed routes taking in restaurants, ethnic eateries and hard-to-find small bars in Perth and Fremantle.

Indigenous Heritage Tour CULTURAL
(☑0405 630 606; www.indigenouswa.com; adult/child $50/15; ⊘1.30pm Mon-Fri) A 90-minute Indigenous-themed stroll around Kings Park. Bookings (essential) can be made

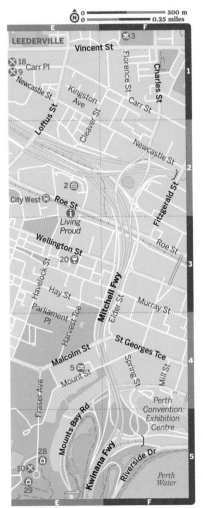

online or through the WA Visitor Centre (p276).

Two Feet & a Heartbeat WALKING
(☑ 1800 459 388; www.twofeet.com.au; per person $35-55) Daytime walking tours of Perth with an emphasis on heritage, culture and architecture, and a popular after-dark 'Small Bar Tour'.

Little Ferry Co BOATING
(☑ 0488 777 088; www.littleferryco.com.au; adult/child single $10/12, return $22/16; ◎ 9.30am-5.30pm) This heritage-style electric ferry travels between the Elizabeth Quay terminal and the cafes and restaurants of Claisebrook Cove. Either take a return trip or return by free CAT bus to the city. Friendly skipper Kevyn provides an interesting commentary, and when the new Perth Stadium opens in early 2018 he hopes to offer transport linking the city and the venue.

See the website for departure times from Elizabeth Quay and Claisebrook Cove for the 30-minute journey.

Highgate & Mt Lawley

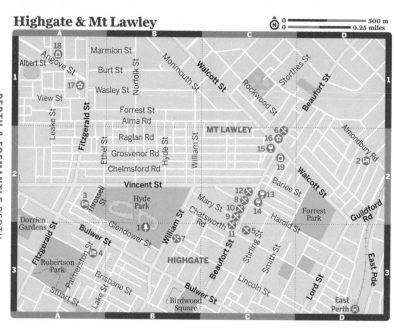

Highgate & Mt Lawley

Segway Tours   TOURS
(🖉1300 80 81 80; www.segwaytourswa.com.au;
Barrack St Jetty; adult/child from $89/79) Options include the Foreshore Tour (90 minutes) and the Riverside Tour (one hour). Full training is given before tours commence.

Beer Nuts   BREWERY
(🖉08-9295 0605; www.beernuts.com.au; per person from $70; ⊙ Wed-Sun) Tours visit Swan Valley microbreweries and a rum distillery.

Captain Cook Cruises   CRUISE
(🖉08-9325 3341; www.captaincookcruises.com.au; adult/child from $40/23) Cruises to the Swan Valley or Fremantle, with an array of add-ons such as meals, craft beer, wine tastings and tram rides. Departures are from Barrack Street Jetty.

Out & About   WINE
(🖉08-9377 3376; www.outandabouttours.com.au; per person from $85) Wine-focused tours of the Swan Valley and historic Guildford. Some

include river cruises, breweries, and cheese and chocolate stops. Also runs day trips to Margaret River.

City Sightseeing Perth Tour BUS
(☑08-9203 8882; www.citysightseeingperth.com; adult/child from $32/12) Hop-on, hop-off double-decker bus tour, with loop routes taking in the central city, Kings Park and Northbridge. Tickets are valid for up to two days.

Golden Sun Cruises CRUISE
(☑08-9325 9916; www.goldensuncruises.com.au; tours from $22) Well-priced cruises and a good option to get to Fremantle. Departures are from Barrack Street Jetty.

Swan Valley Tours FOOD & DRINK
(☑03-9274 1199; www.svtours.com.au; per person from $70) Food- and wine-driven tours that cruise up to and/or drive through the Swan Valley.

✫ Festivals & Events

Perth Cup SPORTS
(www.perthracing.org.au; ⊙1 Jan) New Year's Day sees Perth's biggest day at the races, with the party people heading to 'Tentland' for DJs and daiquiris.

Australia Day Skyworks FIREWORKS
(www.perth.wa.gov.au; ⊙26 Jan) Around 250,000 people come down to the riverside for a whole day of family entertainment, culminating in a 30-minute firework display at 8pm.

Perth International Arts Festival ART
(www.perthfestival.com.au; ⊙mid-Feb–early Mar) Artists such as Laurie Anderson, Dead Can Dance and Sleater-Kinney perform alongside top local talent. Held over 25 days, it spans theatre, classical music, jazz, visual arts, dance, film and literature. Worth scheduling a trip around, especially for nocturnal types.

Kings Park Festival CULTURAL
(www.kingsparkfestival.com.au; ⊙Sep) Held throughout September to coincide with the wildflower displays, the festival includes live music every Sunday, guided walks and talks.

Perth Royal Show FAIR
(www.perthroyalshow.com.au; Claremont Showground; ⊙late Sep-early Oct) A week of funfair rides, spun sugar and show bags full of plastic junk. Oh, and farm animals.

Listen Out MUSIC
(www.listen-out.com.au; Western Parklands; ⊙late Sep) A one-day festival of international and local purveyors of danceable beats.

Awesome International Festival for Bright Young Things ART
(www.awesomearts.com; Perth Cultural Centre; ⊙school holidays Oct) This 13-day contemporary-arts festival celebrates young creativity with exhibitions, film, theatre, dance and wacky instruments. It strikes a balance between international performers and audience participation.

🛏 Sleeping

Hotel options have improved recently, especially around Northbridge – and new luxury international hotels from Westin and Ritz-Carlton are scheduled to open in the CBD and at Elizabeth Quay in 2017 and 2018.

Both the CBD and Northbridge are close to public transport, making hopping out to inner-city suburbs such as Leederville and Mt Lawley straightforward.

🛏 City Centre

Perth City YHA HOSTEL $
(☑08-9287 3333; www.yha.com.au; 300 Wellington St; dm $33-36, r $125, with shared bathroom $100; 🚲@🛜🏊) Occupying an impressive 1940s art-deco building by the train tracks, the centrally located YHA has a slight boarding-school feel in the corridors, but the rooms are clean and there are good facilities including a gym and a bar. Like many Perth hostels, it's popular with FIFO ('fly-in, fly-out') mine workers, so the traditional YHA travellers' vibe has been diminished.

Riverview 42 Mt St Hotel APARTMENT $$
(☑08-9321 8963; www.riverviewperth.com.au; 42 Mount St; apt $130-229; 🚲@🛜) There's a lot of brash new money up here on Mount St, but character-filled Riverview stands out as the best personality on the block. Its refurbished 1960s bachelor pads sit neatly atop a modern foyer and a relaxed cafe. Rooms are sunny and simple; the front ones have river views, while the back ones are quieter.

Pensione Hotel BOUTIQUE HOTEL $$
(☑08-9325 2133; www.pensione.com.au; 70 Pier St; d from $182; 🚲🛜) Formerly the budget-oriented Aarons, this central-city 98-room property now features a boutique sheen as the Pensione Hotel. The standard rooms definitely veer to cosy and (very) compact,

LEE ROGERS / GETTY IMAGES ©

1. Perth nightlife
Hip bars, like Varnish on King (p76), are opening up across the city.

2. Kings Park & Botanic Garden (p56)
Featuring the Lotterywest Federation Walkway that passes through the treetops, Kings Park is Perth's pride and joy.

3. Fremantle
Fremantle has an identity that is entirely separate from Perth and has a host of attractions – including the rejuvenated Fremantle Markets (p88) – making it a draw for tourists in its own right.

4. Perth's beaches
Perth is renowned for its spectacular beaches, including Cottesloe Beach (p57), which is the safest swimming beach.

MEZAIRI / SHUTTERSTOCK ©

but classy decor and a good location are two definite pluses in an expensive city. A few carpets are looking a tad worn, though.

Travelodge Perth HOTEL **$$**

(☑08-9238 1888; www.travelodge.com.au; 417 Hay St; r from $179; ❄️🛜) No surprises here, just unassuming, well-kept rooms, some with views. Occasional online deals are good value.

★Como The Treasury BOUTIQUE HOTEL **$$$**

(☑08-6168 7888; www.comohotels.com/thetreasury; State Buildings, 1 Cathedral Ave; r from $491; ❄️🛜🏊) Judged the world's second-best hotel in late 2016 by the readers of *Condé Nast Traveler* magazine – just a few months after opening – Como The Treasury has 48 luxury rooms that fill the heritage splendour of the 140-year-old State Buildings. Despite the historic backdrop, the property is wonderfully understated and contemporary, with a superb spa and indoor pool.

Terrace Hotel BOUTIQUE HOTEL **$$$**

(☑08-9214 4444; www.terracehotelperth.com.au; 237 St Georges Tce; d from $319; ❄️🛜) The Terrace Hotel fills a heritage-listed terrace house in Perth's historic West End. There are 15 deluxe rooms and suites, all with a clubby, luxurious ambience. Modern accoutrements include huge flat-screen TVs, Apple TV and iPads, and king-sized four-poster beds with Egyptian-cotton linen. The downstairs restaurant is popular for high tea and hosts regular events for Perth's movers and shakers.

Fraser Suites APARTMENT **$$$**

(☑08-9261 0000; http://perth.frasershospitality.com/en; 10 Adelaide Tce; apt from $276; ❄️🛜🏊) At the quieter, eastern end of Perth CBD, Fraser Suites offers elegant, modern apartments that are a good option for families or longer-stay visitors needing kitchen facilities. If you're here for the cricket, the hallowed turf of the WACA is a short stroll away, and when Perth's new stadium opens in early 2018, Fraser Suites will also be well placed.

🛏 Northbridge

Most of Perth's hostels are in Northbridge, and it's possible to walk around and inspect rooms before putting your money down. Note that many hostels have long-term residents working in Perth, and this can alter the ambience for short-term visitors

and travellers. Northbridge also has a few new boutique hotels, which are convenient for the area's good restaurants, bars and nightlife.

Witch's Hat HOSTEL **$**

(☑08-9228 4228; www.witchs-hat.com; 148 Palmerston St; dm $24-30, tw & d $75; ❄️@🛜) Witch's Hat is like something out of a fairy tale. The 1897 building itself could be mistaken for a gingerbread house, and the witch's hat (an Edwardian turret) stands proudly out the front, beckoning the curious to step inside. Dorms are light and uncommonly spacious, and there's a red-brick barbecue area out the back.

Emperor's Crown HOSTEL **$**

(☑08-9227 1400; www.emperorscrown.com.au; 85 Stirling St; dm $24-28, r from $95, with shared bathroom from $90; ❄️@🛜) One of Perth's best hostels has a great position (close to the Northbridge scene without being in the thick of it), friendly staff and high housekeeping standards. It's a bit pricier than most, but it's worth it.

Alex Hotel BOUTIQUE HOTEL **$$**

(☑08-6430 4000; www.alexhotel.com.au; 50 James St; d from $209; ❄️@🛜) The Alex Hotel is stylish evidence of the reinvention of Northbridge as a happening neighbourhood. Classy and compact rooms are decked out in neutral colours, and stacked with fine linen and electronic gear. Relaxed shared spaces include a hip mezzanine lounge, and the roof terrace has great city views. Shadow Wine Bar, the Alex's streetfront restaurant, channels a European bistro.

Pension of Perth B&B **$$**

(☑08-9228 9049; www.pensionperth.com.au; 3 Throssell St; s/d $135/150; ❄️@🛜) Pension of Perth's French style lays luxury on thick, with rich floral rugs, brocade curtains, open fireplaces and gold-framed mirrors. Two doubles with bay windows (and small bathrooms) look out onto the park, and there are two rooms with spa baths. Location-wise, it's just across the road from gorgeous Hyde Park. A town house in Northbridge is also on offer.

Nest on Newcastle BOUTIQUE HOTEL **$$**

(☑08-6151 4000; www.thenestonnewcastle.com.au; 172 Newcastle St; r $190-220; ❄️🛜) Combining a convenient Northbridge location and rooms with design influences as diverse as

'Bali', 'New York' and 'Audrey Hepburn', Nest on Newcastle is one of Perth's newest boutique hotels. Gleaming white tiles make the bathrooms shine and some rooms have compact balconies. Mod cons include Nespresso coffee machines and smart TVs, and there's a rooftop terrace with good views.

Attika APARTMENTS **$$**
(☑08-6168 8598; www.attikahotel.com; 279 Newcastle St; apt from $219; ✳☎) Newly opened Attika features modern studio and one-bedroom apartments a short walk from the good restaurants of Northbridge but far enough away to present no problems with noise. The free CAT bus stops nearby for other Perth journeys, and compact kitchenettes make the property a good medium-stay choice. Attika is popular with business travellers, so weekend rates are cheaper.

East Perth

Wickham Retreat HOSTEL **$**
(☑08-9325 6398; www.facebook.com/wickhamretreat; 25-27 Wickham St; dm $34-38, d $80; @☎) Located in a residential neighbourhood east of the city centre, Wickham Retreat has a quieter vibe than other hostels around town. Most of the guests are international travellers, drawn by the colourful rooms and dorms, and a funky AstroTurf garden. Free food – including rice, fresh bread and vegies – extends travel budgets eroded by Perth's high prices.

Sebel East Perth APARTMENT **$$$**
(☑08-9223 2500; www.accorhotels.com.au; 60 Royal St; apt from $300; ✳☎) Modern and chic apartments with self-contained kitchenettes and a classy hotel vibe. Adjacent Claisebrook Cove Promenade has a few nights' worth of restaurants, cafes and bars.

Highgate & Mt Lawley

★**Durack House** B&B **$$**
(☑08-9370 4305; www.durackhouse.com.au; 7 Almondbury Rd; r $195-215; ☎) It's hard to avoid words like 'delightful' when describing this cottage, set on a peaceful suburban street behind a rose-adorned white picket fence. The three rooms have plenty of old-world charm, paired with thoroughly modern bathrooms. It's only 250m from Mt Lawley station; turn left onto Railway Pde and then take the first right onto Almondbury Rd.

Above Bored B&B **$$**
(☑08-9444 5455; www.abovebored.com.au; 14 Norham St; d $190-200; ✳☎) In a quiet residential neighbourhood, this 1927 Federation house is owned by a friendly TV scriptwriter. The two themed rooms in the main house have eclectic decor, and in the garden there's a cosy self-contained cottage with a kitchenette. In an expensive town for accommodation, Above Bored is great value. Northbridge and Mt Lawley are a short drive away.

Subiaco & Kings Park

Sage Hotel DESIGN HOTEL **$$**
(☑08-6500 9100; www.snhotels.com/sage/west-perth; 1309 Hay St; r $149-246; ✳☎) Handily placed for both the CBD and Kings Park, the newly opened Sage offers modern rooms with iPod docking stations, 48in TVs and cleverly designed bathrooms and work stations. Amenities include a gym, and downstairs is a good Italian restaurant located in a 100-year-old heritage residence.

Richardson HOTEL **$$$**
(☑08-9217 8888; www.therichardson.com.au; 32 Richardson St; r/ste from $295/395; ✳☎⊠) Ship-shaped and shipshape, the Richardson offers luxurious, thoughtfully designed rooms, some with sliding doors to divide them into larger suites. The whole complex has a breezy, summery feel, with pale marble tiles, creamy walls and interesting art. There's an in-house spa centre if you require additional pampering.

Beaches

If you care most for the beach, consider staying at Cottesloe or Scarborough, as public transport to this part of town can be time-consuming.

Ocean Beach Backpackers HOSTEL **$**
(☑08-9384 5111; www.oceanbeachbackpackers.com.au; 1 Eric St; dm/s/d $29/75/84; @☎) Offering (some) ocean views, this big, bright hostel in the heart of Cottesloe is just a short skip from the sand. Rooms are basic, but all have private bathroom, and you'll probably just be here to sleep given the great location. Hire a bike to get around locally, or take advantage of the hostel's free bodyboards and surfboards.

Western Beach Lodge HOSTEL **$**
(☑08-9245 1624; www.westernbeach.com; 6 Westborough St; dm $34, d with shared bathroom $75;

@☎) A real surfer hang-out, this sociable, homey hostel has a good, no-frills feel. Discounts kick in for stays of three nights or longer. Surfboards and boogie boards are available.

Trigg Retreat B&B $$
(☑08-9447 6726; www.triggretreat.com; 59 Kitchener St; r $175; ✳@☎) This classy three-room B&B offers attractive and supremely comfortable queen bedrooms in a modern house a short drive from Trigg Beach. Each has fridge, TV, DVD player and tea- and coffee-making facilities, and there's also a compact guest kitchen. A full cooked breakfast is provided. Also available is a nearby cottage ($240) accommodating up to four people.

Other Areas

Discovery Holiday Parks – Perth CAMPGROUND $
(☑08-9453 6877; www.discoveryholidayparks. com.au; 186 Hale Rd; powered sites $35-45, units $139-159; ✳@☎☀) This well-kept holiday park, 15km out of the city, has a wide range of cabins and smart-looking units, many with deck, TV and DVD player.

🍴 Eating

City Centre

Twilight Hawkers Market STREET FOOD $
(www.twilighthawkersmarket.com; Forrest Chase; snacks & mains around $10; ⊙4.30-9pm Fri mid-Oct–late Apr) Ethnic food stalls bring the flavours and aromas of the world to central Perth on Friday night in spring and summer. Look forward to combining your Turkish *gözleme* (savoury crepe) or Colombian empanadas (deep-fried pastries) with regular live music from local Perth bands.

Le Vietnam VIETNAMESE $
(☑08-6114 8038; www.facebook.com/LeVietnamCafe; 1/80 Barrack St; snacks $7; ⊙6am-3pm Mon-Fri, 8.30am-2pm Sat; ☑) The best *banh mi* (Vietnamese baguettes) in town are served in this narrow, centrally located spot. Classic flavour combos blend chicken, pâté, chilli and lemon grass, while newer spins feature pulled pork, roast pork and crackling. Interesting drinks include Vietnamese coffee and lychee lemonade, and a hearty breakfast or lunch will only cost around 10 bucks.

Nao JAPANESE $
(☑08-9325 2090; www.naojapaneserestaurant. com.au; Equus Arcade, Shop 191/580 Hay St; mains $11-14; ⊙11.30am-6pm Mon-Thu, 11.30am-9pm Fri, noon-5pm Sun) Asian students, CBD desk jockeys and savvy foodies all gravitate to this spot serving the best ramen in town. At peak times you'll need to battle a small queue, but the silky combinations of broth, roast chashu pork and noodles are definitely worth the wait.

Toastface Grillah CAFE $
(☑0409 115 909; www.toastfacegrillah.com; Grand Lane; sandwiches $7-10; ⊙7am-4pm Mon-Fri, 9am-4pm Sat, 10am-4pm Sun) Vibrant street art, excellent coffee and a sneaky laneway location combine with interesting toasted sandwiches such as the 'Pear Grillz' with blue cheese, pear and lime chutney. All this and a not-so-subtle Wu-Tang Clan reference too.

Secret Garden CAFE $
(☑08-9322 5885; www.secretgardencafe.com.au; Murray Mews; mains $10-19; ⊙7am-2.30pm Mon-Sat; ☎) Tucked away down a boho laneway off Murray St, Secret Garden has good coffee, enticing counter food and all-day breakfasts for hangovers. Free wi-fi is the perfect partner to a robust espresso.

Angel Falls Grill VENEZUELAN $$
(☑08-9481 6222; www.angelfallsgrill.com.au; Shop 16, Shafto Lane; mains $14-27; ⊙7am-10pm Mon-Fri, 8am-11pm Sat, 9am-10pm Sun) The pick of Shafto Lane's ethnic eateries, Angel Falls Grill brings a taste of South America to Western Australia. Salads and meat dishes are served with *arepas* (flat breads), and appetisers include empanadas and savoury-topped plantains. Grilled meat dishes from the *parrillada* (barbecue) are packed with flavour, and surprising breakfast options also make Angel Falls a great place to start the day.

La Veen CAFE $$
(☑08-9321 1188; www.laveencoffee.com.au; 90 King St; mains $13-25; ⊙7am-3pm Mon-Sat, 7am-1pm Sun) La Veen's sunny brick-lined space showcases some of the city's best breakfast and lunch dishes. This being Australia, of course *shakshuka* (baked eggs) is on the menu, but La Veen's version, topped with *dukkah* and yoghurt and served with ciabatta toast, is one of Perth's best. It's a worthy coffee stop while browsing nearby fashion and design stores too.

Tiisch Cafe Bistro   CAFE $$
(www.tiisch.com.au; 938 Hay St; mains $14-24; ⊘7am-3pm Mon-Fri) High ceilings inspire a European ambience at this recent CBD opening. A serious approach to drinks includes cold-brew coffee, matcha and green tea, and the breakfast and lunch menus are equally tasty and on trend. Start the day with macadamia-nut granola with coconut *labneh*, or drop by at lunch for the wagyu beef burger with chilli and provolone cheese.

Greenhouse   TAPAS $$
(☑08-9481 8333; www.greenhouseperth.com; 100 St Georges Tce; breakfast $10-18, shared plates $12-32; ⊘7am-late Mon-Fri, from 9am Sat) Ground-breaking design – straw bales, plywood, corrugated iron and exterior walls covered with 5000 pot plants – combines with excellent food at this tapas-style eatery. Middle Eastern and Asian influences inform a sustainably sourced menu including slow-cooked lamb shoulder with miso and eggplant, and fish in a punchy wasabi batter. At night, Greenhouse morphs into a good bar.

★**Long Chim**   THAI $$$
(☑08-6168 7775; www.longchimperth.com; State Buildings, cnr St Georges Tce & Barrack St; mains $28-45; ⊘noon-late; 🍴) Australian chef David Thompson is renowned for respecting the authentic flavours of Thai street food, and with dishes like a fiery chicken *laap* (warm salad with fresh herbs) and roast curry of red duck, there's definitely no dialling back on the flavour for Western palates. The prawns with toasted coconut and betel leaves may well be the planet's finest appetiser.

★**Wildflower**   MODERN AUSTRALIAN $$$
(☑08-6168 7855; www.wildflowerperth.com.au; State Buildings, 1 Cathedral Ave; mains $36-49, 5-course tasting menu without/with wine $145/240; ⊘noon-3pm & 6pm-late Tue-Fri, 6pm-late Sat) Filling a glass pavilion atop the restored State Buildings, Wildflower offers seasonal menus inspired by the six seasons of the Indigenous Noongar people of southwestern WA. There's a passionate focus on Western Australian produce: dishes often include Shark Bay scallops or kangaroo smoked over jarrah embers, as well as indigenous herbs and bush plants like lemon myrtle and wattle seed.

1907   MODERN AUSTRALIAN $$$
(☑0427 260 587; www.1907.com.au; 26 Queen St; mains $28-48, degustation $80-135; ⊘11am-3pm & 6pm-midnight Tue-Sat) Hidden away down a lane, behind a gate and down the side of a building, this classy restaurant has a strong emphasis on local WA produce. Degustation options range from four to seven courses – with optional wine matches – and you can start or end the evening with classy cocktails in 1907's glam Bluzou vodka bar.

Print Hall   MODERN AUSTRALIAN $$$
(☑08-6282 0000; www.printhall.com.au; 125 St Georges Tce; shared plates $14-36, mains $25-36; ⊘11.30am-midnight Mon-Fri, 4pm-midnight Sat) This sprawling complex in the Brookfield Pl precinct includes The Apple Daily, featuring Southeast Asian–style street food, and the expansive Print Hall Bar, with an oyster bar and grilled WA meat and seafood. Don't miss having a drink and Spanish tapas in the rooftop Bob's Bar, named after Australia's larrikin former prime minister Bob Hawke.

SELF-CATERING

The pick of the self-catering crop:

➡ **Boatshed Market** (☑08-9284 5176; www.boatshedmarket.com.au; 40 Jarrad St; ⊘6.30am-8pm) Excellent deli and provedore.

➡ **Chez Jean-Claude Patisserie** (☑08-9381 7968; www.chezjeanclaudepatisserie.com.au; 333 Rokeby Rd; snacks $3-8; ⊘6am-6pm Mon-Fri) Brioche and baguettes.

➡ **City Farm Market** (☑08-9221 7300; www.perthcityfarm.org.au; 1 City Farm Pl; mains $12-15; ⊘8am-noon Sat, cafe 7am-3pm Mon-Fri, to noon Sat) Organic eggs, fruit, vegetables and bread, plus an excellent cafe.

➡ **Kailis Bros** (☑08-9443 6300; www.kailisbrosleederville.com.au; 101 Oxford St; ⊘shop 8am-6pm, cafe 7am-late) Fresh seafood and a cafe.

➡ **Kakulas Bros** (☑08-9328 5285; www.kakulasbros.com.au; 183 William St; ⊘8am-5pm Mon-Sat, 11am-4pm Sun; 🍴) Deli and provisions store.

➡ **Subiaco Farmers Market** (☑0406 758 803; www.subifarmersmarket.com.au; Subiaco Primary School, 271 Bagot Rd; snacks & meals $7-12; ⊘8am-noon Sat) Street eats, organic produce and family entertainment.

Balthazar
MODERN AUSTRALIAN $$$

(☑08-9421 1206; www.balthazar.com.au; 6 The Esplanade; small plates $17-23, large plates $28-38; ⊙noon-late Mon-Fri, 6pm-late Sat) Low-lit, discreet and sophisticated, with a hipster soundtrack and charming staff, Balthazar has an informal, cool vibe that's matched by exquisite food and a famously excellent wine list. The menu is refreshingly original, combining European flavours with an intensely local and seasonal focus. A recent update has reinvented Balthazar as a slightly more relaxed option with superior shared plates.

Trustee
BISTRO $$$

(☑08-6323 3000; www.thetrustee.com.au; 133 St Georges Tce; mains $28-48; ⊙noon-midnight Mon-Fri, from 5.30pm Sat) Occupying a heritage building in central Perth's Brookfield Pl precinct, the Trustee channels a European bistro vibe, with dishes including excellent grilled meats, duck Caesar salad and lamb osso bucco. A spectacular wine list draws Perth's movers and shakers, and the Angel's Cut bar dispenses pricey cocktails and around 100 types of rum.

Northbridge

Chicho Gelato
GELATO $

(www.chichogelato.com; 180 William St; from $5; ⊙noon-10pm Sun-Wed, to 11pm Thu-Sat) 'New-style gelato', the owners reckon, and with innovative flavours like lavender and honeycomb, and smoky Mexican chocolate they certainly have a point. Expect queues in the evening – don't worry, the line moves quickly – and ask about current collaborations with Perth and Fremantle chefs.

Tak Chee House
MALAYSIAN $

(☑08-9328 9445; 1/364 William St; mains $11-18; ⊙11am-3pm & 5-9pm Tue-Sun) With Malaysian students crammed in for a taste of home, Tak Chee is one of the best Asian cheapies along William St. If you don't have a taste for satay, Hainan chicken or *char kway teo* (fried noodles), Thai, Vietnamese, Lao and Chinese flavours are all just footsteps away. Cash only; BYO wine or beer.

Source Foods
CAFE $

(☑08-6468 7100; www.sourcefoods.com.au; 289 Beaufort St; mains $10-19; ⊙7.30am-3pm; 🛜🖉) 🍃 An unassuming corner cafe committed to sustainable practices, Source Food has excellent breakfast options that include a massive spinach-and-feta scramble. The roasted-sweet-potato-and-haloumi quesadilla is a top choice for lunch.

Chu Bakery
CAFE, BAKERY $

(☑08-9328 4740; www.facebook.com/Chu-Bakery-492284474260141; 498 William St; snacks from $5; ⊙7am-4pm Tue-Sun) Chu makes a great stop before or after exploring nearby Hyde Park. The coffee is excellent, the doughnuts superb, and the sourdough bread recommended if you're planning a beachy picnic out at Cottesloe or City Beach. For lunch, a favourite Hyde Park outdoor combo is a takeaway espresso and toast topped with creamy avocado, whipped feta and *sriracha* sauce.

Little Willy's
CAFE $

(☑08-9228 8240; www.facebook.com/LittleWillys; 267 William St; mains $10-19; ⊙6am-4pm Mon-Fri, 8am-4pm Sat & Sun) It's tiny and it's on William St, and it's a go-to spot to grab a footpath table and tuck into robust treats such as the city's best breakfast burrito and Bircher muesli. It's also a preferred coffee haunt for the hip Northbridge indie set. BYO skinny jeans.

Flipside
BURGERS $

(☑08-9228 8822; www.flipsideburgerbar.com.au; 222 William St; burgers $11.50-15.50; ⊙11.30am-9.30pm Mon-Wed, 11.30am-late Thu-Sat, noon-9pm Sun) Gourmet burgers with the option of takeaway to the bar upstairs, Mechanics Institute (p77).

★ Brika
GREEK $$

(☑0455 321 321; www.brika.com.au; 3/177 Stirling St; meze & mains $9-27; ⊙noon-3pm & 5pm-late Fri-Sun, 5pm-late Mon-Thu) Presenting a stylish spin on traditional Greek cuisine, Brika is one of Perth's most appealing restaurants. The whitewashed interior is enlivened by colourful traditional fabrics, and menu highlights include creamy smoked-eggplant dip, slow-cooked lamb, and prawns with saganaki. Definitely leave room for a dessert of *loukoumades* (Greek doughnuts).

If you're pushed for time, grab an espresso, baklava and a souvlaki wrap from Brika's new Filos + Yiros hole-in-the-wall option (open 7.30am to 4pm daily). There's a pleasant park just across the road to sit while you eat.

Hummus Club
MIDDLE EASTERN $$

(☑08-9227 8215; www.thehummusclub.com; 258 William St; mains $14-18; ⊙5-10pm Tue-Sun; 🖉) Formerly operating at markets around

Perth, Hummus Club is now all grown up and, following a successful crowd-funding campaign, has graduated to a bricks-and-mortar location in Northbridge. Creamy hummus is served with pitta bread, and other dishes include lamb kofta, felafel and good salads. Cocktails with Perth craft spirits and Lebanese Almaza beer complement a fun vibe.

Pleased to Meet You
BISTRO, BAR $$

(☑ 08-9227 9238; www.pleasedtomeetyou.com.au; 38 Roe St; shared plates $9-20; ⊗ 5pm-late Mon-Thu, noon-late Fri-Sun) Ticking all the hipster culinary boxes with its dedication to Asian and South American street food, Pleased to Meet You presents bold flavours in a menu that's perfect for sharing over a few cocktails, WA wines or craft beers. Grab a spot at the shared tables and tuck into flavour hits such as coconut ceviche, duck tacos and grilled garlic oysters.

Bivouac Canteen & Bar
CAFE $$

(☑ 08-9227 0883; www.bivouac.com.au; 198 William St; small plates $9-18, large plates $17-32; ⊗ noon-late Tue-Sat) Mediterranean- and North African–influenced cuisine partners with a good wine list, craft beers and artisan ciders here, and Bivouac's utilitarian decor is softened with a rotating roster of work from local artists. Our favourite dish is the flat-bread taco crammed with soft-shell crab, zingy pickles and red-pepper aioli. Refreshing salads include eggplant with tahini, saffron yoghurt, pomegranate and pistachio.

Sauma
INDIAN $$

(☑ 08-9227 8682; www.sauma.com.au; 200 William St; mains $16-28; ⊗ 5.30-10.30pm Tue & Wed, 11.30am-10.30pm Thu-Sun; ☑) The punchy flavours of Indian street food feature at this corner location in Northbridge. Interesting antiques surround the main bar dispensing Indian-inspired cocktails and Swan Valley beers, while the shared tables are full of diners tucking into chai-smoked oysters, chargrilled chilli squid and a terrific goat curry. The two eight-course tasting menus (per person $50 to $60) are good value.

East Perth

★ Restaurant Amusé
MODERN AUSTRALIAN $$$

(☑ 08-9325 4900; www.restaurantamuse.com.au; 64 Bronte St; degustation without/with wine pairing $130/210; ⊗ 6.30pm-late Tue-Sat) The critics have certainly been amused by this degustation-only establishment, regularly rated as one of Australia's finest. Ongoing accolades include being dubbed WA's number-one eatery by *Gourmet Traveller* magazine every year since 2010. Book well ahead and come prepared for a culinary adventure. Look forward to a stellar WA-focused wine list, too.

Highgate, Mt Lawley & Maylands

Veggie Mama
VEGETARIAN $

(☑ 08-9227 1910; www.facebook.com/veggiemama01; cnr Beaufort & Vincent Sts; mains $10-20; ⊗ 8am-7pm Mon & Tue, 8am-9pm Wed-Fri, 9am-5pm Sat & Sun; ☎☑) ☑ Loads of vegan and gluten-free options shine at this cute corner cafe where flavour is definitely not compromised. The menu includes delicious salads, smoothies, vegie curries and burgers; weekend breakfasts are very popular.

Cantina 663
MEDITERRANEAN $$

(☑ 08-9370 4883; www.cantina663.com; 663 Beaufort St; mains $15-28; ⊗ 7.30am-late Mon-Sat, to 3pm Sun) It's a culinary World Cup, featuring Spain, Portugal and Italy, at this cool but casual cantina with tables spilling into the arcade. Service can be a bit too cool for school, but it's worth waiting for dishes such as ravioli with spinach and ricotta, or beef croquettes. A good-value option is 'Design a Menu': eight courses for $40.

El Público
MEXICAN $$

(☑ 0418 187 708; www.elpublico.com.au; 511 Beaufort St; snacks & shared plates $9-18; ⊗ 5pm-midnight Mon-Fri, from 4pm Sat & Sun) Look forward to interesting and authentic spins on Mexican street food, all served as small plates that are perfect for sharing. Menu standouts include duck *carnitas* tacos, grilled octopus, and a sweetcorn sundae with coconut and popcorn for dessert. Bring along a few friends and groove to the occasional DJs over mezcal and great cocktails.

Mrs S
CAFE $$

(☑ 08-9271 6690; www.mrsscafe.com.au; 178 Whatley Cres; mains $11-23; ⊗ 7am-4pm Tue-Fri, 8am-4pm Sat & Sun) Mrs S has a quirky retro ambience, the perfect backdrop for excellent homestyle baking or a lazy brunch. Menus – presented in Little Golden children's books – feature loads of innovative variations on traditional dishes. Weekends are *wildly* popular, so try to visit on a weekday.

Mary Street Bakery CAFE $$

(☑08-499-509-300; www.facebook.com/marystreetbakery; 507 Beaufort St; mains $12-24; ⊘7am-4pm) Crunchy and warm wood-fired baked goods, artisan bread and interesting cafe fare combine with what are quite probably Perth's best chocolate-filled doughnuts at this spacious, sunny addition to the competitive dining scene in Mt Lawley. It's a good way to start the day before exploring the area's retail scene. At lunchtime a concise wine and beer selection also features.

Beaufort Local CAFE $$

(☑08-9328 6299; www.beaufortlocal.com.au; 488 Beaufort St; breakfast $13-24, lunch & dinner $24-37; ⊘7am-late) This Mt Lawley institution is good for a leisurely brekkie over newspapers and a couple of coffees. Go for the spinach-and-ricotta hotcakes, and work out what to order when you come back for dinner. How about the Margaret River lamb with purple basil, broad beans and yoghurt? Adjourn to the garden bar for a few cocktails or craft beers.

St Michael 6003 MODERN AUSTRALIAN $$$

(☑08-9328 1177; www.stmichael6003.com.au; 483 Beaufort St; 3/7 small plates per person $59/89; ⊘6-10pm Tue-Sat, plus noon-3pm Fri) Welcome to one of the city's classiest and most elegant eateries. Like the rest of Perth, the emphasis here is on smaller shared plates, but there's some serious culinary wizardry in the kitchen. Menu highlights could include WA marron (freshwater lobster), scallops, quail and trout. Sign up for the seven-course menu for a leisurely treat.

Must Winebar FRENCH $$$

(☑08-9328 8255; www.must.com.au; 519 Beaufort St; bar snacks $9-24, mains $39-46; ⊘noon-midnight) One of Perth's best wine bars, Must is also one of the city's best restaurants. The Gallic vibe is hip, slick and a little bit cheeky, and the menu marries classic French bistro flavours with the best local produce. Oysters, bar snacks and charcuterie plates are more informal, but equally tasty, distractions.

Mt Hawthorn

New Norcia Bakery BAKERY, CAFE $

(www.newnorciabakery.com.au; 163 Scarborough Beach Rd; mains $14-18; ⊘6.30am-5.30pm) With Perth's best bread, delicious pastries and a bright cafe as well, this place gets crammed on the weekends. There's another more central branch (The Cloisters, Bagot Rd; ⊘7am-

5.30pm Mon-Sat, 7.30am-2.30pm Sun) in Subiaco for takeaway goodies.

Divido ITALIAN $$$

(☑08-9443 7373; www.divido.com.au; 170 Scarborough Beach Rd; mains $38-38, 5-course degustation $79; ⊘11am-late Mon-Sat) Italian but not rigidly so (the chef's of Croatian extraction, so Dalmatian-style doughnuts are served as dessert), this romantic restaurant serves handmade pasta dishes and expertly grilled mains. The five-course degustation menu is highly recommended for a night of culinary adventure. A two-course special for $39.50 is good value and the roast lamb for two diners ($85) is stellar.

Leederville

Market Juicery CAFE $

(☑0458 877 000; www.facebook.com/Themarketjuicery; Shop 2, 139-141 Oxford St; salads $10-12, juices & smoothies $8-9; ⊘7am-3pm Mon-Fri, 8am-2pm Sat; ☑) ☑ Superfood smoothies, cold-pressed juices and zingy salads all feature at this good-value lunch stop amid the funky retailers of Leederville. Wraps and bagels are also appealing. You'll the find it down an arcade behind the magazine store.

Jus Burgers BURGERS $

(☑08-9228 2230; www.jusburgers.com.au; 743 Newcastle St; burgers $12-16; ⊘11am-late) ☑ Tasty, carbon-neutral gourmet burgers. There's another branch in Subiaco (☑08-9381 1895; www.jusburgers.com.au; 1 Rokeby Rd; burgers $12-16; ⊘11am-late).

Sayers CAFE $$

(☑08-9227 0429; www.sayersfood.com.au; 224 Carr Pl; mains $12-28; ⊘7am-4pm) This classy Leederville cafe has a counter groaning under the weight of an alluring cake selection. The breakfast menu includes poached eggs with potato rosti, while lunch highlights include harissa-spiced lamb shoulder with a Lebanese couscous salad and tahini *labneh*. Welcome to one of Perth's best cafes.

Low Key Chow House ASIAN $$

(☑08-9443 9305; www.keepitlowkey.com.au; 140 Oxford St; mains $24-30; ⊘5.30-10.30pm Tue-Fri, noon-3pm & 5.30-10.30pm Sat & Sun) Noisy and bustling – just like the Southeast Asian street-food eateries it references – eating at Low Key Chow House is a fun experience best shared with a group. Sup cold Singha beer or punchy Asian cocktails, and order up a storm from a menu featuring the best of Malaysia, Vietnam, Thailand, Cambodia and Laos.

Duende   TAPAS $$

(☑08-9228 0123; www.duende.com.au; 662 Newcastle St; tapas & mains $15-32; ⊙noon-late Mon-Thu, from 7.30am Fri, from 8.30am Sat & Sun) Sleek Duende occupies a corner site amid the comings and goings of Leederville. Stellar modern-accented tapas are served, so make a meal of it or call in for a late-night glass of dessert wine and *churros*. Alternatively, start the day with an espresso and Duende's sweetcorn and Manchego cheese croquettes. Seven- and 10-course tasting menus are available ($50/65).

⸙ Subiaco

Boucla   CAFE $

(☑08-9381 2841; 349 Rokeby Rd; mains $11-24; ⊙7am-5pm Mon-Fri, to 3.30pm Sat) A locals' secret, this Greek- and Levantine-infused haven is pleasingly isolated from the thick of the Rokeby Rd action. Baklava and cakes tempt you from the corner, and huge tarts filled with blue-vein cheese and roast vegetables spill off plates. The salads are great too.

Meeka   MIDDLE EASTERN $$$

(☑08-9381 1800; www.meekarestaurant.com.au; 361 Rokeby Rd; meze $15-18, mains $31-39; ⊙6pm-late Tue-Sun) In Subiaco's Rokeby Rd restaurant enclave, Meeka combines Modern Australian cuisine with the flavours of the Middle East and North Africa. Standout shared meze dishes include Tasmanian-smoked-salmon terrine, and the seafood tagine with prawn, squid and Pernod sauce integrates French and Moroccan influences. Try the doughnuts with Turkish-delight marshmallow for dessert.

⸙ Cottesloe

Cott & Co Fish Bar   SEAFOOD $$

(☑08-9383 1100; www.cottandco.com.au; 104 Marine Pde; bar snacks & oysters $12-26; mains $28-36; ⊙11am-late) This sleek seafood restaurant and wine bar is part of the renovated and historic Cottesloe Beach Hotel. Settle in with a few local oysters and a glass of Margaret River wine, and ease into a relaxing reverie in front of an Indian Ocean sunset. The pub's formerly rowdy garden bar now channels a whitewashed Cape Cod vibe as The Beach Club.

Il Lido   ITALIAN $$

(www.illido.com.au; 88 Marine Pde; mains $20-42; ⊙7am-late) Il Lido's alfresco area is popular with Cotteslocals and their dogs, but the sunny interior of this self-styled 'Italian canteen' is arguably even better. Breakfast and coffee attract early-bird swimmers, and throughout the day antipasto plates, pasta and risottos, alongside a good beer and wine list, continue the culinary buzz. Maybe linger for cocktails and an Indian Ocean sunset.

🍷 Drinking & Nightlife

A local law change a few years ago has produced a salvo of quirky small bars that are distinctly Melbourne-ish in their hipness. They're sprouting all over the place, including in the formerly deserted-after-dark central city. Northbridge is also a happy hunting ground for more idiosyncratic drinking establishments. Many offer interesting and tasty food, too.

🍺 City Centre

★ Petition Beer Corner   CRAFT BEER

(☑08-6168 7773; www.petitionperth.com/beer; State Buildings, cnr St Georges Tce & Barrack St; ⊙11.30am-late Mon-Sat, from noon Sun) Distressed walls provide the backdrop for craft brews at this spacious bar. There's a rotating selection of beers on tap – check out Now Tapped on Petition's website – and it's a great place to explore the more experimental side of the Australian craft-beer scene. Servings begin at just 150mL, so the curious beer fan will be in heaven.

Halford   COCKTAIL BAR

(☑08-9325 4006; www.halfordbar.com.au; State Buildings, cnr Hay St & Cathedral Ave; ⊙4pm-midnight Sun-Wed, to 2am Thu-Sat) Channeling a cosmopolitan 1950s vibe, Halford is where to come to sip Rat Pack–worthy cocktails, including expertly prepared martinis and other American bar classics. Halford's decor and furnishings have a tinge of retro style too, with shimmering fabrics, mood lighting, and vintage boxing pics lining the walls. Maybe this is the closest a remote Australian city comes to Vegas, baby.

Alfred's Pizzeria   BAR

(www.alfredspizzeria.com.au; 37 Barrack St; ⊙3pm-midnight) Pizza by the slice, a dive-bar vibe (with a touch of *The Godfather*), and craft beer and Aussie wines all combine in this improbably compact space in the CBD. Look forward to checking out the cool B&W photos of heritage NYC, and don't miss the wall-covering murals featuring Axl Rose as Jesus and Madonna as the Virgin Mary.

Lalla Rookh
WINE BAR

(⌨08-9325 7077; www.lallarookh.com.au; Lower Ground Floor, 77 St Georges Tce; ◷11.30am-midnight Mon-Fri, from 5pm Sat) Escape downstairs from the CBD to this cosy bar specialising in wine, craft beer and Italian food. Cocktails also come with a whisper of the Mediterranean, and the all-day menu encourages relaxed grazing over shared dishes (pizza from $18, shared plates from $15). Try the king-prawn pizza partnered with a zesty Feral Hop Hog Pale Ale from the Swan Valley.

Helvetica
BAR

(⌨08-9321 4422; www.helveticabar.com.au; rear 101 St Georges Tce; ◷3pm-midnight Tue-Thu, noon-1am Fri, 6pm-1am Sat) Clever artsy types tap their toes to delicious alternative pop in this bar named after a typeface and specialising in whisky and cocktails. The concealed entry is off Howard St; look for the chandelier in the laneway.

Hula Bula Bar
COCKTAIL BAR

(⌨08-9225 4457; www.hulabulabar.com; 12 Victoria Ave; ◷4pm-midnight Tue-Thu, 4pm-1am Fri, 6pm-1am Sat, 4-10pm Sun; ☏) You'll feel like you're on *Gilligan's Island* in this tiny Polynesian-themed bar, decked out in bamboo, palm leaves and tikis. A cool but relaxed crowd jams in here on weekends to sip ostentatious cocktails out of ceramic monkey's heads.

Varnish on King
COCKTAIL BAR

(⌨08-9324 2237; www.varnishonking.com; 75 King St; ◷11.30am-midnight Mon-Fri, 4pm-midnight Sat) With interesting shopping, cafes and bars, lower King St is an emerging Perth hot spot. Amid the hipster barber shops and single-origin coffee is this brick-lined homage to American whisky. More than 100 are available, and a decent beer and wine list is partnered by grown-up party food such as Texan spiced octopus with squid, zucchini and tarragon.

Wolf Lane
COCKTAIL BAR

(⌨08-9322 4671; www.wolflane.com.au; Wolfe Lane; ◷4pm-1am Fri & Sat) Exposed bricks, classic retro furniture and high ceilings create a pretty decent WA approximation of a

New York loft. A serious approach to cocktails and wine combines with an international beer selection, and quirky bar snacks including Vegemite-and-cheese mini scrolls. Aussie as...

Grosvenor
PUB

(⌨08-9325 3799; www.thegrosvenorperth.com.au; cnr Hay & Hill Sts; ◷11am-midnight) This classic corner pub – complete with wrought-iron balconies and one of Perth's best garden bars – draws a crowd of loyal locals, nearby desk jockeys and thirsty students. Decent wood-fired pizza too.

Ambar
CLUB

(⌨08-9325 3666; www.boomtick.com.au/ambar; 104 Murray St; ◷10pm-5am Fri & Sat) Perth's premier club for breakbeat, drum and bass, and visiting international DJs.

🦊 Northbridge

Northbridge is the rough-edged hub of Perth's nightlife, with pubs and clubs around William and James Sts. Recent openings have lifted the tone of the area. Most pubs have lockouts, so you'll need to be in before midnight. You may need to present photo ID.

★ Sneaky Tony's
BAR

(www.facebook.com/sneakytonys; Nicks Lane; ◷4pm-midnight) On Friday and Saturday you'll need the password to get into this unmarked bar amid street art and Chinese restaurants – don't worry, it's revealed weekly on Sneaky Tony's Facebook page – but once inside park yourself at the long bar and order a rum cocktail. Try the refreshing Dark & Stormy with ginger beer and lime. The entrance is behind 28 Roe St.

Dominion League
BAR

(⌨08-9227 7439; www.dominionleague.com.au; 84 Beaufort St; ◷noon-midnight Tue-Thu, to 2am Fri & Sat) In a quieter location in eastern Northbridge, the Dominion League – named after a 1929 movement pushing for WA to secede from Australia – is a thoroughly grown-up bar with a sophisticated European vibe. Leather sofas and brick walls hint at a gentlemen's-club ambience, while a stellar craft-beer selection combines with a serious wine and cocktail list.

Bar snacks are equally cosmopolitan – think grilled lamb shoulder with tahini yoghurt – and downstairs is a cosy whisky bar.

Alabama Song
BAR

(www.facebook.com/alabamasongbar; Level 1, behind 232 William St; ⊙ 6pm-2am Wed-Sun) Featuring canned brews and over 100 American whiskies and bourbons, Alabama Song is a loads-of-fun, late-night destination down a back lane in Northbridge. Chicken wings and cheeseburgers feature on the bar menu, and on Friday and Saturday nights DJs and local bands rip through rockabilly, honky tonk and country classics. Don't forget your John Deere trucker cap.

Standard
BAR

(☑08-9228 1331; www.thestandardperth.com.au; 28 Roe St; ⊙ 4pm-midnight Mon-Thu, noon-midnight Fri & Sat, noon-10pm Sun) Effortlessly straddling the divide between bar and restaurant, the Standard carries Northbridge's predilection for cool street art right into its colourful interior. Head through to the back and the upper deck for the most raffish ambience, and partake of the considered beer and wine selection and such classy shared plates as kangaroo, Fremantle octopus and zucchini-flower salad.

LOT 20
BAR

(☑08-6162 1195; www.lot20.co; 198-206 William St; ⊙10am-midnight Mon-Sat, to 10pm Sun) LOT 20 is more evidence of the transformation of rough-and-ready Northbridge into the home of more intimate and sophisticated small bars. The brick-lined courtyard is perfect on a warm WA evening, and on cooler nights the cosy interior is best experienced with a few bar snacks, gourmet burgers and WA wine or Aussie craft beer. The entrance is on James St.

Northbridge Brewing Company
MICROBREWERY

(☑08-6151 6481; www.northbridgebrewingco.com.au; 44 Lake St; ⊙8am-10pm Sun-Tue, to midnight Wed-Sat) The four beers brewed here are decent enough, but the real attractions are the occasional on-tap guest beers from around Australia. The outdoor bar adjoining the grassy expanse of Northbridge Plaza is relaxed and easygoing, and various big screens dotted around the multilevel industrial space make this a good spot to watch live sport.

Mechanics Institute
BAR

(☑08-9228 4189; www.mechanicsinstitutebar.com.au; 222 William St; ⊙noon-midnight Mon-Sat, to 10pm Sun) Negotiate the laneway entrance around the corner on James St to discover one of Perth's most down-to-earth small bars. Share one of the big tables on the deck or nab a stool by the bar. Craft beers are on tap, and you can even order in a gourmet burger from Flipside (p72) downstairs.

Ezra Pound
BAR

(☑0415 757 666; www.ezrapound.com.au; 189 William St; ⊙3pm-midnight Tue-Sat, 1-10pm Sun) Down a much-graffitied lane leading off William St, Ezra Pound is favoured by Northbridge's bohemian set. It's the kind of place where you can settle into a red-velvet chair and sip a Tom Collins out of a jam jar. Earnest conversations about Kerouac and Kafka are strictly optional.

Air
CLUB

(☑0415 035 305; www.airclub.com.au; 139 James St; ⊙from 9pm Fri & Sat) Nonstop house, techno and trance.

Metro City
CLUB

(☑08-9228 0500; www.metroconcertclub.com; 146 Roe St) Thumping super-club (capacity 2000), which doubles as a concert venue.

Geisha
CLUB

(☑08-9328 9808; www.geishabar.com.au; 135a James St; ⊙11pm-6am Fri & Sat) A small and pumping, DJ-driven gay-friendly club.

Bird
BAR

(www.williamstreetbird.com; 181 William St; ⊙noon-midnight Mon-Sat, to 11pm Sun) Cool indie bar with local bands, performers and DJs. Upstairs there's a brick-lined deck with city views.

🍸 Highgate, Mt Lawley & Maylands

Swallow
WINE BAR

(☑08-9272 4428; www.swallowbar.com.au; 198 Whatley Cres; ⊙5-10pm Wed-Thu, 4pm-midnight Fri, noon-10pm Sat & Sun) Channeling an art-deco ambience with funky lampshades and vintage French advertising, Swallow is the kind of place you'd love as your local. Wine and cocktails are exemplary, and the drinks list includes Spanish lagers, New Zealand dark beers and WA ciders. Check the website for live music from Thursday to Sunday. Snacks ($10 to $19) are also available.

Five Bar
CRAFT BEER

(☑08-9227 5200; www.fivebar.com.au; 560 Beaufort St; ⊙noon-midnight Mon-Sat, to 10pm Sun) International and Australian craft beers – including seasonal and one-off brews from

WA's best – make Mt Lawley's Five Bar worth seeking out for the discerning drinker. Wine lovers are also well catered for, and the menu leans towards classy comfort food.

Clarence's   COCKTAIL BAR

(☑08-9228 9474; www.clarences.com.au; 506 Beaufort St; ⊙4pm-late Mon-Fri, noon-midnight Sat & Sun) Clarence's combination of small-bar buzz and intimate bistro dining makes it a dependable spot for good times along Mt Lawley's Beaufort St strip. Menu highlights include decent burgers and Freo octopus with pineapple and jalapeño. For $22 you'll get a burger and a beer from 4pm to 10pm weekdays and noon to 4pm weekends. Try the lamb burger with harissa.

Must Winebar   WINE BAR

(☑08-9328 8255; www.must.com.au; 519 Beaufort St; ⊙noon-midnight) With cool French house music pulsing through the air and the perfect glass of wine in your hand (40 offerings by the glass, 500 on the list), Must is hard to beat. Upstairs is an exclusive, bookings-only Champagne bar.

Flying Scotsman   PUB

(☑08-9328 6200; www.facebook.com/ TheFlyingScotto; 639 Beaufort St; ⊙11am-midnight) Old-style pub that attracts the Beaufort St indie crowd. A good spot for a drink before a gig up the road at the Astor (p79).

Velvet Lounge   BAR

(☑08-9328 6200; www.facebook.com/ thevelvetloungeperth; 639 Beaufort St; ⊙noon-midnight) Out the back of the Flying Scotsman (p78) is this small, red-velvet-clad lounge with ska, punk and indie beats. Infinite Jest comedy nights take place Monday at 7pm.

🍷 Leederville

Pinchos   BAR

(☑08-9228 3008; www.pinchos.me; 124 Oxford St; ⊙7am-late) Look forward to Iberian-inspired good times at this corner location amid Leederville's many cafes, restaurants and fast-food joints. Tapas with anchovies, chorizo or goats cheese are perfect drinking fodder with Spanish beer, wine and sherry, and larger shared plates include lamb and pork meatballs, Spanish tortilla and creamy salt-cod-and-saffron croquettes.

Leederville Hotel   PUB

(☑08-9202 8282; www.leedervillehotel.com; 742 Newcastle St; ⊙11am-late) Cool decor and good food ensure nights are huge at The Garden, the Leederville's decent stab at a 21st-century gastropub.

🍷 Subiaco

Juanita's   BAR

(☑08-9388 8882; www.facebook.com/ juanitasbarsubiaco; 341 Rokeby Rd; ⊙2-11pm Tue-Sat, 3-8pm Sun) Welcome to Perth's most eclectic small (and we do mean small) bar. Tapas, shared platters and a concise selection of beer and wine partner with rescued 1960s furniture, walls trimmed with bric-a-brac, and a few outside tables. It's all thoroughly

---

GAY & LESBIAN PERTH

Perth is home to all of Western Australia's gay and lesbian venues. Before you get excited, let's clarify matters: it has precisely two bars and one men's sauna. Many other bars, especially around Highgate and Mt Lawley, are somewhat gay friendly, but it's hardly what you'd call a bustling scene.

For a head's up on what's on, pick up the free monthly newspaper *Out in Perth* (www. outinperth.com). **Pride WA** (www.pridewa.com.au; ⊙Nov) runs PrideFest, a 10-day festival from mid-November culminating in the Pride Parade.

Court (☑08-9328 5292; www.thecourt.com.au; 50 Beaufort St; ⊙noon-midnight Sun-Thu, to 2am Fri & Sat) A large, rambling complex consisting of an old corner pub and a big, partly covered courtyard with a clubby atmosphere. Wednesday is drag night, with kings and queens holding court in front of a young crowd.

Connections (☑08-9328 1870; www.connectionsnightclub.com; 81 James St; ⊙8pm-late Wed-Sat) DJs, drag shows and the occasional bit of lesbian mud wrestling.

Perth Steam Works (☑08-9328 2930; www.perthsteamworks.com.au; 369 William St; $25; ⊙noon-1am Sun-Thu, to 2am Fri & Sat) Gay men's sauna. Entry on Forbes St.

local, very charming, and a refreshing antidote to the flash, renovated pubs elsewhere in Subiaco.

 Other Areas

Dutch Trading Co
CRAFT BEER

(⌨ 08-6150 8329; www.thedutchtradingco.com.au; 243 Albany Hwy; ⊙ 4-11pm Tue-Thu, noon-midnight Fri & Sat, noon-10pm Sun) Located in an up-and-coming eating-and-drinking strip, the Dutch Trading Co combines rustic bar leaners and repurposed sofas with tattooed and bearded bartenders slinging the best of Aussie craft beers. Besides the ever-changing taps, there's a fridge full of international brews, and bar snacks include croquettes with mustard, spicy buttermilk chicken and hearty steak sandwiches.

Hippocampus Metropolitan Distillery
DISTILLERY

(⌨ 08-9212 6209; www.hippocampusmd.com.au; 19 Gordon St; ⊙ 1-8pm Fri) Ten rounds of distillation in a gleaming copper still produce the excellent gin at this West Perth distillery, and on Friday afternoons it morphs into a surprising bar with cocktails and Australian craft beer. Try the infused vodkas or snack on an antipasto platter. (Be sure to pick up a duty-free bottle of Hippocampus gin at Perth Airport as you leave.)

Whipper Snapper Distillery
DISTILLERY

(⌨ 08-9221 2293; www.whippersnapperdistillery.com; 139 Kensington St; tours & tastings $20-75; ⊙ 7am-5pm Mon-Fri, 8am-4pm Sat, 11am-4pm Sun) Look for the vintage aircraft logo on the exterior wall as you visit this combination of urban whisky distillery and sunny coffee shop. The whisky is crafted from 100% WA ingredients, something you'll hear a lot about on an entertaining and informative distillery tour.

Entertainment

Live Music

Badlands Bar
LIVE MUSIC

(⌨ 08-9225 6669; www.badlands.bar; 3 Aberdeen St; ⊙ 7pm-2am) Located on the fringes of Northbridge, Badlands has shrugged off its previous incarnation as a retro 1950s-inspired nightclub to be reborn as the city's best rock venue. The best WA bands are regulars, and if an up-and-coming international band is touring, Badlands is the place to see them before they become really famous. Check online for listings.

Ellington Jazz Club
JAZZ

(⌨ 08-9228 1088; www.ellingtonjazz.com.au; 191 Beaufort St; ⊙ 6.30pm-1am Mon-Thu, to 3am Fri & Sat, 5pm-midnight Sun) There's live jazz nightly in this handsome, intimate venue. Standing-only admission is $10, or you can book a table (per person $15 to $20) for tapas and pizza.

Perth Arena
LIVE MUSIC

(⌨ 08-6365 0700; www.pertharena.com.au; 700 Wellington St) Used for big concerts by major international acts such as Rhianna and the Rolling Stones. It's also used by the Perth Wildcats NBL basketball franchise.

Amplifier
LIVE MUSIC

(⌨ 08-9321 7606; www.amplifiercapitol.com.au; rear 383 Murray St) The good old Amplifier is one of the best places for live (mainly indie) bands. (Part of the same complex is Capitol, used mainly for DJ gigs.)

Moon
LIVE MUSIC

(⌨ 08-9328 7474; www.themoon.com.au; 323 William St; ⊙ 5pm-1am Mon-Thu, noon-late Fri-Sun) Low-key, late-night cafe with singer-songwriters on Wednesday night, jazz on Thursday, and poetry slams on Saturday afternoon from 2pm.

Universal
LIVE MUSIC

(⌨ 08-9227 6771; www.universalbar.com.au; 221 William St; ⊙ 3pm-late Wed-Sun) The unpretentious Universal is one of Perth's oldest bars and much loved by soul, R & B and blues enthusiasts.

Rosemount Hotel
LIVE MUSIC

(⌨ 08-9328 7062; www.rosemounthotel.com.au; cnr Angove & Fitzgerald Sts; ⊙ noon-late) Local and international bands play regularly in this spacious art-deco pub with a laid-back beer garden.

Astor
CONCERT VENUE

(⌨ 08-9370 1777; www.astortheatreperth.com; 659 Beaufort St) The beautiful art-deco Astor still screens the odd film but is mainly used for concerts these days.

Charles Hotel
LIVE MUSIC

(⌨ 08-9444 1051; www.charleshotel.com.au; 509 Charles St) Hosts lots of live music, including the Legendary Perth Blues Club on Tuesday. In recent times it's grown as a venue for touring international acts and Aussie head-liners.

Comedy

Lazy Susan's Comedy Den COMEDY
(☑08-9328 2543; www.lazysusans.com.au; Brisbane Hotel, 292 Beaufort St; ☺8.30pm Tue, Fri & Sat) Shapiro Tuesday offers a mix of first-timers, seasoned amateurs and pros trying out new shtick (for a very reasonable $5). Friday is for more grown-up stand-ups, including some interstaters. Saturday is the Big Hoohaa – a team-based comedy wrassle.

Theatre & Classical Music

Check the *West Australian* newspaper for what's on. Book through www.ticketek.com.au or www.ticketmaster.com.au.

His Majesty's Theatre THEATRE
(☑08-9265 0900; www.ptt.wa.gov.au/venues/his-majestys-theatre; 825 Hay St) The majestic home to the **West Australian Ballet** (☑08-9214 0707; www.waballet.com.au) and **West Australian Opera** (☑08-9278 8999; www.wa-opera.asn.au), as well as lots of theatre, comedy and cabaret.

Perth Concert Hall CONCERT VENUE
(☑08-9231 9999; www.perthconcerthall.com.au; 5 St Georges Tce) Home to the **Western Australian Symphony Orchestra** (WASO; ☑08-9326 0000; www.waso.com.au).

State Theatre Centre THEATRE
(☑08-6212 9200; www.ptt.wa.gov.au/venues/state-theatre-centre-of-wa; 174 William St) This complex includes the 575-seat Heath Ledger Theatre and the 234-seat Studio Underground. It's home to the Black Swan State Theatre Company, Perth Theatre Company and the Barking Gecko young people's theatre (www.barkinggecko.com.au).

Subiaco Arts Centre THEATRE
(☑08-9380 3000; www.ptt.wa.gov.au/venues/subiaco-arts-centre; 180 Hamersley Rd) Indoor and outdoor theatres used for drama and concerts.

Regal Theatre THEATRE
(☑08-9388 2066; www.regaltheatre.com.au; 474 Hay St) Popular musicals and stage shows.

Cinema

Somerville Auditorium CINEMA
(☑08-6488 2000; www.perthfestival.com.au; 35 Stirling Hwy; ☺Dec-Mar) A quintessential Perth experience, the Perth Festival's film program is held here on the University of WA's beauti-ful grounds surrounded by pines. Picnicking before the film is a must.

Rooftop Movies CINEMA
(☑08-9227 6288; www.rooftopmovies.com.au; 68 Roe St; $16; ☺Tue-Sun late Oct-late Mar) Art-house and classic movies screen under the stars on the 6th floor of a Northbridge car park. Deckchairs, wood-fired pizza and craft beer all combine for a great night out. Booking ahead online is recommended and don't be surprised if you're distracted from the on-screen action by the city views.

Moonlight Cinema CINEMA
(www.moonlight.com.au; Synergy Parklands, Kings Park; ☺Dec-Easter) In summer, bring a picnic and a blanket and enjoy a romantic moonlit movie. Booking ahead online is recommended.

Luna CINEMA
(☑08-9444 4056; www.lunapalace.com.au; 155 Oxford St) Art-house cinema in Leederville with Monday double features and a bar. Cheap tickets on Wednesday.

Cinema Paradiso CINEMA
(☑08-9227 1771; www.lunapalace.com.au; 164 James St) Art-house cinema in Northbridge. Cheap tickets on Tuesday.

Camelot Outdoor Cinema CINEMA
(☑08-9386 3554; http://camelot.lunapalace.com.au; Memorial Hall, 16 Lochee St; ☺Dec-Easter) Seated open-air cinema in Mosman Park.

Sport

In WA 'football' means Aussie Rules, and during the Australian Football League (AFL) season it's hard to get locals to talk about anything but the two Western Australian teams: the **West Coast Eagles** (www.west-coasteagles.com.au) and the **Fremantle Dock-ers** (www.fremantlefc.com.au).

Perth Stadium STADIUM
(www.perthstadium.com.au; Victoria Park Dr) Perth's new 60,000-seat riverside stadium is scheduled to open in March 2018 for the beginning of the AFL season. Big concerts and other international sport fixtures are also expected to be held there, and a new Perth Stadium transit station will be opening nearby. It's also envisaged there will be river transport from Elizabeth Quay to key events.

Domain Stadium   STADIUM
(Subiaco Oval; ☑ 08-93812187; www.domainstadium
.com.au; 250 Roberts Rd) The current home of
Aussie Rules football and big concerts, but
it'll be superseded by the new Perth Stadium
when it opens in March 2018.

WACA   STADIUM
(Western Australian Cricket Association; ☑ 08-
9265 7222; www.waca.com.au; Nelson Cres)
Main venue for interstate and international
cricket. From 2018, one-day internation-
als will be held at the new Perth Stadium
(p80).

NIB Stadium   STADIUM
(Perth Oval; ☑ 08-9422 1500; www.nibstadium.
com.au; 310 Pier St) Home to **Perth Glory**
(☑ 08-9492 6000; www.perthglory.com.au) soccer (football) and **Western Force** (☑ 08-9387
0700; www.westernforce.com.au) rugby.

HBF Stadium   STADIUM
(☑ 08-9441 8222; www.hbfstadium.com.au; Stephenson Ave) Home to **West Coast Fever**
(☑ 08-9380 3700; www.westcoastfever.com.au)
netball.

🛍 Shopping

Visit Northbridge for vintage and retro stores
and hit up Leederville and North Perth for design shops and galleries. In the city, the William St mall offers major retailers, while King
St is home to independent clothing designers.

City Centre

78 Records   MUSIC
(☑ 08-9322 6384; www.facebook.com/
78-Records-78432813221; 1st fl, 255 Murray St Mall;
☉ 9.30am-5.30pm Mon-Sat, 11am-5pm Sun) Independent record shop. Also good for vinyl,
and tickets to rock and indie gigs.

Northbridge, Highgate & Mt Lawley

Future Shelter   HOMEWARES
(☑ 08-9228 4832; www.futureshelter.com; 56 Angove St; ☉ 10am-5pm Mon-Sat, noon-3pm Sun)
Quirky clothing, gifts and homewares designed and manufactured locally. Surrounding Angove St is an emerging hip North
Perth neighbourhood with other cafes and
design shops worth browsing.

William Topp   DESIGN
(www.williamtopp.com; 452 William St; ☉ 10am-
6pm Mon-Sat, 11am-4pm Sun) Cool designer
knick-knacks.

Planet Books   BOOKS, MUSIC
(☑ 08-9328 7464; www.planetbooks.com.au; 636-
638 Beaufort St; ☉ 10am-9pm Sun-Thu, 11am-11pm
Fri & Sat) Cool bookshop with prints, posters
and a good range of Australian-themed titles.

Leederville

Atlas Divine   CLOTHING
(☑ 08-9242 5880; www.facebook.com/
AtlasDivine/; 121 Oxford St; ☉ 9am-9pm) Hip
women's and men's clobber: jeans, quirky
tees, dresses etc.

Subiaco & Kings Park

Indigenart   ART
(☑ 08-9388 2899; www.mossensongalleries.com.
au; 115 Hay St; ☉ 11am-4pm Wed-Sat) Indigenous
art from around Australia but with a focus
on WA artists. Works include weavings,
paintings on canvas, bark and paper, and
sculpture.

Aboriginal Art & Craft Gallery   ART
(☑ 08-9481 7082; www.aboriginalgallery.com.au;
Fraser Ave; ☉ 10.30am-4.30pm Mon-Fri, 11am-4pm
Sat & Sun) Work from around WA; more pop-
ulist than high end or collectable.

Aspects of Kings Park   ART, SOUVENIRS
(☑ 08-9480 3900; www.aspectsofkingspark.com.
au; Fraser Ave; ☉ 9am-5pm) Australian art,
craft and books.

Other Areas

æ'lkemi   CLOTHING
(☑ 08-9284 2736; www.aelkemi.com; Times Sq
Centre, 337 Stirling Hwy; ☉ 10am-5pm Tue-Sun)
Top WA designer's signature store, showcasing feminine frocks and distinctive prints.
Adjacent Claremont Quarter is an extensive
mall.

ℹ Orientation

The city of Perth lies along a wide sweep of the
Swan River. The river borders the city centre to
the south and east, and links Perth to its neighbouring port city, Fremantle. Follow the river
north from the city and you'll reach prosperous
nooks such as Claisebrook Cove, lined with
ostentatious houses, cafes and public sculpture.

The ongoing development of the City Link project is improving pedestrian access between the CBD and the Northbridge entertainment enclave, immediately to the north. Here's where you'll find Perth's cultural institutions, most of its hostels and the lively Little Asia restaurant strip.

Continue northeast along Beaufort St and you'll reach the sophisticated suburbs of Highgate and Mt Lawley. Heading west there's Mt Hawthorn and hip Leederville. To the west of the central city rises Kings Park, with well-heeled Subiaco beyond it. Go further west and you'll hit the beaches.

ⓘ Information

EMERGENCY

Police Station (☑13 14 44; www.police.wa.gov. au; 2 Fitzgerald St) Located on the western edge of Northbridge and near the CBD.

Sexual Assault Resource Centre (☑08-9340 1828, freecall 1800 199 888; www.kemh.health. wa.gov.au/services/sarc; ⊘24hr) Provides a 24-hour emergency service.

INTERNET ACCESS

Perth City offers free wi-fi access in Murray St Mall between William St and Barrack St.

State Library of WA (www.slwa.wa.gov.au; Perth Cultural Centre; ⊘9am-8pm Mon-Thu, 10am-5.30pm Fri-Sun; ☎) Free wi-fi and internet access.

MEDIA

Go West (www.gowesternaustralia.com.au) Backpacker magazine with information on seasonal work opportunities.

Urban Walkabout (www.urbanwalkabout.com) Eating, drinking and shopping highlights in key inner-Perth neighbourhoods and Fremantle. Also produces handy mini-guides and maps.

West Australian (www.thewest.com.au) Local newspaper with entertainment and cinema listings.

X-Press Magazine (www.xpressmag.com.au) A good online source of live-music information. Also available as an app.

MEDICAL SERVICES

Lifecare Dental (☑08-9221 2777; www. lifecaredental.com.au; 419 Wellington St; ⊘8am-8pm) In Forrest Chase.

Royal Perth Hospital (☑08-9224 2244; www. rph.wa.gov.au; Victoria Sq) In central Perth.

Travel Medicine Centre (☑08-9321 7888; www.travelmed.com.au; 5 Mill St; ⊘8am-5pm Mon-Fri) Travel-specific advice and vaccinations.

Sexual Assault Resource Centre (p82) Provides a 24-hour emergency service.

MONEY

ATMs are plentiful, and there are currency-exchange facilities at the airport and major banks in the CBD.

POST

Post Office (66 St Georges Tce; ⊘8am-5pm Mon-Fri, 9am-12.30pm Sat)

TOURIST INFORMATION

i-City Information Kiosk (Murray St Mall; ⊘9.30am-4.30pm Mon-Thu & Sat, to 8pm Fri, 11am-3.30pm Sun) Volunteers here answer questions and run walking tours.

WA Visitor Centre (p276) Excellent resource for information across WA.

WEBSITES

Lonely Planet (lonelyplanet.com) Destination information, hotel bookings, traveller forum and more.

Heatseeker (www.heatseeker.com.au) Gig guide and ticketing.

Perth Now (www.perthnow.com.au) Perth and WA news and restaurant reviews.

Scoop (www.scoop.com.au) Entertainment and dining information.

What's On (www.whatson.com.au) Events and travel information.

ⓘ Getting There & Away

BUS

Transwa (☑1300 662 205; www.transwa. wa.gov.au) operates services from the bus terminal at East Perth train station to/from many destinations around the state. These include the following:
- SW1 to Augusta ($53, six hours, 12 per week) via Mandurah, Bunbury, Busselton and Dunsborough.
- SW2 to Pemberton ($55, 5½ hours, thrice weekly) via Bunbury, Balingup and Bridgetown.
- GS1 to Albany ($63, six hours, daily) via Mt Barker.
- GE2 to Esperance ($95, 10 hours, thrice weekly) via Mundaring, York and Hyden.
- N1 to Geraldton ($66, six hours, daily) and on to Northampton and Kalbarri.

South West Coach Lines (☑08-9261 7600; www.southwestcoachlines.com.au) focuses on the southwestern corner of WA, running services from **Elizabeth Quay Busport** (p58) to most towns in the region. Destinations include:
- Dunsborough (four hours, daily) via Mandurah, Bunbury and Busselton.
- Augusta (five hours, daily) via Bunbury, Busselton, Cowaramup and Margaret River.
- Manjimup (five hours, daily except weekends) via Mandurah, Bunbury, Balingup and Bridgetown.

Integrity Coach Lines (☎08-9274 7464; www.integritycoachlines.com.au; Wellington Street Bus Station) runs northbound and southbound services linking Perth to Broome and stopping at key travellers' destinations en route. It also runs services between Perth and Port Hedland via Mt Magnet, Cue, Meekatharra and Newman.

TRAIN

Transwa runs the following services from Perth railway station:

➡ Australind (twice daily) Perth to Pinjarra ($17.50, 1¼ hours) and Bunbury ($32, 2½ hours).

➡ AvonLink (daily) East Perth to Toodyay ($17.50, 1¼ hours) and Northam ($20.50, 1½ hours).

➡ Prospector (daily) East Perth to Kalgoorlie–Boulder ($89, seven hours).

❶ Getting Around

TO/FROM THE AIRPORT

Perth Airport (p271) is served by numerous airlines, including **Qantas** (QF; ☎13 13 13; www.qantas.com.au), and there are daily flights to and from international and Australian destinations. The airport's domestic and international terminals are 10km and 13km east of Perth respectively, near Guildford. Taxi fares to the city are around $45 from each terminal.

Connect (www.perthairportconnect.com.au; 1 way/return $15/30) runs shuttles to/from central accommodation and transport options in the city centre (one way/return $15/30, every 50 minutes). Pay the driver as you board. Bookings are recommended for groups.

Transperth buses 36, 37 and 40 travel to the domestic airport from St Georges Tce (stop 10121), near William St ($4.60, 40 minutes, every 10 to 30 minutes, hourly after 7pm). A free transfer bus links the domestic and international terminals.

CAR & MOTORCYCLE

Driving in the city takes a bit of practice, as some streets are one way and many aren't signposted. There are plenty of car-parking buildings in the central city but no free places to park. For unmetered street parking you'll need to look well away from the main commercial strips and check the signs carefully.

A fun way to gad about the city is on a moped. **Scootamoré** (☎08-9380 6580; www.scootamore.com.au; 356a Rokeby Rd, Subiaco; day/3 days/week/month $45/111/200/400) hires 50cc scooters with helmets (compulsory) and insurance included (for those over 21; $500 excess).

Car-rental companies include **Bayswater** (p274), **Budget** (p274), **Campabout** (p274), **Hertz** (p274) and **Thrifty** (p274). **Britz** (p274) hires out fully equipped 4WDs fitted out as campervans, popular on the roads of northern WA; it has offices in all the state capitals, as well as Perth and Broome, so one-way rentals are possible.

PUBLIC TRANSPORT

Transperth (p276) operates Perth's public buses, trains and ferries. There are Transperth information offices at Perth Station (Wellington St), Perth Busport (between Roe St and Wellington St), Perth underground station (off Murray St) and the Elizabeth Quay Busport (Mounts Bay Rd). There's a good online journey planner.

Fares & Passes

From the central city, the following fares apply for all public transport:

Free Transit Zone (FTZ) Covers the central commercial area, bounded (roughly) by Fraser Ave, Kings Park Rd, Thomas St, Newcastle St, Parry St, Lord St and the river (including the City West and Claisebrook train stations, to the west and east respectively).

Zone 1 Includes the city centre and the inner suburbs ($3).

Zone 2 Fremantle, Guildford and the beaches as far north as Sorrento ($4.60).

Zone 3 Hillarys Boat Harbour (AQWA), the Swan Valley and Kalamunda ($5.50).

Zone 5 Rockingham ($8.10).

Zone 7 Mandurah ($10.70).

DayRider Unlimited travel after 9am weekdays and all day on the weekend in any zone ($12.40).

FamilyRider Lets two adults and up to five children travel for a total of $12.40 on weekends, after 6pm weekdays and after 9am on weekdays during school holidays.

If you're in Perth for a while, consider buying a SmartRider card, covering bus, train and ferry travel. It's $10 to purchase, then you add value to your card. The technology deducts the fare as you go, as long as you tap in and tap out (touch your card to the electronic reader) every time you travel, including within the FTZ. The SmartRider works out 15% cheaper than buying single tickets and automatically caps itself at the DayRider rate if you're avoiding the morning rush hour.

Bus

The Free Transit Zone (FTZ) is served by regular buses and is well covered during the day by the three free Central Area Transit (CAT) services. The Yellow and Red CATs operate east–west routes, Yellow sticking mainly to Wellington St, and Red looping roughly east on Murray St and west on Hay St. The Blue CAT does a figure eight through Northbridge and the southern end of the city; this is the only one to run late – until 1am on Friday and Saturday only. Pick up a copy of the free timetable (widely available on buses and elsewhere) for the exact routes and stops. Buses run every five to eight minutes during weekdays and every 15 minutes on weekends. Digital displays at the stops advise when the next bus is due.

The metropolitan area is serviced by a wide network of Transperth buses. Pick up timetables from any of the Transperth information centres or use the online journey planner. Most buses leave from the city's new **Perth Busport** (58), located between the CBD and Northbridge.

Ferry

A ferry runs every 20 to 30 minutes between the new **Elizabeth Quay Jetty** (p58) and Mends Street Jetty in South Perth – use it to get to the zoo or for a bargain from-the-river glimpse of the Perth skyline. The **Little Ferry Co** (p63) runs scheduled services linking Elizabeth Quay and Claisebrook Cove.

Rottnest Express (Pier 2, Barrack St Jetty; adult/child $105.50/58) runs ferries to Rottnest Island.

Train

Transperth operates five train lines from around 5.20am to midnight weekdays and until about 2am Saturday and Sunday. Your rail ticket can also be used on Transperth buses and ferries within the ticket's zone. You're free to take your bike on the train during non-peak times. The lines and useful stops include:

Armadale Thornlie Line Perth, Burswood.

Fremantle Line Perth, City West, West Leederville, Subiaco, Shenton Park, Swanbourne, Cottesloe, North Fremantle, Fremantle.

Joondalup Line Esplanade, Perth Underground, Leederville.

Mandurah Line Perth Underground, Esplanade, Rockingham, Mandurah.

Midland Line Perth, East Perth, Mt Lawley, Guildford, Midland.

Elizabeth Quay station (p58) is serviced by the Joondalup and Mandurah Lines.

TAXI

Perth has a decent system of metered taxis, though the distances make frequent use costly and on busy nights you may have trouble flagging a taxi down in the street. The two main companies are **Swan Taxis** (☑13 13 30; www. swantaxis.com.au) and **Black & White** (☑13 10 08; www.bwtaxi.com.au); both have wheelchair-accessible cabs. Uber drivers are also common throughout the city.

FREMANTLE

POP 28,100

Creative, relaxed, open-minded: Fremantle's spirit is entirely distinct from Perth's. Perhaps it has something to do with the port and the city's working-class roots. Or the hippies, who first set up home here a few decades ago and can still be seen casually bobbing down the street on old bicycles. Or perhaps it's just that a timely 20th-century economic slump meant that the city retained an almost complete set of formerly grand Victorian and Edwardian buildings, creating a heritage precinct that's unique among Australia's cities today.

Whatever the reason, today's clean and green Freo makes a cosy home for performers, professionals, artists and more than a few eccentrics. There's a lot to enjoy here: fantastic museums, edgy galleries, pubs thrumming with live music and a thriving coffee culture. On weekend nights the city's residents vacate the main drag, leaving it to kids from the suburbs to party hard and loud.

History

This was an important area for the Wadjuk Noongar people, as it was a hub along trading paths. Some of these routes exist to this day in the form of modern roads. Before the harbour was altered, the mouth of the river was nearly covered by a sandbar and it was only a short swim from north to south. The confluence of the river and ocean, where Fremantle now stands, was known as Manjaree (sometimes translated as 'gathering place'). The Fremantle coast was called Booyeembara, while inland was Wallyalup, 'place of the eagle'.

Manjaree was mainly occupied in summer, when the Wadjuk would base themselves here to fish. In winter they would head further inland, avoiding seasonal flooding.

Fremantle's European history began when the ship HMS *Challenger* landed in 1829. The ship's captain, Charles Fremantle, took possession of the whole of the west coast 'in the name of King George IV'. Like Perth, the settlement made little progress until convict labour was used. Convicts constructed most of the town's earliest buildings; some of them, such as the Round House, Fremantle Prison and Fremantle Arts Centre, are now among the oldest in WA.

As a port, Fremantle wasn't up to much until the engineer CY O'Connor created an artificial harbour in the 1890s, destroying the Wadjuks' river crossing in the process. This caused such disruption to their traditional patterns of life that it's said that a curse was placed on O'Connor; some took his later suicide at Fremantle as evidence of its effectiveness.

The port blossomed during the gold rush and many of its distinctive buildings date from this period. Economic stagnation in the 1960s and 1970s spared the streetscape from the worst ravages of modernisation. It wasn't until 1987, when Fremantle hosted the America's Cup, that it transformed itself from a sleepy port town into today's vibrant, artsy city. The cup was lost that year, but the legacy of a redeveloped waterfront remains.

⊙ Sights

★ Fremantle Prison   HISTORIC BUILDING

(☑08-9336 9200; www.fremantleprison.com.au; 1 The Terrace; single day tour adult/child $20/11, combined day tours $28/19, Torchlight Tour $26/16, Tunnels Tour $60/40; ☉9am-5.30pm) With its foreboding 5m-high walls, the old convict-era prison still dominates Fremantle. Daytime tour options include the Doing Time Tour, taking in the kitchens, men's cells and solitary-confinement cells. The Great Escapes Tour recounts famous inmates and includes the women's prison. Book ahead for the Torchlight Tour, focusing on macabre aspects of the prison's history, and the 2½-hour Tunnels Tour (minimum age 12 years), which includes an underground boat ride and subterranean tunnels built by prisoners.

Entry to the gatehouse, including the Prison Gallery, gift shop and Convict Cafe is free. In 2010 the prison's cultural status was recognised as part of the Australian Convict Sites entry on the Unesco World Heritage list.

The first convicts were made to build their own prison, constructing it from beautiful pale limestone dug out of the hill on which it was built. From 1855 to 1991, 350,000 people were incarcerated here, although the highest numbers held at any one time were 1200 men and 58 women. Of those, 43 men and one woman were executed on site, the last of which was serial killer Eric Edgar Cooke in 1964.

★ Western Australian Museum – Maritime   MUSEUM

(☑1300 134 081; www.museum.wa.gov.au; Victoria Quay; adult/child museum $15/free, submarine $15/7.50, museum & submarine $25/7.50; ☉9.30am-5pm) Housed in an intriguing sail-shaped building on the harbour, just west of the city centre, the maritime museum is a fascinating exploration of WA's relationship with the ocean. Well-presented displays range from yacht racing to Aboriginal fish traps and the sandalwood trade. If you're not claustrophobic, take an hour-long tour of the submarine HMAS *Ovens;* the vessel was part of the Australian Navy's fleet from 1969 to 1997. Tours leave every half-hour from 10am to 3.30pm. Booking ahead is recommended.

Various boats are on display in the museum, including *Australia II,* the famous winged-keel yacht that won the America's Cup yachting race in 1983 (ending 132 years of American domination of the competition). Other boats include an Aboriginal bark canoe; an Indonesian outrigger canoe, introduced to the Kimberley and used by Indigenous people; and a pearl lugger used in Broome. Even a classic 1970s panel van (complete with fur lining) makes the cut – because of its status as the surfer's vehicle of choice.

★ Western Australian Museum – Shipwreck Galleries   MUSEUM

(☑1300 134 081; www.museum.wa.gov.au; Cliff St; admission by donation; ☉9.30am-5pm) Located within an 1852 commissariat store, the Shipwreck Galleries are considered the finest display of maritime archaeology in the southern hemisphere. The highlight is the **Batavia Gallery**, where a section of the hull of Dutch merchant ship *Batavia*, wrecked in 1629, is displayed. Nearby is a large stone gate, intended as an entrance to Batavia Castle, which was being carried when the ship sank.

Other items of interest include the inscribed pewter plate left on Cape Inscription by Willem de Vlamingh in 1697, positioned next to a replica of the plate left by Dirk Hartog in 1616 during the first confirmed European landing in WA.

Round House   HISTORIC BUILDING

(☑08-9336 6897; www.fremantleroundhouse.com.au; Captains Lane; admission by donation; ☉10.30am-3.30pm) Built from 1830 to 1831, this 12-sided stone prison is WA's oldest

Fremantle

0 — 400 m
0 — 0.2 miles

Swanbourne St

Stevens Reserve

Solomon St

Stevens St

Fremantle Cemetery (2km)

War Memorial

High St

11

26

Hampton Rd

Ord St

Fremantle Arts Centre (370m)

Knutsford St

Hampton Rd

Fothergill St

Fremantle Prison

1

Attfield St

Alma St

Wray Ave

29

30

41

42

Ellen St

Holdsworth St

32

The Terrace

Fremantle Oval

South Tce

36

Parry St

Queen St

Henderson St

Parry St

45

51

South St

Howard St

South Beach (1.15km)

43

Kings Square

62

Visitor Centre

William St

12

48

Suffolk St

Arundel St

Adelaide St

19

21

23

Mojos (1.8km); Flipside (2km); Mrs Browns (2km)

16

14

54

Norfolk St

35

53

Marine Tce

Cantonment St

63

55

52

50

47

34

Elder Pl

Market St

56

60

Essex St

9

Fremantle

13

39

40

27

59

65

Bannister St

31

58

49

10

Pakenham St

17

57

61

64

28

38

44

Marine Tce

Henry St

46

Fishing Boat Harbour

High St

Mouat St

7

33

15

Phillimore St

Cliff St

6

20

Fisherman's Wharf

8

Western Australian Museum – Shipwreck Galleries

3

Ferry to Rottnest Island (Wadjemup)

Rottnest Express

24

Rottnest Island Visitor Centre

Victoria Quay

25

Swan River

Western Australian Museum – Maritime

2

5

22

18

4

37

Bathers Beach

Arthur Head

Fleet St

Slip St

Victoria Quay Rd

Be.Fremantle (80m)

INDIAN OCEAN

Port Beach (1.7km)

Rous Head

Fremantle

surviving building. It was the site of the colony's first hangings, and was later used for holding Aboriginal people before they were taken to Rottnest Island. On the hilltop outside is the Signal Station, where at 1pm daily a time ball and cannon blast were used to alert seamen to the correct time. The ceremony is re-enacted daily; book ahead if you want to fire the cannon.

To the Indigenous Noongar people, this is a sacred site because of the number of their people killed while incarcerated here. Freedom fighter Yagan was held here briefly in 1832. Beneath is an impressive 1837 Whalers' Tunnel carved through sandstone and used for accessing Bathers Beach, where whales were landed and processed.

Bathers Beach Art Precinct　ARTS CENTRE
(www.facebook.com/bathersbeachartsprecinct; Captains Lane; ⊙opening hours vary) Part of the redevelopment of the Bathers Beach area has been the opening of artists' galleries and studios in heritage cottages and warehouses stretching from near the Round House north and west towards the Western Australian Museum – Maritime (p85).

**Walyalup Aboriginal
Cultural Centre**　CULTURAL CENTRE
(☑08-9430 7906; www.fremantle.wa.gov.au/wacc; 12 Captains Lane; ⊙ 2.30-6.30pm Tue, 10am-2pm Wed-Sat) Various classes and workshops, including language, art and crafts, are held

at this interesting cultural centre. Booking ahead for most is encouraged, so check the program online. As it's part of the Bathers Beach Art Precinct there are also regular Indigenous art exhibitions, with works available for purchase and proceeds going directly to the artists.

Fremantle Arts Centre
GALLERY

(☑08-9432 9555; www.fac.org.au; 1 Finnerty St; ☉10am-5pm) FREE An impressive neo-Gothic building surrounded by lovely elm-shaded gardens, the Fremantle Arts Centre was constructed by convict labourers as a lunatic asylum in the 1860s. Saved from demolition in the 1960s, it houses interesting exhibitions and the excellent Canvas (p92) cafe. During summer there are concerts, courses and workshops.

Fremantle Markets
MARKET

(www.fremantlemarkets.com.au; cnr South Tce & Henderson St; ☉8am-8pm Fri, to 6pm Sat & Sun) FREE Originally opened in 1897, these colourful markets were reopened in 1975 and today draw slow-moving crowds combing over souvenirs. A few younger designers and artists have introduced a more vibrant edge. The fresh-produce section is a good place to stock up on snacks and there's an excellent food court featuring lots of global street eats.

Army Museum of WA
MUSEUM

(☑08-9430 2535; www.armymuseumwa.com.au; Burt St; adult/child $10/7; ☉10.30am-1pm Wed-Sun) Situated within the imposing Artillery Barracks, this little museum pulls out the big guns, literally. Howitzers and tanks line up outside, while inside you'll find cabinets full of uniforms and medals. The WWI galleries were completely redeveloped for the centenary of the war in 2014. Photo ID is required at entry.

PS Arts Space
ARTS CENTRE

(☑08-9430 8145; www.facebook.com/pg/PakenhamStreetArtSpace; 22 Pakenham St; ☉gallery 10am-5pm Tue-Sat) Independent WA artists display often-challenging work in this repurposed heritage warehouse. Occasional events, including pop-up opera, fashion shows and concerts, fill the spacious interior after dark. Drop by or check the Facebook page for what's on.

Gold-Rush Buildings

Fremantle boomed during the WA gold rush in the late 19th century, and many wonderful buildings remain that were constructed during, or shortly before, this period. High St, particularly around the bottom end, has some excellent examples, including several old hotels.

Chamber of Commerce Building
HISTORIC BUILDING

(16 Phillimore St) Continuing its original use since 1873.

St John's Anglican Church
CHURCH

(Kings Sq) Built in 1882.

Fremantle Grammar School
HISTORIC BUILDING

(200 High St) Built as an Anglican public school in 1885.

Town Hall
HISTORIC BUILDING

(Kings Sq) Opened on Queen Victoria's jubilee in 1887.

Samson House
HISTORIC BUILDING

(cnr Ellen & Ord Sts) A well-preserved 1888 colonial home owned by the National Trust.

Esplanade Hotel
HISTORIC BUILDING

(Marine Tce) Attractive colonnaded hotel, built in 1896.

Old German Consulate
HISTORIC BUILDING

(5 Mouat St) Built 1903; now a B&B.

Fremantle Train Station
HISTORIC BUILDING

(Phillimore St) Built from Donnybrook sandstone in 1907; no one can say why the swans are white rather than black.

Customs House
HISTORIC BUILDING

(cnr Cliff & Phillimore Sts) Built in 1908 in Georgian style.

Public Sculptures

Enlivening Fremantle's streets are numerous bronze sculptures, many by local artist Greg James (www.gregjamessculpture.com).

In Fishing Boat Harbour is **To the Fishermen** (Fishing Boat Harbour), a cluster of bronze figures unloading and carrying their catch up from the wharf. There's a lively statue of former member for Fremantle and wartime Labor prime minister **John Curtin** (Kings Sq) (1885–1945) in Kings Sq, outside the Town Hall. Nearby is a portrayal of James's fellow sculptor **Pietro Porcelli** (Kings Sq) (1872–1943) in the act of making a bust.

Bon Scott Statue
STATUE

The most popular of Fremantle's public sculptures is Greg James's statue of Bon Scott (1946–80), strutting on a Marshall amplifier in Fishing Boat Harbour. The AC/DC singer moved to Fremantle with his family in 1956 and his ashes are interred in **Fremantle Cemetery** (Carrington St). Enter the cemetery near the corner of High and Carrington Sts. Bon's plaque is on the left around 15m along the path.

Beaches & Parks

Green spaces around Fremantle include **Esplanade Reserve** (Marine Tce), shaded by Norfolk Island pines and dividing the city from Fishing Boat Harbour. Nearby **Bathers Beach** has recently been revitalised with a good waterfront restaurant and an arts precinct with galleries and studios. Down in South Freo, **South Beach** (Ocean Dr) is sheltered, swimmable, only 1.5km from the city centre and on the free CAT bus route. The next major beach is **Coogee Beach** (Cockburn Rd), 6km further south.

🏃 Activities

Fremantle Trails WALKING
(www.visitfremantle.com.au) Pick up trail cards from the visitor centre (p95) for 11 self-guided walking tours: Art and Culture, Convict, CY O'Connor (the civil engineer who created Fremantle's artificial harbour), Discovery (a Fremantle once-over), Fishing Boat Harbour, Hotels and Breweries, Maritime Heritage, Manjaree (Indigenous) Heritage, Retail and Fashion, Waterfront and Writers.

Oceanic Cruises WHALE WATCHING
(☑08-9325 1191; www.oceaniccruises.com.au; B Shed, Victoria Quay; adult/child $75/29; ⊗mid-Sep–mid-Nov) Departs at 10.15am for a two-hour tour. Days of operation vary by month, so check the website.

STS Leeuwin II BOATING
(☑08-9430 4105; www.sailleeuwin.com; Berth B, Victoria Quay; adult/child $99/69; ⊗Nov–mid-Apr) Take a three-hour trip on a 55m, three-masted tall ship; see the website for details of morning, afternoon and twilight sails. Sailings are usually Saturday and Sunday, but dates vary, so check online.

🧭 Tours

Two Feet & a Heartbeat WALKING
(☑1800 459 388; www.twofeet.com.au; per person $45-60; ⊗10am) Operated by a young, energetic crew, tours focus on Fremantle's often-rambunctious history. The three-hour

'Sailors' Guide to Fremantle' option includes a couple of drink stops.

Fremantle Indigenous Heritage Tours WALKING
(☑0405 630 606; www.indigenouswa.com; adult/child $35/15; ⊗10.30am & 1.30pm Thu & Sat) Highly regarded tour covering the history of Fremantle and the Noongar and Wadjuk people. Book online or through the Fremantle visitors centre.

Fremantle Tram Tours BUS
(☑08-9433 6674; www.fremantletrams.com.au; city circuit adult/child $28/5, Ghostly Tour $85/65) Looking like a heritage tram, this bus departs from the Town Hall on an all-day hop-on, hop-off circuit around the city. The Ghostly Tour, departing 6.45pm to 10.30pm Friday, visits the prison, Round House and Fremantle Arts Centre (former asylum) by torchlight.

Combos include Lunch & Tram (tram plus a lunch cruise on the river; adult/child $95/59), Triple Tour (tram, river cruise and Perth sightseeing bus; $86/33) and Tram & Prison (tram plus Fremantle Prison; $49/16.50).

✨ Festivals & Events

Laneway MUSIC
(www.fremantle.lanewayfestival.com; ⊗early Feb) WA's skinny-jean hipsters party to the planet's up-and-coming indie acts. The ubercool festival takes place around Fremantle's West End and Esplanade Reserve.

Blessing of the Fleet RELIGIOUS
(www.facebook.com/fremantle.blessingfleet; Fishing Boat Harbour, Esplanade Reserve; ⊗late Oct)

FREMANTLE FOR CHILDREN

You can let the littlies off the leash at **Esplanade Reserve**, watch buskers at the **markets**, make sandcastles at **Bathers Beach** (p89) or have a proper splash about at **South** or **Port Beaches**. Older kids might appreciate the creepier aspects of the **prison** (p85) and the innards of the submarine at the **Maritime Museum** (p85), where they can also poke about on actual boats. **Adventure World** (p57) is nearby for funfair rides. Finish up with fish and chips at Fishing Boat Harbour.

An October tradition since 1948, this event was brought to Fremantle by immigrants from Molfetta, Italy. It includes the procession of the Molfettese *Our Lady of Martyrs* statue (carried by men) and the Sicilian *Madonna di Capo d'Orlando* (carried by women) from St Patrick's Basilica (47 Adelaide St) to Fishing Boat Harbour, where the blessing takes place.

Fremantle Festival CULTURAL
(www.fremantle.wa.gov.au/festivals; ⊙late Oct-early Nov) In spring the city's streets and concert venues come alive with parades and performances in Australia's longest-running festival.

🛏 Sleeping

Fremantle Prison YHA Hostel HOSTEL $
(☑08-9433 4305; www.yha.com.au; 6a The Terrace; dm $26-29, d & tw from $76; ✳🛜) Opened in early 2015, Fremantle's former women's prison is now a hostel with dorm-style accommodation and private rooms. Slightly more upmarket options include bathroom, and there are excellent shared spaces often drenched in sun. Interesting photo boards telling the fascinating stories of inmates and the prison are dotted throughout the halls.

Fremantle Beach Backpackers HOSTEL $
(☑08-6219 5355; www.freobackpackers.com.au; 39 High St; dm $29-40, r $100; ✳@🛜) This recently opened backpackers in an old pub is getting good reviews from guests. Rates include a (very) simple breakfast, and quiz nights, movie nights and shared dinners all reinforce a social vibe. Though it's smack-bang in Freo's historic West End, it's a bit of stretch to include 'Beach' in the name...

Pirates HOSTEL $
(☑08-9335 6635; www.piratesbackpackers.com.au; 11 Essex St; dm $27-31, r $70; @🛜) Attracting a diverse international crew, this sun- and fun-filled hostel in the thick of the Freo action is a top spot to socialise. Rooms are small and reasonably basic, but the bathrooms are fresh and clean. The kitchen area is well equipped, there's a shady courtyard, and eye-catching marine murals remind you that an ocean swim is minutes away.

Old Firestation Backpackers HOSTEL $
(☑08-9430 5454; www.old-firestation.net; 18 Phillimore St; dm $18-25, d $55; @🛜) There's entertainment aplenty in this converted fire station: free internet, foosball, movies and a sunny courtyard. Dorms have natural light and afternoon sea breezes, and there's a women-only section. The hippy vibe culminates in late-night guitar-led singalongs around the campfire; bring earplugs if you value sleep.

Woodman Point Holiday Park CAMPGROUND $
(☑08-9434 1433; www.discoveryholidayparks.com.au; 132 Cockburn Rd; sites for 2 people $32-39, d $119-179; ✳@🛜🏊) A particularly pleasant spot, 10km south of Fremantle. It's usually quiet, and its location makes it feel more summer beach holiday than outer-Freo staging post.

★**Fremantle Apartment** APARTMENT $$
(www.thefremantleapartment.com; 7 Leake St; apt $110-160; ✳🛜) Arrayed across three floors and featuring a New York–loft vibe, this spacious apartment is located right in Fremantle's heritage precinct. A massive leather couch and big-screen TV combine with a well-equipped kitchen, and the fridge is usually stocked with a few complimentary chocolate nibbles. Friendly owners Cam and Terri have plenty of ideas on how best to enjoy Fremantle.

Fremantle Colonial Cottages COTTAGE $$
(☑08-9433 4305; www.fremantlecottages.com.au; 6a The Terrace; cottages $250) Located on a grassy terrace with views of Fremantle, these heritage cottages were originally occupied by wardens at the Fremantle women's prison (now the YHA hostel). With bedrooms and bunks, each of the three cottages can accommodate up to six people, and fully equipped kitchens make them a good choice for self-caterers. Wooden floors also make them good for families.

Hougoumont Hotel BOUTIQUE HOTEL $$
(☑08-6160 6800; www.hougoumonthotel.com.au; 15 Bannister St; d $194-260) Standard 'cabin' rooms are definitely compact, but they're very stylish and efficiently designed, and you can't beat the central location of this recently opened boutique hotel. Top-end toiletries, a hip, breezy ambience, and complimentary late-afternoon wine and snacks for guests reinforce the Hougoumont's refreshingly different approach to accommodation. Service from the multinational team is relaxed but professional.

Fothergills of Fremantle   B&B $$

(☑08-9335 6784; www.fothergills.net.au; 18-22 Ord St; r $195-245; 图🛜) Naked bronze women sprout from the front garden, while a life-size floral cow shelters on the veranda of these neighbouring mansions on the hill. Inside, the decor is in keeping with the buildings' venerable age (constructed 1892), including wonderful Aboriginal art and a superb collection of heritage maps of Australia. Breakfast is served in a sunny conservatory.

Terrace Central B&B Hotel   B&B $$

(☑08-9335 6600; www.terracecentral.com.au; 79-85 South Tce; d $175-220; 图@🛜) Terrace Central may be a character-filled B&B at heart, but its larger size gives it the feel of a boutique hotel. The main section is created from an 1888 bakery and an adjoined row of terrace houses, and there are modern one- and two-bedroom apartments out the back. You'll find ample off-street parking and a continental breakfast is served.

Port Mill B&B   B&B $$$

(☑08-9433 3832; www.portmillbb.com.au; 3/17 Essex St; r $199-299; 图🛜) One of the most luxurious B&Bs in town, Port Mill is clearly the love child of Paris and Freo. Crafted from local limestone (it was built in 1862 as a mill), inside it's all modern Parisian style, with gleaming taps, contemporary French furniture and wrought-iron balconies. French doors open out to the sun-filled decks, where breakfast is often served.

Lodging   APARTMENT $$$

(☑08-9430 6568; www.thelodging.co; 215 High St; ste $199-299; 图@) Formerly colonial accommodation with chintzy heritage decor, the Lodging has undergone a sleek designer makeover to re-emerge as a cool and sophisticated place to stay. The four suites now feature minimalist white decor enlivened by big-format B&W photos and colourful rugs, and the spotless bathrooms incorporate subtle art-deco touches. A communal kitchen includes a shared Nespresso machine.

Be.Fremantle   APARTMENT $$$

(☑08-9430 3888; www.befremantle.com.au/; Challenger Harbour, Mews Rd; apt from $250; 图🛜) At the end of a wharf, these sandstone one- to three-bedroom apartments have recently had a stylish makeover to reopen as the Be.Fremantle complex. The more expensive Marina View apartments enjoy the best vistas, and bikes are available for guests to explore Fremantle. A further 24 new apartments opened in mid-2017, so ask about scoring one of those.

🍴 Eating

Although it doesn't have Perth's variety of fine-dining places, eating and drinking your way around town are two of the great pleasures of Freo. People watching from outdoor tables on South Tce is a legitimate lifestyle choice. The Fremantle Markets (p88) are a good place to stock up on fruit and picnic items and have a decent selection of international street eats.

🍴 City Centre

Kakulas Sister   DELI $

(☑08-9430 4445; www.kakulassister.com.au; 29-31 Market St; ⊙9am-5.30pm Mon-Sat, 11.30am-5pm Sun; 🅿) This provedore – packed with nuts, quince paste and Italian rocket seeds – is a cook's dream, and an excellent spot to stock up on energy-filled snacks. If you've been to Kakulas Bros (p71) in Perth's Northbridge, you'll know the deal.

Leake St Cafe   CAFE $

(www.facebook.com/pg/leakestcafeteria; Leake St; mains $10-15; ⊙7.30am-3.30pm; 🅿) 🍃 Access this compact courtyard space by walking through the Kakulas Sister deli (p91), and look forward to some of Freo's best coffee and an ever-changing menu designed by Wade Drummond, a former contestant on Australian *MasterChef*. Healthy flavours could include a salad of roasted eggplant, chickpeas and toasted almonds, sourdough sandwiches, or good-value brown-rice bowls overflowing with Asian spiced chicken.

★ Bread in Common   BISTRO, BAKERY $$

(☑08-9336 1032; www.breadincommon.com.au; 43 Pakenham St; shared platters $15-21, mains $19-26; ⊙9am-10pm Sun-Thu, to 11pm Fri & Sat) Be lured by the comforting aroma of the in-house bakery before staying on for cheese and charcuterie platters, or larger dishes such as lamb ribs, octopus or pork belly. The focus is equally on comfort food and culinary flair, while big shared tables and a laid-back warehouse ambience encourage conversation over WA wines and Aussie craft beers and ciders.

Manuka Woodfire Kitchen
BARBECUE, PIZZA $$

(☑08-9335 3527; www.manukawoodfire.com.au; 134 High St; shared plates $11-38, pizzas $19-21; ☺5-9pm Tue-Fri, noon-3pm & 5-9pm Sat & Sun) Centred on a wood-fired oven, the kitchen at Manuka is tiny, but it's still big enough to turn out some of the tastiest food in town. Pretty well everything is cooked in the oven and the seasonal menu could include Esperance octopus, roast chicken with miso sauce or peppers and basil pesto. The pizzas are also very good.

A proudly local drinks menu includes Margaret River wine, cocktails using craft gin from Perth, and beers from WA's Nail Brewing. The Red Ale is a hoppy marvel.

Raw Kitchen
VEGETARIAN $$

(☑08-9433 4647; www.therawkitchen.com.au; 181a High St; mains $19-28; ☺11.30am-3.30pm Mon-Thu, to 9pm Fri-Sun; ☑) ✿ Vegan, organic and sustainable, and therefore *very* Freo. Reset your chakra and boost your energy levels with the super-healthy but still very tasty food in this funky, brick-lined warehouse. A lot (but not all) of the menu showcases raw ingredients, but taste is never sacrificed. Gluten-free beer and sustainably produced wine mean you don't have to be *too* virtuous.

Canvas
CAFE $$

(☑08-9335 5685; www.canvasatfremantleartscentre.com; Fremantle Arts Centre; mains $15-27; ☺8am-4pm; ☎) Freo's best cafe is in the shaded courtyard of the Fremantle Arts Centre, with a menu channelling Middle Eastern, Spanish and North African influences. Breakfast highlights include baked-egg dishes – try the Israeli-style Red Shakshuka – and lunch presents everything from jerk-chicken wraps to bouillabaisse and Tasmanian salmon. The concise drinks list includes craft beer, ciders and wine.

Moore & Moore
CAFE $$

(☑08-9335 8825; www.mooreandmoorecafe.com; 46 Henry St; mains $13-22; ☺7am-4pm; ☎) An urban-chic cafe that spills into the adjoining art gallery and overflows into a flagstoned courtyard. With great coffee, good cooked breakfasts, pastries, wraps and free wi-fi, it's a great place to linger. Look forward to the company of a few Freo hipsters, and the international crew of students studying at Fremantle's University of Notre Dame.

Mantle
SOUTH AMERICAN $$

(www.themantle.com.au; cnr Beach & James Sts; mains $18-30; ☺4.30-11pm Tue-Fri, 11am-11pm Sat & Sun) Filling a heritage warehouse, the Mantle's three businesses make it worth the 1.5km schlep from central Fremantle. Don Tapa combines South American and Asian flavours, Magna Pizza creates good wood-fired pizza amid the Mantle's rustic industrial ambience, and Alter Ego's hipster bar crew concocts inventive cocktails and serves up frosty craft beer best enjoyed in the raffish, compact courtyard.

Fishing Boat Harbour

Bathers Beach House
MODERN AUSTRALIAN $$$

(☑08-9335 2911; www.bathersbeachhouse.com.au; 47 Mews Rd; mains $32-42, shared platters $42-72; ☺11am-late; ☒) This grand building overlooking Bathers Beach has been reborn as a bustling bistro, with a seafood-heavy menu and chilled wine and craft beer. Oysters come three ways, barramundi partners linguini, and pork belly or wagyu rump are robust meaty options. The deck is Fremantle's best place for a sunset drink, and an adjacent playground is handy for travelling families.

North Fremantle

Flipside
BURGERS $

(☑08-9433 2188; www.flipsideburgers.com.au; 239 Queen Victoria St; burgers $11.50-14.50; ☺11.30am-9pm) Gourmet burgers with the option of dining in next door at Mrs Browns (p93).

Propeller
CAFE $$

(☑08-9335 9366; www.propellernorthfreo.com.au; 222 Queen Victoria St; shared plates & mains $12-28, pizzas $16-26; ☺8am-late) Echoes of Fremantle's maritime heritage fill this sunny cafe and bistro in North Fremantle, but the food is anything but old-fashioned and stuffy. Middle Eastern flavours inform dishes including Moorish skewers, a refreshing fennel-and-blood-orange salad, and rustic wood-fired *manoushe* (Lebanese flat breads). Out the front, good coffee is dispensed from a converted shipping container around a sunny courtyard.

Some of Fremantle's more interesting breakfast dishes are served with bloody Mary or Mimosa cocktails.

South Fremantle

Little Concept
CAFE $

(☑08-6323 1531; www.facebook.com/
TheLittleConcept; 7 Wray Ave; snacks & mains $10-
18; ⊙6.30am-5pm Mon-Sat, 7.30am-3pm Sun; ☑)
🍴 Part of the emerging Wray Ave cafe scene,
the Little Concept is popular with Freo locals
popping in for smoothies, excellent breakfast wraps and stonking slabs of frittata. If
you're feeling a tad coffeed out, come here to
try a wide range of flavoured teas and chais.
Lots of raw and vegan options make this a
healthy choice too.

★Ootong & Lincoln
CAFE $

(☑08-9335 6109; www.ootongandlincoln.com.au;
258 South Tce; mains $12-23; ⊙6am-5pm; ☑)
Catch the free CAT bus to South Fremantle
for a top breakfast spot. Join the locals grab-
bing takeaway coffee or beavering away on
their laptops, and start the day with maca-
damia-and-*dukkah* porridge or pop in from
noon for Mexican corn croquettes. Vintage
1960s furniture and loads of space make it a
great place to linger.

Lenny the Ox
CAFE $$

(☑08-9433 3851; www.facebook.com/LennytheOX;
20 Wray Ave; mains $15-20; ⊙6.30am-5pm) A seri-
ous approach to coffee from bearded hipster
baristas combines with real culinary nous at
this airy cafe. Locals crowd in for excellent
homestyle baking and the first caffeine hit
of the day, before returning for quirky spins
on cafe classics. The *shakshuka* baked eggs
or the potato hash will set you up for the day.

🍷 Drinking & Nightlife

Most of Fremantle's big pubs are lined up
along South Tce and High St. A couple of in-
teresting smaller bars also lurk in North and
South Fremantle, and it's a good destination
for fans of craft beer.

★Norfolk Hotel
PUB

(☑08-9335 5405; www.norfolkhotel.com.au; 47
South Tce; ⊙11am-midnight Mon-Sat, to 10pm Sun)
Slow down to Freo pace at this 1887 pub. In-
teresting guest beers create havoc for the in-
decisive drinker, and the food and pizzas are
very good. The heritage limestone courtyard
is a treat, especially when sunlight peeks
through the elms and eucalypts. Downstairs,
the Odd Fellow channels a bohemian small-
bar vibe and has live music Wednesday to
Saturday from 7pm.

Strange Company
COCKTAIL BAR

(www.strangecompany.com.au; 5 Nairn St;
⊙noon-midnight) Excellent cocktails – try the
spiced daiquiri – WA craft beers and smart
bar food make Strange Company a sophis-
ticated alternative to the raffish pubs along
South Tce. It's still very laid-back, though –
this is Freo, after all – and after-work action
on the sunny terrace segues into after-dark
assignations in Strange Company's cosy in-
terior booths.

Percy Flint's Boozery & Eatery
BAR

(☑08-9430 8976; www.facebook.com/
percyflintsouthfreo; 211 South Tce; ⊙4pm-mid-
night Tue-Thu, noon-midnight Fri-Sun) A relaxed
neighbourhood watering hole, Percy Flint is
very popular with locals. The tap-beer selec-
tion is one of Freo's most interesting, with
brews from around WA, and shared plates
with Mediterranean or Asian flavours are
best enjoyed around the big tables in the
garden courtyard.

Monk
MICROBREWERY

(☑08-9336 7666; www.themonk.com.au; 33 South
Tce; ⊙noon-midnight Mon-Thu, 11am-midnight Fri
& Sat, 11am-10pm Sun) Park yourself on the
spacious front terrace or in the chic interi-
or, partly fashioned from recycled railway
sleepers, and enjoy the Monk's own brews
(*kolsch,* mild, wheat, porter, *rauch,* pale
ale). The bar snacks and pizzas are also
good, and guest beers and regular seasonal
brews always draw a knowledgable crowd of
local craft-beer nerds.

Mrs Browns
BAR

(☑08-9336 1887; www.mrsbrownbar.com.au; 241
Queen Victoria St; ⊙4.30pm-midnight Tue-Thu,
noon-midnight Fri-Sun) Exposed bricks and a
copper bar combine with retro and antique
furniture to create North Fremantle's most
atmospheric drinking den. The music could
include all those cult bands you thought
were *your* personal secret, and an eclectic
menu of beer, wine and tapas targets the
more discerning, slightly older bar hound.
And you can order in burgers from Flipside
next door.

Whisper
WINE BAR

(☑08-9335 7632; www.whisperwinebar.com.au;
1/15 Essex St; ⊙noon-late Wed-Sun) In a lovely
heritage building, this classy French-themed
wine bar also does shared plates of charcute-
rie and cheese.

Little Creatures BREWERY
(☑1800 308 388; www.littlecreatures.com.au;
Fishing Boat Harbour, 40 Mews Rd; ☺10am-mid-
night) Try the Little Creatures Pale Ale and
Pilsner, and other beers and ciders under
the White Rabbit and Pipsqueak labels.
Keep an eye out for one-off Shift Brewers'
Stash beers. It's chaotic at times, but the
wood-fired pizzas ($19 to $24) are worth the
wait. More substantial shared plates ($8 to
$24) include kangaroo with tomato chutney
and marinated octopus. No bookings.

Creatures NextDoor is an adjacent lounge
bar with regular live entertainment and DJs.
Live jazz kicks off at 4.30pm on Sunday, and
there's live comedy on Saturday night from
8pm.

☆ Entertainment

Fly by Night Musicians Club LIVE MUSIC
(☑08-9430 5208; www.flybynight.org; 179 High
St) Variety is the key at Fly by Night, a not-
for-profit club that's been run by musos for
musos for years. All kinds perform here, and
many local bands made a start here. A recent relocation to High St has moved it conveniently closer to central Freo.

Mojos LIVE MUSIC
(☑08-9430 4010; www.mojosbar.com.au; 237
Queen Victoria St; ☺7pm-late) Local and national bands (mainly Aussie rock and indie)
and DJs play at this small place, and there's
a sociable beer garden out the back. First
Friday of the month is reggae night; every
Monday is open-mic night.

Metropolis Fremantle LIVE MUSIC
(☑08-9336 1880; www.metropolisfremantle.com.
au; 58 South Tce) A great space to watch a gig,
Metropolis turns into a nightclub on the
weekends. International and popular Australian bands and DJs perform here.

Newport Hotel LIVE MUSIC
(☑08-9335 2428; www.thenewport.com; 2 South
Tce; ☺noon-midnight Mon-Sat, to 10pm Sun)
Local bands and DJs gig from Friday to
Sunday. The Tiki Beat Bar is worth a kitsch
cocktail or two.

Luna on SX CINEMA
(☑08-9430 5999; www.lunapalace.com.au; Essex
St) Art-house cinema between Essex and
Norfolk Sts. Cheaper tickets on Wednesday.

Hoyts CINEMA
(☑08-9466 4920; www.hoyts.com.au; Collie St)
Blockbuster heaven with cheaper tickets on
Tuesday.

🛍 Shopping

The bottom end of High St features interesting and quirky shopping. Fashion stores
run along Market St, towards the train station. Queen Victoria St in North Fremantle
is the place to go for antiques. Don't forget
Fremantle Markets (p88) for clothes and
souvenirs.

Common Ground Collective DESIGN
(☑0418 158 778; www.facebook.com/cmmngrnd;
82 High St; ☺9am-5pm Mon-Sat, 10am-4pm Sun)
An eclectic showcase of jewellery, apparel
and design, mainly from local Fremantle
artisans and designers. The coffee at the in-
house cafe is pretty damn good too.

MANY 2.0 ARTS & CRAFTS
(52 Adelaide St; ☺10am-5pm Thu-Sun) A boho
mash-up of local artists' studios and pop-up
galleries and shops. Food and drinks also
available.

Didgeridoo Breath ARTS & CRAFTS
(☑08-9430 6009; www.didgeridoobreath.com; 6
Market St; ☺10.30am-5pm) The planet's biggest selection of didgeridoos, Indigenous
Australian books and CDs, and how-to-
play lessons ranging from one hour to four
weeks. You'll probably hear the shop before
you see it.

Aboriginart ART
(☑08-9336 1739; www.aboriginart.com.au; 6 Elder
Pl; ☺10am-4pm Tue-Sun) Contemporary and
collectable art ethically sourced from Indigenous artists living in Australia's Central
and Western Desert areas.

Found ARTS & CRAFTS
(☑08-9432 9555; www.fac.org.au; Fremantle Arts
Centre, 1 Finnerty St; ☺10am-5pm) The Fremantle Arts Centre (p88) shop stocks an inspiring range of WA art and craft.

Japingka ART
(☑08-9335 8265; www.japingka.com.au; 47 High
St; ☺10am-5.30pm Mon-Fri, noon-5pm Sat & Sun)
Specialising in Aboriginal fine art from WA
and beyond. Purchases come complete with
extensive notes about the works and the artists who created them.

Record Finder MUSIC
(☑ 08-9335 2770; www.facebook.com/
The-Record-Finder-232286070119578/; 87 High St;
⊙ 10am-5pm) A treasure trove of old vinyl, including rarities and collectables.

Bodkin's Bootery SHOES
(☑ 08-9336 1484; www.bodkinsbootery.com; 72
High St; ⊙ 9am-5pm Mon-Sat, noon-5pm Sun)
Handcrafted men's and women's boots and hats.

New Edition BOOKS
(☑ 08-9335 2383; www.newedition.com.au; cnr
High & Henry Sts; ⊙ 9am-6pm) Celebrating a sunny corner location, this bookworm's dream has comfy armchairs for browsing, and a superb collection of Australian fiction and non-fiction tomes for sale.

Mills Records MUSIC
(☑ 08-9335 1945; www.mills.com.au; 22 Adelaide
St; ⊙ 9am-5.30pm Mon-Sat, noon-5pm Sun) Music, including some rarities, and concert tickets. Check out the 'Local's Board' for recordings by Freo and WA acts.

Chart & Map Shop MAPS
(☑ 08-9335 8665; www.chartandmapshop.com.
au; 14 Collie St; ⊙ 10am-5pm) Maps and travel guides.

ℹ Information

INTERNET ACCESS

For free wi-fi, try **Moore & Moore** (p92),
or the FREbytes hot spot in the vicinity of the
Town Hall and **library** (☑ 08-9432 9766; www.
frelibrary.wordpress.com; Town Hall, Kings Sq;
⊙ 9.30am-5.30pm Mon, Fri & Sat, to 8pm Tue-
Thu; 🛜).

TOURIST INFORMATION

See www.fremantlestory.com.au for visitor information. Online www.lovefreo.com is a good source of information on local openings and events.

Rottnest Island Visitor Centre (p102) Book bikes and excursions here before you depart Fremantle.

Visitor Centre (☑ 08-9431 7878; www.
visitfremantle.com.au; Town Hall, Kings Sq;
⊙ 9am-5pm Mon-Fri, 9am-4pm Sat, 10am-4pm
Sun) Accommodation and tour bookings, and bike rental.

ℹ Getting There & Away

A taxi fare from **Perth Airport** (p271) (near Guildford) is $65 to $70.

Fremantle sits within zone 2 of **Transperth** (p276), the Perth public-transport system, and is only 30 minutes from Perth by train. There are numerous buses between Perth's city centre and Fremantle, including routes 103, 106, 107, 111 and 158.

Another very pleasant way to get here from Perth is by taking the 1¼-hour river cruise run by **Captain Cook Cruises** (p64).

ℹ Getting Around

There are numerous one-way streets and parking meters in Freo. It's easy enough to travel by foot or on the free CAT bus service, which takes in all the major sights on a continuous loop every 10 minutes from 7.30am to 6.30pm Monday to Thursday, till 9pm Friday, and 10am to 6.30pm on the weekend.

Bicycles (Fremantle Visitor Centre, Kings Sq;
⊙ 9am-5pm Mon-Fri, 9am-4pm Sat, 10am-
4pm Sun) can be rented for free at the visitor centre and are an ideal way to get around Freo's storied streets. A refundable bond of $200 applies.

Car rental is available through **Backpacker** (☑ 08-9430 8869; www.backpackercarrentals.
com.au; 235 Hampton Rd).

Ferries depart Fremantle for Rottnest Island from stops at **Victoria Quay** and **Rous Head**.

Around Perth

POP 285,000

Best Places to Eat

➡ Homestead Brewery (p111)

➡ Flic's Kitchen (p106)

➡ Cervantes Bar & Bistro (p119)

➡ Guildford Hotel (p109)

➡ Ostro Eatery (p104)

Best Places to Sleep

➡ Cervantes Lodge & Pinnacles Beach Backpackers (p118)

➡ Amble Inn (p118)

➡ Rottnest Island Authority Cottages (p101)

➡ Lancelin Lodge YHA (p117)

➡ Centrebreak Beach Stay (p120)

Why Go?

Although Western Australia is huge, you don't have to travel too far from Perth to treat yourself to a taste of what the state has to offer. A day trip could see you frolicking with wild dolphins, snorkelling with sea lions, scooping up brilliant-blue crabs or spotting bilbies in the bush. Active types can find themselves canoeing, rafting, surfing, windsurfing, sandboarding, diving, skydiving and ballooning. Those who prefer pursuits less likely to ruffle the hair can linger at vineyards or craft breweries, settle down for a culinary feast, or explore historic towns classified by the National Trust. To the north is the spectacular landscape of the Pinnacles Desert.

When to Go

Mandurah

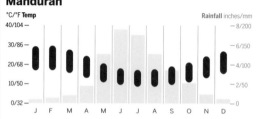

Mar Good beach weather and a fine time to spot thrombolites in Lake Clifton.

Aug Wildflowers start to bloom; brave paddlers take on the Avon River Descent.

Sep Catch the ferry to Rottnest Island for music, film and comedy at the annual Rottofest.

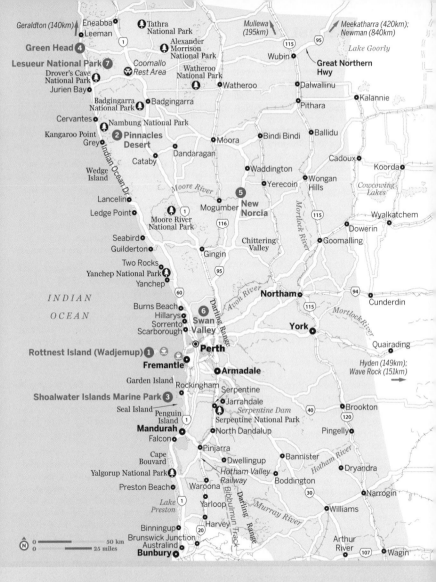

Around Perth Highlights

1 Cycling your way to a private slice of coastal paradise on **Rottnest Island** (Wadjemup; p98), then spending the afternoon swimming, sunning and snorkelling.

2 Enjoying a sublime sunset over the other-worldly **Pinnacles Desert** (p118).

3 Hanging out with penguins in **Shoalwater Islands Marine Park** (p103) off Rockingham.

4 Splashing about with sea lions in **Green Head** (p120) a few hours north of Perth.

5 Exploring the intriguing monastery town of **New Norcia** (p114).

6 Getting your foodie fix at the vineyards, breweries and artisan producers of the **Swan Valley** (p110).

7 Immersing yourself in the wonderful wildflowers of **Lesueur National Park** (p118).

ROTTNEST ISLAND

POP 475

'Rotto' has long been the family-holiday playground of choice for Perth locals. Although it's only about 19km offshore from Fremantle, this car-free, off-the-grid slice of paradise, ringed by secluded beaches and bays, feels a million miles away.

Cycling around the 11km-long, 4.5km-wide island is a real pleasure, and it's easy to discover your own sandy beach. You're bound to spot quokkas, the island's only native land mammals. Also relatively common are New Zealand fur seals off magical **West End**, dolphins, and – in season – whales. King skinks are also regularly seen sunning themselves on the roads.

Snorkelling, fishing, surfing and diving are also all excellent on the island. There's not a lot to do here that's not outdoors, so postpone your day trip if the weather is bad. It can be quite unpleasant when the wind really kicks up.

History

The island was originally called Wadjemup (place across the water), but Wadjuk oral history recalls that it was joined to the mainland before being cut off by rising waters. Modern scientists date that occurrence to before 6500 years ago, making these memories some of the world's oldest. Archaeological finds suggest that the island was inhabited 30,000 years ago, but not after it was separated from the mainland.

Dutch explorer Willem de Vlamingh claimed discovery of the island in 1696 and named it Rotte-nest ('rat's nest' in Dutch) because of the king-sized 'rats' (which were actually quokkas) he saw there.

From 1838 the island was used as a prison for Aboriginal men and boys from all around the state. At least 3670 people were incarcerated here, in harsh conditions, with around 370 dying (at least five were hanged). Although there were no new prisoners after 1903 (by which time holidaymakers from the mainland had already discovered the island), some existing prisoners served their sentences here until 1931. Even before the prison was built, Wadjemup was considered a 'place of the spirits', and it's been rendered even more sacred to Indigenous people because of the hundreds of their own, including prominent resistance leaders, who died here. Many avoid it to this day.

During WWI, approximately a thousand men of German or Austrian extraction were incarcerated here, their wives and children left to fend for themselves on the mainland. Ironically, most of the 'Austrians' were actually Croats who objected to Austro-Hungarian rule of their homeland. Internment resumed during WWII, although at that time it was mainly WA's Italian population that was imprisoned.

There's an ongoing push to return the island to its original name. One suggested compromise is to adopt a dual name, Wadjemup/Rottnest.

◉ Sights

Most of Rottnest's historic buildings, built mainly by Aboriginal prisoners, are grouped around Thomson Bay, where the ferry lands.

Salt Store   HISTORIC BUILDING
(Colebatch Ave; ☺10am-3pm) **FREE** A photographic exhibition in this 19th-century building looks at a different chapter of local history: when the island's salt lakes provided all of WA's salt (between 1838 and 1950). It's also the meeting point for walking tours.

Vlamingh's Lookout   VIEWPOINT
Not far away from Thomson Bay (go up past the old European cemetery), this unsigned vantage point offers panoramic views of the island, including its salt lakes. It's on View Hill, off Digby Dr.

Quod   HISTORIC SITE
(Kitson St) Built in 1864, this octagonal building with a central courtyard was once the Aboriginal prison block but is now part of the Rottnest Lodge hotel. During its time as a prison several men would share a 3m by 1.7m cell, with no sanitation (most of the deaths here were due to disease). The only part of the complex that can be visited is a small whitewashed chapel. A weekly Sunday service is held at 9.30am.

Aboriginal Burial Ground   CEMETERY
Adjacent to the Quod (p98) is a wooded area where hundreds of Aboriginal prisoners are buried in unmarked graves. Until relatively recently, this area was used as a camping ground, but it's now fenced off with signs asking visitors to show respect for what is regarded as a sacred site. Plans are under consideration to convert the area into a memorial, in consultation with Aboriginal elders.

Rottnest Museum   MUSEUM
(Kitson St; admission by gold-coin donation; ⊙11am-3.30pm) Housed in the old hay-store building, this little museum tells the island's natural and human history, warts and all, including dark tales of shipwrecks and incarceration.

Oliver Hill Battery   HISTORIC SITE
The Oliver Hill battery was built in the 1930s and played a major role in the WWII defence of the WA coastline and Fremantle harbour.

🏃 Activities

Most visitors come for Rottnest's beaches and aquatic activities. The Basin (p100) is the most popular beach for family-friendly swimming as it's protected by a ring of reefs. Other popular spots are **Longreach Bay** and **Geordie Bay**, though there are many smaller secluded beaches such as **Little Parakeet Bay**.

Skydive Geronimo   SKYDIVING
(☑1300 449 669; www.skydivegeronimo.com.au; Rottnest Airport; 10,000/14,000/15,000ft $389/489/539; ⊙8am-3pm Sat & Sun, by appointment weekdays) Take an island leap of faith and land on the beach. Bookings essential; minimum age 12.

Oliver Hill Train & Tour   RAIL
(☑08-9432 9300; www.rottnestisland.com; adult/child $29/16.50) This trip (departing from the train station at 1.30pm) takes you by train to historic Oliver Hill battery (p99) and includes the Gun & Tunnels tour run by Rottnest Voluntary Guides (p101).

Scenic Joy Flights   SCENIC FLIGHTS
(☑1300 895 538, 0411 264 547; www.rottnest.aero/scenic-rottnest; 10/20/35min $45/75/110) Spectacular flights over the island, departing from Rottnest Airport.

Rottnest Island Bike Hire   CYCLING
(☑08-9292 5105; www.rottnestisland.com; cnr Bedford Ave & Welch Way; bikes per half-/full-day from $16/30; ⊙8.30am-4pm, to 5.30pm summer) Also rents masks, snorkels and fins, and surfboards.

Snorkelling & Diving

Excellent visibility, temperate waters, coral reefs and shipwrecks make Rottnest a top spot for scuba diving and snorkelling. There are snorkel trails with underwater plaques at Little Salmon Bay and Parker Point. The Basin, Little Parakeet Bay, Longreach Bay and Geordie Bay are also good. Rottnest Island Bike Hire (p99) hires out masks, snorkels and fins, as well as kayaks, surfboards, paddleboards and scooters. The only wreck that's accessible to snorkellers without a boat is at Thomson Bay.

The Australasian Diving Academy (p61) organises wreck-diving trips here.

Surfing

The best surf breaks are at Strickland, Salmon and Stark Bays, towards the western end of the island.

Birdwatching

Rottnest is ideal for twitchers because of the varied habitats: coast, lakes, swamps, heath, woodlands and settlements. Coastal birds include pelicans, gannets, cormorants, bar-tailed godwits, whimbrels, fairy terns, bridled terns, crested terns, oystercatchers and majestic ospreys. For more, grab a copy of *A Bird's Eye View of Rottnest Island* from the visitor centre (p102).

👉 Tours

Check times online at www.rvga.asn.au or at the Salt Store (p98), or call the visitor centre (p102).

Grand Island Tour   BUS
(☑08-9432 9300; www.rottnestisland.com/tours; adult/child incl lunch $69/55; ⊙departs 11am) A 3½-hour in-depth exploration of the island that includes lunch. Book online or at the visitor centre (p102) when you arrive. Buses depart from the main bus stop in Thomson Bay.

Discovery Tour   BUS
(☑1300 467 688; www.rottnestexpress.com.au; adult/child $45/22; ⊙departs 11.15am & 1.40pm) Ninety-minute tours of the island with an informative and entertaining commentary. Coaches depart from the main bus stop in Thomson Bay.

Segway Tours   TOURS
(☑1300 808 180; www.segwaytourswa.com.au; Kingstown Barracks, cnr Kingstown Rd & Hospital Lane; 1hr/90min $79/115; ⊙tours depart 9am, 11am, 12.30pm & 2.30pm) Choose from the popular 90-minute off-road Fortress Adventure Tour or the 60-minute Settlement Explorer Tour taking in the history of Rottnest's original settlement. If you just want to zip around on a Segway, sign up for 25 minutes ($40) in the Segway Experience Zone. Participants must be at least nine years old.

AROUND PERTH ROTTNEST ISLAND

Rottnest Island (Wadjemup)

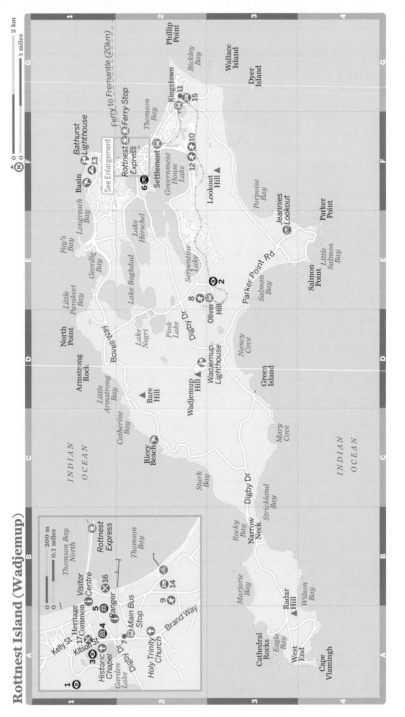

Rottnest Island (Wadjemup)

Charter 1 BOATING
(✆0428 604 794; www.charter1.com.au; adult/child $229/149; ⊗mid-Sep–Apr) Briny excursions departing from Fremantle include full-day sails incorporating kayaking and snorkelling.

Rottnest Voluntary Guides WALKING
(✆08-9372 9757; www.rvga.asn.au) FREE Free, themed walks leave from the central Salt Store daily, with topics including History, Reefs, Wrecks and Daring Sailors, Vlamingh Lookout and Salt Lakes, and the Quokka Walk. The outfit also runs tours of Wadjemup Lighthouse (p100) (adult/child $9/4) and Oliver Hill Gun & Tunnels (adult/child $9/4); you'll need to make your own way there for the last two.

Adventure Rottnest CRUISE
(✆1300 467 688; www.rottnestexpress.com.au; adult/child $55/27; ⊗mid-Sep–late Apr) Ninety-minute cruises around the coast with a special emphasis on spotting wildlife. Packages are also available from Perth (adult/child $152/76) and Fremantle (adult/child $132/66). Check the website for other options incorporating the Discover Rottnest coach tour and snorkelling tours.

Island Explorer Tour BUS
(✆08-9432 9300; www.rottnestisland.com; adult/child/family $20/12/50; ⊗departs every 1¼hr 8.45am-3pm) Handy hop-on, hop-off coach service stopping at 18 locations around the island. Includes a limited commentary and is a great way to get your bearings when you first arrive.

★☆ Festivals & Events

Rotto is the site of annual school leavers' and end-of-uni-exams parties, a time when the island is overrun by kids 'getting blotto on Rotto'. Depending on your age, it's either going to be the best time you've ever had or the worst – check the calendar before proceeding.

Rottofest MUSIC
(www.rottofest.com.au; ⊗Sep) The annual Rottofest immerses the island in a day of music, film and comedy.

🛏 Sleeping

Rotto is wildly popular in summer and during school holidays, when accommodation is booked out for months in advance. Prices can rise steeply at these times. Check websites for off-peak deals combining transport to the island, especially for weekday visits.

Kingstown Barracks Youth Hostel HOSTEL $
(✆08-9432 9111; www.rottnestisland.com; Kingstown Rd; dm/f $53/117) This hostel is located in old army barracks that still have a rather institutional feel and few facilities. Check in at the visitor centre (p102) before you make the 1.8km walk, bike or bus trip to Kingston.

Allison Tentland CAMPGROUND $
(✆08-9432 9111; www.rottnestisland.com; Thomson Bay; sites $38) Camping on the island is restricted to this leafy camping ground with barbecues. Be vigilant about your belongings, especially your food – cheeky quokkas have been known to help themselves.

**Rottnest Island
Authority Cottages** COTTAGE $$
(✆08-9432 9111; www.rottnestisland.com; cottages $189-322) There are more than 250 villas and cottages for rent around the island. Some have magnificent beachfront positions

QUOKKAS

These cute little docile bundles of fur have suffered a number of indignities over the years. First Willem de Vlamingh's crew mistook them for rats as big as cats. Then the British settlers misheard and mangled their name (the Noongar word was probably *quak-a* or *gwaga*). But, worst of all, a cruel trend of 'quokka soccer' by sadistic louts in the 1990s saw many kicked to death before a $10,000 fine was imposed; occasional cases are still reported. On a more positive note, the phenomenon of 'quokka selfies' briefly illuminated the internet in 2015 with various Rottnest marsupials achieving minor global fame on Instagram. Google 'Rottnest quokka selfies' to see the best of #quokkaselfie.

These marsupials of the macropod family (relatives of kangaroos and wallabies) were once found throughout the southwest but are now confined to mainland forests and a population of 8000 to 10,000 on Rottnest Island. Don't be surprised if one approaches looking for a titbit. Just say no, as human food isn't good for them.

and are palatial; others are more like beach shacks. Prices rise by around $60 for Friday and Saturday, and they increase by up to $120 in peak season (late September to April). Check online for the labyrinthine pricing schedule.

Karma Rottnest Lodge HOTEL $$
(☑1300 7688 6378; www.karmagroup.com; Kitson St; r $210-320; ⏸🌊) It's claimed there are ghosts in this complex, which is based around the former Quod (p98) prison building and boys' reformatory school. If that worries you, ask for a room in the new section, looking onto a salt lake. Older rooms are comfortable but fairly compact and basic. Services and amenities include bar, restaurant and spa treatments. Rates are best midweek.

Hotel Rottnest HOTEL $$$
(☑08-9292 5011; www.hotelrottnest.com.au; 1 Bedford Ave; r $270-320; ❄️🌊) Based around the former summer-holiday pad for the state's governors (built in 1864), the former Quokka Arms has been transformed by a stylish renovation. The whiter-than-white

rooms in an adjoining building are smart and modern, if a tad pricey. Some have beautiful sea views.

🍴 Eating

Most visitors to Rotto self-cater. The **general store** (☑08-9292-5017; www.rottnestgeneralstore.com.au; Thomson Bay; ⏰8am-6pm) is a small supermarket (and also stocks liquor), but if you're staying a while, it's better to bring supplies with you. Another option is to pre-order food from the general store, and they'll equip your accommodation with food and drinks before your arrival. Rottnest's small township has cafes and a good bakery.

Hotel Rottnest PUB FOOD $$
(☑08-9292 5011; www.hotelrottnest.com.au; 1 Bedford Ave; mains $23-37, pizzas $20-26; ⏰11am-late) It's hard to imagine a more inviting place for a sunset pint of Little Creatures than the AstroTurf 'lawn' of this chic waterfront hotel. A big glass pavilion creates an open and inviting space, and bistro-style food and pizzas are reasonably priced given the location and ambience. Bands and DJs regularly boost the laid-back island mood during summer.

Aristos SEAFOOD $$$
(☑08-9292 5171; www.aristosrottnest.com.au; Colebatch Ave; breakfast $10-23, lunch & dinner mains $27-46; ⏰8am-late) An upmarket but pricey option for seafood, steaks and salads, fish and chips, burgers, ice cream or excellent coffee. Push the boat (way) out with a seafood platter for two people ($155).

ℹ️ Information

At the Thomson Bay settlement, behind the main jetty, there's a shopping area with an ATM.
Visitor Centre (☑08-9372 9732; www.rottnestisland.com; Thomson Bay; ⏰7.30am-5pm Sat-Thu, to 7pm Fri, extended hours summer) Handles check-ins for all of the island authority's accommodation. There's a bookings counter at the Fremantle office (Map p86; ☑08-9432 9300; www.rottnestisland.com; E Shed, Victoria Quay), near where the ferry departs.
Ranger (☑08-9372 9788) For fishing and boating information.

ℹ️ Getting There & Away

There is a fee per adult/child/family of $18/6.50/42.50 to visit the island. This fee is included in ferry costs but payable separately if you're visiting the island on a private boat.

AIR

Rottnest Air-Taxi (☑1300 895 538; www.rottnest.aero) Flies from Jandakot airport. Prices for whole planes cost from $250, working out to around $83 per person.

BOAT

Ferry services to the island:

Rottnest Express (☑1300 467 688; www.rottnestexpress.com.au) Ferries from Perth's **Barrack Street Jetty** (p84) (1¾ hours, once daily), Fremantle (30 minutes, five times daily) and North Fremantle (30 minutes, three times daily). Packages including bike hire, snorkelling equipment, meals, accommodation and tours are all available. Services increase in summer and during school holidays. The Perth and Fremantle departure points are handy to train stations.

Rottnest Fast Ferries (☑08-9246 1039; www.rottnestfastferries.com.au; adult/child $85.50/48.75) Departs from Hillarys Boat Harbour (40 minutes; three times daily), around 40 minutes' drive north of Perth. See www.hillarysboatharbour.com.au for public-transport details. An additional 6pm ferry departs on Friday night in summer. Packages also available.

❶ Getting Around

BIKE

Rottnest is just big enough (and has just enough hills) to make a day's ride good exercise. Electric bikes (half-/full-day $40/60) are also available.

Bikes can be booked in advance online or on arrival through **Rottnest Island Bike Hire** (p99). Photo ID must be shown.

The ferry companies also hire bikes as part of an island package, and they have them waiting for visitors on arrival. The visitor centre hires bikes, too.

BUS

A free shuttle runs between Thomson Bay, the main accommodation areas and the airport, departing roughly every 35 minutes, with the last bus at 8pm.

The **Island Explorer** (p101) is a handy hop-on, hop-off coach service stopping at 18 locations around the island. It includes a commentary and is a great way to get your bearings when you first arrive. Between Geordie Bay and Thomson Bay it's free.

ROCKINGHAM

POP 135,000

Just 46km south of Perth, Rockingham has good beaches and the Shoalwater Islands Marine Park, where you can observe dolphins, sea lions and penguins in the wild.

Rockingham was founded in 1872 as a port, although this function was taken over by Fremantle in the 1890s. There's still a substantial industrial complex to the north, at Kwinana.

Most places of interest are stretched along Rockingham Beach.

◉ Sights & Activties

Shoalwater Islands Marine Park   NATURE RESERVE
(www.parks.dpaw.wa.gov.au/park/shoalwater-islands; ⊙closed for nesting Jun–mid-Sep) 🏊 Just a few minutes' paddle, swim or boat ride away from the shore is strictly protected **Penguin Island**, home to penguins, silver gulls, boardwalks, swimming beaches and picnic tables. Apart from birdwatching (pied cormorants, pelicans, crested and bridled terns, oystercatchers), day visitors can also swim and snorkel.

The Penguin Island ferry (p104) is run by Rockingham Wild Encounters (p103). Tickets that combine the ferry with entry to the penguin feeding at the island's **discovery centre** (adult/child $23/18.50) are available.

At low tide it's possible to wade the few hundred metres to the island across the sandbar. However, take heed of warning signs, as people have drowned here after being washed off the bar during strong winds and high tides.

West Coast Dive Park   DIVING
(☑08-9592 3464; www.westcoastdivepark.com.au; permits per day/week $25/50) Diving within the Shoalwater Islands Marine Park became even more interesting after the sinking of the *Saxon Ranger*, a supposedly jinxed 400-tonne fishing vessel. Permits to dive at this site are available from the visitor centre (p104). Contact the Australasian Diving Academy (p61) about expeditions here and to the wrecks of three other boats, two planes and various reefs in the vicinity.

☞ Tours

Rockingham Wild Encounters   WILDLIFE
(☑08-9591 1333; www.rockinghamwildencounters.com.au; cnr Arcadia Dr & Penguin Rd; ⊙Sep–May) 🏊 The only operator licensed to take people to Penguin Island near Rockingham, this outfit also runs other low-impact tours. The most popular is the **dolphin swim** (per

person $205 to $225), which lets you interact with some of the marine park's 200 wild bottlenose dolphins. Swimming with dolphins can disturb them, so an alternative is the two-hour **dolphin-watch tour** (adult/child $85/50).

There's also a 45-minute penguin and sea-lion cruise in a glass-bottomed boat. Pick-ups can be arranged from Perth hotels.

Capricorn Seakayaking KAYAKING
(☑ 0427 485 123; www.capricornseakayaking.com.au; per person $180; ⊙ late Sep–late Apr) Runs full-day sea-kayaking tours around Penguin and Seal Islands. Also includes wildlife watching and snorkelling.

✕ Eating

★ Ostro Eatery CAFE $$
(☑ 08-9592 8957; www.ostroeatery.com.au; 11a Rockingham Beach Rd; mains $15-28; ⊙ 7.30am-3pm Mon-Wed, 7.30am-late Thu-Sun) This weekday cafe with big shared tables morphs into a sociable evening option later in the week. The blue-swimmer-crab omelette is a great way to start the day, and from Thursday to Sunday there are sophisticated dinner options, including Exmouth prawns and beef-cheek ravioli. Cold-pressed juices and house-made sodas complement a concise selection of beer and wine.

Rustico CAFE $$
(☑ 08-9528 4114; www.rusticotapas.com.au; 61 Rockingham Beach Rd; shared plates $14-26, pizzas $17; ⊙ 4-9pm Tue, noon-10pm Wed-Sun) This stylish cafe is renowned for its authentic Spanish-style food. Sit on the corner terrace with ocean views, and tuck into sweetcorn-and-cheese croquettes or pan-seared squid. A six-course degustation (per person $59) showcases salmon, scallops and pork belly, and wines are also available to partner each course. Cocktails, sangria and craft beer all contribute to a fun vibe.

ℹ Information

Visitor Centre (☑ 08-9592 3464; www.rockinghamvisitorcentre.com.au; 19 Kent St; ⊙ 9am-5pm) Has accommodation listings.

ℹ Getting There & Around

Rockingham sits within zone 5 of the Perth public-transport system, **Transperth** (p276). Regular trains depart from Rockingham station, via the Mandurah line, to Perth Underground/Esplanade ($8.10, 34 minutes) and Mandurah ($5.50, 18 minutes).

Rockingham station is around 4km southeast of Rockingham Beach and around 6km east of Mersey Point, from where the **Penguin Island Ferry** (Mersey Point Jetty; adult/child $15/12.50; ⊙ hourly 9am-3pm mid-Sep–May) departs; catch bus 551 or 555 to the beach or stay on the 551 to Mersey Point.

PEEL REGION

Taking in swaths of jarrah forest, historic towns and the increasingly glitzy coastal resort of Mandurah, the Peel Region can easily be tackled as a day trip from Perth or as the first stopping point of a longer expedition down the South Western Hwy (Rte 1).

As you enter the Peel, you'll pass out of Wadjuk country and into that of their fellow Noongar neighbours, the Pinjarup (or Binjareb) people.

Mandurah

POP 84,537

Shrugging off its fusty retirement-haven image, Mandurah has made concerted efforts to reinvent itself as an upmarket beach resort, taking advantage of its new train link to Perth's public-transport network. And, although its connected set of redeveloped 'precincts' and 'quarters' may sound a little pretentious, the overall effect is actually pretty cool. You can wander along the waterfront from the Ocean Marina (boats, cafes and the Dolphin Quay indoor market), past the Venetian Canals (glitzy apartments linked by Venetian-ish sandstone bridges), through the Boardwalk and Cultural Precinct (more eateries, visitor centre, cinema, arts centre) to the Bridge Quarter (still more restaurants and bars).

Mandurah Bridge spans the Mandurah Estuary, which sits between the ocean and the large body of water known as the Peel Inlet. It's one of the best places in the region for fishing, crabbing, prawning (March and April) and dolphin spotting.

◉ Sights & Activities

Several beautiful beaches are within walking distance of the Mandurah waterfront.

Town Beach BEACH
Town Beach is just across from the marina, at the southern end of Silver Sands resort. It's perhaps the best of the ocean beaches.

DWELLINGUP

Dwellingup is a small, forest-shrouded township with character, 100km south of Perth. Its reputation as an activity hub has been enhanced by the hardy long-distance walkers and cyclists passing through on the Bibbulmun Track and the Munda Biddi Trail respectively.

Visit the **Forest Heritage Centre** (⌂08-9538 1395; www.forestheritagecentre.com.au; 1 Acacia St; adult/child $5.50/3.50; ⊙10am-3pm) for displays on local flora and fauna and a shop selling pieces crafted by the resident woodwork artists. The **Hotham Valley Railway** (⌂08-6278 1111; www.hothamvalleyrailway.com.au; Forest Train adult/child $28/14, Restaurant Train $92, Steam Ranger $40/20; ⊙Forest Train departs 10.30am & 2pm Sat & Sun, Restaurant Train 7.45pm Sat, Steam Ranger 10.30am & 2pm Sun May-Oct) chugs along 8km of forest track on a 90-minute return trip, and **Dwellingup Adventures** (⌂08-9538 1127; www.dwellingupadventures.com.au; cnr Marrinup & Newton Sts; 1-person kayaks & 2-person canoes per 3hr $30; ⊙8.30am-5pm) can arrange bike, kayak and canoe rental, and also book self-guided canoeing and mountain biking excursions, and guided white-water-rafting tours (per person $150, from June to October).

Pop into the **Blue Wren Cafe** (⌂08-9538 1234; www.facebook.com/DwellingupBlueWrenCafe; 53 McLarty St; mains $15-18; ⊙8am-7pm Tue-Sun, to 5pm Mon) for excellent homemade pies and consider **Lewis Park Chalets'** (⌂08-9538 1406; www.lewisparkchalets.com.au; 99 Irwin Rd; d $150) rural ambience for an overnight stay.

Swimming Area BEACH

There's a designated, boat-free swimming area on the far side of the estuary, just north of Mandurah Bridge. Here dolphins have been known to swim up to kids for a frolic.

Doddi's Beach BEACH

West of the mouth of the estuary is family-friendly Doddi's Beach, facing the ocean.

Mandurah Cruises CRUISE

(⌂08-9581 1242; www.mandurahcruises.com.au; Boardwalk) Take a one-hour Dolphin & Scenic Canal Cruise (adult/child $28/14; departs on the hour from 10am to 4pm), a half-day Murray River Lunch Cruise ($89/55; Wednesday and Saturday) and, through December, a one-hour Christmas Lights Canal Cruise ($33/18), that gawps at millionaires' mansions under the pretence of admiring their festive displays.

Mandurah Boat & Bike Hire BOATING, CYCLING

(⌂08-9535 5877; www.mandurahboatandbikehire.com.au; Boardwalk) Chase the fish on a four-seat dinghy or six-seat pontoon (per hour/day from $55/350). Also hires out bikes (per hour/day $10/40). If you're keen to get active on the water, ask about kayak and SUP (stand-up paddleboard) hire.

🛌 Sleeping

Dolphin Point B&B B&B $$

(⌂08-9581 5813; www.dolphinpointbandb.com.au; 26 Bermuda Pl, Halls Head; ste/apt from $170/270; ❄☎) With a waterfront location right in the heart of Mandurah's famed canals, Dolphin Point B&B is a great place to wind down and wave at the excursion boats as they putter past. Options include a comfortable suite and a self-contained apartment with a full kitchen. Both have water views, and the apartment also has a barbecue for relaxed evening meals.

Seashells Resort RESORT $$

(⌂08-9550 3000; www.seashells.com.au; 16 Dolphin Dr; apt from $195; ❄☄) Seashells' apartments are cool and spacious, and there's a beach on its doorstep and a lovely infinity-lipped pool just metres away. Check into one of the luxury beachfront villas and you may not want to leave.

Mandurah Ocean Marina Chalets MOTEL $$

(⌂08-9535 8173; www.marinachalets.com.au; 6 The Lido; studios & chalets $117-175; ❄☎) The ambience is a bit like a British holiday camp, but the chalets and motel units are spotless and modern, with fully equipped kitchens. There's a shared barbecue area and crab-cooking facility, and the canals and restaurants of Ocean Marina and Dolphin Quay are a short walk away.

🍴 Eating

Restaurants and cafes abound on the Boardwalk, at Dolphin Quay, and back in the older, more established area of Mandurah.

DRYANDRA WOODLAND

With small populations of threatened numbats, woylies and tammar wallabies, this isolated remnant of eucalypt forest 164km southeast of Perth hints at what the wheat belt was like before large-scale land clearing and feral predators wreaked havoc on ecosystems. With numerous walking trails, it makes a great getaway from Perth.

The excellent **Barna Mia Animal Sanctuary** (adult/child/family $20/10/50), home to endangered bilbies, boodies, woylies and marla, conducts 90-minute after-dark torchlight tours, providing a rare opportunity to see these creatures up close. Book through **Parks & Wildlife** (☑08-9881 9222; www.parks.dpaw.wa.gov.au; 7 Wald St, Narrogin; ⊙8.30am-4pm) for post-sunset tours on Monday, Wednesday, Friday and Saturday and book early for peak periods.

The **Lions Dryandra Village** (☑08-9884 5231; www.dryandravillage.org.au; adult/child $30/15, 2-/4-person cabins $70/90, 8-12-person cabins $130) is a 1920s forestry camp with self-contained renovated woodcutters' cabins and the attention of nearby grazing wallabies.

★ **Flic's Kitchen**   MODERN AUSTRALIAN **$$**
(☑08-9535 1661; www.flicskitchen.com; 3/16 Mandurah Tce; breakfast $10-23, shared plates $16-24; ⊙8am-late Wed-Sat, to 3pm Sun; ☑) Perfectly located to catch the afternoon sun, this recent opening infused with cosmopolitan cool has outdoor seating and a versatile menu covering breakfast, lunch and dinner. Highlights include corn hotcakes with chipotle-spiced chicken for brunch, and Mandurah-crab croquettes as the sun goes down. Expect a good beer and wine list and vegan and paleo menu options.

Peninsula   BISTRO **$$**
(☑08-9534 9899; www.thepenmandurah.com. au/; 1 Marco Polo Dr; mains $22-40, bar snacks $10-24; ⊙11am-9.30pm) There's been a pub on this spot since 1911, but 'The Pen's' latest 2016 reincarnation has turned it into a sleek 21st-century watering hole. Huge picture windows allow brilliant marine views from the restaurant serving upscale mains, while the absolute waterside beer garden is great for frosty pints of Tiger beer and crab tacos with daikon and *sriracha* dressing.

🍷 Drinking & Nightlife

DPM Cafe   CAFE
(☑0459 982 710; www.facebook.com/ dawnpatrolmobilecafe; 14 Mandurah Tce; ⊙6am-4pm Mon, Tue, Thu & Fri, 6am-noon Wed, 7am-noon Sat & Sun) The best coffee in town is at this funky hole-in-the-wall place a short stroll from the estuary. Partner it with a toasted sourdough sandwich for a good-value lunch.

Brighton Hotel   PUB
(☑08-9534 8864; www.brightonmandurah.com. au; 10-12 Mandurah Tce; ⊙10am-late Mon-Sat, to 10pm Sun) Watch the sun set over the estuary with a glass of wine, and return after 8pm at the weekend to move to the DJs. Decent meals for lunch and dinner complete the picture for a classic Aussie pub.

ℹ Information

Visitor Centre (☑08-9550 3999; www. visitpeel.com.au; 75 Mandurah Tce; ⊙9am-5pm) On the estuary boardwalk.

ℹ Getting There & Away

Mandurah is 72km from central Perth; take the Kwinana Fwy and follow the signs.

TRAIN

Mandurah sits within the outermost zone (7) of the Perth public-transport system and is the terminus of Transperth's Mandurah line. There are direct trains from Mandurah to Perth Underground/Esplanade ($10.70, 50 minutes) and Rockingham ($8.10, 18 minutes).

BUS

Transwa (☑1300 662 205; www.transwa. wa.gov.au) coach routes include the following:
➡ SW1 (12 per week) to East Perth ($17.50, 1½ hours), Bunbury ($17.50, two hours), Busselton ($27, 2¾ hours), Margaret River ($35, four hours) and Augusta ($38, 4¾ hours).
➡ SW2 (three times weekly) to Balingup ($29, three hours), Bridgetown ($32, 3½ hours) and Pemberton ($44, 4½ hours).
➡ GS3 (weekly) to Denmark ($69, 7¼ hours) and Albany ($75, eight hours).

SOUTHERN WHEAT BELT

A beautiful forest, rare marsupials, stunning ancient granite formations, salt lakes, interesting back roads and the unique Wave Rock are the scattered highlights of this widespread farming region.

Hyden & Wave Rock

Large granite outcrops dot the Central and Southern Wheat Belts, and the most famous of these is Wave Rock. The nearest town is Hyden, a sleepy bush settlement including motel, cafe, bakery and petrol station.

⊙ Sights

Wave Rock   LANDMARK
The multicoloured cresting swell of Wave Rock is 350km from Perth. Formed some 60 million years ago by weathering and water erosion, the granite outcrop is streaked with colours created by run-off from local mineral springs. To get the most out of Wave Rock, obtain the *Walk Trails at Wave Rock and The Humps* brochure from the visitor centre.

Parking at Wave Rock is $10 per car, or you can park at Hippos Yawn (no fee) and follow the shady track back along the rock base to Wave Rock (1km).

Mulka's Cave & the Humps   CAVE
The superb Mulka's Cave is an important rock-art site, with 450 stencils and handprints. The more adventurous can choose from two walking tracks. The Kalari Trail (1.6km return) climbs onto a huge granite outcrop (one of the Humps) with excellent views, somehow wilder and more impressive than Wave Rock, while the Gnamma Trail (1.2km return) stays low and investigates natural waterholes with panels explaining Noongar culture. The site is 16km from Wave Rock.

🛏 Sleeping

Wave Rock Cabins & Caravan Park   CABIN **$**
(✐ 08-9880 5022; www.waverock.com.au; unpowered/powered sites from $30/48, cabins & cottages from $140; ✳ ✉) Accommodation can fill up quickly, so phone ahead for a spot amid the gum trees here.

Wave Rock Motel   MOTEL **$$**
(✐ 08-9880 5052; www.waverock.com.au; 2 Lynch St, Hyden; s/d from $105/150; ✳ ✉) In Hyden,

4km east of Wave Rock, the Wave Rock Motel has well-equipped rooms, a comfy lounge with fireplace, and a bush bistro where you can barbecue steaks and chicken on an indoor grill.

ℹ Information

Visitor Centre (✐ 08-9880 5182; www.waverock.com.au; Wave Rock; ⊙ 9am-5pm) Also has a good cafe and quirky local souvenirs.

ℹ Getting There & Away

This area is best explored with your own vehicle, ideally on the way to somewhere else. If heading to/from the Nullarbor, take the 300km unsealed direct Hyden–Norseman Rd, which will save 100km or so. Look for the brochure *The Granite and Woodlands Discovery Trail* at the Norseman or Wave Rock visitor centres.

Transwa (✐ 1300 662 205; www.transwa.wa.gov.au) runs bus GE2 from East Perth to Hyden ($55, five hours) and on to Esperance ($53, five hours) every Tuesday, returning on Thursday. **Western Travel Bug** (✐ 08-9486 4222; www.travelbug.com.au; adult/child $185/135; ⊙ Tue, Thu & Sat) offers a very long one-day tour from Perth three times a week.

DARLING RANGE

Commonly known as the Perth Hills, this forest-covered escarpment provides the city with a green backdrop and offers great spots for picnics, barbecues, bushwalking and rubbing shoulders with wild kangaroos. Leafy suburbs nestle at its feet, along with a few dozen wineries.

Kalamunda

Kalamunda is a well-heeled township on the crest of the Darling Range. The area began as a timber settlement, but it's since become a quieter residential haven close to the city (it's a 30-minute drive from Perth).

For walkers, Kalamunda is the northern terminus of the **Bibbulmun Track**, which starts near the shops and heads into the forest of **Kalamunda National Park**.

From Zig-Zag Dr, just north of Kalamunda off Lascelles Pde, there are fantastic views over Perth to the coast. The drive through the forested hills to Mundaring via Mundaring Weir Rd is also wonderful, but watch out for kangaroos.

◉ Sights

Araluen Botanic Park GARDENS

(☑08-9234 2200; www.araluenbotanicpark.com.
au; 362 Croyden Rd, Roleystone; adult/child $6/3;
⊙9am-6pm) South of Kalamunda, just off
Brookton Hwy, is Araluen Botanic Park. Constructed in the 1920s by the Young Australia
League (YAL) as a bush retreat, the park was
neglected for years and became overgrown.
The state government purchased it in 1990
and has since restored its elaborate garden
terraces, waterfalls and ornamental pool.
The spring tulip displays are wonderful.

✖ Eating

Jack & Jill CAFE $$

(☑08-9293 3023; www.facebook.com/
Jackandjillkalamunda; 18 Haynes St; mains $8-
23; ⊙8am-3pm Tue-Sun) Giving Kalamunda's
sleepy main street a bit of a shake-up, Jack
& Jill's modern take on cafe dining includes
a great eggs Benedict with pulled pork, and
the delicate strawberry friands are also worthy of a stop. Look forward to meeting the
locals at the big shared tables.

Kalamunda Farmers Market MARKET $

(www.kalamundafarmersmarket.com; Central
Mall; ⊙8am-noon Sun) One of the Perth area's
best farmers markets, with up to 70 stalls.
There's lots of street eats, so definitely come
hungry.

❶ Getting There & Away

From Perth's Elizabeth Quay Busport,
Transperth buses 283, 295, 296, 298 and 299 all
head to Kalamunda ($5.50, 47 minutes).

Mundaring

POP 38,300

Located 35km east of Perth, Mundaring is a
laid-back spot with a small artists community. Bisected by the busy Great Eastern Hwy,
the township itself isn't particularly interesting, but it's a short drive to national parks
and the Mundaring Weir.

◉ Sights

Mundaring Weir DAM

South of Beelu National Park is Mundaring
Weir, a dam built 100 years ago to supply
water to the goldfields more than 500km to
the east. The reservoir is a blissful spot, with
walking trails and a well-positioned pub.
Come dusk, the whole area swarms with
kangaroos.

Mundaring Arts Centre GALLERY

(☑08-9295 3991; www.mundaringartscentre.com.
au; 7190 Great Eastern Hwy; ⊙10am-5pm Tue-Fri,
11am-3pm Sat & Sun) Exhibits and sells the
work of local artists.

Lake Leschenaultia LAKE

(⊙8.30am-dusk) East of Mundaring and
north of the Great Eastern Hwy, near Chid-
low, is freshwater Lake Leschenaultia, a picturesque former railway dam complete with
a swimming pontoon.

Beelu National Park NATIONAL PARK

(☑08-9295 2244; www.parks.dpaw.wa.gov.au)
Immediately south of Mundaring is Beelu
National Park, part of a continuous swath
of forest that includes Kalamunda National Park. The Perth Hills National Parks
Centre (p108) hosts Nearer to Nature
kids programs with a flora-and-fauna spin.
There's a good camping ground (adult/child
$7.50/2.20), well positioned for the Bibbul-
mun Track, which passes nearby.

From November to April, kick back in a
deck chair at the open-air **Kookaburra Cinema** (☑08-9295 6190; www.kookaburracinema.
com.au; Allen Rd; adult/child $15/10), just across
the road from the park centre.

John Forrest National Park NATIONAL PARK

(☑08-9290 6100; www.parks.dpaw.wa.gov.au;
per car $12) The 16-sq-km John Forrest Na-
tional Park, west of Mundaring, was the
state's first national park. Protected areas of jarrah and marri trees are scattered
about granite outcrops, waterfalls and a
pool.

⮠ Sleeping

Mundaring Weir Hotel HOTEL $

(☑08-9295 1106; www.mundaringweirhotel.com.
au; Weir Village Rd; r $120-145; ⊕❄) Overlook-
ing the weir, this 1898 pub has bucketloads
of ramshackle character. Rooms are simple
but tidy, with DVD players and microwaves.
The rooms also open onto an amphitheatre,
which mainly functions as a beer garden but
occasionally hosts concerts and Sunday-af-
ternoon music sessions and barbecues.
Rooms are cheapest Sunday to Thursday,
and there's a good restaurant (mains $21 to
$32).

❶ Information

Perth Hills National Parks Centre (☑08-
9295 2244; www.dpaw.wa.gov.au; Allens Rd;
⊙9am-4pm) Hosts Nearer to Nature kids

programs with a flora-and-fauna spin. Located off Mundaring Weir Rd.

Visitor Centre (☑08-9295 0202; www.mundaringtourism.com.au; 7225 Great Eastern Hwy; ◷9.30am-4pm Mon-Sat, 10.30am-2.30pm Sun) Good for accommodation bookings including B&Bs and lodges in the Perth Hills.

❶ Getting There & Away

You can reach Mundaring from Perth on public transport in just over an hour by taking a train to Midland and then bus 320 ($6.50). From town it's another 6km to Mundaring Weir.

SWAN VALLEY

Perthites love to swan around this semirural valley on the city's eastern fringe to partake of the finer things in life: booze, nosh and the great outdoors. Perhaps in tacit acknowledgement that its wines will never compete with the state's more prestigious regions (it doesn't really have the ideal climate), the Swan Valley compensates with plenty of galleries, breweries, provedores and restaurants.

The Swan Valley vibe is more low-key and relaxed than that of Margaret River. There are more than 40 vineyards, concentrated mainly along busy West Swan Rd (the road leading north from the Guildford Visitor Centre (p110) and the Great Northern Hwy (running parallel to the east). Look for the free *Food & Wine Trail Guide* at the Guildford Visitor Centre (p110).

Guildford

POP 1822

The centre of Guildford town is Stirling Sq, at the intersection of Swan and Meadow Sts. There's a cluster of historic buildings opposite the square and a colonial mansion just east of town, by the river.

History

Guildford is built at the confluence of three rivers and was an important meeting and ceremonial place for the Wadjuk people. When the British arrived and travelled up the Swan, access to fresh water led them to establish one of their first settlements here. In 1833, four years after the colony's

founding, resistance leader Yagan was shot and decapitated in the Swan Valley.

The fertile valley land was soon being used for farming. Vines were first planted in the 1830s at Houghton's, but it was after the arrival of Croatian settlers (from around 1916) that the farmland was increasingly transformed into a wine-production area.

◎ Sights & Activities

Various heritage walks start from the Old Courthouse; get information from the visitor centre (p110) or download a trail card from its website.

Taylor's Cottage   HISTORIC BUILDING
(Swan St) This 1863 cottage is in the grounds of the Old Courthouse (1866). Admission is included with **gaol** (Old Courthouse, Swan St; $5; ◷10am-2pm Thu-Sat) entry.

Woodbridge House   HISTORIC BUILDING
(☑08-9274 2432; www.nationaltrust.org.au/places/woodbridge; Ford St; adult/child $5/3; ◷1-4pm Thu-Sun Aug-Jun) An 1885 colonial mansion overlooking the river.

✖ Eating

★ **Guildford Hotel**   PUB FOOD $$
(☑08-6336 9766; www.theguildfordhotel.com.au; 159 James St; mains $21-26; ◷11am-late) The Guildford Hotel only reopened in 2016, following a 2008 fire, but the flash makeover has been worth the wait. Smart design choices have retained many historic features, but the ambience is definitely modern and cosmopolitan. Local beers and wines feature in the cool garden bar, while meals in the sunny, brick-lined interior include smoked barbecue meats and good burgers.

Rose & Crown   PUB FOOD $$
(☑08-9347 8100; www.rosecrown.com.au; 105 Swan St, Guildford; mains $25-38; ◷8am-11pm) WA's oldest still-operating pub (1841) has a wonderful leafy beer garden and lots of different spaces to explore inside. Have a beer in the cellar bar, where there's a convict-built well, and check out the sealed-off tunnel that used to connect the hotel with the river. Try the hearty rabbit pie with a pint of Feral Brewing's 'The Local'.

Jezebelle   CAFE $$
(☑08-6278 3538; www.jezebelle.com.au; 127 James St, Guildford; tapas & shared plates $11-29, breakfast $13-24; ◷5.30-10pm Wed-Thu, from noon Fri, from 8am Sat & Sun) An exciting selection of

AROUND PERTH GUILDFORD

WA, Spanish and Italian wines partner with interesting tapas and shared plates at Guildford's Jezebelle. Tacos, paella and quesadillas all feature, with calamari, prawns and lamb the flavoursome stars. Leave room for a dessert of churros (Spanish doughnuts). Leisurely weekend breakfasts are equally classy.

❶ Information

Visitor Centre (☑08-9207 8899; www. swanvalley.com.au; Old Courthouse, cnr Swan & Meadow Sts; ⊘9am-4pm) Information and maps, plus an interesting display on local history.

❶ Getting There & Away

As the gateway to the Swan Valley, Guildford falls within zone 2 of Perth's public-transport system, and it costs only $4.60 to get here by bus or train on the Midland Line from Perth, East Perth or Mt Lawley station.

For Whiteman Park, catch a train on the Midland Line from Perth to Bassendean Station. Switch to a bus to Ellenbrook and get off at Lord St (bus stop 15529).

Around the Swan Valley

Perthites love to swan around this semirural valley on the city's eastern fringe to partake of the finer things in life: booze, nosh and the great outdoors. Perhaps in tacit acknowledgement that its wines will never compete with the state's more prestigious regions (it doesn't really have the ideal climate), the Swan Valley compensates with plenty of galleries, breweries, provedores and restaurants.

The Swan Valley vibe is more low-key and relaxed than that of Margaret River. There are more than 40 vineyards, concentrated mainly along busy West Swan Rd (the road leading north from the Guildford Visitor Centre (p110)) and the Great Northern Hwy (running parallel to the east). Look for the free *Food & Wine Trail Guide* at the Guildford Visitor Centre.

◉ Sights

Gomboc Gallery GALLERY
(☑08-9274 3996; www.gomboc-gallery.com.au; 50 James Rd, Middle Swan; ⊘10am-5pm Wed-Sun) FREE One of WA's best commercial galleries, surrounded by an intriguing sculpture park.

Whiteman Park PARK
(www.whitemanpark.com; West Swan; ⊘8.30am-6pm) Located in Caversham in West Swan, at 26 sq km this is Perth's biggest park, with over 30km of walkways and bike paths, and numerous picnic and barbecue spots. There are also train and tram rides for the kids. Enter the park from Lord St or Beechboro Rd.

Caversham Wildlife Park ZOO
(☑08-9248 1984; www.cavershamwildlife. com.au; Unit B, 99 Lord St; adult/child $25/11; ⊘9am-5.30pm, last entry 4.30pm) Part of the Whiteman Park estate, this wildlife park features cassowaries, echidnas, kangaroos, koalas, potoroos, quokkas and native birds. Say g'day to Neil, the very laid-back southern hairy wombat. There are also farm shows for the kids.

Revolutions MUSEUM
(☑08-9209 6040; www.whitemanpark.com.au; admission by gold-coin donation; ⊘10am-4pm) Museum celebrating transport in WA with horse-drawn wagons, camels, trains, boats and planes.

Motor Museum of WA MUSEUM
(☑08-9249 9457; www.motormuseumofwa.asn. au; 99 Lord St; adult/child $10/7; ⊘10am-4pm Mon-Fri, to 5pm Sat & Sun) Vintage cars and motorbikes in Whiteman Park.

✖ Eating

Lamont's TAPAS $$
(☑08-9296 4485; www.lamonts.com.au; 85 Bisdee Rd, Millendon; tapas $12.50-23; ⊘10am-5pm Thu-Sun) Look forward to lazy tastings and heaving plates of tapas under an open sky. The wine's very good, much of it grown in the Lamont's Margaret River vineyard.

RiverBank Estate MODERN AUSTRALIAN $$$
(☑08-9377 1805; www.riverbankestate.com.au; 126 Hamersley Rd, Caversham; mains $38-45; ⊘tastings 10am-4pm, restaurant 11.30am-2.30pm) The pick of the region's restaurants, RiverBank winery is a wonderful place to while away a few hours over excellent Modern Australian cuisine. It's a little more dressed up than most other places and there's live jazz on the first Saturday of the month. Note that there's a charge for tastings if you're not dining in the restaurant.

Sandalford BISTRO $$$
(www.sandalford.com; 3210 West Swan Rd, Caversham; tours $25, mains $38-45; ⊘tastings 10am-5pm, tours noon, lunch noon-3pm; P) Sandalford

has the nicest surrounds of any of the Swan Valley wineries, and plays host to weddings and major concerts. Main dishes are stylish and elegant, and there's also a menu of shared plates like octopus, grilled halloumi cheese and arancini.

Cheese Barrel CHEESE

(☑08-9296 4539; www.thecheesebarrel.com.au; 920 Great Northern Hwy; platters $35-65; ☺11am-5pm Mon & Tue, 10am-5pm Wed-Sun) Share a gourmet cheeseboard and an excellent wine flight from the adjacent Olive Farm Wines with your travelling companions, and stock up on cheeses from around the world for on-the-road dining. Sign up for an enjoyable cheesemaking course (from $197) to craft camembert or marinated feta; see www.thecheesemaker.com.au for details and timing of full-day courses.

🍷 Drinking

★**Homestead Brewery** CRAFT BEER

(☑08-6279 0500; www.mandoonestate.com.au/homestead/about-us; 10 Harris Rd, Caversham; ☺10am-5pm Mon-Thu, 10am-late Fri, from 7.30am Sat & Sun) Located in the grounds of the award-winning Mandoon Estate winery, Homestead is the Swan Valley's newest craft brewery and one of WA's best. Standout

brews include Kaiser's Choice, a zingy Hefeweizen wheat beer. Visit on weekend afternoons for garden picnics and Mediterranean-style deli food inspired by the owners' Croatian heritage. Pizzas and superior burgers and bar snacks are available daily.

★**Feral Brewing Company** CRAFT BEER

(☑08-9296 4657; www.feralbrewing.com.au; 152 Haddrill Rd; ☺11am-5pm Sun-Thu, to late Fri & Sat) Here's your chance to try some of Australia's best craft beers. Head brewer Brendan Varis is regularly lauded, with his always-interesting brews including the iconic Hop Hog Pale Ale. Feral's barrel-aged and sour brews are also excellent when paired with Feral's robust pub-grub menu. Try the Barrique Okarma, a *barrique*-fermented black India pale ale (IPA).

Mash CRAFT BEER

(☑08-9296 5588; www.mashbrewing.com.au; 10250 West Swan Rd, Henley Brook; ☺11am-5pm Mon & Tue, to late Wed-Sun) A lively bar-like atmosphere showcases craft lager, ales, wheat beer and cider. Interesting seasonal brews are always worth trying. The hoppy Copycat American IPA was judged Aussie's best beer in 2014, and the limited-edition Barley Wine is dangerously easy to drink despite measuring a stonking 9.5% alcohol. Make sure

Darling Range, Swan Valley & Avon Valley

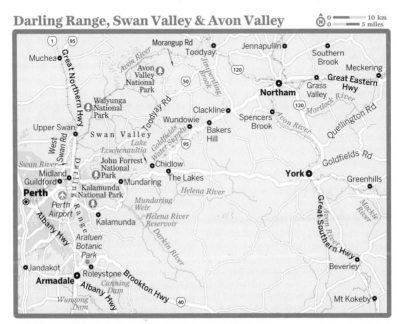

NORTHAM'S AVON RIVER FESTIVAL

Sleepy Northam comes alive in early August with the **Avon River Festival** (www.avondescent.com.au; ⊘early Aug). Events including a street parade, markets and fireworks are followed by the Avon Descent, a gruelling 133km white-water event for power dinghies, kayaks and canoes. If you're passing through at other times, check out the heritage architecture along Northam's main street and stop for Mediterranean-influenced food at **Cafe Yasou** (☑08-9622 3128; www.cafeyasou.com.au; 175 Fitzgerald St; mains $11-22; ⊘8am-4pm Mon-Fri, to noon Sat).

someone else is driving after you have one of those.

ⓘ Getting There & Around

As the gateway to the Swan Valley, Guildford falls within zone 2 of Perth's public-transport system, and it costs only $4.60 to get here by bus or train on the Midland Line from Perth, East Perth or Mt Lawley station.

For Whiteman Park, catch a train on the Midland Line from Perth to Bassendean Station. Switch to a bus to Ellenbrook and get off at Lord St (bus stop 15529).

To get around the Swan Valley you'll need to drive or take a tour. Another option is to rent a **bike**, but the area is surprisingly spread out.

Perth Electrical Bike Hire (☑0401 077 405; www.facebook.com/Perth-Electric-Bike-Hire-176805015710848; 1235 Great Northern Hwy; push/electric bikes per day $30/45) Both pushbikes and electric bikes are available here. Bikes can be delivered to/from the **Visitor Centre** (p110) in Guildford and Guildford's Transperth train station.

AVON VALLEY

The lush, green Avon Valley – with its atmospheric homesteads featuring big verandahs, rickety wooden wagons and moss-covered rocks – was 'discovered' by European settlers in early 1830 after food shortages forced Governor Stirling to dispatch Ensign Dale to search the Darling Range for arable land. What he found was the upper reaches of the Swan River, but he presumed it was a separate river – which is why its name changes from the Swan to the Avon in Walyunga National Park. The valley was very soon settled, just a year after Perth was founded, and many historic stone buildings still stand proudly in the towns and countryside in the area.

This country traditionally belongs to the Balardung, one of the Noongar peoples.

⊙ Sights

Avon Valley National Park   NATIONAL PARK (www.parks.dpaw.wa.gov.au; per car $12, campsites adult/child $7.50/2.20; ⊘8am-4pm) Featuring granite outcrops, forests and wonderful fauna, this national park is accessed from Toodyay and Morangup Rds. The Avon River flows through the centre of the park in winter and spring but is usually dry at other times. There are campsites with basic facilities (eg pit toilets and barbecues).

The park is the northern limit of the jarrah forests, and the jarrah and marri are mixed with wandoo woodland. Bird species include rainbow bee-eaters, honeyeaters, kingfishers and rufous treecreepers. In the understorey, honey possums and western pygmy possums hide among the dead leaves, and skinks and geckos scuttle about.

Accommodation in the park is limited to campsites. The nearest supermarkets and cafes are in York and Northam. Private transport is needed to travel to and access the park.

York
POP 2100

York is the most atmospheric spot in the Avon Valley and is a wonderful place to while away a couple of hours. Avon Tce is lined with restored heritage buildings, and the entire town has been classified by the National Trust.

Only 97km from Perth, York is the oldest inland town in WA, first settled in 1831, just two years after the Swan River Colony. The settlers here saw similarities between the Avon Valley and their native Yorkshire, so Governor Stirling bestowed the name York.

Convicts were brought to the region in 1851 and contributed to the development of the district; the ticket-of-leave hiring depot was not closed until 1872, four years after the transportation of convicts to WA ceased.

York prospered during the gold rush, servicing miners who were heading to Southern Cross, a goldfields town 273km to the east. Most of the town's buildings date from this time.

◎ Sights & Activities

Residency Museum
MUSEUM

(☑08-9641 1765; www.theyorksociety.com/residency-museum; Brook St; adult/child $5/3; ⊙1-3pm Tue, Wed & Thu, 11am-3.30pm Sat & Sun) Built in 1858, this museum houses some intriguing historical exhibits and poignant old black-and-white photos of York.

Motor Museum
MUSEUM

(☑08-9641 1288; www.yorkmotormuseum.com; 116 Avon Tce; adult/child $9/4; ⊙9.30am-3pm) A must for vintage-car enthusiasts.

Holy Trinity Church
CHURCH

(Newcastle St) By the Avon River, this church was completed in 1854 and features stained-glass windows designed by WA artist Robert Juniper, as well as a rare pipe organ.

Skydive Express
SKYDIVING

(☑08-9444 4199; www.skydive.com.au; 3453 Spencers Brook Rd; tandem jumps 8000/14,000ft $259/399) The Avon Valley is WA's skydiving centre; the drop zone is about 3km from town. Weekdays usually offer the best rates.

⊨ Sleeping & Eating

Faversham House
B&B $$

(☑08-9641 1366; www.favershamhouse.com.au; 24 Grey St; r $125-255; ❈☎) If you've ever wished you were 'to the manor born', indulge your fantasies in this grand stone mansion (1840). The rooms in the main house are large, TV-free and strewn with antiques; some have four-poster beds. All have smallish bathrooms. The cheaper rooms are in the old servants' quarters (naturally). Breakfast often features poached fruit and croissants with homemade jam.

Jules Cafe
CAFE $

(☑08-9641 1832; 121 Avon Tce; snacks & mains $10-18; ⊙8am-4pm Mon-Sat; ☑) ✿ Putting a colourful spin on heritage York since 1990, Jules Cafe channels a Lebanese heritage for top-notch kebabs, falafel and Middle Eastern sweets. A funky new-age accent is introduced with organic, veggie and gluten-free options, and juices and fruit smoothies are perfect in summer.

ℹ Information

Visitor Centre (☑08-9641 1301; www.avonvalleywa.com.au; Town Hall, 81 Avon Tce; ⊙10am-4pm)

ℹ Getting There & Away

Transwa (☑1300 662 205; www.transwa.wa.gov.au) Transwa coach routes include the following: GE2 (three per week) to East Perth ($17.50, 1½ hours), Mundaring ($14, 47 minutes), Hyden ($42, 3¼ hours) and Esperance ($85, 8½ hours), and GS2 to Northam ($8, 33 minutes, six per week), Mt Barker ($58, 5¼ hours, four per week) and Albany ($63, six hours, four per week).

Toodyay

POP 1100

Historic Toodyay, only 85km northeast of Perth, is a popular weekend destination for browsing the bric-a-brac shops or having a beer on the verandah of an old pub. As you'd expect of a town classified by the National Trust, it has plenty of charming heritage buildings. Originally known by the name Newcastle, Toodyay (pronounced '2J') came from the Aboriginal word *duidgee* (place of plenty); the name was adopted around 1910.

◎ Sights

St Stephen's Church
CHURCH

Tinged with Gothic influences, this 1862 church is towered over by a sprawling gum tree reckoned to be around 400 years old.

Connor's Mill
MUSEUM

(Stirling Tce; $3; ⊙9am-4pm) Start at the top of this aged flour mill (1870) and descend through three floors of chugging machinery and explanatory displays that cover the milling process, along with local history. Entry is through the neighbouring visitor centre.

Newcastle Gaol
MUSEUM

(17 Clinton St; $3; ⊙10am-3pm) Built in the 1860s using convict labour, the jail complex includes a courtroom, cells and stables. A gallery tells the story of famed bushranger Moondyne Joe.

Coorinja
WINERY

(☑08-9574 2280; Toodyay Rd; ⊙10am-5pm Mon-Sat) Operating continuously since the 1870s, this winery specialises in fortified wines, including port, sherry, muscat and Marsala. It's 6km out of town, on the road to Perth.

⭐ Festivals & Events

Moondyne Festival
CULTURAL
(www.moondynefestival.com.au; ⊙1st Sun May) Costumed heritage hijinks in honour of Moondyne Joe (1826–1900), Western Australia's most infamous bushranger, who had a knack for escaping from prison: he did so on multiple occasions.

Toodyay International Food Festival
FOOD & DRINK
(www.toodyayiff.wix.com/home; ⊙1st Sat Aug) Held the day before the Avon Descent (p112). Stalls include the best of Perth's ethnic-food purveyors and there's a growing array of food trucks.

Toodyay Agricultural Show
FAIR
(⊙early Oct) Lots of well-bred animals on display and a great insight into local lifestyles.

✗ Eating

Toodyay Bakery
CAFE $
(⊉08-9574 2617; www.facebook.com/toodyaybakery; 123 Stirling Tce; snacks $3-6; ⊙7am-3pm) The Toodyay Bakery has been around for decades, but recent refurbishment has given it an artisan and gourmet makeover. The excellent sourdough bread and chicken and mushroom pies are famous around the Avon Valley, so stock up for on-the-road picnics or grab a sunny outdoor table and partner an espresso with a salted-caramel doughnut.

Cola Café & Museum
CAFE $
(⊉08-9574 4407; www.colacafe.com.au; 128 Stirling Tce; snacks $10-19; ⊙9am-4.30pm; 🗟) Coca-Cola memorabilia runs amok here. Order a cola spider (Coke with a scoop of ice cream) and a big burger and play 'name that song' with the retro tunes.

ℹ Information

Visitor Information Centre (⊉08-9574 2435; www.toodyay.com; 7 Piesse St; ⊙9am-4pm) Tourist information and accommodation bookings.

ℹ Getting There & Away

Transwa (⊉1300 662 205; www.transwa.wa.gov.au) Toodyay is a stop on the Transwa AvonLink and Prospector lines, with trains to East Perth ($17.50, 1¼ hours, seven per week), Northam ($8, 20 minutes, 12 per week) and Kalgoorlie ($80, 5½ hours, four per week).

NEW NORCIA

POP 70

The idyllic monastery settlement of New Norcia, 132km from Perth, consists of a cluster of ornate, Spanish-style buildings set incongruously in the Australian bush. Founded in 1846 by Spanish Benedictine monks as an Aboriginal mission, the working monastery today holds prayers and retreats, alongside a business producing boutique breads and gourmet goodies.

◉ Sights

New Norcia Museum & Art Gallery
MUSEUM, GALLERY
(⊉08-9654 8056; www.newnorcia.wa.edu.au; Great Northern Hwy; combined museum & town tours adult/family $25/60; ⊙10am-4.30pm) New Norcia Museum & Art Gallery traces the history of the monastery and houses impressive art, including contemporary exhibitions and one of the country's largest collections of post-Renaissance religious art. The gift shop sells souvenirs, honeys, preserves, and breads baked in the monks' wood-fired oven.

Abbey Church
CHURCH
Inside the abbey church, try to spot the native wildlife in the sgraffito artworks that depict the Stations of the Cross. Look hard, as there's also an astronaut.

☞ Tours

Town Tours
TOURS
(⊉08-9654 8056; www.newnorcia.wa.edu.au; adult/child $15/10; ⊙11am & 1.30pm) Guided two-hour town tours offer a look at the abbey church and the frescoed college chapels; purchase tickets from the museum.

🛏 Sleeping

New Norcia Hotel
HOTEL $
(⊉08-9654 8034; www.newnorcia.wa.edu.au; Great Northern Hwy; s/d with shared bathroom incl breakfast from $80/100; ⊙11am-2pm & 6-8.30pm) New Norcia Hotel harks back to a more genteel time, with sweeping staircases, high ceilings, understated rooms and wide verandahs. An international menu ($15 to $36) is available at the bar or in the elegant dining room. Be sure to try the selection of dips served with New Norcia's own wood-fired sourdough bread.

Sit outside on the terrace and sample the delicious but deadly New Norcia Abbey Ale, a golden Belgian-style ale brewed especially for the abbey. Sunday is a good day to visit,

KWONGAN WILDFLOWERS

Take any road inland from the Turquoise Coast and you'll soon enter the Kwongan heathlands, where, depending on the season, the roadside verges burst with native wildflowers such as banksia, grevillea, hakea, calothamnus, kangaroo paw and smokebush. While Lesueur National Park (p118) is an obvious choice for all things botanical, consider some of the following options.

Badgingarra National Park Three-and-a-half kilometres of walking trails, kangaroo paws, banksias, grass trees, verticordia and a rare mallee. The back road linking Badgingarra and Lesueur is particularly rich in flora. Obtain details from the Badgingarra Roadhouse. There's also a picnic area on Bibby Rd.

Alexander Morrison National Park Named after WA's first botanist. There are no trails, but you can drive through slowly on the Coorow Green Head Rd, which has loads of flora along its verge all the way from Lesueur. Expect to see dryandra, banksia, grevillea, smokebush, leschenaultia and honey myrtle.

Tathra National Park Tathra has similar flora to Alexander Morrison National Park, and the drive between the two is rich with banksia, kangaroo paw and grevillea.

Coomallo Rest Area Orchids, feather flowers, black kangaroo paws, wandoo and river red gums can be found upstream and on the slopes of the small hill.

Brand Hwy (Rte 1) The route's not exactly conducive to slow meandering, but the highway verges are surprisingly rich in wildflowers, especially either side of Eneabba.

If you're overwhelmed and frustrated by not being able to identify all these strange new plants, consider staying at Western Flora Caravan Park (☑08-9955 2030; wflo-racp@activ8.net.au; Brand Hwy, North Eneabba; unpowered/powered sites $28/32, d $65, on-site vans $80, chalets $130), where the enthusiastic owners run free two-hour wildflower walks across their 65-hectare property every day at 4.30pm.

---

either for a leisurely breakfast or for popular wood-fired pizzas in the evening. Note that rooms are $20 to $35 more expensive on Saturday nights.

Monastery Guesthouse GUESTHOUSE $
(☑08-9654 8002; www.newnorcia.wa.edu.au; full board suggested donation $80) The abbey offers lodging in the Monastery Guesthouse, within the walls of the southern cloister. Guests can join in prayers with the monks (and men can dine with them).

WILDFLOWER WAY

Inland east from Geraldton, Rte 123 leads to wheat silos, wildflowers and little one-pub towns that are a hive of activity between August and September as minibuses full of senior travellers zoom around hunting blossoms.

Moora

POP 2574

Tall gums, broad streets, a couple of galleries and a railway line (wheat trains only) define this agricultural service centre. To see WA wildflowers being dried and shipped around the country, visit the Western Wildflower Farm (☑08-9651 8060; www.westwayswildflowers.com.au; 2187 Price's Rd, Coomberdale; ◷9am-5pm Mon-Sat) FREE, 19km north of Moora. It's a worthwhile stop if you're heading out on a wildflower pilgrimage, as the friendly owners can supply maps showing where the best local displays area.

The Moora Caravan Park (☑08-9651 0000; Dandaragan St; unpowered/powered sites $20/30, chalets $120-140) offers offers basic, shady sites, and some comfortable modern chalets, and the visitor centre (☑08-9653 1053; www.moora.wa.gov.au; Moora Railway Station, 34 Padbury St; ◷8.45am-4pm Mon-Fri, 10am-noon Sat) can book B&Bs and provide information on heritage walks and more local maps for seeing wildflowers.

The best coffee in town is at the Wheatbelt Gallery (☑0429 372 637; www.facebook.com/wheatbeltgallery; Padbury St; ◷9am-5pm Tue-Sat), opposite the visitor centre. There's also pizza and toasted sandwiches, and it doubles as a bar some evenings.

Wongan Hills

POP 1462

From the direction of New Norcia, take the back road via Yerecoin and you'll pass the intriguing **Lake Ninan**, a huge salt pan. Wongan Hills, with its gently undulating country and myriad verticordias, makes a pleasant change from the flat wheat-belt towns, and there are plenty of trails for bushwalkers. The area is also known for its wildflowers.

Wongan Hills Hotel HOTEL $
(☑ 08-9671 1022; www.facebook.com/WonganHills-Hotel; 5 Fenton Pl; hotel s/d $70/90, motel d $120) Art-deco Wongan Hills Hotel offers classic hotel rooms, some opening onto the upstairs verandah, and modern motel rooms in a separate building. Meals (mains $20 to $35) are typical pub fare, including good pizzas, and there's a friendly bar.

SUNSET COAST

The coast road north of Perth leads to some popular spots for travellers. Within an hour's drive, Perth's outer suburbs give way to the bushland oasis of Yanchep National Park, with wonderful wildlife and walking trails.

The coastline ranges from tranquil bays at Guilderton, good for swimming and fishing, to windswept beaches at Lancelin, with excellent conditions for windsurfing and kitesurfing.

Yanchep

POP 2482

Yanchep and its close neighbour Two Rocks are effectively Perth's northernmost suburbs. The town was developed extensively during the 1980s by (now convicted fraudster) Alan Bond, and the legacy of this era includes a large marina and some dubious bits of sculpture (dolphins, a dragon and a giant Neptune). The highlights for travellers are the natural and cultural attractions of Yanchep National Park.

Yanchep National Park NATIONAL PARK
(☑ 08-9303 7759; www.parks.dpaw.wa.gov.au; Wanneroo Rd; per car $12; ⊙ visitor centre 9.15am-4.30pm) The woodlands and wetlands of Yanchep National Park are home to fauna including koalas, kangaroos, emus and cockatoos. The free *Wild About Walking* brochure outlines nine walking trails, from the 20-minute Dwerta Mia walk to the four-day Coastal Plain walk. Register with the park centre for longer walks. To get up close and personal with koalas, stroll along the 240m-long Koala Boardwalk. The park also features splendid caves, which can be viewed on 45-minute tours (adult/child $10/5).

On Saturday and Sunday, local Noongar guides run excellent tours (prior booking essential) showcasing their traditional culture, including the importance of the park's plants and animals, and spear and boomerang demonstrations.

Yanchep Inn MOTEL $
(☑ 08-9561 1001; www.yanchepinn.com.au; hotel r $60-85, old motel r $115, new motel r $170-210; ❋) Within the national park, Yanchep Inn is more attractive from the outside than it is on the inside. The inn has basic rooms with shared facilities and a cafe downstairs. Rooms in the newer of the two motel blocks, with lake views and rammed-earth walls, are more comfortable but perhaps a little overpriced. Rates jump by $25 to $55 at weekends.

Guilderton

POP 150

Some 43km north of Yanchep, Guilderton is a popular and staggeringly beautiful family-holiday spot. Children paddle safely near the mouth of the Moore River, while adults enjoy fishing and surfing on the ocean beach.

The name comes from the wreck of the *Vergulde Draeck*, part of the Dutch East India Company fleet, which ran aground nearby in 1656, reputedly carrying a treasure in guilders. Its original name was Gabbadah, meaning 'mouth of water', although many older Perthites still refer to it as Moore River.

Guilderton Caravan Park CARAVAN PARK $
(☑ 08-9577 1021; www.guildertoncaravanpark.com.au; 2 Dewar St; unpowered/powered sites $30/45, chalets $165) Has self-contained chalets, but you'll need your own linen.

There's a compact volunteer-run visitor centre (with erratic hours) next door to the caravan park.

Lancelin

POP 670

Afternoon offshore winds and shallows and a protective outlying reef make Lancelin perfect for windsurfing and kitesurfing, attracting action seekers from around the world. In January wind worshippers descend for the Lancelin Ocean Classic (p117) windsurfing race, starting at Ledge Point to the south.

The coral and limestone reef, no-fishing zone and dazzling white sands also make Lancelin a great snorkelling spot, while the mountainous soft, white dunes on the edge of town are good for sandboarding.

ℹ Getting There & Away

From Lancelin, Integrity (p273) buses leave from Lancelin Lodge YHA at 11.30pm on Tuesday and Thursday to Cervantes ($34, one hour), Jurien Bay ($34, 1¼ hours) and Geraldton ($50, four hours). Heading south, buses travel to Perth ($34, two hours), leaving Lancelin at 4.55am on Saturday and Monday mornings.

🏃 Activities

Makanikai Kiteboarding KITESURFING
(☑0406 807 309; www.makanikaikiteboarding.com; lessons from $200) Run lessons in the fine art of kiteboarding and hires out gear; accommodation packages are also available.

Have a Chat General Store OUTDOORS
(☑08-9655 1054; 104 Gingin Rd; sandboard hire per 2hr $10; ⊙7am-6pm) Hires sandboards.

✨ Festivals & Events

Lancelin Ocean Classic SPORTS
(☑08-9314 3820; www.lancelinoceanclassic.com.au; ⊙Jan) Thousands flock to tiny Lancelin each year for this world-famous windsurfing event. Held over four days, the event covers wave sailing on the Thursday and Friday, the marathon on Saturday and the Sunday slalom.

🛏 Sleeping & Eating

★**Lancelin Lodge YHA** HOSTEL $
(☑08-9655 2020; www.lancelinlodge.com.au; 10 Hopkins St; dm/d/f $33/90/130; @🅿🍽🏊) This laid-back hostel is well equipped and welcoming, with wide verandahs and lots of communal spaces. The excellent facilities include big kitchen, barbecue, wood-fired pizza oven, swimming pool, ping-pong table, volleyball court and free use of bikes and boogie boards. New owners have effortlessly maintained the standards of previous years. This is still one of WA's best hostels.

Ledge Point Holiday Park CARAVAN PARK $
(☑1300 856 088; www.lphp.com.au; 742 Ledge Point Rd; 2-person sites $45, chalets & studios $115-180; @🛜) About 10 minutes' drive south of Lancelin, with excellent facilities and spotless accommodation ranging from caravan and camping sites to chalets and studios. Lots of family-friendly attractions include pedal carts and a jumping pillow. Ledge Point's beach – good for fishing and swimming – is around 500m away.

Windsurfer Beach Chalets APARTMENT $$
(☑08-9655 1454; www.lancelinaccommodation.com.au; 1 Hopkins St; d from $170) These self-contained two-bedroom chalets are near the windsurfing beach and are a good choice for groups of friends and families (each chalet sleeps up to six). They're functional and well equipped, and have a sun terrace backing onto a grassy area. The operators can also arrange accommodation in Lancelin and nearby Ledge Point in a variety of self-contained holiday homes.

★**Endeavour Tavern** PUB FOOD $$
(☑08-9655 1052; www.endeavourtavern.com.au; 58 Gingin Rd; mains $23-32; ⊙10.30am-10pm Sun-Thu, to midnight Fri & Sat) A classic beachfront Aussie pub with a beer garden overlooking the ocean. The casual eatery serves pubgrub classics and tasty burgers and salads. Naturally, the seafood is popular and very good.

TURQUOISE COAST

Stretching north of Lancelin to Port Denison, the relaxed Turquoise Coast is dotted with sleepy fishing villages, stunning beaches, extraordinary geological formations, rugged national parks and incredibly diverse flora. Offshore marine parks and island nature reserves provide a safe breeding habitat for Australian sea lions and other endangered species, while crayfishing brings in the dollars. Once somewhat isolated, the whole area has been brought within easy reach of Perth by the completion of the final section of Indian Ocean Dr between Lancelin and Cervantes.

ℹ Getting There & Away

Integrity (☑1800 226 339; www.integritycoachlines.com.au) runs three times a week along the coast between Perth and Geraldton and on to Exmouth and Broome.

Cervantes & Pinnacles Desert

POP 480

Heading north from Lancelin on Indian Ocean Dr, you will pass the tiny fishing-shack villages of Wedge Island (http://wedgewa.com.au) and Grey, where access was previously 4WD-only along the beach. Pressure from developers and government mean the future of these communities is uncertain, and although there are no facilities for tourists, you're welcome to wander.

The laid-back crayfishing town of Cervantes, 198km north of Perth, makes a pleasant overnight stop for enjoying the Pinnacles Desert and a good base for exploring the flora of the Kwongan (p115), the inland heathland of Lesueur National Park and Badgingarra National Park. There are also some lovely beaches on which to while away the time.

◎ Sights

Just south of Cervantes, turn off for Lake Thetis, where living stromatolites – the world's oldest organisms – inhabit the shoreline. Nearby Hansen Bay Lookout has excellent views across the coast.

In Cervantes town, walkways wend along the coastline and provide beach access.

★**Nambung National Park**　　NATIONAL PARK
(per car $12) Situated 19km from Cervantes, Nambung is home to the spectacular **Pinnacles Desert**, a vast, alien-like plain studded with thousands of limestone pillars. Rising eerily from the desert floor, the pillars are remnants of compacted seashells that once covered the plain and, over millennia, subsequently eroded. A loop road runs through the formations, but it's more fun to wander on foot, especially at sunset, full moon or dawn, when the light is sublime and the crowds evaporate.

Nearby **Kangaroo Point** and **Hangover Bay** make nice picnic spots, with barbecues and tables. The latter has the better swimming.

Lesueur National Park　　NATIONAL PARK
(per car $12) This botanical paradise, 50km north of Cervantes, contains a staggering 820 plant species, many of them rare and endemic, such as the pine banksia (*Banksia tricupsis*) and Mt Lesueur grevillea (*Grevillea batrachioides*). Late winter sees the heath erupt into a mass of colour, and

the park is also home to the endangered Carnaby's cockatoo. An 18km circuit drive is dotted with lookouts and picnic areas. Flat-topped **Mt Lesueur** (4km return walk) has panoramic coastal views.

⚱ Activities

Many Perth-based companies offer day trips to the Pinnacles.

Pinnacle Helicopter Flights　　SCENIC FLIGHTS
(☑0428 880 066; www.pinnaclehelicopterflights.com.au; Pinnacles Discovery Centre, Nambung National Park; per person $135-300) Spectacular flights allow you to see the beauty of the Pinnacles and the WA coastline from the air.

⊨ Sleeping

★**Cervantes Lodge
& Pinnacles Beach Backpackers**　　HOSTEL $
(☑1800 245 232; www.cervanteslodge.com.au; 91 Seville St, Cervantes; dm $33, d $135, d with shared bathroom $90; @🛜) This relaxing hostel has a wide verandah, small and tidy dorms, a nice communal kitchen and a cosy lounge area. Bright, spacious en-suite rooms, some with views, are next door in the lodge. There's a good on-site cafe too – open to outside guests during the day – and affable co-owner Tony is always up for a chat.

RAC Cervantes Holiday Park　　CARAVAN PARK $
(☑08-9652 7060; www.parksandresorts.rac.com.au/park/cervantes-holiday-park; 35 Aragon St, Cervantes; sites $30-32, cabins & units $90-225; 🛜⚊) Fantastic location right behind the dunes with plenty of shady, grassy sites and an on-site cafe. New chalets and a swimming pool and recreation room opened in early 2017.

★**Amble Inn**　　B&B $$
(☑0429 652 401; www.amble-inn.com.au; 2150 Cadda Rd, Hill River; d from $160; ⚹🛜) High up on the heathland, about 25km east of Cervantes, this hidden gem of a B&B has beautiful thick stone walls, wide verandahs and superbly styled rooms. Watch the sunset over the coast from the nearby hill with a glass of your complimentary wine.

Cervantes Holiday Homes　　APARTMENT $$
(☑08-9652 7115; www.cervantesholidayhomes.com.au; cnr Malaga Ct & Valencia Rd, Cervantes; cottages from $140; ⚹) These well-equipped, fully self-contained cottages are great value, especially for groups.

Eating

Cervantes Bar & Bistro PUB FOOD **$$**
(☑08-9652 7009; www.facebook.com/
cervantesbarandbistro; 1 Cadiz St, Cervantes; mains
$21-35; ⊙11am-midnight Mon-Sat, to 10pm Sun)
This welcoming pub offers meals that are
a cut above the fare in most other regional
WA towns. Local seafood is the star – lobster,
squid, mussels and oysters all feature – and
a decent array of tap beers goes well with
Aussie culinary classics, including steak
sandwiches and chicken parmigiana. Quite
probably the coldest beers on the Turquoise
Coast too.

Lobster Shack SEAFOOD **$$**
(☑08-9652 7010; www.lobstershack.com.au; 11
Madrid St, Cervantes; ⊙shop 8am-5pm, cafe 11am-
3pm, tours noon-3pm) Craving crayfish? They
don't come much fresher than at this lob-
ster-factory-turned-lunch spot, where half
a delicious grilled cray, chips and salad will
set you back around $40. Cheaper lobster
and octopus burgers ($20) and fish and
chips are also on offer. Self-guided factory
tours and takeaway frozen seafood are also
available.

ⓘ Information

Post Office and Visitor Centre (☑08-9652
7700, freecall 1800 610 660; www.visitpin-
naclescountry.com.au; Cadiz St, Cervantes;
⊙9am-5.30pm Mon-Fri, to 5pm Sat & Sun)
Grab a copy of the *Turquoise Coast Self Drive
Map* from Cervantes' combined post office and
visitor centre, which also supplies accommodation and tour information.

ⓘ Getting There & Away

Integrity (p117) runs three times a week
to Perth ($44, three hours), Dongara ($34,
two hours), Geraldton ($42, three hours) and
Exmouth ($183, 14 hours). **Transwa** runs twice
weekly to Perth ($34, three hours), Dongara
($22, two hours) and Geraldton ($40, three
hours).

Jurien Bay

POP 1500
The largest town on the Turquoise Coast
is likely to become quite a lot bigger after
being selected as a regional 'Super Town'.
Home to a hefty fishing fleet and lots of big
houses, it's already rather spread out; however, there's a nice long swimming beach
and great snorkelling and diving opportunities. Anglers have a choice of jetties and

the lengthy foreshore walkway links several
pleasant parks.

⚲ Activities

Snorkelling Trail SNORKELLING
(⊙Sep-May) FREE Around 25m off the beach
near the piles of the old jetty, this underwater trail marked by buoys guides snorkellers
around a reef slowly becoming inhabited by
marine flora and fauna. The depth of the
water is around 2m to 3m, and interpretive
plinths on the sea floor provide information.
Snorkelling gear can be rented in town.

Skydive Jurien Bay SKYDIVING
(☑08-96521320,1300293766; www.skydivejurien-
bay.com; 65 Bashford St; 8000/10,000/14,000ft
jumps $300/350/450) To see the coastline
from the air and land on the beach, see the
team at Skydive Jurien Bay.

ⓒ Tours

Turquoise Safaris FISHING, SNORKELLING
(☑0458 905 432; www.turquoisesafaris.com.au;
Shop 1, Roberts St Arcade; fishing half-/full-day
per person $150/220, snorkelling & sea lions adult/
child $90/60) Offers half- and full-day fish-
ing charters and trips viewing sea lions and
then time spent snorkelling. Turquoise Safaris also has a handy 4WD-recovery service if
you get stuck in the sand or in WA's red dirt.

Jurien Bay Adventure Tours ADVENTURE
(☑1300 462 383; www.jurienbayadventuretours.
com.au; tours per person $39-99) Versatile one-
stop shop for hire of bikes, sandboards, paddleboards and snorkelling gear, and guided
tours covering everything from the Pinnacles and the crayfishing industry south at
Cervantes, to exploring the nearby Stockyard
Gully caves or Mt Lesueur, or going by 4WD
to the best sandboarding spots in the area. All
tours depart from the visitor centre (p120).

🛏 Sleeping

Jurien Bay Tourist Park CARAVAN PARK **$**
(☑08-9652 1595; www.jurienbaytouristpark.com.
au; Roberts St; sites $38, chalets $145-170; 🐾)
There are comfortable chalets right behind
the beach, although the tent sites are set
back against the main road. A $20 single-
night surcharge applies to the chalets.

**Jurien Bay
Holidays** ACCOMMODATION SERVICES **$$$**
(☑08-9652 2055; www.jurienbayholidays.com;
Shop 1a, 34 Bashford St) Check here for holiday
rentals.

✕ Eating

Jetty Cafe   CAFE **$**
(☑ 08-9652 1999; 1 Roberts St; meals $10-19;
☺ 7.30am-5pm) In a great position next to
the caravan park, Jetty serves up decent
brekkies, burgers and grilled fish.

Beach Bistro   CAFE **$$**
(☑ 08-9652 1513; www.beachbistro.com.au; 2/1
Roberts St; lunch $15-22, dinner $21-36; ☺ 11am-
8pm Wed-Mon) For a beer or wine with lunch
or dinner, try the eclectic international
menu at the laid-back Beach Bistro. Quiz
night from 7pm on occasional Thursdays is
always fun, and the $20 beer-and-a-burger
deal on a Monday night is good value.

ℹ Information

Turquoise Coast Visitor Centre (☑ 08-9652
0870; www.facebook.com/TurquoiseCoastWA;
67 Bashford St; ☺ 9am-5pm Mon-Fri, to 1pm
Sat) The excellent new Turquoise Coast Visitor
Centre can advise on activities, transport and
accommodation in Jurien Bay and the sur-
rounding Dandaragan Shire.

Green Head & Leeman

On the way to Green Head from Jurien Bay,
stop at Grigson Lookout for a panoramic
view of the coast and the Kwongan heath-
lands (p115). Tiny **Green Head** (popu-
lation 280) has several beautiful bays; the
horseshoe-shaped **Dynamite Bay** is the
most spectacular and is sheltered for swim-
mers. There's good fishing, snorkelling,
surfing and windsurfing here and at nearby
Leeman (population 400).

Heading north on Indian Ocean Dr, un-
marked side roads lead to lonely beaches
and rocky cliffs begging to be explored.

☞ Tours

Sea Lion Charters   WILDLIFE
(☑ 0427 931 012; sealioncharters@hotmail.com; 24
Bryant St, Green Head; morning tours adult/child
$150/75) A magical experience interacting
in shallow water with playful sea lions who
mimic your every move. It helps to be a good
snorkeller. Wetsuits cost extra and booking
ahead is essential.

🛏 Sleeping

Green Head Caravan Park   CARAVAN PARK **$**
(☑ 08-9953 1131; www.greenheadcaravanpark.
com.au; 9 Green Head Rd, Green Head; unpowered/
powered sites $28/37, cabins & vans $90-110)   A
relaxed and shady park on the road into
town.

Centrebreak Beach Stay   GUESTHOUSE **$$**
(☑ 08-9953 1896; www.centrebreakbeachstay.
com.au; Lot 402, Ocean View Dr, Green Head; dm/
d/f $35/150/190; 🛜) Centrebreak has a room
to suit everyone, from clean, small dorms
to a two-bedroom apartment. The on-site
licensed Osprey Bar & Lounge serves up
burgers, seafood and steaks (meals $15 to
$40) for lunch and dinner.

Margaret River & the Southwest Coast

POP 120,000

Best Places to Eat

➡ Rustico at Hay Shed Hill (p135)

➡ Piari & Co (p129)

➡ Eagle Bay Brewing Co (p131)

➡ Wills Domain (p135)

➡ Tall Timbers (p144)

Best Places to Sleep

➡ Empire Retreat & Spa (p134)

➡ Acacia Chalets (p140)

➡ Burnside Organic Farm (p137)

➡ Wildwood Valley Cottages (p134)

➡ Foragers (p145)

Why Go?

The farmland, forests, rivers and coast of the lush, green southwestern corner of Western Australia contrast vividly with the stark, sunburnt terrain of much of the state. On land, world-class wineries and craft breweries beckon, and tall trees provide shade for walking trails and scenic drives. Offshore, bottlenose dolphins and whales frolic, and devoted surfers search for – and often find – their perfect break.

Unusually for WA, distances between the many attractions are short, and driving time is mercifully limited, making it a fantastic area to explore for a few days – you will get much more out of your stay here if you have your own wheels. Summer brings hordes of visitors, but in the wintry months from July to September the cosy pot-bellied stove rules and visitors are scarce, and while opening hours can be somewhat erratic, prices are much more reasonable.

When to Go
Margaret River

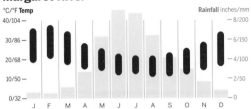

Jan Follow the party crowds from the Southbound festival to the beach.

Mar–Apr Catch the surf festival in Margaret River, and the Nannup Music Festival.

Aug Head to empty beaches, Margaret River wineries and Busselton's film festival.

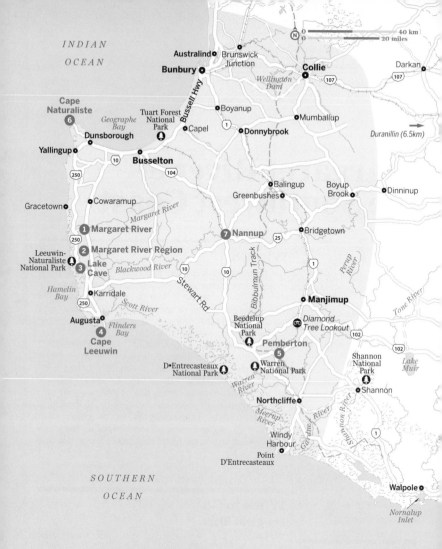

Margaret River & the Southwest Coast Highlights

➊ Sampling the first-class wine, food and architecture of the vineyards of **Margaret River** (p130).

➋ Getting active amid the dramatic seascapes and landscapes of the **Margaret River region** (p137).

➌ Exploring the labyrinthine limestone caverns along Caves Rd, especially beautiful **Lake Cave** (p139).

➍ Fronting up to the impressive coastline at Augusta's **Cape Leeuwin Lighthouse** (p141), at the confluence of the Indian and Southern Oceans.

➎ Sinking into the dappled depths of the karri forests surrounding **Pemberton** (p144).

➏ Revelling in wild and beautiful coastal scenery of **Cape Naturaliste** (p129).

➐ Canoeing from the forest to the sea along the Blackwood River, starting at **Nannup** (p142).

GEOGRAPHE BAY

Turquoise waters and 30km of excellent swimming beaches define this gorgeous bay. Positioned between the Indian Ocean and a sea of wine, the beachside towns of Busselton and Dunsborough attract hordes of holidaymakers. By WA standards, attractions are close together, making it perfect for leisurely touring. Accommodation prices can rise around 30% during summer and school holidays.

For 55,000 years the area from Geographe Bay to Augusta was inhabited by the Wardandi, one of the Noongar peoples. They lived a nomadic life linked to the seasons, heading to the coast in summer to fish, and journeying inland during the wet winter months.

The French connection to many of the current place names dates from an early-19th-century expedition by the ships *Le Géographe* and *Naturaliste*. Thomas Vasse, a crewman who was lost at sea, is remembered in the name of a village, river, inlet and Margaret River winery.

Bunbury

POP 67,090

The southwest's only city is morphing from an industrial port into a seaside holiday destination. From Bunbury, the main route south branches to the Bussell Hwy (for Margaret River), and the South Western Hwy (to the southern forests and south coast). It's also the southernmost stop on the train network and a hub for regional buses.

The town centre has basically one main street (Victoria), and a few blocks to the west lies the beach. Immediately to the north, the redeveloped port features waterside restaurants.

The city lies at the western end of Leschenault Inlet. The area was named Port Leschenault after the botanist on Nicolas Baudin's ship *Le Géographe* in 1803, but British Governor James Stirling renamed it Bunbury after a lieutenant in charge of the original military outpost. The first British settlers arrived in 1838.

Sights

Bunbury Wildlife Park   ZOO
(☑08-9721 8380; www.bunburywildlifepark.com.au; Prince Philip Dr; adult/child $9.80/5; ⊙10am-5pm) Parrots, kangaroos, wallabies, possums, owls and emus all feature. Across the road, the Big Swamp wetlands has good walking tracks and stops for birdwatching. Head south on Ocean Dr, turn left at Hayward St and continue through the roundabout to Prince Philip Dr.

Dolphin Discovery Centre   WILDLIFE RESERVE
(☑08-9791 3088; www.dolphindiscovery.com.au; Koombana Beach; adult/child $10/5; ⊙9am-2pm May-Sep, 8am-4pm Oct-Apr) Around 60 bottlenose dolphins live in the bay year-round, their numbers increasing to 260 in summer. This centre has a beachside zone where dolphins regularly come to interact with people in the shallows and you can wade in alongside them, under the supervision of trained volunteers.

If you want to up your chances, there are 1½-hour Eco Cruises (1½hr cruise adult/child $54/40; ⊙11am mid-Oct–Apr, 11.30am May–mid-Oct) and three-hour Swim Encounter Cruises (3hr cruises $165; ⊙7.30am mid-Oct–mid-Dec & Feb-Apr, 7.30am & 11.30am mid-Dec–Jan).

There are no guarantees of a close encounter, but they are more likely in the early mornings between November and April. Entry tickets are valid for three separate visits, a good option if you're in town for a few days.

Volunteers must commit to at least six weeks' full-time involvement.

Bunbury Regional Art Galleries   GALLERY
(☑08-9792 7323; www.brag.org.au; 64 Wittenoom St; ⊙10am-4pm) FREE Housed in a restored pink convent (1897), this excellent gallery has a collection that includes works by Australian art luminaries Arthur Boyd and Sir Sidney Nolan.

St Mark's (Old Picton) Church   CHURCH
(cnr Charterhouse Cl & Flynn St, East Bunbury) Built in 1842 using wattle and daub construction, this is WA's second-oldest church.

🏃 Activities

Mangrove Boardwalk   WALKING
Mangrove Boardwalk (enter off Koombana Dr) meanders through the most southerly mangroves in WA, rich with more than 70 species of bird. Interpretive signs provide information about this 2500-year-old ecosystem.

Tuart Forest   WALKING
This stretch of forest lined with tall trees runs along the southern end of Ocean Dr.

Bunbury

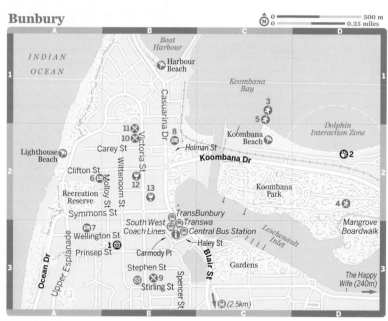

Bunbury

⊙ Sights
1 Bunbury Regional Art Galleries............. B3
2 Dolphin Discovery Centre...................... D2

⊕ Activities, Courses & Tours
3 Eco Cruises..C1
4 Mangrove Boardwalk D2
5 Swim Encounter Cruises C1

⊜ Sleeping
6 Clifton A2

7 Dolphin Retreat YHA..............................A3
8 Mantra..B2

⊗ Eating
9 Café 140...B3
10 Market Eating House.............................B2
11 Sala Wine Bar & Kitchen.......................B2

⊖ Drinking & Nightlife
12 Lost Bills B2
13 Yours or Mine..B2

☞ Tours

**Ngalang Wongi Aboriginal
Cultural Tours** CULTURAL
(☑ 0457 360 517; www.ngalangwongi.com.au;
adult/child from $50/25) Local man Troy Ben-
nell shares his Noongar culture and heritage
on a town tour incorporating the Indigenous
history of the Bunbury area, and a walking
tour around the Mangrove Boardwalk and
Koombana Bay finishing at the Dolphin Discovery Centre.

🛏 Sleeping

Bunbury Glade Caravan Park CARAVAN PARK $
(☑ 08-9721 3800; www.glade.com.au; Timper-
ley Rd; 2-person sites $30-40, cabins $80-120;

❄ @ ♠ ⛨) This spotless park is a five-min-
ute drive from the centre of town on Blair St,
the main road heading south.

Dolphin Retreat YHA HOSTEL $
(☑ 08-9792 4690; www.dolphinretreatbunbury.
com.au; 14 Wellington St; dm/s/d $31/57/82;
@ ♠) Around the corner from the beach,
this small hostel is in a labyrinthine old
house with hammocks and a barbecue on
the back verandah. It's popular with longer-
term residents working in the area.

Mantra APARTMENT $$
(☑ 08-9721 0100; www.mantra.com.au; 1 Hol-
man St; apt from $210; ❄ @ ♠ ⛨) The Mantra
has sculpted a set of modern studios and

apartments around four grain silos by the harbour. Deluxe rooms have spa baths and full kitchens.

Clifton MOTEL $$
(☑08-9721 4300; www.theclifton.com.au; 2 Molloy St; r $150-275; ☜) For luxurious heritage accommodation, go for the top-of-the-range rooms in the Clifton's historic Grittleton Lodge (1885). Good-value motel rooms are also available.

✖ Eating

★ **Market Eating House** MODERN AUSTRALIAN $$
(☑08-9721 6078; www.marketeatinghouse. au; 9 Victoria St; shared plates $12-18, mains $35-42; ☺5.30pm-late Wed-Thu, noon-late Fri & Sat, 9am-4pm Sun) More evidence that Bunbury's dining scene has definitely become more interesting across recent years, the Market Eating House focuses on a custom-made wood-fired grill that is used for everything from chicken and fish to pork and beef. Turkish and Middle Eastern flavours underpin many dishes, and smaller shared plates include plump ricotta dumplings and hummus topped with lamb.

Sala Wine Bar & Kitchen TAPAS $$
(☑08-9701 9504; www.facebook.com/ salawinelounge; 5 Victoria St; shared plates $10-24; ☺4pm-midnight Thu & Fri, noon-midnight Sat & Sun) Shared small plates and a stellar collection of craft beer and wine combine at this Victoria St venue with a relaxed heritage ambience. Menu highlights include coconut prawns, smoked scallops and Japanese-style *karaage* fried chicken. The rotating beer taps usually include WA brews, and top-notch cocktails include a very refreshing mojito.

Café 140 CAFE $$
(☑08-9721 2254; www.cafe140.com.au; 140 Victoria St; mains $13-32; ☺7am-4.30pm Mon-Thu, to midnight Fri, 8am-2pm Sat & Sun) Hip, onto-it staff make the funky Café 140 a top spot for a leisurely Bunbury breakfast. Try the Indian-inspired salmon kedgeree omelette. Later in the day, gourmet burgers, charcuterie platters and grilled Turkish sandwiches combine with a concise beer and wine list. Pop next door to the recently added wood-fired bakery for crunchy and still-warm sourdough loaves and great doughnuts.

Happy Wife CAFE $$
(☑08-9721 7706; www.thehappywife.com.au; 98 Stirling St; mains $11-24; ☺6.30am-3.30pm Mon-Fri, 7.30am-2.30pm Sat) Grab a spot in the garden of this Cape Cod–style cottage just a short drive from the centre of town. Excellent homestyle baking and regular lunch specials make it worth seeking out. Try the slow-roasted pork salad or the duck and sweet potato parcel.

☕ Drinking & Nightlife

Yours or Mine BAR
(☑08-9791 8884; www.facebook.com/ yoursorminel; 26 Victoria St; shared plates $18-28, mains $24-42; ☺noon-3pm & 5pm-midnight Mon-Thu, noon-midnight Sat & Sun) Bunbury's Monday-night dining scene is pretty quiet, but Yours or Mine comes to the rescue with small-bar style and tasty shared plates. The service was a bit hit-and-miss during our visit, but the South American–influenced food, including pulled-pork tacos, was worth the wait. Check the website for nightly specials and occasional Sunday-afternoon live music.

Lost Bills BAR
(www.facebook.com/pg/lostbillsishere; 41 Victoria St; ☺4-11pm Wed-Thu, 3pm-midnight Fri & Sat, 2-8pm Sun) Lost Bills' compact brick-lined space is enlivened by quirky artwork – look out for Snoop Dogg as a hot dog. A good wine and cocktail list and four guest taps with beer and cider from around WA are also valid reasons to visit Bunbury's pretty accurate approximation of a small bar in Sydney or Melbourne.

❶ Information

Visitor Centre (☑08-9792 7205; www. visitbunbury.com.au; Carmody Pl; ☺9am-5pm Mon-Sat, 10am-2pm Sun) Located in the historic train station (1904). Bikes can be rented and there are free historic walking tours every Wednesday at 10am.

❶ Getting There & Away

BUS

Coaches stop at the **central bus station** (p124), next to the visitor centre, or at the **train station** (p124).

Transwa (p124) routes include the following:
➡ SW1 (12 weekly) to East Perth ($32.45, 3¼ hours), Mandurah ($17.50, two hours), Busselton ($9.90, 43 minutes), Margaret River ($17.50, two hours) and Augusta ($26.50, 2½ hours).

➡ SW2 (three weekly) to Balingup ($14.45, 53 minutes), Bridgetown ($17.50, 1¼ hours) and Pemberton ($29.40, 2¼ hours).

➜ GS3 (daily) to Walpole ($47, 4½ hours), Denmark ($52, 5½ hours) and Albany ($60, six hours).

South West Coach Lines (☑08-9261 7600; www.southwestcoachlines.com.au) Runs services to/from Perth's Elizabeth Quay Busport ($35, 2½ hours, three daily), Busselton ($12, 1¼ hours, four daily), Dunsborough ($21, 1¾ hours, daily) and Bridgetown ($19, 1¾ hours, daily).

TransBunbury Runs buses (30 minutes) between the central bus station and train station ($2.90; no Sunday service). Look for bus number 827.

TRAIN

Bunbury is the terminus of the **Transwa** (p124) Australind train line, with two daily services to Perth ($31.45, 2½ hours) and Pinjarra ($17.50, 1¼ hours).

Tuart Forest National Park

The tuart is a type of eucalypt that only grows on coastal limestone 200km either side of Perth, and this 20-sq-km strip squeezed between the Bussell Hwy and the Indian Ocean is the last pure tuart forest left. An alternative route to Busselton from Bunbury leads through the shade cast by these giants, some more than 33m tall.

Turn off the highway at Tuart Dr, 4km southwest of Capel. After 11km, turn right into Layman Rd for **Wonnerup House** (☑08-9752 2039; www.nationaltrust.org.au; 935 Layman Rd; adult/child $5/3; ☺10am-4pm Thu-Mon), a National Trust homestead (1859). Continue past the seaside village of Wonnerup and follow the coast to Busselton.

Busselton

POP 31,767

Unpretentious and uncomplicated, Busselton is what passes for the big smoke in these parts. Surrounded by calm waters and white-sand beaches, its outlandishly long jetty is its most famous attraction. The family-friendly town has plenty of diversionary activities for lively kids, including sheltered beaches, water slides and animal farms.

◉ Sights

Busselton Jetty LANDMARK
(☑08-9754 0900; www.busseltonjetty.com.au; adult/child $3/free, return train adult/child $13/6.50, Interpretive Centre free; ☺Interpretive Centre 8.30am-5pm Sep-Apr, 9am-5pm May-Aug) Busselton's 1865 timber-piled jetty – the southern hemisphere's longest (1841m) – reopened in 2011 following a $27-million refurbishment. A little train chugs along to the **Underwater Observatory** (adult/child incl train $33/16.50; ☺9am-4.25pm), where tours take place 8m below the surface; bookings are essential. There's also an Interpretive Centre, an attractive building in the style of 1930s bathing sheds, about 50m along the jetty. A new option to explore the underwater world around the jetty's historic piles, offered by Dive Busselton Jetty (p126), is wearing a self-contained breathing apparatus called a SeaTREK helmet.

ArtGeo Cultural Complex GALLERY
(☑08-9751 4651; www.artgeo.com.au; 6 Queen St; ☺10am-4pm) Grouped around the old courthouse (1856), this complex includes tearooms, wood turners, an artist-in-residence and the Busselton Art Society's gallery, selling works by local artists.

Busselton Museum MUSEUM
(☑08-9754 2166; www.busseltonmuseum.org.au; Peel Tce; adult/child $8/3; ☺10am-4pm Wed-Mon) Local history in an old butter factory.

🏃 Activities

Capel Vale WINE
(☑08-9727 1986; www.capelvale.com.au; Mallokup Rd; ☺cellar door 10am-4.30pm, restaurant 11.30am-3pm Thu-Mon) Geographe Bay wine region's best-known winery is conveniently located halfway between Bunbury and Busselton. Capel Vale offers free tastings and Match restaurant overlooking the vines. It's located off the Bussell Hwy on the opposite side of the highway from Capel village.

Dive Busselton Jetty DIVING
(☑1800 994 210; www.divebusseltonjetty.com.au; underwater walks $165, snorkelling/diving from $29/99; ☺underwater walks Dec-Apr) Offers snorkelling and dive trips around the jetty, and also a walk along the ocean floor around Busselton Jetty's wooden piles while wearing a self-contained breathing helmet called a SeaTREK apparatus. The experience is open to everyone – you can leave your glasses on and your hair won't get wet – and the underwater view includes coral and fish. Book ahead for the popular underwater walks.

Dive Shed DIVING
(☑08-9754 1615; www.diveshed.com.au; 21 Queen St) Runs regular dive charters along the

jetty, to Four Mile Reef (a 40km limestone ledge about 6.5km off the coast) and to the scuttled navy vessel HMAS *Swan* (off Dunsborough).

👉 Tours

Southwest Eco Discoveries ECOTOUR
(☑0477 030 322, 0477 049 722; www.southwestecodiscoveries.com.au; tours $45-95) Brothers Ryan and Mick White run tours exploring around Geographe Bay and Cape Naturaliste. Options include morning tours discovering the stunning coastline, afternoon tours with a wine and gourmet focus, and evening outings to see endangered woylies and other nocturnal marsupials. Tour pick-ups can be made from accommodation in Busselton, Dunsborough and Cowaramup, and from Margaret River by availability and arrangement.

🎉 Festivals & Events

CinéfestOZ FILM
(www.cinefestoz.com; ⊙late Aug) Busselton briefly morphs into St-Tropez with this oddly glamorous festival of French and Australian cinema, including lots of Australian premieres and the odd Aussie starlet.

Southbound MUSIC
(www.southboundfestival.com.au; ⊙late Dec) Celebrate the end of the year with three days of alternative music and camping just after Christmas.

🛏 Sleeping

Accommodation sprawls along the beach for several kilometres either side of the town centre, so check the location if you don't have transport. During school holidays, the population increases fourfold and accommodation prices soar.

Beachlands Holiday Park CARAVAN PARK $
(☑08-9752 2107; www.beachlands.com.au; 10 Earnshaw Rd, West Busselton; sites per 2 people $51, chalets from $156; ❄🐾🏊) This excellent family-friendly park offers a wide range of accommodation amid shady trees, palms and flax bushes. Deluxe spa villas ($185) have corner spas, huge TVs, DVD players and full kitchens.

Observatory Guesthouse B&B $$
(☑08-9751 3336; www.observatoryguesthouse.com; 7 Brown St; d $150; ❄🐾) A five-minute walk from the jetty, this friendly B&B has four bright, cheerful rooms. They're not overly big, but you can spread out on the communal sea-facing balcony and front courtyard.

Aqua DESIGN HOTEL $$$
(☑08-9750 4200; www.theaquaresort.com.au; 605 Bussell Hwy; apt from $480; ❄🐾🏊) Down a driveway framed by peppermint trees and with direct beach access, the luxury beach houses at Aqua are a grand option for families or a pair of couples travelling together. Bedrooms and bathrooms are stylish and understated, but the real wow factor comes in the stunning lounges and living areas. Facilities include a beachfront infinity pool and a spa and sauna.

🍴 Eating & Drinking

Laundry 43 CAFE $$
(☑08-9754 1503; www.laundry43.com.au; 43 Prince St; shared plates $14-29; ⊙4pm-late Tue-Thu, 11am-late Fri & Sat) Brick walls and a honey-coloured jarrah bar form the backdrop for Margaret River beers and wines, great cocktails, and classy shared plates and bigger dishes. Definitely get ready to linger longer than you planned. Ask about occasional special degustation menus.

Goose CAFE $$
(☑08-9754 7700; www.thegoose.com.au; Geographe Bay Rd; breakfast $13-22, shared plates & mains $11-35; ⊙7am-10pm; 🐾) Near the jetty, stylish Goose is a cool and classy cafe, bar and bistro. The drinks list bubbles away with WA craft beer and wine, and a versatile menu kicks off with eggy breakfasts, before graduating to shared plates including Vietnamese pulled-pork sliders, and larger dishes such as steamed mussels and seafood chowder.

Fire Station CRAFT BEER
(☑08-9752 3113; www.firestation.bar; 68 Queen St; ⊙4-11pm Tue-Wed, 11.30am-midnight Thu-Sat, 11.30am-10pm Sun) Park yourself in the cosy interior or outside under the market umbrellas and enjoy one of the southwest's best selections of wine and craft beer. The tasty food menu includes classic drinking dishes like spicy chicken wings and cheese and chilli croquettes, and weekly specials include Thursday's Bao & Beer deal with $7 pints and Asian steamed buns from 4pm.

ℹ Information

Visitor Centre (☑08-9752 5800; www.margaretriver.com; end of Queen St, Busselton foreshore; ⊘9am-5pm Mon-Fri, to 4.30pm Sat & Sun) On the waterfront near the pier. Bikes can be rented for exploring Busselton's foreshore.

ⓘ Getting There & Away

Buses link Busselton to the north and south. **South West Coach Lines** (☑08-9753 7700; www.southwestcoachlines.com.au; Peel Tce) Runs services to/from Perth's Elizabeth Quay Busport ($40, 3¾ hours, three daily), Bunbury ($12, one hour, three daily), Dunsborough ($12, 30 minutes, three daily) and Margaret River ($12, 50 minutes, three daily).

Transwa (☑1300 662 205; www.transwa. wa.gov.au) The SW1 service (12 weekly) stops on Peel Tce heading to/from East Perth ($38, 4¼ hours), Bunbury ($12, 43 minutes), Dunsborough ($8.25, 28 minutes), Margaret River ($14.45, 1½ hours) and Augusta ($17.50, 1¾ hours).

Following a recent expansion of Busselton airport, interstate flights are expected to launch in 2018.

Dunsborough

POP 3400

Smaller and less sprawling than Busselton, Dunsborough is a relaxed, beach-worshipping town that goes bonkers towards the end of November when about 7000 'schoolies' descend. When it's not inundated with drunken, squealing teenagers, it's a thoroughly pleasant place to be. The beaches are better than Busselton's, but accommodation is more limited.

The name Dunsborough first appeared on maps in the 1830s, but to the Wardandi people it was always Quedjinup, meaning 'place of women'.

🏃 Activities

Naturaliste Charters　　　WHALE WATCHING (☑08-9750 5500; www.whales-australia.com; 25/27 Dunn Bay Rd; adult/child $90/50; ⊘10am & 2pm Sep–mid-Dec) Two-hour whale-watching cruises from September to early December. From December to January, the emphasis switches to an **Eco Wilderness Tour** showcasing beaches, limestone caves with Indigenous art, and wildlife, including dolphins and New Zealand fur seals. Tours also run out of Augusta from late May to August.

Cape Dive　　　DIVING (☑08-9756 8778; www.capedive.com; 222 Naturaliste Tce; ⊘9am-5pm) There is excellent diving

in Geographe Bay, especially since the decommissioned Navy destroyer HMAS *Swan* was purposely scuttled in 1997 for use as a dive wreck. Marine life has colonised the ship, which lies at a depth of 30m, 2.5km offshore.

🛏 Sleeping

As well as motels and a hostel, there are many options for self-contained rentals in town depending on the season. The visitor centre (p129) has listings.

Dunsborough Beachouse YHA　　　HOSTEL **$** (☑08-9755 3107; www.dunsboroughbeachouse. com.au; 205 Geographe Bay Rd; dm $34-36, s/d $60/92; @ 🛜) On the Quindalup beachfront, this friendly hostel has lawns stretching languidly to the water's edge. It's an easy 2km cycle from the town centre.

Dunsborough Central Motel　　　MOTEL **$$** (☑08-9756 7711; www.dunsboroughmotel.com. au; 50 Dunn Bay Rd; r $130-175; 🛜🞬) Centrally located in Dunsborough town, this well-run motel is good value, especially if you can snare an online midweek discount, which leaves more of your travel budget to enjoy the nearby wineries and breweries.

Dunsborough Rail Carriages & Farm Cottages　　　COTTAGE **$$** (☑08-9755 3865; www.dunsborough.com; Commonage Rd; rail carriages/cottages from $135/170; 🛜) Refurbished rail carriages are dotted about this big bush block near Quindalup, as are self-contained timber cottages, which are spacious for families. Kids will have fun with the friendly sheep and chooks.

🍴 Eating

Wild & Woods　　　CAFE **$$** (☑08-9755 3308; www.wildandwoods.com.au; 2/237 Naturaliste Tce; mains $12-25; ⊘8am-4pm Tue-Fri, to 3pm Sat, to 2pm Sun) Wild & Woods' Australia-meets-Scandinavia decor is a relaxing backdrop for good cafe fare – try the apricot and macadamia muesli for breakfast – and interesting counter food like felafel wraps. There's a handy providore section for picking up local gourmet produce, and juices and smoothies provide a healthy balance to the region's vineyards and craft breweries.

Pourhouse　　　BISTRO **$$** (☑08-9759 1720; www.pourhouse.com.au; 26 Dunn Bay Rd; mains $19-34; ⊘4pm-late) Hip but not pretentious, with comfy couches, weekend DJs and an upstairs terrace for summer. The pizzas are excellent, and top-notch burgers come in a locally baked sourdough bun. A considered approach to beer includes rotating taps from the best of WA's craft breweries and lots of bottled surprises. Check the Facebook listing to see what's pouring. Two-for-one burgers on Wednesdays.

★**Piari & Co**   BISTRO, BAR $$$
(☑08-9756 7977; www.piariandco.com.au; 5/54 Dunn Bay Rd; small plates $21-23, mains $34-42; ☺5-11pm Tue-Sat) This relaxed and stylish bistro has a strong emphasis on local and seasonal produce. Small plates include Shark Bay prawns wrapped in ham, and a punchy combination of beef tartare and horseradish. Mains such as lamb rump and fish go well with a drinks list proudly showcasing Margaret River wines and craft beer. Bookings recommended.

❶ Information

Visitor Centre (☑08-9752 5800; www. margaretriver.com; 1/31 Dunn Bay Rd; ☺9am-5pm Mon-Fri, 9.30am-4.30pm Sat & Sun) Information and bookings.

❶ Getting There & Away

Buses link Dunsborough north to Perth and further south through Margaret River to Albany and the southwest.

South West Coach Lines (☑08-9753 7700; www.southwestcoachlines.com.au; Seymour Blvd) Runs services to/from Perth's Elizabeth Quay Busport ($46, 4½ hours, daily), Bunbury ($21, 1¾ hours, daily) and Busselton ($12, 30 minutes, three daily).

Transwa (☑1300 662 205; www.transwa. wa.gov.au; Seymour Blvd) The SW1 (12 weekly) service stops at the visitor centre, heading to/from East Perth ($41.25, 4½ hours), Bunbury ($14.45, 1¼ hours), Busselton ($8.25, 28 minutes), Margaret River ($9.90, 49 minutes) and Augusta ($17.50, 1¼ hours).

Cape Naturaliste

Northwest of Dunsborough, Cape Naturaliste Rd leads to the excellent beaches of **Meelup**, **Eagle Bay** and **Bunker Bay**, and on to Cape Naturaliste. There are walks and lookouts along the way; pick up brochures from Dunsborough's visitor centre before heading out. Whales and hammerhead sharks like to hang out on the edge of Bunker Bay, where the continental shelf drops 75m. There's excellent snorkelling on the edge of the shelf at Shelley Cove.

Bunker Bay is home to Bunkers Beach Cafe (p130), serving an adventurous menu with Asian and Mediterranean flavours just metres from the sand.

The Cape Naturaliste lighthouse (p130), built in 1903, can be visited on tours and there's also a free museum and a cafe. Above and Below (adult/child $30/15) packages are available, combining entry to Ngilgi Cave (p133).

Sights

Leeuwin-Naturaliste National Park   NATIONAL PARK
(Caves Rd) Despite the vast areas of aridity it contains, Western Australia also boasts a startling variety of endemic wildflowers. The Leeuwin-Naturaliste National Park explodes with colour in the spring months. The leached, sandy soils of Western Australia produce a surprising variety of vividly coloured wildflowers.

The demanding environment prevents any one species predominating, leaving a gorgeous array of fantastically evolved orchids, sundews, kangaroo paws and the like to flourish in their exclusive niches. Their striking colours and shapes developed as a means of attracting the attentions of the few pollinators found in the area. Walking in the 155-sq-km Leeuwin-Naturaliste National Park in spring (September to November), it's possible to see orchids, banksias, clematis, cowslips and many other species, including the improbably named prickly moses.

RED TAILS IN THE SUNSET

Between Cape Naturaliste and Cape Leeuwin is the most southerly breeding colony of the red-tailed tropicbird (*Phaethon rubricauda*) in Australia. From September to May, look for it soaring above Sugarloaf Rock, south of Cape Naturaliste. The viewpoint can be reached by a 3.5km boardwalk from the Cape Naturaliste lighthouse or by Sugarloaf Rd.

The tropicbird is distinguished by its two long, red tail streamers – almost twice its body length. Bring binoculars to watch this small colony soar, glide, dive and then swim with their disproportionately long tail feathers cocked up.

Cape Naturaliste Lighthouse   LIGHTHOUSE
(☑08-9780 5911; www.margaretriver.com; adult/
child $14/7; ⊙tours every 30min 9.30am-4pm)
Built in 1903, this lighthouse can be visited
on tours. There's also a free museum and a
cafe. Above and Below (adult/child $30/15)
packages combining lighthouse entry with
Ngilgi Cave (p133) are also available.

🏃 Activities

Cape to Cape Track   WALKING
(www.capetocapetrack.com.au) Stretching from
Cape Naturaliste to Cape Leeuwin, the
135km Cape to Cape Track passes through
the heath, forest and sand dunes of the
Leeuwin-Naturaliste National Park (p129),
all the while providing Indian Ocean views.
Most walkers take about seven days to complete the track, staying in a combination of
national-park camp sites and commercial
caravan parks along the way, but you can
walk it in five days or break up the route
into day walks.

☞ Tours

Cape to Cape Tours   WALKING
(☑0459 452 038; www.capetocapetours.com.au;
per couple from $1300) Negotiate the entire
route or just parts of the stunning Cape to
Cape coastal walk on self-guided and guided
itineraries. Trips include camping or lodge
accommodation and excellent meals, and
options from three to eight days are available. Various day tours exploring the Margaret River region are also offered.

🍴 Eating

Bunkers Beach Cafe   CAFE $$
(☑08-9756 8284; www.bunkersbeachcafe.com.
au; Farm Break Lane; breakfast $14-25, lunch $29-
38; ⊙8.30am-4pm) Bunker Bay is home to
Bunkers Beach Cafe, serving an adventur-
ous menu with Asian and Mediterranean
flavours just metres from the sand.

MARGARET RIVER WINE REGION

With vineyard restaurants, artisan food
producers, and some of Australia's most
spectacular surf beaches and rugged coast-
line, the Margaret River wine region packs
attractions aplenty into a compact area.
Sleepy Yallingup conceals excellent beaches,
restaurants and luxe accommodation, Mar-

garet River township is the region's bustling
foodie heart, and the best of the area's win-
eries are focused around Cowaramup and
Wilyabrup. Throughout the area, an excel-
lent craft-beer scene bubbles away, and the
road further south to the windswept Cape
Leeuwin Lighthouse at Augusta is studded
with spectacular underground caves.

☞ Tours

Margaret River Brewery Tours   FOOD & DRINK
(☑0458 450 120; www.mrbt.com.au; tours $70-
110; ⊙noon-6pm) Four craft breweries are
visited on these small-group minibus tours
helmed by the super-friendly Jules. The $70
'Mid Strength' option allows participants to
buy their own drinks as they go, while the
$110 'Full Strength' tour includes a six-brew
tasting paddle at each stop. Both options in-
clude an excellent lunch, and cider drinkers
can also be catered for.

Taste the South   WINE
(☑0438 210 373; www.tastethesouth.com.au; per
person from $95) Wine and craft-beer tours.
Up to five breweries can be visited, and the
special Hits with Kids tour combines chil-
dren-friendly vineyards with activities, in-
cluding lamb feeding, sheep shearing and a
chocolate factory.

Wine for Dudes   WINE
(☑0427 774 994; www.winefordudes.com; tours
$105) Includes a brewery, a chocolate factory,
four wineries, a wine-blending experience
and lunch.

Margaret River Tours   WINE
(☑0419 917 166; www.margaretrivertours.com)
Runs winery tours (half-/full-day $85/150)
and can arrange charters.

Margies Big Day Out   WINE
(☑0416 180 493; www.margaretrivertourswa.com.
au; tours $95) Three wineries, two breweries,
cheese, chocolate and lunch.

Harvest Tours   WINE
(☑0429 728 687; www.harvesttours.com.au; adult/
child from $105/65) Food and wine tour with
an emphasis on organic, sustainable and
ethical producers.

Bushtucker Tours   TOURS
(☑08-9757 9084; www.bushtuckertours.com;
adult/child $95/40) The four-hour tour com-
bines walking and canoeing up the Marga-
ret River, and features aspects of Aboriginal
nal culture along with uses for flora, and

a bush-tucker lunch. Also runs a Winery & Brewery Tour (adult/child $100/40) around Margaret River.

✦ Festivals & Events

Drug Aware Pro SPORTS
(www.worldsurfleague.com; ⊙Apr) Pro-surfing competition with concerts and fashion shows.

Margaret River Gourmet Escape FOOD & DRINK
(www.gourmetescape.com.au; ⊙late Nov) From Rick Stein, Nigella Lawson and Heston Blumenthal to MasterChef's George Cal-

ombaris and Matt Preston, the Gourmet Escape food and wine festival attracts the big names in global and Australian cuisine. Look forward to three days of food workshops, tastings, vineyard events and demonstrations.

❶ Getting There & Away

Margaret River is easily reached by bus from Perth. To drive from Perth to Margaret River township takes around three hours.

South West Coach Lines (☑ 08-9261 7600; www.southwestcoachlines.com.au) Runs services between Busselton and Augusta, stopping

---

GETTING CRAFTY IN MARGARET RIVER

The Margaret River region's wine credentials are impeccable, but the area is also a destination for craft-beer fans. Many breweries serve bar snacks and lunch.

Eagle Bay Brewing Co (☑08-9755 3554; www.eaglebaybrewing.com.au; Eagle Bay Rd, Dunsborough; ⊙11am-5pm) A lovely rural outlook; interesting beers and wines served in modern, spacious surroundings; and excellent food, including crisp wood-fired pizzas ($20 to $25). Keep an eye out for Eagle Bay's Single Batch Specials.

Black Brewing Co (☑08-9755 6500; www.blackbrewingco.com.au; 3517 Caves Rd, Wilyabrup; 4-beer tasting paddle $20; ⊙11am-late) Black Brewing's well-made beers are approachable for beginner craft-beer fans – just don't expect any bold hop bombs – and brews like the crisp and citrusy extra pale ale (XPA) and rich milk stout go well with dishes inspired by Asian street food. Also sharing the spectacular location on a private lake is Vintner Black winery, specialising in chardonnay and cabernet sauvignon.

Cheeky Monkey Brewery (☑08-9755 5555; www.cheekymonkeybrewery.com.au; 4259 Caves Rd, Margaret River; ⊙10am-6pm) Set around a pretty lake, Cheeky Monkey has an expansive restaurant and lots of room for the kids to run around. Try the Hatseller Pilsner with bold New Zealand hops or the Belgian-style Hagenbeck Pale Ale. Decent food and apple and pear ciders mean you'll make a day of it.

Beer Farm (☑08-9755 7177; www.beerfarm.com.au; 8 Gale Rd, Metricup; ⊙noon-5pm Mon-Thu, to 7pm Fri-Sun) Located in a former milking shed down a sleepy side road, the Beer Farm is Margaret River's most rustic brewery. Loyal locals crowd in with their children and dogs, supping on the Beer Farm's own brews – try the hoppy Rye IPA – and there's a food truck and plenty of room for the kids (and dogs) to run around.

Bootleg Brewery (☑08-9755 6300; www.bootlegbrewery.com.au; Puzey Rd, off Yelverton Rd, Wilyabrup; ⊙11am-6pm) More rustic than some of the area's flashier breweries, but lots of fun with a pint in the sun – especially with live bands on Saturday. Try the award-winning Raging Bull Porter – a West Australian classic – or the US West Coast–style Speakeasy IPA. The food is also very good.

Cowaramup Brewing Company (☑08-9755 5822; www.cowaramupbrewing.com.au; North Treeton Rd, Cowaramup; ⊙11am-6pm) Modern microbrewery with an award-winning Pilsner and a moreish English-style Special Pale Ale. Four other beers and occasional seasonal brews also feature.

Colonial Brewing Co (☑08-9758 8177; www.colonialbrewingco.com.au; 56 Osmington Rd; ⊙11am-6pm Sat-Thu, to 11pm Fri) This modern microbrewery has rural views and an excellent range of authentic beers including a *witbier* with coriander and mandarin, and a hop-fuelled India pale ale (IPA). Our favourite is the refreshing German-style *kolsch*. Look for regular seasonal special brews and settle in with a pizza on the deck. On Friday nights it's often packed and a fun place to be.

Margaret River Wine Region

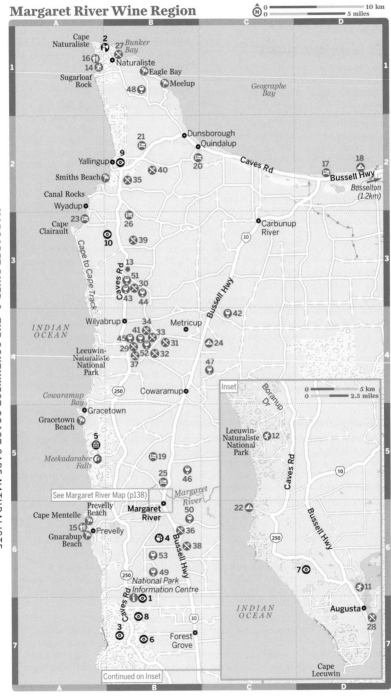

See Margaret River Map (p138)

Inset

Continued on Inset

Margaret River Wine Region

at Cowaramup and Margaret River, and linking with Perth on the weekends.

Transwa (☎1300 662 205; www.transwa.wa.gov.au) The SW1 service (12 weekly) from Perth to Augusta stops at Yallingup and Margaret River, with three coaches weekly continuing to Pemberton.

Yallingup & Around

POP 1070

Beachside Yallingup is a mecca for both surfers and wine aficionados. You're permitted to let a 'wow' escape when the surf-battered coastline first comes into view. For romantic travellers, Yallingup means 'place of love' in the Wardandi Noongar tongue.

Beautiful walking trails follow the coast between here and Smiths Beach. Canal Rocks, a series of rocky outcrops forming a natural canal, are just past Smiths Beach.

⊙ Sights & Activities

Ngilgi Cave CAVE
(☎08-9755 2152; www.margaretriver.com; Yallingup Caves Rd; adult/child $22.50/12; ⊙9am-5pm) Between Dunsborough and Yallingup, this 500,000-year-old cave is associated with Wardandi spirituality with the victory of the good spirit Ngilgi over the evil spirit Wolgine. To the Wardandi people it became a kind of honeymoon location. A European man first stumbled upon it in 1899 while looking for his horse. Formations include the white **Mother of Pearl Shawl** and the equally beautiful **Arab's Tent** and **Oriental Shawl**. Tours depart every half-hour. Check online for other options.

More adventurous caving options include the two-hour Ancient Riverbed Tour (adult/child $60/39), the 45-minute Express Adventure Tour (adult/child $47/29), the 2½-hour Explorer Tour (adult/child $88/52), the three-hour Crystal Crawl Tour (adults only, $110) and the four-hour Ultimate Ngilgi

> ### TOP FIVE SURF SPOTS
> ➧ Margaret River Mouth
> ➧ Southside
> ➧ Three Bears
> ➧ Yallingup
> ➧ Injidup Car Park

Adventure (adults only, $158). The Above & Below ticket (adult/child $30/15) includes entry to the Cape Naturaliste Lighthouse (p130).

Well-marked bushwalks start from here.

Wardan Aboriginal Centre
CULTURAL CENTRE, GALLERY

(☑08-9756 6566; www.wardan.com.au; Injidup Springs Rd, Yallingup; experiences adult/child $20/10; ☻10am-4pm daily mid-Oct–mid-Mar, 10am-4pm Mon, Wed-Fri & Sun mid-Mar–mid-Jun & mid-Aug–mid-Oct, experiences Sun, Mon, Wed & Fri) ✐ Offers a window into the lives of the local Wardandi people. There's a gallery (free admission), an interpretive display on the six seasons that govern the Wardandi calendar (adult/child $8/3), and the opportunity to take part in various experiences, including making stone tools and throwing boomerangs and spears. A guided bushwalk explores Wardandi spirituality and the uses of various plants for food, medicine and shelter.

Yallingup Surf School
SURFING

(☑08-9755 2755; www.yallingupsurfschool.com) Offers 90-minute lessons for beginners (one-hour lesson $50, three hours $125) and private coaching ($110).

📯 Tours

Koomal Dreaming
TOURS

(☑0413 843 426; www.koomaldreaming.com.au; adult/child from $55/25) Yallingup local and Wardandi man Josh Whiteland runs tours showcasing Indigenous food, culture and music, usually also including bushwalking and exploration of the Ngilgi Cave.

🍳 Courses

Wildwood Valley Cooking School
COOKING

(☑08-9755 2120; www.wildwoodvalley.com.au; 1481 Wildwood Rd, Wildwood Valley Cottages; per person $140; ☻Dec-Mar) Set amid the shaded grounds of the Wildwood Valley Cottages (p134), the cooking school with Sioban and Carlo Baldini offer hands-on classes in Thai or Italian cuisine. Sioban's CV includes cooking at Longrain and living in Tuscany. Cooking classes are $140 per person and options include Wood Fired cooking and Taste of Tuscany. The classes are wildly popular with Perth visitors, so check the schedule online and book early. Most classes occur on a Wednesday, Friday or Saturday, but this does vary.

🛏 Sleeping

Yallingup Beach Holiday Park
CARAVAN PARK $

(☑08-9755 2164; www.yallingupbeach.com.au; Valley Rd; sites per 2 people $40, cabins $115-165; ☎) You'll fall asleep to the sound of the surf here, with the beach just across the road.

Caves House
HOTEL $$

(Hotel Yallingup; ☑08-9750 1888; www.caveshousehotelyallingup.com.au; 18 Yallingup Beach Rd; d $170, ste $280-410; ☎) Sunday to Thursday rates at this restored heritage hotel are good value, and it's an atmospheric spot for a drink, with live gigs from 5pm on Friday and Sunday afternoons. Over summer, some of Australia's biggest touring bands sometimes drop by, and outdoor movies add to a laid-back holiday vibe.

★ Wildwood Valley Cottages
COTTAGE $$$

(☑08-9755 2120; www.wildwoodvalley.com.au; 1481 Wildwood Rd; cottages from $250; ☎) Luxury cottages trimmed by native bush are arrayed across 120 acres, and the property's main house also hosts the Wildwood Valley Cooking School (p134) with Sioban and Carlo Baldini. Look out for grazing kangaroos as you meander up the unsealed road to reception.

Injidup Spa Retreat
BOUTIQUE HOTEL $$$

(☑08-9750 1300; www.injidupsparetreat.com.au; Cape Clairault Rd; ste from $650; ❄✖) ✐ The region's most stylish and luxurious accommodation, Injidup perches atop an isolated cliff south of Yallingup. A striking carved concrete and iron facade fronts the car park, while inside there are heated polished-concrete floors, 'eco' fires and absolute sea views. Each of the 10 suites has its own plunge pool. It's off Wyadup Rd.

Empire Retreat & Spa
SPA HOTEL $$$

(☑08-9755 2065; www.empireretreat.com; Caves Rd; ste $295-575; ❄☎) Everything about the intimate Empire Retreat is stylish, from the cool Scandi-inspired design to the attention to detail and service. The rooms are built around a former farmhouse, and a rustic but sophisticated ambience lingers. Check online for good packages combining accommodation and spa treatments.

✗ Eating

Yallingup Woodfired Bread   BAKERY $
(189 Biddle Rd; bread from $4; ☺7am-6pm Mon-Sat) Look out for excellent sourdough, rye bread and fruit loaves at local shops and the Margaret River Farmers Market, or pick up some still-warm loaves at the bakery near Yallingup.

Wills Domain   BISTRO $$$
(☑08-9755 2327; www.willsdomain.com.au; cnr Brash & Abbey Farm Rds; mains $31-42, 5-/7-course degustation $85/99; ☺tastings 10am-5pm, lunch noon-3pm) Restaurant, gallery and wonderful hilltop views over vines. An innovative seven-course tasting menu (with/without wine match $139/99) is also available.

Studio Bistro   MODERN AUSTRALIAN $$$
(☑08-9756 6164; www.thestudiobistro.com.au; 7 Marrinup Dr; small plates $15-20, mains $28-39, degustation menu with/without wine matches $135/95; ☺10am-5pm Wed-Mon, 6pm-late Sat; ☑) 🥢 Studio Bistro's gallery focuses on Australian artists, while the garden restaurant showcases subtle dishes such as pan-fried fish with cauliflower cream, radicchio, peas and crab meat. Five-course degustation menus are offered on Friday and Saturday nights. Bookings recommended.

Cowaramup & Wilyabrup

POP 988

Cowaramup (Cow Town to some) is a couple of blocks of shops lining Bussell Hwy. Wilyabrup to the northwest is where the Margaret River wine industry began in the 1960s. This area has the highest concentration of wineries, and pioneers Cullen Wines and Vasse Felix are still leading the way.

🍳 Courses

Cape Lodge   COOKING
(☑08-9755 6311; www.capelodge.com.au; 3341 Caves Rd, Wilaybrup; $145) Cooking classes with renowned chef Michael Elfwing take place at this lovely country lodge around every second Saturday. Menus harnessing WA produce have a seasonal focus, and the experience includes a three-course lunch. Check

the website for what's coming up and consider booking an overnight accommodation package as well (from $395).

🛏 Sleeping

Taunton Farm Holiday Park   CARAVAN PARK $
(☑1800 248 777; www.tauntonfarm.com.au; Bussell Hwy, Cowaramup; sites $45, cottages $130-160; ☎) There are plenty of farm animals for the kids to meet at one of Margaret River's best family-oriented camping grounds. For caravan and tenting buffs, the amenities blocks are spotless, and farm-style self-contained cottages are also scattered about.

Noble Grape Guesthouse   B&B $$
(☑08-9755 5538; www.noblegrape.com.au; 29 Bussell Hwy, Cowaramup; s $140-160, d $150-190; ❄☎) Noble Grape is more like an upmarket motel than a traditional B&B. Rooms offer a sense of privacy and each has a verdant little garden courtyard.

✗ Eating

Margaret River Nougat Company   SWEETS $
(☑08-9755 5539; www.margaretrivernougat.com.au; cnr Tom Cullity Dr & Miamup Rd, Cowaramup; ☺9.30am-5pm) Visit the modern lakeside tasting room for award-winning French-style nougat. Our favourite flavours are the salted caramel and liquorice. Wines can also be sampled and purchased.

Providore   DELI $
(☑08-9755 6355; www.providore.com.au; 448 Tom Cullity Dr, Wilyabrup; ☺9am-5pm) Voted one of Australia's Top 100 Gourmet Experiences by *Australian Traveller* magazine – given its amazing range of artisan produce, including organic olive oil, tapenades and preserved fruits, we can only agree. Look forward to loads of free samples.

★ Rustico at Hay Shed Hill   TAPAS $$$
(☑08-9755 6455; www.rusticotapas.com.au; 511 Harmans Mill Rd, Wilyabrup; shared plates $17-28, pizzas $27-29, degustation from $85; ☺11am-5pm) Vineyard views from Rustico's deck provide the background for a Spanish-influenced menu using the best of southwest Australian produce. Albany rock oysters are paired with Margaret River riesling, pork belly comes with Pedro Ximénez sherry, and paella is crammed with chicken from Mt Barker and local seafood. Consider a leisurely six-course degustation with wine matches from Hay Shed Hill vineyard.

MARGARET RIVER & THE SOUTHWEST COAST COWARAMUP & WILYABRUP

Vasse Felix BISTRO $$$
(☑08-9756 5050; www.vassefelix.com.au; cnr Caves Rd & Tom Cullity Dr, Cowaramup; mains $37-39, five-course menu $95; ⊙cellar door 10am-5pm, restaurant 10am-3pm) Vasse Felix winery is considered by many to have the best fine-dining restaurant in the region, the big wooden dining room reminiscent of an extremely flash barn. The grounds are peppered with sculptures, while the gallery displaying works from the Holmes à Court collection is worth a trip in itself.

Knee Deep in Margaret River BISTRO $$$
(☑08-9755 6776; www.kneedeepwines.com.au; 61 Johnson Rd, Wilyabrup; mains $34-40, 4-course menu $70; ⊙cellar door 10am-5pm, lunch noon-3pm) 🍴 Small and focused could be the motto here. Only a handful of mains are offered – crafted with locally sourced, seasonal produce – and the open-sided pavilion provides a pleasantly intimate vineyard setting. The $70 'Trust the Chef' four-course option is worth the splurge.

Cullen Wines BISTRO $$$
(☑08-9755 5656; www.cullenwines.com.au; 4323 Caves Rd, Cowaramup; mains $25-38; ⊙10am-4pm Fri-Tue) 🍴 Grapes were first planted here in 1966, and Cullen has an ongoing commitment to organic and biodynamic principles in both food and wine. Celebrating a relaxed ambience, Cullen's food is excellent, with many of the fruits and vegetables sourced from its own gardens. Booking ahead is recommended, especially on weekends.

Margaret River Chocolate Company SWEETS $
(☑08-9755 6555; www.chocolatefactory.com.au; Harman's Mill Rd; ⊙9am-5pm) Watch truffles being made and sample chocolate buttons.

🍷 Drinking & Nightlife

Stormflower Vineyard WINERY
(www.stormflower.com.au; 3503 Caves Rd, Wilyabrup; ⊙11am-5pm) A rustic, relaxed but modern alternative to some of Margaret River's more grandiose tasting rooms and formal wine estates. The compact organic vineyard is just 9 hectares, and Stormflower's cabernet shiraz is highly regarded.

Ashbrook WINERY
(☑08-9755 6262; www.ashbrookwines.com.au; 379 Tom Cullity Dr, Wilyabrup; ⊙10am-5pm) Ashbrook grows all of its grapes on-site. Its award-winning rieslings are rightly lauded.

Thompson Estate WINERY
(☑08-9755 6406; www.thompsonestate.com; 299 Tom Cullity Dr, Wilyabrup; ⊙11am-5pm Tue-Sun) A small-scale producer with an architectural-award-winning tastings and barrel room.

Margaret River
POP 4500

Although tourists usually outnumber locals, Margaret River still feels like a country town. The advantage of basing yourself here is that after 5pm, once the wineries shut up shop, it's one of the few places with any vital signs. Plus, it's close to the incredible surf of Margaret River Mouth and Southside, and the swimming beaches at Prevelly and Gracetown.

Margaret River spills over with tourists every weekend and gets very, *very* busy at Easter and Christmas (when you should book weeks, if not months, ahead). Accommodation prices tend to be cheaper midweek.

🛌 Sleeping

Wharncliffe Mill Bush Retreat GUESTHOUSE $
(☑08-9758 8227; www.wharncliffemill.com.au; McQueen Rd, Bramley National Park; sites $34, dm $25-30, safari tents & cabins $95-180; @🛜) 🍴 Set amid shaded forests and around a former timber mill, Wharncliffe has accommodation ranging from simple shared dorms to safari tents and cosy wooden cabins. Solar power and sustainable environmental practices are encouraged, and there's plenty of excellent advice on local opportunities for bushwalking and mountain biking. Margaret River township is just 2km away, and mountain bikes can be hired (half-/full-day $15/25).

Margaret River Lodge HOSTEL $
(☑08-9757 9532; www.margaretriverbackpackers.com.au; 220 Railway Tce; dm $30-32, r with/without bathroom $87/76; @🛜🏊) About 1.5km southwest of the town centre, this clean, well-run hostel has a pool, volleyball court and football field. Dorms share a big communal kitchen, and a quieter area with private rooms has its own little kitchen and lounge.

Edge of the Forest MOTEL $$
(☑08-9757 2351; www.edgeoftheforest.com.au; 25 Bussell Hwy; r $165-175; ❄🛜) Just a pleasant stroll from Margaret River township, the rooms here have stylish bathrooms and a chic Asian theme. The friendly owners have lots of local recommendations, and the leafy

shared garden is perfect for an end-of-day barbecue. The spacious front unit is a good option for families.

★ **Burnside Organic Farm**　　BUNGALOW **$$$**
(☑08-9757 2139; www.burnsideorganicfarm.com. au; 287 Burnside Rd; d $350; ❄️🐾) Welcome to the perfect private retreat after a day cruising the region's wine, beer and food highlights. Bungalows made from rammed earth and limestone have spacious decks and designer kitchens, and the surrounding farm hosts a menagerie of animals and organic orchards. Guests can pick vegetables from the garden. Minimum two-night stay.

✗ Eating

Margaret River Farmers Market　　MARKET **$**
(☑0438 905 985; www.margaretriverfarmers- market.com.au; Lot 272 Bussell Hwy, Margaret River Education Campus; ⊗8am-noon Sat) 🐾 The region's organic and sustainable artisan producers come to town every Saturday. It's a top spot for breakfast. Check the website for your own foodie hit list.

Margaret River Bakery　　CAFE **$**
(☑08-9757 2755; 89 Bussell Hwy; mains $10-18; ⊗7am-4pm Mon-Sat; 🍴) 🐾 Elvis on the stereo, retro furniture and kitsch needlework art – the MRB has a rustic, playful interior. It's the perfect backdrop to the bakery's honest homestyle baking, often with a veg or gluten-free spin. Soak up the previous day's wine tasting with terrific burgers and pies.

Swings Taphouse　　BISTRO, WINE BAR **$$**
(☑08-9758 7155; www.swings.com.au; 85 Bussell Hwy; shared plates $13-32 pizzas $22-25; ⊗7am-late) Local wine served from taps, craft beer, shared tapas plates and gourmet pizzas combine at this cosmopolitan spot at the northern end of Margaret River township. It's also a good spot for a leisurely breakfast. Try the house-smoked salmon, carrot, quinoa and orange blossom. Bloody Marys and Mimosas kick off at 10am for a restorative hair of the dog.

Larder　　DELI **$$**
(☑08-9758 8990; www.larder.biz; 2/99 Bussell Hwy; ⊗9.30am-6pm Mon-Sat, 10.30am-4pm Sun)

ACTIVE MARGARET RIVER

Much of the Margaret River experience is based around sybaritic pleasures, but to balance the virtue-vs-vice ledger, get active amid the region's stunning scenery. Surfing, swimming and walking are obvious choices, but there's also caving, diving and kayaking – to name a few.

Cape to Coast (☑0418 808 993; www.capestocoast.com.au; half-/full-day $80/160) Mountain biking, reef snorkelling and 'coasteering' – a combination of rock climbing, shore scrambling and leaping off cliffs into the ocean – all combine in these fun and active tours.

Dirty Detours (☑08-9758 8312; www.dirtydetours.com; tours $80-105) Runs guided mountain-bike rides, including through the magnificent Boranup Forest, as well as a Sip 'n' Cycle cellar-door tour. Multiday tours are also available.

Dirt Skills (☑0402 305 104; www.dirtskillsmargaretriver.com; per person $65-70; ⊗Sat) If you're serious about getting active amid Margaret River's growing mountain-biking scene, consider a training hook-up with these guys. Beginner and intermediate riders are all welcome, and if there's at least two of you, a special Trail Guiding session will help you find the region's best tracks. Bikes can also be hired.

Edge Tours (☑0413 892 036; www.edgetours.com.au; per person from $175) Rock climbing, abseiling, caving and sea kayaking.

Margaret River Climbing (☑0415 970 522; www.margaretriverclimbingco.com.au; half-/full-day $130/250) Caving, rock climbing and abseiling.

Margaret River Surf School (☑0401 616 200; www.margaretriversurfschool.com; group/individual lessons from $50/120, 3-/5-day course from $120/185) Group and individual lessons for both surfing and stand-up paddleboarding. Three- and five-day courses are the best option if you're serious about learning to surf.

Margaret River Kitesurfing & Windsurfing (☑0419 959 053; www.mrkiteandsail.com.au; 2hr for 2 people from $220) Instruction and gear rental. Lessons take place on flat and sheltered waters around Augusta and Australind or Bunbury.

Margaret River

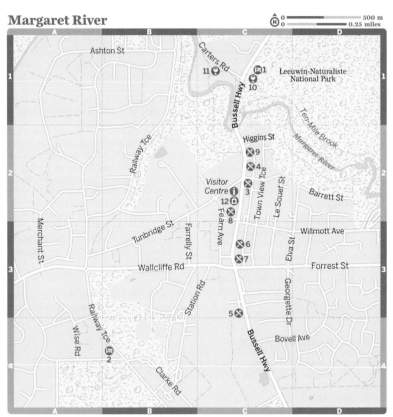

Showcasing local Margaret River produce and gourmet foods, the Larder also sells takeaway meals ($15 to $18) – a good option for dinner – and comprehensive breakfast packs, picnic hampers and barbecue fixings ($50 to $95). Occasional cooking classes complete the tasty menu.

Morries Anytime
CAFE $$

(☑08-9758 8280; www.morries.com.au; 2/149 Bussell Hwy; tapas $11-14; mains $21-34; ⊙noon-late) Settle into the clubby, cosmopolitan atmosphere of Morrie's for lunch, or come back later for cocktails and tapas or dinner. Local beers from Colonial Brewing are on tap, and the menu smartly channels both Asian and European flavours.

Settler's Tavern
PUB FOOD $$

(☑08-9757 2398; www.settlerstavern.com; 114 Bussell Hwy; mains $16-35; ⊙11am-midnight Sun-Fri, from 10am Sat) There's live entertainment

Thursday to Sunday at Settler's, so pop in for good pub grub and a beer, or choose a wine from the extensive list. Dinner options are limited in Margaret River, and Settler's is often wildly popular with locals and visitors. Try the excellent local seafood with a pint of the pub's own Great White Ale.

Miki's Open Kitchen
JAPANESE $$$

(☑08-9758 7673; www.facebook.com/mikisopenkitchen; 131 Bussell Hwy; small plates $12-17, large plates $31-36; ⊙6pm-late Tue-Sat) Secure a spot around the open kitchen and enjoy the irresistible theatre of the Miki's team creating innovative Japanese spins on the best of WA seafood and produce. Combine a Margaret River wine with the $60 multi-course tasting menu for the most diverse experience, and settle in to watch the laid-back Zen chefs work their tempura magic. Bookings recommended.

Margaret River

⭐ **Temper Temper**   SWEETS
(📞08-9757 3763; www.tempertemper.com.au;
2 Rosa Brook Rd; ⊙9am-5pm) This colourful
shrine to chocolate features a tasting area
where you can try loads of free samples
showcasing the difference between cacao
from Cuba, Venezuela, Sumatra and Madagascar, and also enticingly rich slabs with
thoroughly adult and addictive flavours like
pink peppercorn or liquorice. If you're buying souvenirs for the folks back home, you
could certainly do worse.

🍷 Drinking & Nightlife

Brewhouse   MICROBREWERY
(📞08-9757 2614; www.brewhousemargaretriver.
com.au; 35 Bussell Hwy; ⊙11am-7pm Mon-Sat,
to 10pm Sun) Finally, a craft-beer place you
can walk to from Margaret River township.
Around 900m north of town, the Brewhouse
is nestled amid karri forest with a rustic bar
and restaurant serving three guest beers
and six of its own brews. Try the Inji Pale
Ale with the chilli salt squid, and check out
live music on Sundays from 4pm.

**Margaret River
Distilling Company**   DISTILLERY
(📞08-9757 9351; www.distillery.com.au; Maxwell
St, off Carters Rd; ⊙10am-7pm) Limeburners
Single Malt whisky, Tiger Snake Sour Mash,
Great Southern Gin and White Shark Vodka
can all be sampled at this edge-of-the-forest
tasting room. There are also local beers to go
with pizzas and shared platters.

🛍 Shopping

Margaret River Artisan Store   ARTS & CRAFTS
(📞0448 733 799; www.margaretriverartisanstore.
com; 2/110 Bussell Hwy; ⊙10am-5pm Mon-Sat
& to 1pm Sun) Clothing, design and arts and
crafts all feature at this eclectic shop where
the majority of items are sourced from

local Margaret River designers, jewellers
and artists.

ℹ Information

Visitor Centre (📞08-9780 5911; www.
margaretriver.com; 100 Bussell Hwy; ⊙9am-
5pm) Bookings and information plus displays
on local wineries.

ℹ Getting Around

Margaret River Beach Bus (📞08-9757 9532;
www.margaretriverbackpackers.com.au)
Minibus linking the township and the beaches
around Prevelly ($10, three daily); summer
only, bookings essential.

Around Margaret River

West of the Margaret River township, the
coastline provides spectacular surfing and
walks. Prevelly is the main settlement, with
a few places to sleep and eat. Most of the
sights are on Caves Rd or just off it.

◉ Sights

CaveWorks & Lake Cave   CAVE
(📞08-9757 7411; www.margaretriver.com; Conto
Rd; single cave adult/child $22.50/12; ⊙9am-
5pm, Lake Cave tours hourly 9.30am-3.30pm) The
main ticket office for **Lake Cave, Mammoth Cave** (www.margaretriver.com; Caves Rd;
adult/child $22.50/12; ⊙9am-5pm) and Jewel
Cave (p141), CaveWorks also has excellent displays about caves, cave conservation
and local fossil discoveries. You'll also find
an authentic model cave and a 'cave crawl'
experience. Behind the centre is Lake Cave,
the prettiest of them all, where limestone
formations are reflected in an underground
stream. The vegetated entrance to this cave
is spectacular and includes a karri tree with
a girth of 7m.

Lake Cave is the deepest of all the caves open to the public. There are more than 300 steps down to the entrance (a 62m drop).

CaveWorks is 20km south of Margaret River, off Caves Rd. Single-cave tickets include entry to CaveWorks. The Three Cave Pass (adult/child $55/24), covering CaveWorks and all three caves, is valid for seven days.

Calgardup Cave
CAVE

(☑08-9757 7422; www.parks.dpaw.wa.gov.au; Caves Rd; adult/child $18/9; ⊙9am-4.15pm) This self-guided cave is managed by the Department of Parks and Wildlife (DPAW), which provides helmets and torches. Calgardup Cave has a seasonal underground lake and is an attractive illustration of the role of the caves in the ecosystem – a stream transports nutrients to the creatures living in the cave, while tree roots hang overhead.

Giants Cave
CAVE

(www.parks.dpaw.wa.gov.au; Caves Rd; adult/child $18/9; ⊙10am-1pm Oct-Apr & 9.30am-3.30pm during school & public holidays) This self-guided cave is managed by the Department of Parks and Wildlife (DPAW), which provides helmets and torches. Features steep ladders and scrambles.

Ellensbrook Homestead
HISTORIC BUILDING

(☑08-9755 5173; www.nationaltrust.org.au; Ellensbrook Rd; adult/child $4/2; ⊙10am-4pm Thu-Sat) Around 8km northwest of Margaret River, Ellensbrook (1857) was the first home of settlers Alfred and Ellen Bussell. The Wardandi people welcomed them, gave them Noongar names and led them to this sheltered site. The basic ramshackle house is constructed of paperbark, driftwood, timber, lime, dung and hair. Between 1899 and 1917, Edith Bussell, who farmed the property alone for many years, established an Aboriginal mission. Children were taught to read and write, and two became beneficiaries of Edith's will.

Eagles Heritage
WILDLIFE RESERVE

(☑08-9757 2960; www.eaglesheritage.com.au; 341 Boodjidup Rd; adult/child $17/10; ⊙10am-4.15pm Sat-Thu) Housing Australia's largest collection of raptors, this centre, 5km south of Margaret River, rehabilitates many birds of prey each year. There are free flight displays at 11am and 1.30pm.

🏃 Activities

Boranup Drive
SCENIC DRIVE

This 14km diversion runs along an unsealed road through Leeuwin-Naturaliste National Park's beautiful karri forest. Near the southern end there's a lookout offering sea views.

🛏 Sleeping

Llewellin's
B&B $$

(☑08-9757 9516; www.llewellinsguesthouse.com.au; 64 Yates Rd; r $218-268; 🐾) It may be a Welsh name, but the style is French provincial in the four upmarket yet homely guestrooms.

Surfpoint
GUESTHOUSE $$

(☑08-9757 1777; www.surfpoint.com.au; Reidle Dr, Gnarabup; d from $140, without bathroom from $115; @🐾🏊) This airy place offers the beach on a budget. The rooms are clean and well presented, and there's an enticing little pool. Private rooms with en suite facilities are good value, and energetic new owners have done a great job with recent renovations. Shared spaces include a very comfortable lounge and a full kitchen. Stylish apartments nearby are also available.

★Acacia Chalets
CHALET $$$

(☑08-9757 2718; www.acaciachalets.com.au; 113 Yates Rd; d $260-280; ❄) Private bushland, complete with marsupial locals, conceals three luxury chalets that are well located to explore the region's vineyards, caves and rugged nearby coastline. Limestone walls and honey-coloured jarrah floors are combined in some of the area's best self-contained accommodation. Spacious decks are equipped with gas barbecues.

🍴 Eating

Common
BISTRO $$

(☑08-9757 1586; www.thecommonbistro.com.au; 1 Resort Pl, Gnarabup; mains $18-35; ⊙4pm-late Mon-Fri, noon-late Sat & Sun) Pizza, burgers and hearty mains come with a side order of salty maritime breezes at this relaxed bistro a short walk from the surf at Gnarabup. Pair the barramundi fillet and garlic roasted potatoes with a glass of Margaret River sauvignon blanc, or settle with craft beer and cocktails on the huge outdoor deck with ocean views.

White Elephant Cafe
CAFE $$

(☑08-9757 1990; www.whiteelephantcafe.com.au; Gnarabup Rd, Gnarabup; mains $13-24; ⊙7.30am-3pm) Combining a simple pavilion and a spacious deck, White Elephant's location just metres from the cobalt waters of Gnarabup beach offers some of the best dining views around Margaret River. Wraps and burgers go well with good smoothies and juices, and the cafe is open later in summer for the best of Indian Ocean sunsets.

Watershed Premium Wines BISTRO $$$
(☑08-9758 8633; www.watershedwines.com.au; cnr Bussell Hwy & Darch Rd; cafe $18-26, restaurant $34-42; ☺10am-5pm) Famous for its 'Awakening' cabernet sauvignon, and regularly rated one of WA's best vineyard restaurants, Watershed offers dining options that include an informal cafe and a classier restaurant with expansive views of a compact lake and trellised vines.

🍷 Drinking & Nightlife

Stella Bella WINERY
(☑08-9758 5000; www.stellabella.com.au; 205 Rosabrook Rd; ☺10am-5pm) No bells and whistles, just excellent wines with the prettiest labels in the region.

Leeuwin Estate WINERY
(☑08-9759 0000; www.leeuwinestate.com.au; Stevens Rd; mains $32-45; ☺10am-5pm, dinner Sat) An impressive estate with tall trees and lawns gently rolling down to the bush, Leeuwin Estate's Art Series chardonnay is one of Australia's best. Behind-the-scenes tours, wine flights and tastings ($25 to $55) are all available and international open-air concerts are regularly held here. Don't miss visiting the downstairs gallery of excellent Australian art that has been used on Leeuwin's colourful labels.

Voyager Estate WINERY
(☑08-9757 6354; www.voyagerestate.com.au; Stevens Rd; ☺10am-5pm) The formal gardens and Cape Dutch–style buildings delight at Voyager Estate, the grandest of Margaret River's wineries. Tours of the estate are available ($35 to $200 including tastings and lunch). Tastings only start at $25 per person.

ℹ Information

National Park Information Centre (☑08-9757 7422; www.parks.dpaw.wa.gov.au; Calgardup Cave, Caves Rd; ☺9am-4.15pm)

Augusta & Around
POP 1700

Augusta is positioned at the mouth of the Blackwood River, 5km north of Cape Leeuwin, and quite separate from the main wine region. There are a few vineyards, but the vibe here is less epicurean and more languid.

◎ Sights & Activities

Operators running boat trips up the Blackwood River include **Absolutely Eco River Cruises** (☑0419 975 956; cdragon@westnet.com.au; Victoria Pde; adult/child $30/15; ☺Oct-May) and **Miss Flinders** (☑0409 377 809; Victoria Pde; adult/child $30/15; ☺Oct-May).

Cape Leeuwin Lighthouse LIGHTHOUSE
(☑08-9780 5911; www.margaretriver.com; adult/child $8/5; ☺9am-4.30pm) Wild and windy Cape Leeuwin, where the Indian and Southern Oceans meet, is the most southwesterly point in Australia. It takes its name from a Dutch ship that passed here in 1622. The lighthouse (1896), WA's tallest, offers magnificent views of the coastline. Tours leave every 40 minutes from 9am to 4.20pm (adult/child $20/13) – expect a short wait during the holiday season. The Augusta Icons Pass (adult/child $36/12) combines admission to the lighthouse with Jewel Cave.

Jewel Cave CAVE
(☑08-9780 5911; www.margaretriver.com; Caves Rd; adult/child $22.50/12; ☺tours hourly 9.30am-3.30pm) The most spectacular of the region's caves, Jewel Cave has an impressive 5.9m straw stalactite, so far the longest seen in a tourist cave. Fossil remains of a Tasmanian tiger (thylacine), believed to be 3500 years old, were discovered here. It's located near the south end of Caves Rd, 8km northwest of Augusta. The interesting interpretive galleries of the Jewel Cave Preservation Centre have been recently added. Access to the cave is by guided tours only.

Blackwood River Houseboats OUTDOORS
(☑08-9758 0181; www.blackwoodriverhouseboats.com.au; Westbay) Take care of your accommodation, river cruise and fishing trip all at once with a houseboat holiday. The houseboats are easy to drive and available for two-night/three-day hire (weekend $1000 to $1900) or for weekly hire ($2300 to $3800). A midweek rental will give you three nights for the weekend price of two nights.

Naturaliste Charters WHALE WATCHING
(☑08-9750 5500; www.whales-australia.com.au; adult/child $90/$50; ☺whale watching mid-May–Aug) 🐋 This operator runs two-hour whale-watching cruises departing Augusta. During May, the emphasis switches to an

MARGARET RIVER & THE SOUTHWEST COAST AUGUSTA & AROUND

Eco Wilderness Tour showcasing beaches and wildlife, including dolphins, New Zealand fur seals and lots of seabirds.

Sleeping

Baywatch Manor HOSTEL $
(☑08-9758 1290; www.baywatchmanor.com.au; 9 Heppingstone View; dm $8, d $130, d without bathroom $100; @❷☎) Clean, modern rooms with creamy brick walls and pieces of antique furniture. There is a bay view from the deck and, in winter, a roaring fire in the communal lounge. Some doubles have compact balconies.

Hamelin Bay Holiday Park CARAVAN PARK $
(☑08-9758 5540; www.hamelinbayholidaypark.com.au; Hamelin Bay West Rd; 2-person sites $30-49, cabins & cottages $110-300) Absolute beachfront, northwest of Augusta. This secluded place gets very busy during holiday times.

Georgiana Molloy Motel MOTEL $$
(☑08-9758 1255; www.augustasmolloymotel.com.au; 84 Blackwood Ave; r $130-140) The decor is a little dated, but the spacious, self-contained units are standout value, each with a small garden area.

✗ Eating

Colourpatch Café CAFE
(☑08-9758 1295; 38 Albany Tce; snacks & mains $10-20; ☺9am-3pm, to 7pm for takeaways) Watch the Blackwood River meet the waters of Flinders Bay at the self-styled 'last eating house before the Antarctic', which sells fish from the ocean across the road.

❶ Information

Visitor Centre (☑08-9780 5911; www.margaretriver.com; cnr Blackwood Ave & Ellis St; ☺9am-5pm) Information and bookings. Ask about seeing local wildflowers around September to November.

SOUTHERN FORESTS

The tall forests of WA's southwest are simply magnificent, with towering gums (karri, jarrah, marri) sheltering cool undergrowth. Between the forests, small towns bear witness to the region's history of logging and mining. Many have redefined themselves as small-scale tourist centres where you can take walks, wine tours, canoe trips and trout- and marron-fishing expeditions.

❶ Getting There & Away

Transwa (☑1300 662 205; www.transwa.wa.gov.au) coach routes include the following:
➡ SW1 (three weekly) to Nannup and Pemberton from East Perth, Bunbury, Busselton, Margaret River and Augusta.
➡ SW2 (three weekly) to Balingup, Bridgetown, Manjimup and Pemberton from East Perth, Mandurah and Bunbury.
➡ GS3 (daily) to Balingup, Bridgetown, Manjimup and Pemberton from Perth, Bunbury, Walpole, Denmark and Albany.

South West Coach Lines (☑08-9261 7600; www.southwestcoachlines.com.au) runs services to the following:
➡ Nannup from Busselton (twice weekdays) and Bunbury (weekdays).
➡ Balingup, Bridgetown and Manjimup from Bunbury, Mandurah and Perth (daily).

Nannup

POP 500

Nannup's historic weatherboard buildings and cottage gardens have an idyllic bush setting on the Blackwood River. The Noongar-derived name means 'a place to stop and rest'; it's also a good base for bushwalkers and canoeists.

Sporadic but persistent stories of sightings of a striped wolflike animal, dubbed the Nannup tiger, have led to hopes that a Tasmanian tiger may have survived in the surrounding bush (the last known Tasmanian tiger, or thylacine, died in Hobart Zoo in 1936).

🏃 Activities

Blackwood River Canoeing CANOEING
(☑08-9756 1209; www.blackwoodrivercanoeing.com; hire per day from $25) Trips access the largely untouched jarrah forests framing southwest Australia's longest river, and multiday expeditions incorporate overnight camping. Blackwood River Canoeing provides equipment, basic instruction and transfers for canoeing paddles and longer expeditions. The best time to paddle is in late winter and early spring, when the water levels are up.

🎉 Festivals & Events

Nannup Music Festival MUSIC
(☑08-9756 1511; www.nannupmusicfestival.org; ☺early Mar) Held in early autumn, focusing on folk and world music. Buskers are encouraged. Check the website for ride-sharing

opportunities if you don't have your own transport.

🛌 Sleeping & Eating

Holberry House   B&B **$$**
(☑08-9756 1276; www.holberryhouse.com; 14 Grange Rd; r $165-220; 🛜🏊) The decor might lean towards granny-chic, but this large house on the hill has charming hosts and comfortable rooms. It's surrounded by large gardens dotted with quirky sculptures (open to nonguests for $4).

Pickle & O   CAFE **$**
(☑08-9756 1351; 16 Warren Rd; snacks $7-12; ⊘9.30am-4pm Sun-Fri, to 3pm Sat; 🛜🏊) 🍴 Good fair-trade coffee, huge slabs of cheese-cake, and smoked trout kebab wraps are all tasty reasons to stop in at this quirky combination of health-food store and organic, sustainable cafe. An associated gift shop next door was acting as the local information office at the time of writing.

Nannup Bridge Cafe   CAFE **$$**
(☑08-9756 1287; www.facebook.com/nannupbridgecafe; 1 Warren Rd; breakfast & lunch $9-24, dinner $16-34; ⊘9am-2pm Tue-Sun, 6-8pm Thu-Sat) This riverfront cafe morphs into a bistro at night from Thursday to Saturday. Standout dishes include the pork belly and the sticky-date pudding.

Bridgetown

POP 2400

◉ Sights

Bridgedale House   HISTORIC BUILDING
(Hampton St; gold-coin donation; ⊘10am-2pm Sat & Sun) Bridgetown's old buildings include Bridgedale House, built of mud and clay by the area's first settler in 1862, and since restored by the National Trust.

🎉 Festivals & Events

Blues at Bridgetown Festival   MUSIC
(☑08-9761 2921; www.bluesatbridgetown.com.au; ⊘Nov) Blues at Bridgetown Festival is held on the second weekend of November.

🛌 Sleeping & Eating

Bridgetown Riverside Chalets   CHALET **$$**
(☑08-9761 1040; www.bridgetownchalets.com.au; 11347 Brockman Hwy; chalets from $150) On a rural riverside property, 5km up the road to Nannup, these four stand-alone wooden chalets (complete with pot-bellied stoves and washing machines) sleep up to six in two bedrooms.

Barking Cow   CAFE **$$**
(☑08-9761 4619; 88 Hampton St; breakfast $11-18, lunch $13-21; ⊘8am-2.30pm Mon-Sat; 🖉) Colourful, cosy, and serving the best coffee in town, the Barking Cow is also worth stopping at for daily vegetarian specials and world-famous-in-Bridgetown gourmet burgers.

Cidery   CAFE **$$**
(☑08-9761 2204; www.thecidery.com.au; 43 Gifford Rd; mains $10-25; ⊘11am-4pm Sat-Thu, to 8pm Fri) Craft beer from the Blackwood Valley Brewing Company, cider and light lunches are all enjoyed on outdoor tables. On Friday nights from 5.30pm there's live music. Try the easy-drinking mid-strength Summer Ale.

ℹ Information

Visitor Centre (☑08-9761 1740; www.bridgetown.com.au; 154 Hampton St; ⊘9am-5pm Mon-Fri, 10am-3pm Sat, 10am-1pm Sun) Includes apple-harvesting memorabilia and a surprisingly interesting display of jigsaws from around the world in the attached heritage museum.

Manjimup

POP 4300

Surrounded by spectacular forest, Manjimup is at the heart of WA's timber industry. For foodies it's known for something very different: truffles. During August especially, Manjimup's black Périgord truffles make their way onto top Australian menus.

◉ Sights

★**Truffle & Wine Co**   FARM
(☑08-9777 2474; www.truffleandwine.com.au; Seven Day Rd; ⊘10am-4pm, cafe 11am-3pm) To discover how the world's most expensive produce is harvested, follow your snout to the Truffle & Wine Co. Join a 2½-hour truffle hunt with the clever truffle-hunting Labradors from Friday to Sunday from June to August (adult/child $90/81; definitely book ahead). Throughout the year there are plenty of truffle products to sample, and the attached provedore and cafe serves up tasting plates ($10 to $15) and truffle-laced mains ($25 to $40), including seafood ravioli and mushroom risotto.

Four Aces
FOREST

(Graphite Rd) These four 300-plus-year-old karri trees sit in a straight line; stand directly in front and they disappear into one. There's a short loop walk through the surrounding karri glade, or a 1½-hour loop bushwalking trail from the Four Aces to One Tree Bridge.

Diamond Tree Lookout
VIEWPOINT

Nine kilometres south of Manjimup along the South Western Hwy is the Diamond Tree Lookout. Metal spikes allow you to climb this 52m karri, and there's a nature trail nearby.

Sleeping

Diamond Forest Cottages
COTTAGE $$

(☑08-9772 3170; www.diamondforest.com.au; 29159 South Western Hwy; chalets $180-220; ❄️🛜) South of Manjimup, before the turn-off to Pemberton, is this collection of well-equipped wooden chalets with decks, scattered around a farm. Turkeys and sheep wander around, and it has a petting zoo and daily animal-feeding for the kids. Sunday to Thursday stays offer the best rates.

✕ Eating

★ Tall Timbers
BISTRO $$

(☑08-9777 2052; www.talltimbersmanjimup.com. au; 88 Giblett St; tapas $10-19, mains $19-44; ⊘9am-10pm Mon-Fri, from 8am Sat & Sun) Tall Timbers' upscale pub food stretches from gourmet burgers to confit duck, but its real point of difference is wines from all southwest Australia. More than 40 wines are available, many from boutique vineyards that don't have cellar doors, and a special dispensing system allows visitors to purchase samples from just 25ml and pair them with tapas or cheese platters.

ⓘ Information

Visitor Centre (☑08-9771 1831; www. manjimupwa.com; Giblett St; ⊘9am-5pm) Located in Manjim Park and offering accommodation and transport bookings.

Pemberton

POP 760

Hidden deep in the karri forests, drowsy Pemberton produces excellent wine. If Margaret River is WA's Bordeaux, Pemberton is its Burgundy – producing excellent chardonnay and pinot noir, among other varietals.

Wine tourism isn't as developed here, with some of the better names only offering tastings by appointment. Grab a free map listing cellar-door opening hours from the visitor centre (p146).

The national parks circling Pemberton are impressive. Aim to spend a day or two driving the well-marked Karri Forest Explorer tracks, walking the trails and picnicking in the green depths.

⊙ Sights

Big Brook Arboretum
NATURE RESERVE

FREE Showcase of big trees from all around the world. Pick up a Karri Forest Explorer map from the Pemberton visitor centre.

Fine Woodcraft Gallery
ARTS CENTRE

(☑08-9776 1741; www.facebook.com/ PembertonFineWoodcraftGallery; Dickinson St; ⊘9am-5pm) In lush gardens, the Fine Woodcraft Gallery has truly beautiful pieces, all mastercrafted from salvaged timber. It also has a good cafe offering hearty breakfasts and lunches and the opportunity to purchase house-made smoked meats and charcuterie from Pemberton's Holy Smoke. Try the excellent tasting platter for $32.

✹ Activities

Pemberton Tramway
RAIL

(☑08-9776 1322; www.pemtram.com.au; adult/child $28/14; ⊘10.45am & 2pm Mon-Sat; 👪) Built between 1929 and 1933, the tram route travels through lush karri and marri forests to Warren River. A commentary is provided and it's a fun – if noisy – 1¾-hour return trip.

Pemberton Pool
SWIMMING

(Swimming Pool Rd) **FREE** Surrounded by karri trees, this natural pool is popular on a hot day – despite the warning sign (currents, venomous snakes). They breed them tough around here. Nearby is the trailhead for tracks making up the Pemberton Mountain Bike Park (p144).

Pemberton
Mountain Bike Park
MOUNTAIN BIKING

(www.pembertonvisitor.com.au/pages/pemberton-mountain-bike-park) Nearby Pemberton Pool (p144) is the trailhead for tracks making up the Pemberton Mountain Bike Park. Trail maps can be downloaded off the website.

Pemberton Wine Centre　WINE

(☑08-9776 1211; www.pembertonwine.com.au; 388 Old Vasse Rd; ☺noon-5pm) At the very heart of Warren National Park, this centre offers tastings of local wines and can compile a mixed case of your favourites.

Mountford　WINE

(☑08-9776 1345; www.mountfordwines.com.au; Bamess Rd; ☺10am-4pm) 🌿 The wines and ciders produced here are all certified organic, plus there's a gallery on-site. It's located north of Pemberton and is easily incorporated into the Karri Forest Explorer circuit.

🖝 Tours

**Pemberton Hiking
& Canoeing**　HIKING, CANOEING

(☑08-9776 1559; www.hikingandcanoeing.com.au; half-/full-day $50/100) 🌿 Environmentally sound tours in Warren and D'Entrecasteaux National Parks and to the Yeagarup sand dunes. Specialist tours (wildflowers, frogs, rare fauna) are also available, as are night canoeing trips ($50) to spot nocturnal wildlife.

Donnelly River Cruises　BOATING

(☑08-9777 1018; www.donnellyrivercruises.com.au; adult/child $65/35) 🌿 Cruises through 12km of D'Entrecasteaux National Park to the cliffs of the Southern Ocean.

**Pemberton Discovery
Tours**　TOURS, MOUNTAIN BIKING

(☑08-9776 0484; www.pembertondiscoverytours.com.au; 12 Brockman St; adult/child $155/55; ☺10am-5pm Mon-Sat, to 2pm Sun) 🌿 Half-day 4WD tours to the Yeagarup sand dunes and the Warren River mouth. Other tours focus on local vineyards, breweries and cideries, and the wild coastal scenery of D'Entrecasteaux National Park. Visit its central Pemberton location for local information and mountain-bike hire, including details of nearby tracks and recommended rides.

🛏 Sleeping

Pemberton Backpackers YHA　HOSTEL $

(☑08-9776 1105; www.yha.com.au; 7 Brockman St; dm/s/d $33/70/77; @☎) The main hostel in Pemberton's main street is given over to seasonal workers, but you'll need to check in there for a room in the separate cottage (8 Dean St) that's set aside for travellers. It's cute and cosy, but book ahead as it only has three rooms, one of which is a six-person dorm.

Best Western Pemberton Hotel　HOTEL $$

(☑08-9776 1017; www.pembertonhotel.bestwestern.com.au; 66 Brockman St; r from $150; ☎) Attached to a classic country pub, the comfortable accommodation occupies a striking extension of rammed earth and cedar. The pub's friendly bistro is the best place for an evening meal in town.

Marima Cottages　COTTAGE $$

(☑08-9776 1211; www.marima.com.au; 388 Old Vasse Rd; cottages $200-225) Right in the middle of Warren National Park, these four country-style rammed-earth-and-cedar cottages with pot-bellied stoves and lots of privacy are luxurious getaways. Look forward to marsupial company at dusk.

Pump Hill Farm Cottages　COTTAGE $$

(☑08-9776 1379; www.pumphill.com.au; Pump Hill Rd; cottages $150-205; ☎) Families love this farm property, where kids are taken on a daily hay ride to feed the animals. Child-free folk will enjoy the ambience of the private, well-equipped cottages too.

**Old Picture Theatre
Holiday Apartments**　APARTMENT $$

(☑08-9776 1513; www.oldpicturetheatre.com.au; cnr Ellis & Guppy Sts; apt $170-210; ❈☎) The town's old cinema has been revamped into well-appointed, self-contained, spacious apartments with lots of jarrah detail and black-and-white movie photos. It offers good value for money and includes an on-site spa.

Foragers　COTTAGE $$$

(☑08-9776 1580; www.foragers.com.au; cnr Roberts & Northcliffe Rds; cottages $270-290; ❈) Choose between very nice, simple karri cottages, or leap to the top of the ladder with the luxury eco-chalets. The latter are light and airy, with elegant, contemporary decor, eco-conscious waste-water systems and a solar-passive design. You're also right on hand to enjoy culinary treats at the adjacent Foragers Field Kitchen (p146).

🍴 Eating & Drinking

Millhouse Cafe　CAFE $$

(☑08-9776 1776; www.facebook.com/Pembertonmillhousetearooms; 14 Brockman St; breakfast $10-21, lunch $10-16; ☺8am-4pm) Now under new management, this cafe is situated in a cosy heritage cottage with wraparound verandahs and provides good coffee and surprising spins on breakfast. Regular marron specials and trout are on offer for lunch, and local art is displayed on the walls. On Thursdays, Thai meals ($19 to $22) are often available in the cafe until 3pm and for take-away until 6pm.

Foragers Field Kitchen INTERNATIONAL $$$
(☑08-9776 1580; www.foragers.com.au; cnr Roberts & Northcliffe Rds; dinner $80, cooking classes $85; ☺dinner 7pm Sat) 🍴 Join renowned chef Sophie Zalokar at one of her regular four-course Saturday-night set dinners – menus always include seasonal and local southwest WA produce – or sign up for one of her monthly cooking classes (usually on a Friday night). Check the website's events calendar for dates. Booking at least 48 hours ahead is preferred.

Jarrah Jacks CRAFT BEER
(☑08-9776 1333; www.jarrahjacks.com.au; Lot 2 Kemp Rd; ☺11am-5pm Thu-Sun) Reopened under new ownership, this craft brewery features vineyard views, six craft beers and tasty locally sourced food from a seasonal menu. Try the Swinging Axe Ale, a robust 6% Red Ale, or take it easy with the mid strength 2.9% Arthur's Hop Ale. Sampling trays are also available for hoppy variety, and you can also try wines from Pemberton's Woodsmoke Estate.

ⓘ Information

Visitor Centre (☑08-9776 1133; www.pembertonvisitor.com.au; Brockman St; ☺9am-4pm) Includes a pioneer museum and karri-forest discovery centre.

Department of Parks & Wildlife (☑08-9776 1207; www.dpaw.wa.gov.au; Kennedy St; ☺9am-4.30pm) Information on local parks and bushwalks. Ask about the latest situation in Shannon National Park following the 2015 bushfires.

Shannon National Park

The 535-sq-km **Shannon National Park** (entry per car/motorcycle $12/6) is on the South Western Hwy, 53km south of Manjimup. Until 1968 Shannon was the site of WA's biggest timber mill. Areas of this park were badly damaged by forest fires in 2015, and at the time of writing access to the park was not possible. Check with the Department of Parks & Wildlife online or in Pemberton on the current situation.

🏃 Activities

The 48km **Great Forest Trees Drive** is a one-way loop, split by the highway. Start at the park day-use area on the north of the highway. From here there's an easy 3.5km walk to the Shannon Dam and a steeper 5.5km loop to Mokare's Rock, with a boardwalk and great views.

Further along, the 8km (return) Great Forest Trees Walk crosses the Shannon River. Off the southern part of the drive, boardwalks look over stands of giant karri at **Snake Gully** and **Big Tree Grove**.

In the park's southwest, a 6km (return) walking track links Boorara Tree with a lookout point over Lane Poole Falls.

🛏 Sleeping

Shannon National Park Campground CAMPGROUND $
(www.parks.dpaw.wa.gov.au; sites per adult/child $10/6.60) There is a sizeable camping ground with showers in the spot where the original timber-milling town used to be. Following the fires in 2015 it was closed for redevelopment. Check with Department of Parks & Wildlife (p146) in Pemberton on the current status.

Southern Western Australia

POP 55,000

Best Places to Eat

➡ Kirby's at Rickety Gate (p152)

➡ Maleeya's Thai Cafe (p158)

➡ Pepper & Salt (p152)

➡ Boston Brewery (p152)

➡ Fish Face (p163)

Best Places to Sleep

➡ Cape Howe Cottages (p151)

➡ Beach House at Bayside (p155)

➡ Esperance B&B by the Sea (p163)

➡ Lily (p159)

➡ 1849 Backpackers (p155)

Why Go?

Standing above the waves and cliffs of the rugged south coast is an exhilarating experience. And on calm days, when the sea is aquamarine and white-sand beaches lie pristine and welcoming, it's a different type of magnificent. Even busy summer holiday periods in the Great Southern are relaxed. It's just that bit too far from Perth for the holiday hordes. Winter months bring pods of migrating whales, while the spectacular tingle trees of Walpole's Valley of the Giants are more super-sized evidence of nature's wonder.

For a change from the great outdoors, Albany – the state's earliest European settlement – has colonial and Anzac history, and Denmark has excellent wine, craft beer and good food. Inland, the peaks and plains of Stirling National Park are enlivened by wildflowers from September to November, while orca visit remote Bremer Bay from February to April.

Further west, Esperance is the gateway to stunning coastal scenery.

When to Go

Esperance

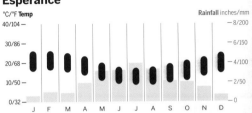

Jan The best beach weather – and it's not as hot or crowded as the west coast.

Sep Go wild for wildflowers and whales.

Dec Perfect weather for the Stirling Range and Porongurup National Parks.

Southern Western Australia Highlights

1 Walking among and above the giant tingle trees in the **Valley of the Giants** (p149) Tree Top Walk.

2 Competing to see who can spot the most whales in (p154) in Albany, from where soldiers departed for WWI.

3 Understanding the sacrifices made by brave soldiers 100 years ago at the **National Anzac Centre**

Albany's **King George Sound** (p155).

4 Hiking among the tall trees and spectacular granite outcrops of **Porongurup National Park** (p158).

5 Wandering through wild flowers in **Fitzgerald River National Park** (p159).

6 Feeling exhilarated on an exciting boat trip to see orcas in **Bremer Bay** (p160).

7 Swimming, surfing and soaking up the sun on the squeaky-clean beaches of **Cape Le Grand National Park** (p164).

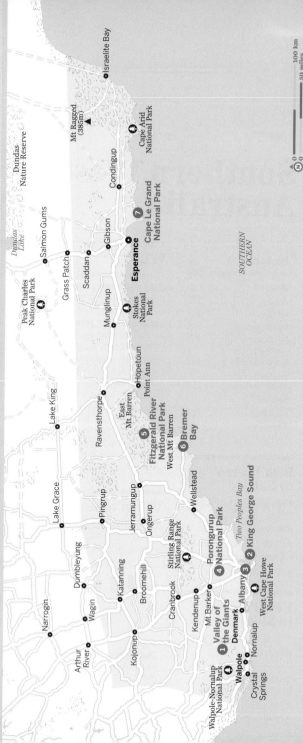

Walpole & Nornalup

POP 320 & 50

The peaceful twin inlets of Walpole (population 320) and Nornalup (population 50) make good bases from which to explore the heavily forested Walpole Wilderness Area – an immense wilderness incorporating a rugged coastline, several national parks, marine parks, nature reserves and forest conservation areas – covering a whopping 3630 sq km. Walpole is the bigger settlement, and it's here that the South Western Hwy (Rte 1) becomes the South Coast Hwy.

◉ Sights

Walpole-Nornalup National Park   NATIONAL PARK

(www.parks.dpaw.wa.gov.au) Giant trees include red, yellow and Rate's tingles (all types of eucalypt, or gum, trees). Good walking tracks include a section of the Bibbulmun Track, which passes through Walpole to Coalmine Beach. Scenic drives include the Knoll Drive, 3km east of Walpole; the Valley of the Giants Rd; and through pastoral country to Mt Frankland, 29km north of Walpole. Here you can climb to the summit for panoramic views or walk around the trail at its base.

Opposite Knoll Drive, Hilltop Rd leads to a giant tingle tree; this road continues to the Circular Pool on the Frankland River, a popular canoeing spot. You can hire canoes from Nornalup Riverside Chalets.

★Valley of the Giants   NATURE RESERVE

(☑08-9840 8263; www.valleyofthegiants.com.au; Valley of the Giants Rd; Tree Top Walk adult/child $21/10.50; ⊗9am-5pm) In the Valley of the Giants is the spectacular Tree Top Walk. A 600m-long ramp rises from the valley, allowing visitors access high into the canopy of the giant tingle trees. At its highest point, the ramp is 40m above the ground. It's on a gentle incline so it's easy to walk and is accessible by assisted wheelchair. At ground level, the Ancient Empire boardwalk (admission free) meanders through veteran red tingles, up to 16m in circumference and 46m high.

Conspicuous Cliffs   LANDMARK

Midway between Nornalup and Peaceful Bay, Conspicuous Cliffs is a good spot for whale-watching from July to November. It features a hilltop lookout and a steepish 800m walk to the beach.

⛵ Tours

★WOW Wilderness Ecocruises   CRUISE

(☑08-9840 1036; www.wowwilderness.com.au; adult/child $45/15) The magnificent landscape and its ecology are brought to life with anecdotes about Aboriginal settlement, salmon fishers and shipwrecked pirates. The 2½-hour cruise through the inlets and river systems leaves at 10am daily; book at the visitor centre (p150).

Naturally Walpole Eco Tours   ECOTOUR

(☑08-9840 1111; Walpole Visitor Centre) Half-day tours exploring the Walpole Wilderness (adult/child $70/35) and the Tree Top Walk ($80/40).

🛏 Sleeping

As well as hostels, campgrounds and chalets, there are bush camping sites in the Walpole Wilderness Area, including at Crystal Springs and Fernhook Falls.

Tingle All Over YHA   HOSTEL $

(☑08-9840 1041; www.yha.com.au; 60 Nockolds St, Walpole; dm/s/d $31/54/74; @🛜) Help yourself to lemons and chillies from the garden of this clean, basic option near the highway. Lots of advice on local walks is on offer and the owners are super-friendly.

Rest Point Holiday Village   CARAVAN PARK $

(☑08-9840 1032; www.restpoint.com.au; Rest Point; 2-person sites $32, cabins $115-140) Set on wide lawns with direct water frontage, this spacious holiday park has shade for campers and a range of self-contained accommodation.

Walpole Lodge   HOSTEL $

(☑08-9840 1244; www.walpolelodge.com.au; Pier St, Walpole; dm/s $27/45, d $65-90; @🛜) This popular place is basic, open plan and informal, with great info boards and casual, cheery owners. En-suite rooms are excellent value.

Nornalup Riverside Chalets   CHALET $$

(☑08-9840 1107; www.nornalupriversidechalets.com.au; Riverside Dr, Nornalup; chalets $115-190) Stay a night in sleepy Nornalup in these comfortable, colourful self-contained chalets, just a rod's throw from the fish in the Frankland River. The chalets are well spaced out, giving a feeling of privacy.

Riverside Retreat   CHALET $$

(☑08-9840 1255; www.riversideretreat.com.au; South Coast Hwy, Nornalup; chalets $150-210) On the banks of the beautiful Frankland River, these well-equipped chalets are great value, with pot-bellied stoves for cosy winter warmth, and tennis and canoeing as outdoor pursuits. Expect frequent visits from the local wildlife.

✗ Eating

Nornabar   BISTRO $$
(☑08-9840 1407; 6684 South Coast Hwy; tapas $10-13, mains $23-34; ☺8am-late Wed-Sat & 8am-3pm Tue & Sun) Nornalup's former tearooms have been reborn as a light, sunny bar and cafe soundtracked with cool jazz and enlivened by colourful local art. There's a concise selection of local Great Southern wines available, and the menu stretches from chicken, ricotta and tarragon meatballs to a delicate salad of poached WA tiger prawns. A compact beer garden completes a versatile offering.

Top Deck Cafe   CAFE $$
(25 Nockolds St, Walpole; mains $15-27; ☺9am-2pm & 5.30-9pm; 🛜) Tucked away in Walpole's main road, Top Deck kicks off with breakfast, and graduates to dinner options, including spinach-and-feta pie and a daily curry special. Booking for dinner is recommended to check they'll be open.

Thurlby Herb Farm   CAFE $$
(☑08-9840 1249; www.thurlbyherb.com.au; 3 Gardiner Rd; snacks & mains $8-24; ☺9am-5pm Mon-Fri) Thurlby offers light lunches and cakes accompanied by fresh-picked herbal teas, as well as other herb-based products including soap and aromatherapy treatments. It's north of Walpole on the way to Mt Frankland National Park.

ℹ Information

Visitor Centre (☑08-9840 1111; www.walpole. com.au; South Coast Hwy, Walpole; ☺9am-5pm) In the Pioneer Cottage.

THE ROAD TO MANDALAY

About 13km west of Walpole, at Crystal Springs, is an 8km gravel road to **Mandalay Beach**, where the *Mandalay*, a Norwegian barque, was wrecked in 1911. The wreck eerily appears every 10 years or so after storms. See the photos at Walpole **visitor centre**. The beach is glorious, often deserted, and accessed by a boardwalk across sand dunes and cliffs. It's part of D'Entrecasteaux National Park.

ℹ Getting There & Away

Departing from the visitor centre, **Transwa** (☑1300 662 205; www.transwa.wa.gov.au) bus GS3 heads daily to/from Bunbury ($47, 4½ hours), Bridgetown ($26.50, 3¼ hours), Pemberton ($20.50, 1¾ hours), Denmark ($14.45, 42 minutes) and Albany ($23, 1½ hours).

Denmark

POP 2800

Denmark's beaches and coastline, river and sheltered inlet, forested backdrop and hinterland have attracted a varied, creative and environmentally aware community. Farmers, ferals, fishers and families all mingle during the town's four market days each year.

Denmark was established to supply timber to the early goldfields. Known by the Minang Noongar people as Koorabup (place of the black swan), there's evidence of early Aboriginal settlement in the 3000-year-old fish traps found in Wilson Inlet.

◉ Sights & Activities

Surfing & Fishing

Surfers and anglers should head to ruggedly beautiful **Ocean Beach**. Accredited local instructor Mike Neunuebel gives surfing lessons (p150).

Surf Lessons   SURFING
(☑0401 349 854; www.southcoastsurfinglessons. com.au; 2hr lessons incl equipment from $60) Surfing lessons from Mike Neunuebel on Ocean Beach. October to June is the best time to learn.

Walking

To get your bearings, walk the **Mokare Heritage Trail** (a 3km circuit along the Denmark River), or the **Wilson Inlet Trail** (12km return, starting at the river mouth), which forms part of the longer **Nornalup Trail**. The **Mt Shadforth Lookout** has fine coastal views, and lush **Mt Shadforth Rd**, running from town to the South Coast Hwy west of town, makes a great scenic drive. A longer pastoral loop is via **Scotsdale Rd**. Attractions include alpaca farms, wineries, dairy farms, and arts-and-crafts galleries.

Swimming

William Bay National Park, about 20km west of town, offers sheltered swimming in gorgeous **Greens Pool** and **Elephant Rocks**, and has good walking tracks. Swing by **Bartholomews Meadery** (☑08-9840 9349; www.honeywine.com.au; 2620 South Coast Hwy; ice cream from $5; ☺9.30am-4.30pm) for a post-beach treat of mead (honey wine) or delicious home-made honey-rose-almond ice cream ($5).

🕝 Tours

Poornati Aboriginal Tours CULTURAL
(☑0415 840 216, 0412 786 588; www.poornati. com.au; adult/child $150/60) Day tours focus on the Noongar Indigenous cultural history of Kinjarling (Albany) and Kwoorabup (Denmark) and include foraging and tasting bush tucker, as well as local art and traditional song and dance. Vibrational healing day tours are also available, incorporating ancient Noongar healing techniques.

Denmark Wine Lovers Tour WINE
(☑0427 482 400; www.denmarkwinelovers. com.au; half-/full-day per person from $70/88) Full-day and half-day tours taking in Denmark wineries or heading further afield to Porongurup or Mt Barker. Check out the website to see which vineyards can be included in the mix. Ice cream and craft beer can also be included as stops on Denmark tours.

🎉 Festivals & Events

Market Days FAIR
(www.denmarkarts.com.au) Four times a year (mid-December, early and late January and Easter) Denmark hosts riverside market days with craft stalls, music and food.

Festival of Voice MUSIC
(www.denmarkfestivalofvoice.com.au; ☺Jun) Performances and workshops on the WA Day long weekend, which incorporates the first Monday in June.

🛏 Sleeping

Blue Wren Travellers' Rest YHA HOSTEL $
(☑08-9848 3300; www.denmarkbluewren.com. au; 17 Price St; dm/d/f $40/100/135) Great info panels cover the walls, and it's small enough (just 20 beds) to have a homey feel. Bikes can also be rented – $20 per day – and the friendly new owner is an affable South African who reckons Denmark is a great place to call home.

Denmark Rivermouth
Caravan Park CARAVAN PARK $
(☑08-9848 1262; www.denmarkrivermouthcara-vanpark.com.au; Inlet Dr; 2-person sites $34, cabins

& chalets $135-210) Ideally located for nautical pursuits, this caravan park sits along Wilson Inlet beside the boat ramp. Some of the units are properly flash, although they are quite tightly arranged. It also has a kids' playground and kayaks for hire. Look forward to pelicans cruising the nearby estuary most afternoons.

31 on the Terrace BOUTIQUE HOTEL $$
(☑08-9848 1700; www.denmarkaccommodation. com.au; 31 Strickland St; r $85-175; ❋) Good-value, stylish en-suite rooms – some with balconies – fill this renovated corner pub in the centre of town. Compact apartments sleep up to five people.

★**Cape Howe Cottages** COTTAGE $$$
(☑08-9845 1295; www.capehowe.com.au; 322 Tennessee Rd S; cottages $180-290; ❋) For a remote getaway, these five cottages in bushland southeast of Denmark really make the grade. They're all different, but the best is only 1.5km from dolphin-favoured Lowlands Beach and is properly plush – with a BBQ on the deck, a dishwasher in the kitchen and laundry facilities.

Celestine Retreat CHALET $$$
(☑08-9848 3000; www.celestineretreat.com; 413 Mt Shadforth Rd; d $239-289; ❋) With just four spa chalets scattered over 13 hectares, there are stunning ocean and valley views at this luxury retreat. Romance is also on the agenda, with private spas, fluffy bathrobes and high-end bathroom goodies. There is usually a two-night stay minimum.

🍴 Eating

Denmark Bakery BAKERY $
(☑08-9848 2143; www.denmarkbakery.com.au; Strickland St; pies $6-8; ☺7am-5pm) Prize-winning pies lauded across WA. Try the spicy Vinda-Roo with everyone's favourite marsupial given a spicy subcontinental spin.

Mrs Jones CAFE $$
(☑0467 481 878; www.mrsjonescafe.com.au; 12 Mt Shadforth Rd; mains $12-19; ☺7am-4pm) Denmark's best coffee is at this spacious spot with high ceilings and exposed beams. Settle in with locals and tourists for interesting cafe fare, often with an Asian or Mediterranean spin. Try the hearty *shakshuka* baked eggs for breakfast or the robust harissa-spiced lamb burger for lunch. There's a good selection of vegan and gluten free menu options.

★**Kirby's at**
Rickety Gate   MODERN AUSTRALIAN $$$
(☑08-9840 9967; www.ricketygateestate.com.au; 1949 Scotsdale Rd; 2/3 courses $70/80; ☺noon-4pm Sat & Sun & 6.30-10pm 1st Sat of month) Our pick of the vineyard restaurants along Scotsdale Rd's easygoing rural loop, Kirby's offers lunches on Saturday and Sunday afternoons and Saturday dinner once a month. The menu changes with the seasons, but could include slow-braised beef cheek or chicken breast wrapped in pancetta. Booking ahead is recommended, and wines from the adjacent Rickety Gate Estate are also available.

★**Pepper & Salt**   MODERN AUSTRALIAN, ASIAN $$$
(☑08-9848 3053; www.pepperandsalt.com.au; 1564 South Coast Hwy, Forest Hill Vineyard; mains $39-44; ☺noon-3pm Thu-Sun, from 6pm Fri) With his Fijian-Indian heritage, chef Silas Masih's knowledge of spices and herbs is wonderfully showcased in his fresh and vibrant food. Highlights include king prawns with chilli popcorn and lime mayonnaise, or the excellent tapas platter ($69), which effortlessly detours from Asia to the Middle East. Bookings essential.

🍸 **Drinking & Nightlife**

★**Boston Brewery**   CRAFT BEER
(☑08-9848 1555; www.willoughbypark.com.au; Willoughby Park Winery, South Coast Hwy; pizzas $17-18, mains $25-38; ☺10am-7pm Mon-Thu, to 10pm Fri & Sat, to 9pm Sun) The industrial chic of the brewery gives way to an absolute edge-of-vineyard location, where wood-fired pizzas, meals and bar snacks go well with Boston's core portfolio of seven beers. The Willoughby Park Winery is also on site, and there's live music from 4pm to 8pm every second Saturday. See if any seasonal brews are available.

Denmark Tavern   PUB
(☑08-9848 1084; www.thedenmarktavern.com.au; 135 South Coast Hwy; ☺10.30am-late Mon-Sat, from 11am-10pm) Excellent pub food (mains $22 to $38), including great local seafood, and some of Western Australia's best craft brews, with beers from Denmark-based Artisan Brewing often on tap. The Denmark Tavern is around 1km west of central Denmark.

Howard Park   WINERY
(☑08-9848 2345; www.burchfamilywines.com.au; Scotsdale Rd; ☺10am-4pm) Excellent Great Southern winery located in a pleasant rural location along Scotsdale Rd.

Forest Hill   WINERY
(☑08-9848 2399; www.foresthillwines.com.au; cnr South Coast Hwy & Myers Rd; ☺10.30am-5pm Thu-Sun) Hosts the excellent Pepper & Salt (p152) restaurant.

ℹ **Information**

Visitor Centre (☑08-9848 2055; www.denmark.com.au; 73 South Coast Hwy; ☺9am-5pm) Information, accommodation bookings, and a display on the local wine scene. Bikes (half/full day $22/33) and body boards can also be hired of you're feeling active.

ℹ **Getting There & Away**

Transwa (☑1300 662 205; www.transwa.wa.gov.au; Holling Rd) Transwa bus service GS3 heads daily to/from Bunbury ($53, 5½ hours), Bridgetown ($35, 4¾ hours), Pemberton ($29, 2¾ hours), Walpole ($14, 42 minutes) and Albany ($10, 42 minutes).

Albany
POP 37,233
Established shortly before Perth in 1826, the oldest European settlement in the state is now the bustling commercial centre of the southern region. Albany is a mixed bag comprising a stately and genteel decaying colonial quarter, a waterfront in the midst of sophisticated redevelopment and a hectic sprawl of malls and fast-food joints. Less ambivalent is its spectacular coastline, from Torndirrup National Park's surf-pummelled cliffs to Middleton Beach's white sands and the calm waters of King George Sound.

The town is in an area that's seen the violence of weather and whaling. Whales are still a part of the Albany experience, but these days are hunted with a camera lens.

The Bibbulmun Track (p155) ends (or starts) here, just outside the visitor centre.

History
The Minang Noongar people called this place Kinjarling (the place of rain) and believed that fighting Wargals (mystical giant serpents) created the fractured landscape.

Initial contacts with Europeans were friendly, with over 60 ships visiting between 1622 and 1826. The establishment of a British settlement was welcomed as it regulated the behaviour of sealers and whalers, who had been kidnapping, raping and murdering Minang people. Yet by the end of the

Albany

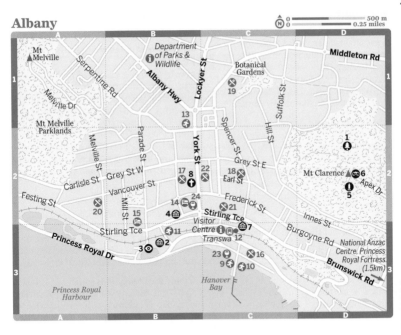

Albany

⊙ Sights
1 Albany Heritage Park	D2
2 Albany Residency Museum	B3
3 Brig Amity	B3
4 Courthouse	B2
5 Desert Mounted Corps Memorial	D2
6 Mt Clarence	D2
7 Old Post Office	C3
8 St John's Anglican Church	B2
Western Australian Museum – Albany	(see 2)

⊙ Activities, Courses & Tours
9 Albany Ocean Adventures	C3
10 Albany Whale Tours	C3
11 Alkoomi Wines	B3
12 Busy Blue Bus	C3
13 Southcoast Diving Supplies	B1

⊜ Sleeping
14 1849 Backpackers	B2
15 Albany Harbourside	B2

⊗ Eating
16 Albany Boatshed Markets	C3
17 Albany Farmers Market	B2
18 Earl of Spencer	C2
19 Lime 303	C1
20 Vancouver Street Cafe	A2
21 White Star Hotel	C2
22 York Street Cafe	C2

⊕ Drinking & Nightlife
23 Due South	C3
24 Liberté	B2

19th century, every shop in Albany refused entry to Aboriginal people, and their control over every aspect of their lives (including the right to bring up their own children) had been lost.

For the British, Albany's raison d'être was its sheltered harbour, which made it a whaling port right up to 1978. During WWI it was the mustering point for transport ships for Australian and New Zealand Army Corps (Anzac) troops heading for Egypt and the Gallipoli campaign.

In late 2014, Albany commemorated the centenary of the departure of over 40,000 Anzac soldiers to the Great War, and the opening of the National Anzac Centre has seen the city develop into an important destination for travellers interested in WWI history.

◉ Sights

Albany Heritage Park   PARK
(www.nationalanzaccentre.com.au/visit/alba-ny-heritage-park) Inaugurated in 2014, the Albany Heritage Park incorporates the National Anzac Centre, Princess Royal Fortress, Padre White Lookout, Desert Mounted Corps Memorial and the Ataturk Memorial.

★ National Anzac Centre   MUSEUM
(☑ 08-6820 3500; www.nationalanzaccentre.com.au; 67 Forts Rd, Albany Heritage Park; adult/child $24/10; ☺ 9am-5pm) Opened for Albany's Anzac centenary commemorations in late 2014, this superb museum remembers the men and women who left by convoy from Albany to fight in WWI. Excellent multimedia installations provide realism and depth to the exhibitions, and there is a profound melancholy in the museum's location overlooking the same expansive body of water the troop ships left from.

Visitors are assigned one of 32 photographs remembering actual soldiers and nurses upon entry – including a German soldier and a Turkish soldier – and they can then follow their life story on interactive installations. The exact fate of each of the people in the 32 photographs is poignantly not revealed until the final stages of the museum.

Princess Royal Fortress   HISTORIC SITE
(Forts Rd; incl with entry to National Anzac Centre; ☺ 9am-5pm) As a strategic port, Albany was historically regarded as being vulnerable to attack. Built in 1893 on Mt Adelaide, this fort was initially constructed as a defence against potential attacks from the Russians and French, and the restored buildings, gun emplacements and views are very interesting. From the fortress take the Convoy Walk for excellent views of King George Sound and signage showing where each ship was anchored before its departure to the Egypt and Gallipoli campaigns of WWI.

Mt Clarence   VIEWPOINT
There are fine views over the coast and inland from Mt Clarence, which sits atop the Albany Heritage Park. On top of Mt Clarence is the Desert Mounted Corps Memorial (p154).

Desert Mounted Corps Memorial MONUMENT
(Albany Heritage Park) Memorial to WWI soldiers who fought at the Nek in the Gallipoli campaign of 1915. The memorial was originally erected in Port Said, Egypt. However, it was irreparably damaged during the Suez crisis in 1956, and this copy was made from masonry salvaged from the original. Excellent views over King George Sound.

Western Australian Museum – Albany   MUSEUM
(www.museum.wa.gov.au; Residency Rd; by donation; ☺ 10am-4.30pm) This branch of the state museum is split between two neighbouring buildings. The newer Eclipse building has a childrens' discovery section, a lighthouse exhibition and usually excellent visiting displays. The restored 1850s home of the resident magistrate illuminates Minang Noongar history, local natural history and seafaring stories.

Brig Amity   SHIP
(adult/child $5/2; ☺ 10am-4.30pm) This full-scale replica of the brig that carried Albany's first British settlers from Sydney in 1826 was completed for the city's 150th anniversary. Around the brig is a heritage area worth exploring.

Albany Residency Museum   MUSEUM
(☑ 08-9841 4844; www.museum.wa.gov.au; Residency Rd; by donation; ☺ 10am-5pm) One of Albany's most impressive buildings how houses the Albany Residency Museum. Built in the 1850s as the home of the resident magistrate, the museum has displays telling seafaring stories, explaining local natural history, and showing Aboriginal artefacts.

Great Southern Distillery   DISTILLERY
(☑ 08-9842 5363; www.distillery.com.au; 252 Frenchman Bay Rd; tours $15; ☺ cellar door 10am-5pm) Limeburners Single Malt whisky is the star at this waterfront distillery, but brandy, gin, absinthe and grappe also feature. Tours on weekends – phone ahead to check on timing and availability – include tastings, and there's a cafe offering tapas, local beer and snacks.

Historic Buildings
Near the foreshore is Albany's historic precinct. Take a stroll down Stirling Tce – noted for its Victorian shopfronts, **Courthouse** (184 Stirling Tce) and **Old Post Office** (31-39 Stirling Tce) – and up York St to **St John's Anglican Church** (Lower York St). A guided walking-tour brochure is available from the visitor centre.

Beaches
East of the town centre, the beautiful Middleton and Emu Beaches face King George Sound and share one long stretch of family-friendly sand. In winter, you'll often see pods of mother whales and their calves here. Head around Emu Point to Oyster Harbour

for swimming pontoons and even calmer waters.

A clifftop walking track hugs much of the waterfront between the town centre and Middleton Beach. Boardwalks continue along Emu Beach.

🏃 Activities

Hiking

Bibbulmun Track HIKING
(www.bibbulmuntrack.org.au) Taking around eight weeks, the 963km Bibbulmun Track goes from Kalamunda, 20km east of Perth, through mainly natural environment to Walpole and Albany. Terrain includes jarrah and marri forests, wildflowers, granite outcrops, coastal heath country and spectacular coastlines. Comfortable camp sites are spaced regularly along the track, and the best time to do it is from August to October.

Whale Watching

Albany Ocean Adventures WHALE WATCHING
(📞0428 429 876; www.whales.com.au; 5a Toll Pl; adult/child $88/50; ⊙Jul-Oct) Regular whale-watching trips in season.

Albany Whale Tours WHALE WATCHING
(📞08-9845 1068; www.albanywhaletours.com.au; Albany Waterfront Marina, cnr Princess Royal Dr & Toll Pl; adult/child $95/55; ⊙Jun-Oct) Regular whale-watching trips in season.

Flightseeing

Skyhook Helicopters SCENIC FLIGHTS
(📞08-9844 4019; www.skyhookhelicopters.com. au; flights from $140) Options include 10-minute scenic flights around Albany harbour or longer options taking in Albany's stunning coastal scenery and landing at the lighthouse on historic Breaksea Island, around 8km from Albany in King George Sound.

Diving

Southcoast Diving Supplies DIVING
(📞08-9841 7176; www.divealbany.com.au; 84b Serpentine Rd) Southcoast Diving Supplies will show you the underwater world.

👉 Tours

Busy Blue Bus BUS
(📞08-9842 2133; www.busybluebus.com.au; ⊙adult/child from $135/108) Full- and half-day tours taking in Albany's Anzac history, the city's whaling heritage, or further afield to the Great Southern vineyards or Castle Rock and the Granite Skywalk in the Porongurup National Park.

Kalgan Queen BOATING
(📞08-9844 3166; www.albanyaustralia.com; Emu Point; adult/child $85/50; ⊙9am Sep-Jun) Four-hour cruises up the Kalgan River in a glass-bottomed boat explain the history and wildlife of the area.

🛏 Sleeping

1849 Backpackers HOSTEL $
(📞08-9842 1554; www.albanybackpackersaccommodation.com.au; 45 Peels Pl; dm/s/d $30/63/80; @🛜) Big flags from many nations provide a colourful international welcome at this well-run hostel. A huge, modern kitchen, sunny rooms and a laid-back social ambience make this one of Western Australia's best places to stay for budget travellers. Make sure you book in for 1849's free barbecue on Sunday night.

Emu Beach Holiday Park CARAVAN PARK $
(📞08-9844 1147; www.emubeach.com; 8 Medcalf Pde, Emu Point; sites $40, chalets $140-200; ✼) Families love the Emu Beach area, and this friendly holiday park includes a BBQ area and a kids' playground.

Albany Harbourside APARTMENT $$
(📞08-9842 1769; www.albanyharbourside.com. au; 8 Festing St; d $169-239; ✼🛜) Albany Harbourside's portfolio includes spacious and spotless apartments on Festing St, and three other self-contained options arrayed around central Albany. Decor is modern and colourful, and some apartments have ocean views.

Coraki Holiday Cottages RENTAL HOUSE $$
(📞08-9844 7068; www.corakicottages.com.au; 16 Nanarup Rd; cottages from $125) On the edge of Oyster Bay, between the King and Kalgan Rivers, these light, bright, private cottages with bush surrounds are great value.

★ Beach House at Bayside BOUTIQUE HOTEL $$$
(📞08-9844 8844; www.thebeachhouseatbayside. com.au; 33 Barry Ct, Collingwood Park; r $280-375; ✼🛜) Positioned right by the beach and the golf course in a quiet cul-de-sac, midway between Middleton Beach and Emu Point, this modern accommodation offers wonderful service. Rates include breakfast, afternoon tea, and evening port and chocolates. The friendly owners have their fingers on the pulse of Albany's dining scene, and a second property a few doors away is equally comfortable.

✖ Eating

Albany Boatshed Markets MARKET $
(☑ 0458 433 248; www.albanyboatshedmarkets.
com; Princess Royal Dr, the Boatshed; ⊙ 10am-
1pm Sun) Local produce, arts and crafts, and
wines from around the Great Southern area.

Albany Farmers Market MARKET $
(☑ 0417 983 428; www.albanyfarmersmarket.com.
au; Collie St; ⊙ 8am-noon Sat) Weekly market
with gourmet food and local artisan produce.

Three Anchors PUB FOOD $$
(☑ 08-98411 600; www.threeanchors.com.au;
2 Flinders Pde, Middleton Beach; mains $18-34;
⊙ 7am-10pm) Located under towering Nor-
folk pines on the edge of Middleton Beach,
Three Anchors is a versatile all-day eatery
just metres from the sand. Try the juicy
lamb kofta burger for lunch, or enjoy a lei-
surely breakfast in the courtyard. Sunday
sessions offer live music from 4pm to 7pm,
and craft beers from Albany's Wilson Brew-
ery Company are often on tap.

Vancouver Street Cafe CAFE $$
(☑ 08-9841 2475; www.facebook.com/Vancou-
verCafeAlbany/; 65 Vancouver St; mains $12-24;
⊙ 8am-3.30pm Mon-Fri, to 3pm Sat & Sun) This
heritage cafe features balcony views and
delicious home baking. Toasted Turkish
sandwiches combine with bigger dishes
such as Moroccan lamb balls with pilaf and
honey yoghurt, and good-value platters are
a relaxed way to recharge over lunch. One
of WA's best eggs Benedict seals the deal for
breakfast.

White Star Hotel PUB FOOD $$
(☑ 08-9841 1733; www.whitestarhotel.com.au; 72
Stirling Tce; mains $21-39; ⊙ 11am-late) With
good beers on tap, excellent pub grub, a
beer garden and lots of live music, this old
pub gets a gold star. Sunday-night folk and
blues gigs are a good opportunity to share a
pint with Albany's laid-back locals. The sur-
rounding Stirling Tce area has other good
cafes and restaurants, with outdoor seating
during spring and summer.

Craft beers from the Albany Brewing
Company are brewed on site. Our favourite
is the Hopback Ale. Look for the breaching
humpback on the tap badge when you're
ordering.

York Street Cafe CAFE $$
(☑ 08-9842 1666; www.184york.com; 184 York
St; mains $12-22; ⊙ 7am-4pm; 🛜) The food is
excellent at this cosmopolitan and versatile

cafe on the main strip. Breakfast options include a terrific egg, bacon and hash-brown
wrap and an Asian-style omelette, while
Thai fishcakes and gourmet burgers are
lunchtime highlights.

Earl of Spencer PUB FOOD $$
(☑ 08-9847 4262; www.facebook.com/TheEarlOf-
Spencer; cnr Earl & Spencer Sts; mains $23-36;
⊙ 11.30am-late) Locals crowd in for the Earl's
famous pie-and-pint deal or hearty lamb
shanks. Live bands are regular visitors on
weekends, often with a jaunty Irish brogue.
Occasional guest taps from WA craft brew-
ers make it a good destination for travelling
beer fans.

Lime 303 MODERN AUSTRALIAN $$$
(☑ 08-9841 1400; www.dogrockmotel.com.au;
303 Middleton Rd; mains $32-42; ⊙ dinner 6pm-
late, tapas 4.30-9pm) Pretty flash for regional
WA, Lime 303 showcases local produce in
dishes such as spiced aubergine moussaka,
confit duck leg and hearty lamb rump with
artichoke hash. More informal bar tapas are
available from 4.30pm.

🍷 Drinking & Nightlife

Due South PUB
(☑ 08-9841 8526; www.duesouthalbany.com.au; 6
Toll Pl; ⊙ 11am-late) Due South's bar is nattily
concealed in a colourful shipping container,
and the best place for a sunset drink is this
bustling waterfront tavern's outdoor deck.
There are decent craft beers on tap and local Albany wines, and the pub food menu is
available throughout the day – handy in a
town where many places take a break between lunch and dinner.

Liberté WINE BAR
(☑ 08-9847 4797; www.facebook.com/Liberte-
bar; 162 Stirling Tce; ⊙ noon-midnight Mon-Sat)
Housed in the corner bar of a heritage pub,
Liberté is a surprisingly hip addition to Albany's eating and drinking scene. The ragtag
decor channels a louche Parisian cafe and
velvet-trimmed speakeasy, while top cocktails, Great Southern wines and craft beers
partner interesting French-Vietnamese bar
food, such as steamed buns with soft shell
crab, truffled egg and *sriracha* mayonnaise.

ℹ Information

Department of Parks & Wildlife (☑ 08-9842
4500; www.parks.dpaw.wa.gov.au; 120 Albany
Hwy; ⊙ 8am-4.30pm Mon-Fri) For national-
park information.

Visitor Centre (☑ 08-9841 9290; www.amazin-galbany.com; Proudlove Pde; ⊙ 9am-5pm) In the old train station.

❶ Getting There & Away

Transwa (☑ 1300 662 205; www.transwa. wa.gov.au) State-wide WA bus services stop at the visitor centre.

Around Albany

Discovery Bay   MUSEUM
(☑ 08-9844 4021; www.discoverybay.com.au; 81 Whaling Station Rd; adult/child/family $32/12/75; ⊙ 9am-5pm) When the Cheynes Beach Whaling Station ceased operations in November 1978, few could have guessed that the formerly gore-covered decks would eventually be covered in tourists discovering the area's bleakly fascinating story. An attached museum screens films about sharks and whales, and displays giant skeletons, harpoons, whaleboat models and scrimshaw (etchings on whalebone). Outside there's the rusting *Cheynes IV* whale chaser and station equipment to inspect. Free guided tours depart on the hour from 10am to 3pm.

Part of the wider Discovery Bay complex is a new Australian wildlife park and botanic garden (adult/child $15/8) with plants endemic to the area. There are good ocean views from the elevated sight, but the fledgling gardens need a few years to develop more, and the animals – including koalas, pademelons and wallaroos – are cared for in fairly compact areas.

◉ Sights

Torndirrup National Park   NATIONAL PARK
(Frenchman Bay Rd; per motorcycle/car $6/12) Covering much of the peninsula enclosing the southern reaches of Princess Royal Harbour and King George Sound, this national park features windswept, ocean-bashed cliffs. **The Gap** is a natural cleft in the rock, channelling surf through walls of granite. A spectacular new viewing platform provides superb access. Close by is the **Natural Bridge**. National park fees apply and there is a kiosk for paying by credit card. Alternatively passes are available at the Albany's visitor centre.

Further east, the **Blowholes** are spectacular. Rocky coves such as Jimmy **Newells Harbour** and **Salmon Holes** are popular with surfers. Better for swimmers are **Misery Beach** or **Frenchman Bay** on the peninsula's more sheltered side. There's a

---

ALBANY TO ESPERANCE ALTERNATIVES

The rural 480km of South Coast Hwy (Rte 1) between Albany and Esperance is a relatively unpopulated stretch. Break up the first leg by taking the Albany Hwy (Rte 30) to Mt Barker, and then head east to Porongurup. Then travel north through the Stirling Ranges, and turn east again through Ongerup, and rejoin the highway at Jerramungup. This route adds 57km to the trip.

At Ongerup, the **Yongergnow Malleefowl Centre** (☑ 08-9828 2325; www.yongergnow.com.au; adult/child $10/5; ⊙ 10am-4pm Tue-Sat) is devoted to the conservation of a curious endangered bird that creates huge mounds to incubate its chicks.

Near Jerramungup is **Fitzgerald River National Park** – base yourself at Hopetoun or Bremer Bay to explore the national park. Note that Bremer Bay is best reached by taking the South Coast Hwy from Albany.

---

challenging 10km-return **bushwalk** (five hours plus) over Isthmus Hill to Bald Heads.

Two Peoples Bay   NATURE RESERVE
(Two Peoples Bay Rd) Around 20km east of Albany, Two Peoples Bay is a scenic 46-sq-km nature reserve with a good swimming beach.

Waychinicup National Park   NATIONAL PARK
(Cheyne Beach Rd; park admission free, camp site adult/child $7.50/2.20) In a beautiful spot by the Waychinicup River, where Gilbert's potoroos and scrub birds are often seen.

Mt Barker

POP 1770

Mt Barker (50km north of Albany) is the gateway to the Porongurup and Stirling Range National Parks. It's also the hub for the local wine industry. Pick up the *Mt Barker Wineries* map from the town's visitor centre in the old railway station and visit www.mountbarkerwine.com.au.

Around 5km south of town, **Mt Barker** has excellent views. Southwest of Mt Barker, on the rolling grounds of the Egerton-Warburton estate, is the photogenic **St Werburgh's Chapel** (1872).

Mt Barker Police Station Museum MUSEUM
(www.mountbarkertourismwa.com.au/police_station;
Albany Hwy; adult/child $5/free; ⊙10am-3pm Sat
& Sun) Mt Barker has been settled since the
1830s and the convict-built 1868 police station
and gaol have been preserved as a museum.

Nomads Guest House GUESTHOUSE **$**
(☑08-9851 2131; www.nomadsguesthouse-
wa.com.au; 12 Morpeth St; s/d/yurts/chalets
$70/90/100/110; 🛜) A surprising sight is the
authentic Mongolian yurt (felt tent) and
gallery of Mongolian and Chinese art in the
grounds of Nomads Guest House. The owners frequently rescue orphaned joeys (baby
kangaroos), so don't be surprised to see a
few temporary marsupial visitors in the
main house.

West Cape Howe Wines WINERY
(☑08-9892 1444; www.westcapehowewines.com.au;
14923 Muir Hwy; ⊙cellar door 10am-5pm Mon-Fri &
11am-4pm Sat & Sun) In lovely grounds around
10km west of Mt Barker, West Cape Howe
Wines are regular award winners for their
riesling, merlot and cabernet sauvignon.

Plantagenet Wines WINERY
(☑08-9851 3111; www.plantagenetwines.com; Albany Hwy; ⊙10am-4.30pm) Plantagenet Wines'
cellar door is conveniently situated in the
middle of Mt Barker town.

Porongurup National Park

The 24-sq-km, 12km-long Porongurup
National Park (p158) has 1100-million-
year-old granite outcrops, panoramic views,
beautiful scenery, large karri trees and some
excellent bushwalks. Porongurup is also part
of the Great Southern wine region and there
are 11 wineries in the vicinity. See www.
porongurup.com.

Porongurup National Park NATIONAL PARK
(entry per car/motorcycle $12/6) Bushwalks
range from the 100m **Tree-in-the-Rock**
stroll to the harder **Hayward and Nancy
Peaks** (5.5km loop). The **Devil's Slide** (5km
return) passes through karri forest to the
stumpy vegetation of the granite zone. These
walks start from the main day-use area (Bol-
ganup Rd). **Castle Rock Trail to Balancing
Rock** (3km return) starts further east, signposted off the Mt Barker–Porongurup Rd.

The **Castle Rock Granite Skywalk Trail**
(4.4km return, two hours) negotiates a steep
and spectacular path up the rock. The final
200m ascent to the summit incorporates a
steep rocky scramble and a vertical 7m ladder.

🛏 Sleeping & Eating

There is limited accommodation around the
national park. See www.porongurup.com for
listings of a caravan park and B&Bs. It's a
short drive from Mt Barker, and Albany is
around 54km from Porongurup.

★ **Maleeya's Thai Cafe** THAI **$$**
(☑08-9853 1123; www.maleeya.com.au; 1376
Porongurup Rd; mains $25-33; ⊙11.30am-3pm &
6-9pm Fri-Sun; ☑) 🍃 Foodies and chefs ven-
ture to Porongurup for some of WA's most
authentic Thai food. Curries, soups and stir-
fries all come punctuated with fresh herbs
straight from Maleeya's garden, and oth-
er ingredients are organic and free range.
Bookings recommended.

Porongurup National Park

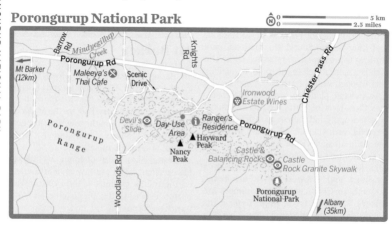

Ironwood Estate Wines
WINERY

(☑ 08-9853 1126; www.ironwoodestatewines.com.au; 2191 Porongurup Rd; ☺ 11am-5pm Wed-Mon) Bailey, the friendly labradoodle, usually welcomes visitors who come to enjoy the stunning Porongurup views at Ironwood's tasting room and cafe. Our favourite wine is the flinty and fruity Riesling. Light meals ($12 to $15), including salmon quiche, are available along with coffee, tea and cakes.

Stirling Range National Park

Rising abruptly from surrounding flat and sandy plains, the Stirling Range's propensity to change colour through blues, reds and purples captivates photographers during the spectacular wildflower season from late August to early December. It's also recognised by the Noongar people as a place of special significance – a place where the spirits of the dead return. Every summit has an ancestral being associated with it, so it's appropriate to show proper respect when visiting.

This 1156-sq-km **national park** (☺ entry per car/motorcycle $12/6) consists of a single chain of peaks pushed up by plate tectonics to form a range 10km wide and 65km long. Running most of its length are isolated summits, some knobbly and some perfect pyramids, towering above broad valleys covered in shrubs and heath. Bluff Knoll (Bular Mai), at 1095m, is the highest point in the southwest.

Park fees are charged at the start of Bluff Knoll Rd.

The Stirlings are renowned for serious **bushwalking**. Keen walkers can choose from **Toolbrunup** (for views and a good climb; 1052m, 4km return) and **Bluff Knoll** (a well-graded tourist track; 1095m, 6km return). **Mt Hassell** (848m, 3km return) and **Talyuberlup** (783m, 2.6km return) are popular half-day walks.

Challenging walks cross the eastern sector include those from **Bluff Knoll to Ellen Peak** (three days), or the shorter traverse from **The Arrows to Ellen Peak** (two days).

Stock up on food in Mt Barker or Albany if you're camping. If you're staying at the Lily, evening meals are available for in-house guests.

Stirling Range Retreat
CARAVAN PARK $

(☑ 08-9827 9229; www.stirlingrange.com.au; 8639 Chester Pass Rd; unpowered/powered 2-person sites $32/36, cabins $95-149, units $160-195;

✳ @ ☲) � On the park's northern boundary, this shaded area offers camp sites, cabins and vans, and self-contained, rammed-earth units. Wildflower and orchid bus tours and walkabouts (three hours, $49 per person) are conducted from mid-August to the end of October. The swimming pool only opens from November to April.

Mount Trio Bush Camping & Caravan Park
CARAVAN PARK $

(☑ 08-9827 9270; www.mttrio.com.au; Salt River Rd; unpowered/powered sites per person $14/18) Rustic bush campground on a farm property close to the walking tracks, north of the centre of the park. It has hot showers, a kitchen, free gas BBQs and a campfire pit. Guided walks, from 90 minutes to one day in length, are on offer.

★ Lily
COTTAGE $$

(☑ 08-9827 9205; www.thelily.com.au; Chester Pass Rd; cottages $159-189) These cottages, 12km north of the park, are grouped around a working windmill. Accommodation is self-contained, and meals are available for guests at the neighbouring restaurant. Call to enquire which nights the restaurant is open to the public and to arrange mill tours ($50, minimum of four people). There's also private accommodation in a restored 1944 Dakota DC3 aircraft ($249).

Fitzgerald River National Park

Midway between Albany and Esperance, this gem of a national park (entry per car/motorcycle $12/6) has been declared a Unesco Biosphere Reserve. Its 3300 sq km contain half of the orchid species in WA (more than 80, 70 of which occur nowhere else), 22 mammal species, 200 species of bird and 1700 species of plant (20% of WA's described flora species).

Walkers will discover beautiful coastline, sand plains, rugged coastal hills (known as 'the Barrens') and deep, wide river valleys. In season, you'll almost certainly see whales and their calves from the shore at **Point Ann**, where there's a lookout and a heritage walk that follows a short stretch of the 1164km **No 2 rabbit-proof fence**.

Bookending the park are the sleepy coastal settlements of Bremer Bay and Hopetoun, both with white sand and shimmering waters.

You'll need your own transport. A 4WD vehicle is strongly recommended. The three main 2WD entry points to the park are from

Stirling Range National Park

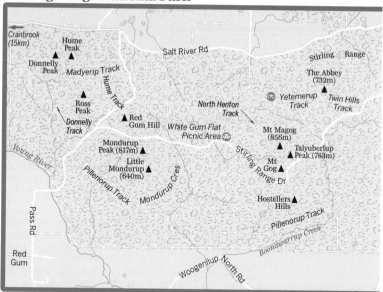

the South Coast Hwy (Quiss Rd and Pabelup Dr), Hopetoun (Hamersley Dr) and Bremer Bay (along Swamp and Murray Rds). All roads are gravel, and likely to be impassable after rain, so check locally before you set out.

Quaalup Homestead CAMPGROUND $
(☑ 08-9837 4124; www.whalesandwildflowers.com.au; 1 Gairdner Rd; sites per person from $12, cabins $115-125) 🅟 This 1858 homestead is secluded deep within the park's southern reaches. Electricity is solar generated, and forget about mobile-phone coverage. Accommodation includes a bush camp site with gas BBQs and cosy units and chalets.

Bremer Bay

POP 250

Edged with brilliant white sand and translucent green waters, this sleepy fishing and holiday hamlet is 61km from the South Coast Hwy. From July to November, the bay is a cetacean maternity ward for southern right whales, and orca are seen from February to mid-April.

Bremer Canyon
Killer Whale Expeditions WHALE WATCHING
(☑ 08-9750 5500; www.whales-australia.com.au/bremer-killer-whales; Bremer Bay Boat Harbour;

per person $385; ⊙ late Jan–mid-Apr) From late January to mid-April, orca are regular visitors to the deep and nutrient-rich waters of the Bremer Canyon. Excursions departing from Bremer Bay wharf run from 8.30am to 4.30pm, and booking ahead is strongly recommended. Transport is available from Albany with Busy Blue Bus (p155). Operators Naturaliste Charters are supporting Riggs Australia (www.riggsaustralia.com) in passive research on the Bremer Canyon whales.

The best eating in town is at the Bremer Bay Beaches Resort & Tourist Park (p160), and there a few other cafes also. Groceries are expensive, so stock up before you arrive.

Bremer Bay Beaches Resort
& Tourist Park CARAVAN PARK $
(☑ 08-9837 4290; www.bremerbaybeaches.com.au; Wellstead Rd; 2-person sites from $45, cabins & chalets $150-210; 🛜 🌊) This park has shady campsites and a well-equipped shared kitchen. It's a 1.5km walk through the dunes to the beach. There's also a seasonal pizzeria and very good espresso coffee.

Visitor Centre TOURIST INFORMATION
(☑ 08-9837 4171; www.bremerbaycrc.com.au/; Mary St; ⊙ 9am-4.30pm Mon-Fri; 🛜) The visitor centre in the shire library also has in-

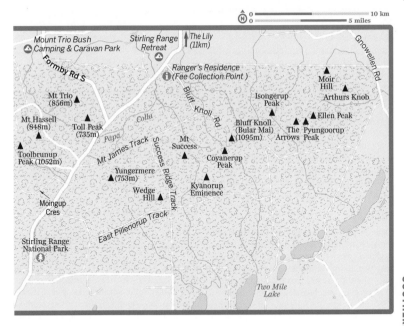

ternet access. Holiday homes can be booked through the visitor centre, and the website lists B&B options.

There is no public transport to Bremer Bay, and visitors need their own vehicle. Busy Blue Bus (p155) in Albany run tours to see the orca.

Hopetoun

POP 590

Once as sleepy as Bremer Bay, Hopetoun has nearly doubled in size in recent years due to the opening of a nickel mine. The beauty of the beaches hasn't changed, but there are now more eating options and the local pub fills up with young workers in dusty overalls. From the jetty at the end of the main drag (Veal St) there are wonderful views. Beside it is a child-friendly beach with a swimming pontoon. The old train route between Ravensthorpe and Hopetoun is now a heritage walking track.

The world's longest fence – the 1833km-long **No 1 rabbit-proof fence** – enters the sea at Starvation Bay; it starts at Eighty Mile Beach on the Indian Ocean, north of Port Hedland. The fence was built during the height of the rabbit plague between 1901 and 1907. However, the bunnies beat the fence-builders to the west side, so it wasn't as effective a barrier as hoped.

To the west of town, separating it from Fitzgerald River National Park, is the almost landlocked **Culham Inlet** (great for fishing – especially for black bream). To the east is the scenic but in parts extremely rough Southern Ocean East Drive, heading to beaches with camp sites at **Mason Bay** and **Starvation Bay**. If you're in a 2WD vehicle, don't head to Esperance this way.

Hopetoun Motel & Chalet Village MOTEL **$$**
(☑08-9838 3219; www.hopetounmotel.com.au; 458 Veal St, Hopetoun; r $140-200; ☏) Rammed-earth complex with comfy beds and quality linen.

Toun Beach Cafe CAFE **$$**
(☑08-9838 3918; Veal St; lunch $10-17, dinner $26-30; ☺8.30am-2.30pm & 5.30-8pm Tue-Sat, to 2pm Sun) This friendly combination of cafe and gift shop offers burgers, pasta and other light meals.

If you're heading on to Esperance, instead of doubling back to the turnoff at Ravensthorpe, take Jerdacuttup Rd (past the airport) instead. Bus transport to Hopetoun is limited to Transwa's (www.transwa.wa.gov. au) midweek GE4 service linking Albany and Esperance.

Esperance

POP 9600 / ☑08

Framed by aquamarine waters and pristine white beaches, Esperance sits in solitary splendour on the Bay of Isles. But despite its isolation, families still travel from Perth or Kalgoorlie just to plug into the easygoing vibe and great beach life. For travellers taking the coastal route across the continent, it's the last sizeable town before the Nullarbor.

Picture-perfect beaches dot the even more remote national parks to the town's southeast, and the pristine environment of the 105 islands of the offshore Recherche Archipelago are home to fur seals, penguins and sea birds.

History

Esperance's indigenous name, Kepa Kurl (water boomerang), refers to the shape of the bay. Archaeological finds on Middle Island suggest that it was occupied before the last Ice Age, when it was still part of the mainland.

Esperance received its current name in 1792 when the *Recherche* and *Espérance* sailed through the archipelago and into the bay to shelter from a storm. In the 1820s and 1830s the Recherche Archipelago was home to Black Jack Anderson – Australia's only pirate. From his base on Middle Island he raided ships and kept a harem of Aboriginal women, whose husbands he had killed. He was eventually murdered in his sleep by one of his own men.

Although the first settlers came in 1863, it wasn't until the gold rush of the 1890s that the town really became established as a port. Since the 1950s Esperance developed as an agricultural centre, and it continues to export grain and minerals.

◎ Sights & Activities

Esperance Museum   MUSEUM
(☑08-9071 1579; www.esperancemuseum.com.au; cnr James & Dempster Sts; adult/child $8/3; ◐1.30-4.30pm) Glass cabinets are crammed with quirky collections of sea shells, frog ornaments, tennis rackets and bed pans. Bigger items include boats, a train carriage and the remains of the USA's spacecraft *Skylab*, which made its fiery re-entry at Balladonia, east of Esperance, in 1979.

Museum Village   HISTORIC BUILDING
(cnr Dempster & Kemp Sts) The museum consists of galleries and cafes occupying various restored heritage buildings; markets are held here every second Sunday morning. Aboriginal-run **Kepa Kurl Art Gallery** (☑08-9072 1688; www.kepakurl.com.au; cnr Dempster & Kemp Sts; ◐10.30am-3.30pm Tue-Fri, market Sun) has reasonably priced works by local and Central Desert artists.

Lake Warden Wetland System   NATURE RESERVE
Esperance is surrounded by extensive wetlands, which include seven large lakes and over 90 smaller ones. The 7.2km-return **Kepwari Wetland Trail** (off Fisheries Rd) takes in **Lake Wheatfield** and **Woody Lake**, with boardwalks, interpretive displays and good birdwatching. **Lake Monjingup**, 14km to the northwest along the South Coast Hwy, is divided by Telegraph Rd into a conservation area (to the west) and a recreation area (to the east). It has recently been temporarily closed due to bushfire damage; check its current status before visiting.

Cannery Arts Centre   GALLERY
(☑08-9071 3599; www.canneryartscentre.com.au; 1018 Norseman Rd; gold-coin donation; ◐10am-2pm Mon-Sat, 1-4pm Sun) Has artist studios, interesting exhibitions and a shop selling local artwork.

Great Ocean Drive   SCENIC DRIVE
Many of Esperance's most dramatic sights can be seen on this well-signposted 40km loop. Starting from the waterfront, it heads southwest along the breathtaking stretch of coast that includes a series of popular surfing and swimming spots, including **Blue Haven Beach** and **Twilight Cove**. Stop at rugged **Observatory Point** and the lookout on **Wireless Hill**. A turn-off leads to the **wind farm**, which supplies about 23% of Esperance's electricity. Walking among the turbines is surreal when it's windy.

☞ Tours

Esperance Island Cruises   BOATING
(☑08-9071 5757; wwww.esperancecruises.com.au; 72 The Esplanade; adult/child $100/65; ◐9am-12.30pm) Scenic wildlife cruises for spotting sea lions, New Zealand fur seals, dolphins, Cape Barren geese and sea eagles. Snorkelling equipment and a light morning tea are also provided.

Eco-Discovery Tours   DRIVING
(☑0407 737 261; www.esperancetours.com.au) Runs 4WD tours along the sand to Cape Le Grand National Park (half/full day $105/195, minimum of two/four people) and two-hour circuits of Great Ocean Dr (adult/child $60/45).

Woody Island Tours BOATING
(📞 0484 327 580; www.woodyisland.com.au; full-day
ferry adult/child $40/30, half-day guided trip adult/
child $65/55; ⊗ mid-Dec–Jan, mid-Apr–early May)
Half-day boat trips incorporating a guided island walk, snorkelling, morning tea and the
opportunity to spot local wildlife, including
fur seals, sea lions, dolphins and Cape Barren
geese. Alternatively, for independent fishing,
swimming and bushwalking on the island,
catch a ferry at 7am and return at 3pm.

Esperance Diving & Fishing DIVING, FISHING
(📞 08-9071 5111; www.esperancedivingandfishing.
com.au; 72 The Esplanade) Takes you wreck
diving on the *Sanko Harvest* (two-tank dive
including all gear $260) or charter fishing
throughout the archipelago. Also gear hire
and dive courses.

🛏 Sleeping

Woody Island Eco-Stays CAMPGROUND $
(📞 0484 327 580; www.facebook.com/woodyis-
landecotours; ⊗ mid-Dec–Jan, mid-Apr–early May)
🏊 At the time of writing, accommodation
on this nature reserve island was closed for
renovation but was due to open again in late
2017. Options will include leafy camp sites
and canvas-sided bush huts. Power is mostly solar, and rainwater supplies the island
– both are highly valued. Allow for an $80
return ferry transfer as well.

Check the website to get the latest information on Woody Island's reopening.

Blue Waters Lodge YHA HOSTEL $
(📞 08-9071 1040; www.yha.com.au; 299 Goldfields
Rd; dm/d/tr $33/67/91) On the beachfront
about 1.5km from the town centre, this rambling place feels institutional, and many of
the guests are long-stay residents working
in the area. Bikes can be hired to ride along
the beach.

★ Esperance B&B by the Sea B&B $$
(📞 08-9071 5640; www.esperancebb.com; 34
Stewart St; s/d $130/190; ❀) This great-value
beachhouse has a private guest wing and
the views from the deck overlooking Blue
Haven Beach are breathtaking, especially at
sunset. It's just a stroll from the ocean and
a five-minute drive from central Esperance.

Driftwood Apartments APARTMENT $$
(📞 0428 716 677; www.driftwoodapartments.com.
au; 69 The Esplanade; apt $165-220; ❀) Each of
these seven smart blue-and-yellow apartments, right across from the waterfront, has
its own BBQ and outdoor table setting. The

two-storey, two-bedroom units have decks
and a bit more privacy.

Clearwater Motel Apartments MOTEL $$
(📞 08-9071 3587; www.clearwatermotel.com.au;
1a William St; s $120, d $140-195; ❀) The bright
and spacious rooms and apartments here
have balconies and are fully self-contained,
and there's a well-equipped shared BBQ
area. It's just a short walk from both the wa-
terfront and town.

✖ Eating & Drinking

★ Fish Face SEAFOOD $$
(📞 08-9071 1601; www.facebook.com/FishFaceEs-
perance; 1 James St; mains $15-20; ⊗ 4.30-8.30pm
Thu-Tue) Seafood is the star at Fish Face, with
superior fish and chips, grilled prawns and
squid, and scallops and oysters served up
in stylish surroundings. Good sides include
caesar salads, tasty buckwheat noodles with
a ponzu dressing, and a healthy carrot and
quinoa salad. Specials could include surf and
turf, seafood risotto or Tasmanian salmon.

Taylor's Beach Bar & Cafe CAFE $$
(📞 08-9071 4317; Taylor St Jetty; mains $16-34;
⊗ 8am-10pm Wed-Sun; 🐾) This sprawling cafe
by the jetty serves cafe fare, burgers, seafood
and salads. Locals hang out at the tables on
the grass or read on the covered terrace.
Focaccia sandwiches are good value and it's
good for a glass of wine or chilled pint of
Lucky Bay Brewing's refreshing *kolsch* beer.
Ask about occasional live music – usually on
Sunday afternoons.

Pier Hotel PUB FOOD $$
(📞 08-9071 1777; www.thepierhotelesperance.com;
47 The Esplanade; mains $22-38; ⊗ 11.30am-late)
Lots of beers on tap, wood-fired pizzas and
good-value bistro meals conspire to make the
local pub a firm favourite with both locals
and visitors. The Pale Ale from Esperance's
very own Lucky Bay Brewing is usually on
tap, and there's live music most weekends.

Ocean Blues CAFE $$
(📞 08-9071 7107; www.facebook.com/ocean-
blues6450; 19 The Esplanade; mains $11-35; ⊗ 7am-
2pm daily & 5.30pm-late Mon-Tue & Thu-Sat) Wan-
der in sandy-footed and order a simple lunch
(burgers, salads, sandwiches) from this un-
pretentious eatery. Dinners are more adven-
turous, representing good value for the price.

Lucky Bay Brewery MICROBREWERY
(📞 0447 631 115; www.facebook.com/luckybay-
brewing; Barook Rd; tastings $10; ⊗ 2-5.30pm

Fri-Sun) Look for Lucky Bay's beers in bars around Esperance – watch for the kangaroo tap badge – or make the journey 12km west to their simple brewery and tasting room. Two-litre growlers are available for takeaway, and Nigel the friendly brewmaster will guide you through beers, including the refreshing Skippy Rock *kolsch*, Belgian-style Homestead *saison* or hoppy Cyclops India pale ale (IPA).

S'Juice JUICES
(☑0417 986 869; 1 The Esplanade, Tanker Jetty Headland; juices & smoothies $7-9; ⊙9am-4pm Mon-Fri, to 3pm Sat & Sun) Colourful caravan with excellent juices and smoothies, and a few warming soups in cooler months. Usually located in the car park near Tanker Jetty. Check out the Facebook page.

Coffee Cat CAFE
(☑0417 968 177; ⊙7am-2pm Mon-Fri) Parked up near Esperance's Tanker Jetty, WA's hippest mobile coffee caravan also serves up yummy home-baked cakes and muffins. Grab an early-morning java to fuel a stroll along Esperance's recently redeveloped and very impressive esplanade. During summer the surrounding area often attracts a few other food trucks.

❶ Information

Visitor Centre (☑08-9083 1555; www.visitesperance.com; cnr Kemp & Dempster Sts; ⊙9am-5pm Mon-Fri, to 4pm Sat, to 2pm Sun) In the museum village with a handy 24-hour information touch screen also.

Parks & Wildlife (☑08-9083 2100; www.parks.dpaw.wa.gov.au; 92 Dempster St; ⊙8am-4.40pm Mon-Fri) National parks information.

❶ Getting There & Away

AIR
Esperance Airport (Coolgardie-Esperance Hwy) is 18km north of the town centre. **Rex** (Regional Express; ☑13 17 13; www.rex.com.au) flies between Perth and Esperance.

BUS
Transwa (☑1300 662 205; www.transwa.wa.gov.au) services stop at the visitor centre.
➼ GE1 to/from East Perth ($95, 10¼ hours, three weekly).
➼ GE2 to/from East Perth ($95, 10 hours), Mundaring ($93, 9¼ hours), York ($85, 8½ hours) and Hyden ($60, five hours) – all three times weekly.
➼ GE3 to/from Kalgoorlie ($60, five hours, three weekly), Coolgardie ($58, 4¾ hours, weekly) and Norseman ($32, 2¼ hours, three weekly).

❶ Getting Around

Rent a car from **Avis** (☑08-9071-3998; www.avis.com.au; 63 The Esplanade; ⊙8.30am-5pm Mon-Fri & to noon Sat) if you wish to explore Cape Le Grand National Park or the spectacular Great Ocean Drive. There is a branch at the Esperance airport too.

Around Esperance

◉ Sights

Cape Le Grand National Park NATIONAL PARK
(entry per car/motorcycle $12/6, sites adult/child $10/2.20) Good fishing, swimming and camping can be found at **Lucky Bay** and **Le Grand Beach**, and day-use facilities at gorgeous **Hellfire Bay**. Make the effort to climb **Frenchman Peak** (a steep 3km return, allow two hours), as the views from the top and through the rocky 'eye', especially during the late afternoon, are superb.

The 15km Le Grand Coastal Trail links the bay, or you can do shorter stretches between beaches.

Cape Arid National Park NATIONAL PARK
(entry per car/motorcycle $12/6, sites adult/child $10/2.20) Whales (in season), seals and Cape Barren geese are seen regularly here. Most of the park is 4WD-accessible only, although the Thomas River Rd leading to the shire camp site suits all vehicles. There's a challenging walk to the top of Tower Peak on Mt Ragged (3km return, three hours).

Stokes National Park NATIONAL PARK
(entry per car/motorcycle $12/6) Most of this park's 107 sq km is covered in scrub and coastal heath, sheltering kangaroos and birds. You might also spot seals. It's a popular spot for anglers, and there's a bush **campground** (camp sites adult/child $10/2.20), which is 2WD accessible.

❷ Drinking & Nightlife

Lucky Bean Cafe CAFE
(☑0418 913 414; www.facebook.com/luckybeancafe; Lucky Bay; ⊙9.30am-4pm Thu-Mon Oct-Apr, open daily in school holidays) This spring-and-summer-only beachfront caravan may be the most spectacular place you ever have a coffee and a muffin. You may even get lucky and see marsupial visitors on Lucky Bay's glorious sandy arc while sipping your 'Kangacino'.

Monkey Mia &
the Central West

POP 55,000

Best Places
for Sunset

➡ Steep Point (p176)

➡ Fishermens Lookout (p167)

➡ Red Bluff (p175)

➡ Shark Bay Hotel (p178)

➡ HMAS Sydney II Memorial (p168)

Best Places
to Sleep

➡ Gnaraloo Station (p182)

➡ Dongara Breeze Inn (p167)

➡ Eco Abrolhos (p173)

➡ Monkey Mia Dolphin Resort (p179)

➡ Hamelin Outback Station Stay (p176)

Why Go?

The pristine coastline and sheltered turquoise waters of World Heritage–listed Shark Bay draw tourists and marine life from around the world. Aside from the dolphins of Monkey Mia, the bay's submerged sea-grass meadows host dugongs, rays, sharks and turtles. On land, rare marsupials take refuge in remote national parks, and limestone cliffs, red sand and salt lakes litter a stark interior.

Further south, the gorges of Kalbarri invite adventurers to explore their depths, while wildflowers carpet the plains, and ospreys wheel away from battered Indian Ocean cliffs as humpback whales migrate south.

Veggies are ripening in Carnarvon as anglers and boardriders check the tides, and windsurfers are waiting for the 'Doctor' (strong afternoon sea breeze) to blow. In Geraldton, cool cafes, weekend markets and an excellent museum combine with Indian Ocean views along the city's wonderfully revamped foreshore.

When to Go
Monkey Mia

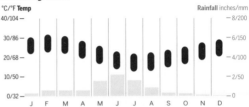

Jun–Aug The winter swells pump the breaks off Gnaraloo and Quobba.

Aug & Sep Kalbarri and surrounds erupt in wildflowers.

Nov–Feb Windsurfers clutch their sails from Geraldton to Carnarvon.

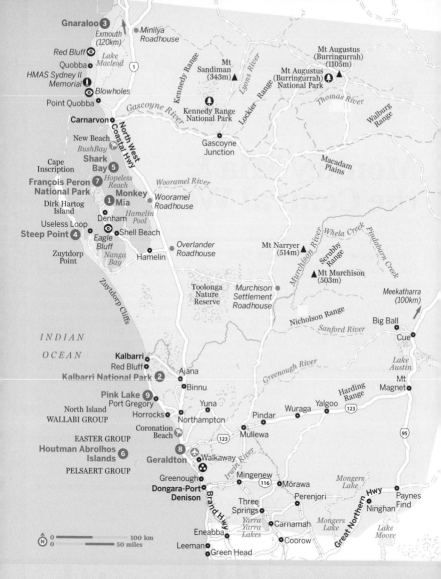

Monkey Mia & the Central West Highlights

① Watching the wild dolphins feed at **Monkey Mia** (p179).

② Taking in gorgeous viewpoints, or canoeing or abseiling the deep gorges, at **Kalbarri National Park** (p174).

③ Surfing the Tombstones break at **Gnaraloo** (p182).

④ Driving out to the mainland's most westerly tip, **Steep Point** (p176).

⑤ Scouting for dugongs on a boat trip out of Monkey Mia in **Shark Bay** (p175).

⑥ Diving on ancient shipwrecks, or taking in the reef from the air, at the **Houtman Abrolhos Islands** (p173).

⑦ Spotting marine life from a coastal walk in the **Francois Peron National Park** (p177).

⑧ Checking out the first-rate foreshore regeneration in **Geraldton** (p168) and getting a dose of 'city' treats.

⑨ Checking out the surrealist rosy hues of **Pink Lake** (p171).

ℹ️ Getting There & Away

AIR

Regional airlines connect Perth with small airports at Geraldton, Shark Bay and Carnarvon.

Qantas (📞13 13 13; www.qantas.com.au) and **Virgin Australia** (📞13 67 89; www.virginaustralia.com) fly between Perth and Geraldton; **Skippers** (📞1300 729 924; www.skippers.com.au) flies between Perth, Shark Bay and Carnarvon.

BUS

From Perth, **Transwa** (📞1300 662 205; www.transwa.wa.gov.au) buses run as far north as Kalbarri. **Integrity** (📞08-9274 7464; www.integritycoachlines.com.au) services run three times a week from Perth to Port Hedland or Broome, stopping at Dongara, Geraldton and Carnarvon and offering shuttle connections from the North West Coastal Hwy to Kalbarri and Shark Bay.

BATAVIA COAST

From tranquil Dongara-Port Denison to the remote, wind-scoured Zutydorp Cliffs stretches a dramatic coastline steeped in history, littered with shipwrecks and rich in marine life. While the region proved the undoing of many early European sailors, today modern fleets make the most of a lucrative crayfish industry, and travellers hunt down empty beaches.

Dongara-Port Denison

POP 3700

Pretty little Dongara and Port Denison, twin seaside towns some 360km from Perth, make an idyllic spot to break up a long drive. Surrounded by beautiful beaches, walking trails and historic buildings, the towns are divided by the Irwin River and have a laid-back atmosphere. Port Denison has good beaches and a marina filled with fishing boats, while Dongara's main street, shaded by enormous, century-old Moreton Bay fig trees, offers the best eating.

◉ Sights & Activities

From the visitor centre (p168), pick up the free *Thungara Trails* brochure outlining six **walking trails** that follow the river and/or coastline. A good place to start exploring is from the **Irwin River Estuary Nature Park** (Church St, Dongara).

There are also a handful of walking-trail brochures available for a small fee (around $2) that describe themed itineraries (history, birdlife etc).

The visitor centre rents out sandboards ($25 per day) for sand-dune fun, while Dongara Breeze Inn has bikes, snorkelling gear, golf clubs, surfboards and kayaks for hire.

Fishermens Lookout VIEWPOINT
(off Point Leander Dr, Port Denison) Commonly referred to as 'the Obelisk' by locals, this monument just southwest of the Port Denison marina has excellent views, especially at sunset.

🛏️ Sleeping & Eating

Note that accommodation is more expensive during public and school holidays.

★**Dongara Breeze Inn** GUESTHOUSE $
(📞08-9927 1332; www.breezeinn.com.au; 32 Waldeck St, Dongara; dm/s/d without bathroom $30/80/90; ❄️🛜) The cheapest beds in town look onto a gorgeous leafy garden at this friendly, popular guesthouse, which has stylish doubles with a chic Asian ambience, rustic dorms (in a vintage railway carriage) and free bike use for guests. All rooms share good kitchen and bathroom facilities – but it's the garden with its chill-out spaces that holds the most appeal.

Dongara Top Tourist Park CARAVAN PARK $
(📞08-9927 1210; www.dongaratouristpark.com.au; 8 George St, Port Denison; unpowered/powered sites from $26/37, 1-/2-bedroom cabins $114/160) There are good caravan parks in the area, but the best camping option has shaded, spacious sites behind South Beach. The two-bedroom cabins on the hill have great views, the studio cabins are quite upmarket, and there's a fabulous lush pergola for barbecuing and outdoor dining.

Starfish Cafe CAFE $
(📞0448 344 215; White Tops Rd, Port Denison; mains $12-25; ⊗8am-2pm Wed-Sun) Tucked away in the South Beach car park, this casual snack-shack offers coffee, cooked brekkies, winter soups and summer salads.

Priory Hotel PUB FOOD $$
(📞08-9927 1090; www.prioryhotel.com.au; 11 St Dominics Rd, Dongara; mains $15-45; ⊗noon-9pm) There's a touch of *Picnic at Hanging Rock* about this leafy former nunnery and ladies college with its period furniture, polished floorboards, black-and-white photos and

MONKEY MIA & THE CENTRAL WEST DONGARA-PORT DENISON

wide verandahs. Sundays bring roasts and wood-fired pizza, several nights offer live music, and steaks and burgers are available every evening. Meals are served noon to 2pm Wednesday to Sunday, and 5.45pm to 8pm nightly.

ℹ Information

Visitor Centre (☑08-9927 1404; www. dongaraportdenison.com.au; 9 Waldeck St, Dongara; ⊙8.30am-4.30pm Mon-Fri, 10am-1pm Sat)

Geraldton

POP 40,000

Capital of the midwest, sun-drenched 'Gero' is surrounded by excellent beaches offering myriad aquatic opportunities – swimming, snorkelling, surfing and, in particular, windsurfing and kitesurfing. The largest town between Perth and Darwin has huge wheat-handling and fishing industries that make it independent of the fickle tourist dollar, and seasonal workers flood the town during crayfish season.

In parts, Geraldton is still something of a work in progress, as the town's focus shifts to the waterfront and leaves a few empty lots ripe for development. The fantastically revamped waterfront is a masterclass in creating fun public spaces, and Gero blends big-city sophistication with small-town friendliness, offering a strong arts culture and a blossoming foodie scene.

◉ Sights

★**Foreshore**   WATERFRONT
Geraldton's foreshore is a great example of waterfront redevelopment: loads of beach space and grassy spots, walking paths, picnic shelters, free barbecues, playgrounds (including a water-play park), cafes and event spaces. Check out the fun 'Rubik's cube' public toilets at the northern end, and the wonderful 'emu eggs' art sculpture from local Indigenous artists.

★**HMAS Sydney II Memorial**   MONUMENT
(www.hmassydneymemorial.com.au; Gummer Ave; ⊙24hr) FREE Commanding the hill overlooking Geraldton is this moving, multifaceted memorial commemorating the 1941 loss of the *Sydney* and its 645 men after a skirmish with the German raider *Kormoran*. Note the cupola over the pillared sanctuary – it comprises 645 steel gulls, representing the

lives lost. Free guided tours are available at 10.30am daily.

★**Western Australian Museum –
Geraldton**   MUSEUM
(☑08-9431 8393; www.museum.wa.gov.au; 2 Museum Pl; by donation; ⊙9.30am-3pm) At one of the state's best museums, intelligent multimedia displays relate the area's natural, cultural and Indigenous history. The Shipwreck Gallery documents the tragic story of the *Batavia,* while 3D video footage reveals the sunken wrecks of HMAS *Sydney II* and the *Kormoran.* A highlights tour is offered daily at 11.30am.

**Cathedral of St Francis Xavier
Church**   CHURCH
(☑08-9921 3221; www.geraldtondiocese.org.au; Cathedral Ave; ⊙generally 8am-5pm) Geraldton's cathedral, built between 1916 and 1938, is arguably the finest example of the architectural achievements of the multi-skilled Monsignor John Hawes. The cathedral's striking features include imposing twin towers with arched openings, a central dome, Romanesque columns and boldly striped walls.

The cathedral is generally open for visitors from about 8am (after Mass at 7am) until 5pm (6pm on weekends, before a 6pm Mass). Tours are held at 10am Monday and Friday, and 4pm Wednesday.

Geraldton Regional Art Gallery   GALLERY
(☑08-9964 7170; artgallery.cgg.wa.gov.au; 24 Chapman Rd; ⊙10am-4pm Mon-Sat) FREE With an excellent permanent collection, including paintings by Norman Lindsay and Elizabeth Durack, this petite gallery also presents provocative contemporary work and regular touring exhibitions.

🏃 Activities

Most activities are water-based, but there is also a network of bike paths, including the 10km-long coastal route from **Tarcoola Beach to Chapman River**. Grab the Local Travelsmart map from the visitor centre (p171). Bikes can be hired from **Revolutions** (☑08-9964 1399; www.revolutionsgeraldton.com.au; 268 Marine Tce; bike hire per half/full day $25/30; ⊙9am-5.30pm Mon-Fri, to 2pm Sat, 10am-2pm Sun), right by the foreshore.

The best surfing conditions are from April to October, when there is little wind and ideal swell. The windy season is roughly

Geraldton

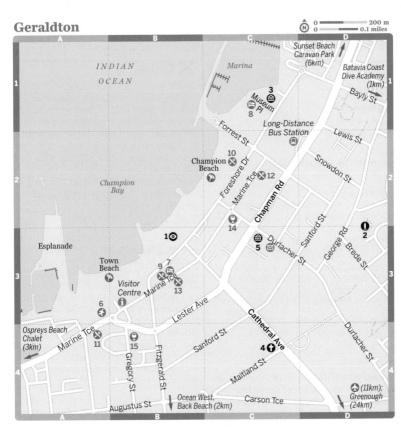

November to April – this is when wind-based water sports are at their best.

One of the best activities is a tour to the beautiful Abrolhos Islands (p173), 60km offshore.

Companies offering flights to the islands also offer scenic flights around the Geraldton area. See **G-Spot Xtreme** (☑ 0428 122 726; www.gspotxtreme.com.au), **KiteWest** (☑ 0449 021 784; www.kitewest.com.au; lessons per hr from $70) and **Midwest Surf School** (☑ 0419 988 756; http://surf2skool.com; lessons from $60, board hire from $20) for above-the-water action, while the **Batavia Coast Dive Academy** (☑ 08-9921 4229; www.facebook.com/bataviacoastdive; 118 North West Coastal Hwy; local dives $200; ☺ 8.30am-5pm Mon-Fri, 8am-2pm Sat, 10am-noon Sun) can arrange PADI courses and chartered trips to the Houtman Abrolhos Islands.

★☆ Festivals

Sunshine Festival CULTURAL
(www.sunshinefestival.com.au; ☺ Oct) It started in 1959 as a tomato festival, but now Geraldton's celebrations include dragon-boat races, parades, sand sculptures and parties. It's held over a week in early October. Sunshine guaranteed.

🛏 Sleeping

★ **Foreshore Backpackers** HOSTEL $
(☑ 08-9921 3275; www.foreshorebackpackers.com.au; 172 Marine Tce; dm/s/d without bathroom $35/55/75; @ 🛜) This rambling central hostel is full of hidden nooks, sunny balconies and world-weary travellers. It's very close to beaches, bars and cafes, and a good place to find a job, lift or travel buddy. It's well run, too, with bright, fresh decor that's a cut above. Discounts for stays longer than one night.

Geraldton

Sunset Beach Holiday Park CARAVAN PARK $
(☎1800 353 389; www.sunsetbeachpark.com.au; 4 Bosley St; powered sites $38, cabins $110-152; ☎) About 6km north of the CBD, Sunset Beach has roomy, shaded sites just a few steps from a lovely beach, and an ultramodern camp kitchen with a huge TV. Decor in some of the cabins is pretty dated.

Ocean West APARTMENT $$
(☎08-9921 1047; www.oceanwest.com.au; 1 Hadda Way; 1-/2-/3-bedroom apt from $140/195/245; ✱🤫⛶) Don't let the '60s brick put you off; these fully self-contained units have all been renovated in fresh monochrome, making them one of the better deals in town (especially for families or groups). Facilities are excellent; the wildly beautiful back beach is just across the road.

Mantra Geraldton APARTMENT $$
(☎08-9956 1300; www.mantra.com.au; 221 Foreshore Dr; 1-/2-bedroom apt from $189/239; ✱🤫⛶) The pick of the upmarket options, for its marina-side location and proximity to museums, the foreshore and town centre. It offers a selection of modern apartments (one- to three-bedroom, all with balcony, kitchen and laundry), polished facilities and

Skeetas (☎08-9964 1619; www.skeetas.com.au; 3/219 Foreshore Dr; mains $20-46; ☎7am-9.30pm) restaurant downstairs.

Eating

Quiet Life CAFE $
(☎0484 314 364; www.quietlifecoffee.com.au; 287 Marine Tce; bagels $8-12; ☎7am-4pm Thu-Tue) Sit outside under the grapevine at this sweet old cottage, now a hipster-fied cafe serving up outstanding speciality coffee and delicious filled bagels (the chicken with slaw and bacon jam is top-notch). There's an additional brunch menu from Thursday to Sunday; keep an eye out for Friday-night 'After Dark' events.

Jaffle Shack CAFE $
(☎08-9949 9755; www.facebook.com/TheJaffleShack; 188 Marine Tce; jaffles $6-12; ☎7am-3pm) The humble jaffle (toasted sandwich) is showcased at this rustic, surfer-chic cafe. Fillings range from classic Aussie combos such as Vegemite and cheese or baked beans, to prosciutto with garlic mushrooms. Leave room for a dessert jaffle (like apple with almond and ricotta). Ice-cream milkshakes and damn fine coffee too. There's a second **shack** (www.facebook.com/TheJaffleShack; Foreshore Dr; jaffles $6-12; ☎7.30am-4pm) on the foreshore.

★ Saltdish CAFE $$
(☎08-9964 6030; 35 Marine Tce; breakfast $8-25, lunch $22-30; ☎7am-4pm Mon-Fri, plus 6-9pm Fri & Sat) The hippest cafe in town serves innovative, contemporary brekkies, light lunches and industrial-strength coffee, plus home-baked sweet treats. The menu is an ode to local produce and accomplished cooking, from Exmouth prawn and spring-pea risotto to tempura-fried Atlantic cod. It's also open for dinner on Friday and Saturday nights (two courses for $55). BYO wine or beer.

★ The Provincial MODERN AUSTRALIAN $$
(☎08-9964 1887; 167 Marine Tce; pizza $13-20, mains $18-34; ☎4.30pm-late Tue-Sat) Stencil art adorns this cool little taste of the city, an atmospheric bar serving up tasty share plates, wood-fired pizzas and more. It's a loungey spot with smooth tunes, outdoor courtyard, cocktail specials, and live music most Friday and Saturday nights.

🍷 Drinking & Nightlife

There's an assortment of pubs offering live music on weekends (local artists plus vis-

PINK LAKE

More commonly referred to as 'Pink Lake', Hutt Lagoon is an arresting sight near the seaside villages of Horrocks and Port Gregory. Yes, the saltwater here is pink, due to the presence of the algae *Dunaliella salina*. The algae is a source of beta-carotene, which is harvested here and used in food colouring and make-up.

You can see the lake from George Grey Dr (the road south of Kalbarri), but take the turn-off to Port Gregory for the best viewpoints. You can also take popular sightseeing flights over the lake from Kalbarri and Geraldton.

iting Perth bands) and various cheap meal deals to lure in the punters. See Facebook pages to see what live music is on offer. And check out The Provincial (p170), too, for a smooth lounge-bar vibe.

Geraldton Hotel　　　　　　　　　　PUB
(✆08-9921 3700; www.geraldtonhotel.com.au; 19 Gregory St; ⏰10am-10pm Sun-Thu, to midnight Fri & Sat) Winning features of this landmark old pub (dating from 1860) include a huge palm-tree-lined courtyard, $10 meal deals, and live music on weekends, including popular Sunday-afternoon sessions.

Freemasons Hotel　　　　　　　　　　PUB
(✆08-9964 3457; www.thefreemasonshotel.wix-site.com/home#; cnr Marine Tce & Durlacher St; ⏰5.30-9pm Mon-Tue, 11am-9pm Wed-Thu, 11am-10pm Fri-Sun) The heritage-listed Freo has been serving beer to thirsty travellers since the 1800s. Nowadays it's a popular hang-out, with live music, DJs and open-mic nights complemented by a good range of bar meals.

ℹ Information

Visitor Centre (✆08-9956 6670; www.visitgeraldton.com.au; 246 Marine Tce; ⏰9am-5pm Mon-Fri, to 1pm Sat & Sun) Top location at the foreshore, with helpful staff. Accommodation, tour and transport bookings.

ℹ Getting There & Around

Geraldton is 420km north of Perth.

Virgin Australia and Qantas both fly daily between Perth and Geraldton. The airport is 12km east of the city centre, on the road to Mullewa and Mt Magnet.

The **long-distance bus station** (p169) is at the old railway station on Chapman St; a Trans-wa booking office is here.

All fares listed are one way.

Transwa (www.transwa.wa.gov.au) Runs buses between Perth and Geraldton ($66, six to 8½ hours) taking one of four possible routes. The twice-weekly coastal option runs via Indian Ocean Drive. Inland options run via Rte 1, Rte 115, or Rtes 95 and 116. The most frequent service is via the Brand Hwy (Rte 1); it offers connection to Kalbarri ($30; 2½ hours) three times a week. Transwa also has a twice-weekly service from Geraldton to Meekatharra ($79, seven hours).

Integrity (www.integritycoachlines.com.au) Runs three bus services per week linking Geraldton to Perth ($63, six hours), Carnarvon ($115, 6½ hours) and Exmouth ($156, 11½ hours).

Kalbarri

POP 2000

Magnificent sandstone cliffs terminate at the Indian Ocean. The beautiful Murchison River snakes through tall, steep gorges before ending treacherously at Gantheaume Bay. Wildflowers line paths frequented by kangaroos, emus and thorny devils, while whales breach just offshore, and rare orchids struggle in the rocky ground. To the north, the towering line of the limestone Zuytdorp Cliffs remains aloof, pristine and remote.

Kalbarri is surrounded by stunning nature, and there's great surfing, swimming, fishing, bushwalking, horse riding and canoeing both in town and in Kalbarri National Park (p174). While its vibe is mostly low-key, Kalbarri is stretched to the limit in school holidays.

◉ Sights

Aside from the beaches, Kalbarri's biggest drawcards lie in the national park (p174) that surrounds the town to the northeast and the south. Be sure to admire the views from lookouts at coastal cliffs and river gorges.

Foreshore　　　　　　　　　　WATERFRONT
In town, the river foreshore is lovely for a stroll or cycle – it has children's playgrounds (behind the town beach and by the jetty), picnic tables, barbecues, and fine swimming areas at the west end of town.

Rainbow Jungle　　　　　　　　BIRD SANCTUARY
(✆08-9937 1248; www.rainbowjunglekalbarri.com; Red Bluff Rd; adult/child/family $16/8/42; ⏰9am-5pm Mon-Sat, to 4pm Sun) Bird fans (and kids)

Kalbarri

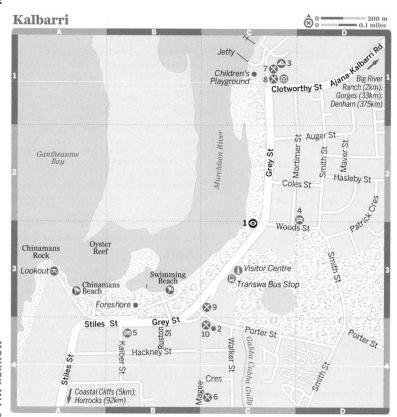

will enjoy this bird park south of town – it's an Australian parrot breeding centre, and there's all manner of colourful feathered creatures to admire (local lorikeets and cockatoos, but also South American macaws). It has a walk-through aviary, a lookout tower to climb and a small cafe. Look for outdoor movie evenings at the park's Cinema Parrotiso (adult/child $18/10), held in the school holidays.

Pelican Feeding   WATERFRONT
(Foreshore; ⊗8.45-9.15am) FREE Kalbarri's most popular attraction takes place every morning on the waterfront. Look for the compact wooden viewing area and wait for the hungry birds to rock up.

🏃 Activities

Just south of town are turn-offs to a string of **beaches** (all are great for sunset-watching), connected by the 8km **Melaleuca Cycle-Walk Trail**.

Kalbarri

◎ Sights
1 Pelican Feeding C3

🏃 Activities, Courses & Tours
2 Reefwalker Adventure Tours C4

🛏 Sleeping
3 Anchorage Caravan Park..................... C1
4 Kalbarri Backpackers YHA D2
5 Pelican Shore Villas B4

⊗ Eating
6 Finlay's Fresh Fish BBQ C4
7 Gorges Café... C1
8 Jetty Seafood Shack C1
9 Kalbarri Motor Hotel........................... C3
10 Restaurant Upstairs C4

Blue Holes is the best place for snorkelling, while **Jakes Bay** draws surfers (Jakes Point is an elevated area for watching the

HOUTMAN ABROLHOS ISLANDS

Better known as 'the Abrolhos', this archipelago of 122 islands and coral reefs 60km off the coast of Geraldton is home to amazing wildlife, including sea lions, green turtles, carpet pythons, seabirds and the Tammar wallaby.

Much of the flora is rare, endemic and protected, and the surrounding reefs offer great diving and snorkelling thanks to the warm Leeuwin Current, which allows tropical species such as *Acropora* (staghorn) coral to flourish further south than normal. In fact, the Abrolhos Islands are the southernmost coral reefs in the Indian Ocean; they are clustered into three main groups (Wallabi, Easter and Pelsaert) and spread from north to south across 100km of ocean.

The name Abrolhos is thought to derive from the Portuguese expression *Abre os olhos*, meaning 'keep your eyes open'. These gnarly reefs have claimed many ships over the years, including the ill-fated Dutch East India Company's *Batavia* (1629) and *Zeewijk* (1727). You can dive on some wreck sites, as well as follow a number of self-guided dive trails.

How to Visit

Unless you have your own boat (see the *Abrolhos Islands Information Guide* for details on visiting requirements and moorings), you'll need to take a tour.

There are non-permanent inhabitants of the islands – these are the families who fish commercially for western rock lobster. There is also some pearl farming done in the surrounding waters. You'll see the locals' rustic houses and jetties from the air, and it's a beautiful sight.

Because the general public can't stay overnight, divers (and surfers and fishers) normally need a multi-day boat charter. If you're content with a day trip where you can bushwalk, picnic and snorkel, then flying in is your best bet (and the aerial views are truly spectacular).

Tours generally depart from Geraldton. Two airlines offer tours and day trips: **Shine Aviation** (☑08-9923 3600; www.shineaviation.com.au; Geraldton Airport; 4hr/6hr Abrolhos tour $235/255) and **Geraldton Air Charter** (☑08-9923 3434; www.geraldtonaircharter. com.au; Geraldton Airport; 4hr/6hr Abrolhos tour $240/260) fly from the Geraldton airport 12km east of town and offer similar services and prices. The most popular tour is to land on East Wallabi Island and snorkel off the pristine beach here – four- and six-hour tours are available. Shorter, cheaper flights (flightseeing only, no landing; $215 for 90 minutes) are possible, or you can combine a visit to East Wallabi Island with flightseeing over Kalbarri and Hutt Lagoon (aka Pink Lake; from $455).

Kalbarri Scenic Flights (☑08-9937 1130; www.kalbarriaircharter.com.au; Kalbarri Airport, off Ajana-Kalbarri Rd; flights & tours $84-315) offers flightseeing ($245) or a five-hour tour including landing ($255), departing from Kalbarri.

Divers should contact Batavia Coast Dive Academy (p169) in Geraldton, which can help get a boat together (from $300 per person per day).

Eco Abrolhos (☑08-9964 5101; www.ecoabrolhos.com.au; 3-/5-day cruise incl meals from $1176/1960) is run by a crayfisherman with longstanding connections to the Abrolhos. The company offers liveaboard boat tours, departing from Geraldton between March and October and taking in snorkelling, diving, fishing, wildlife spotting and shore excursions around the islands. The vessel can accommodate 38 passengers in air-con cabins with en suites.

surfers and any visiting dolphins). **Wittecarra Beach** draws fishing fans, and **Red Bluff Beach** is ideal for swimming. South of here is Red Bluff itself, the start of the southern section of Kalbarri National Park (p174).

Wildflowers bring visitors in spring – with the right conditions, the season can last from mid-June into November. Look for wildflowers along Stiles Rd, the Ajana-Kalbarri Rd, and near the airport. The visitor centre (p174) publishes wildflower updates in season and doles out up-to-date advice.

☞ Tours

Kalbarri is an outdoor adventure hub and excursions on offer include **Kalbarri Quadbike Safaris** (☑08-9937 1011; www.kalbarriquadsafaris.com.au; off Ajana-Kalbarri Rd; driver/passenger from $80/40), whale-watching with **Reefwalker Adventure Tours** (☑08-9937 1356; www.reefwalker.com.au; office: Porter St; whale-watching tour adult/child $85/55) (from June to November) and abseiling in the gorges of Kalbarri National Park with **Kalbarri Abseil** (☑08-9937 1618; www.kalbarriabseil.com; adult/child $90/80).

For interesting full- and half-day tours combining canoeing, bushwalking and swimming, contact **Kalbarri Adventure Tours** (☑08-9937 1677; www.kalbarritours.com.au; adult/child from $75/50).

Ask at the visitor centre also about canoeing, boat rental, horse riding, wilderness cruises and scenic flights.

🛏 Sleeping & Eating

Anchorage Caravan Park   CARAVAN PARK $
(☑08-9937 1181; www.kalbarrianchorage.com.au; cnr Anchorage Lane & Grey St; sites $35-45, cabins $80-90; ☒) The best option for campers, Anchorage has roomy, nicely shaded sites that overlook the rivermouth. Standard cabins have a kitchen and are family-sized, but they're budget affairs (no bathroom, BYO linen or hire it).

Kalbarri Backpackers YHA   HOSTEL $
(☑08-9937 1430; www.kalbarribackpackers.com; cnr Woods & Mortimer Sts; dm/d $29/77; @🖙☒) The great location (one block back from the beach) and the friendly hosts win brownie points; the facilities themselves are a bit run-down. Still, there's a pool, a barbecue and an outdoor kitchen, and you can hire bikes ($20 per day), snorkels and boogie boards.

Pelican Shore Villas   APARTMENT $$
(☑08-9937 1708; www.pelicanshorevillas.com.au; cnr Grey & Kaiber Sts; villas $150-207; ✳🖙☒) This complex of 18 modern and stylish villas have the best view in town and lovely grounds. All units have full kitchen and laundry; choose from two- or three-bedroom options.

Jetty Seafood Shack   FISH & CHIPS $
(☑08-9937 1067; Grey St; meals $11-25, burgers $9-14; ⊙4.30-8.30pm) Excellent fish and chips, bumper burgers and takeaway salads (to make you feel at least slightly healthy).

Pop across the road and dine at one of the outdoor picnic tables.

★**Finlay's Fresh Fish BBQ**   SEAFOOD $$
(☑08-9937 1260; www.finlaysfreshfishbbq.com; 24 Magee Cres; mains $15-45; ⊙5.30-10pm Tue-Sun) Fresh local seafood comes simply prepared at this super-quirky Kalbarri institution, and often with piles of chips and lashings of mayonnaise-packed salads. Don't miss the walls packed with a few decades' of kitsch Australiana and Oz popular culture. It's not all seafood – steak and burgers available too. BYO drinks.

★**Gorges Café**   CAFE $$
(☑08-9937 1200; 166 Grey St; meals $10-30; ⊙7am-2pm Wed-Mon) Just opposite the jetty, Gorges has excellent breakfasts and lunches, and bright friendly service. Look forward to the best coffee in town, ace eggy breakfasts and delicious lunchtime dishes like fish cakes, Thai beef salad or club sandwiches.

Kalbarri Motor Hotel   PUB FOOD $$
(☑08-9937 1400; 50 Grey St; pizzas $18-25, mains $22-38) The garden bar is our favourite spot for a sunset beer, and there's occasional live bands on Friday and Saturday nights. The menu is a roll-call of well-prepared classic hits, from spag bol to surf 'n' turf, but there are surprises in the Asian menu (eg, Vietnamese chicken curry) and the WA crayfish options. Meals served noon to 2.30pm and 6pm to 8.30pm.

Restaurant Upstairs   MODERN AUSTRALIAN $$$
(☑08-9937 1033; 2 Porter St, upstairs; mains $27-44; ⊙6pm-late Wed-Mon) Stick to the core menu of seafood and Asian-influenced mains, and you'll be satisfied at the classiest dining spot in town. Book ahead and ask for a spot on the balcony. Good desserts and a decent wine list seal the deal. Small kids not welcome.

ℹ Information

There are ATMs at the shopping centre on Porter St, and by the post office opposite the jetty on Grey St.

Visitor Centre (☑08-9937 1104; www.kalbarri.org.au; Grey St; ⊙9am-5pm Mon-Sat, to 1pm Sun) Books accommodation, tours and bus tickets.

Kalbarri National Park

With its magnificent river red gums and Tumblagooda sandstone, rugged Kalbarri

National Park (www.parks.dpaw.wa.gov.au/park/kalbarri; admission per car $12) contains almost 2000 sq km of wild bushland, stunning river gorges and savagely eroded coastal cliffs. It contains abundant wildlife, including 200 species of birds, and spectacular wildflowers between July and November.

There are two faces to the park: coastal cliffs line the coast south of Kalbarri, with great lookouts and walking trails connecting them. Inland are the river gorges.

◉ Sights

Coastal Cliffs

A string of lookouts dot the coast south of Kalbarri (accessed from George Grey Dr). Most lookouts are just a short walk from car-parking areas; a few have trails down to small beaches below. From July to November, you may spot migrating whales.

For an invigorating walk, take the **Bigurda Trail** (8km one way) following the clifftops between Natural Bridge and Eagle Gorge.

Closer to town are Pot Alley, Rainbow Valley, Mushroom Rock and Red Bluff. **Red Bluff** is the closest part of the park to town, and is accessible via a walking trail from Kalbarri (5.5km one way). From the lookout there are wonderful views of the Zuytdorp Cliffs to the north, and sunsets here are stunning.

River Gorges

The river gorges are east of Kalbarri, accessed from the Ajana-Kalbarri Rd. Roads travel to car-park areas with shaded picnic facilities, basic toilets and short walking paths (from 200m to 1.2km return) to dramatic lookouts.

Travel east of town for 11km to reach the first park turn-off. After a period of disruptive closures (from December 2016 to July 2017), a newly sealed, 20km road grants access to the park's favourite sites.

At the T-intersection, turn left to reach **West Loop Lookout** (where a new **Skywalk** was under construction at the time of research) and the Loop Lookout. From the Loop Lookout, a 1km return path leads to the park's most iconic attraction, the superb **Nature's Window** (a rock formation that perfectly frames the Murchison River below).

Bring lots of water if you want to walk the unshaded **Loop Trail** (9km return), accessed from Nature's Window.

Turning right at the T-intersection leads to **Z-Bend** with a breathtaking lookout (1.2km return), or you can continue steeply down to the gorge bottom (2.6km return).

Head back to Ajana-Kalbarri Rd and travel a further 24km east to reach the second set of sights. Turn off the road and you'll quickly reach the **Ross Graham Lookout**, where you can access the river's edge (1.4km return). Nearby **Hawks Head** has more great views – it's named after the shape of the rock structure seen from the lookout.

ℹ Information

For information, visit the Kalbarri **visitor centre** (p174) or the Department of Parks & Wildlife website (www.parks.dpaw.wa.gov.au). The Kalbarri tourist brochure (published annually) has excellent maps and details of all the walks.

Take water if you're visiting the gorges, and note that temperatures in this part of the park can be high – hike in the early part of the day.

SHARK BAY

The World Heritage–listed area of Shark Bay, stretching from Kalbarri to Carnarvon, consists of more than 1500km of dazzling coastline: turquoise lagoons, barren finger-like peninsulas, hidden bays, white-sand beaches, towering limestone cliffs and numerous islands. It's the westernmost part of the Australian mainland, and one of WA's most biologically rich habitats, with an array of plant and animal life found nowhere else on earth. Lush beds of sea-grass and sheltered bays nourish dugongs, sea turtles, humpback whales, dolphins, stingrays, sharks and more.

On land, Shark Bay's biodiversity has benefited from Project Eden, an ambitious ecosystem-regeneration program that has sought to eradicate feral animals and reintroduce endemic species. Shark Bay is also home to the amazing stromatolites of Hamelin Pool.

History

The Malgana, Nhanda and Inggarda peoples originally inhabited the area, and visitors can take Indigenous cultural tours to learn about 'Country'.

Shark Bay played host to early European explorers (and shipwrecks), and many geographical names display this legacy. In 1616, Dutch explorer Dirk Hartog nailed a pewter dinner plate (now in Amsterdam's Rijksmuseum) to a post on the island that now bears his name.

ℹ Getting There & Away

Shark Bay airport is located between Denham and Monkey Mia. **Skippers Aviation** (www.skippers.com.au) flies to/from Perth a handful of times weekly.

Integrity (www.integritycoachlines.com.au) buses run along the coast between Perth and Broome a few days a week, but don't make it up to Denham or Monkey Mia. They do, however, stop at the Overlander Roadhouse on the North West Coastal Hwy, 130km from Denham. **Shark Bay Car Hire** (☑08-9948 3032, 0427 483 032; www.carhire.net.au/shuttle-service/; 65 Knight Tce, Denham; shuttle $72, car/4WD hire per day from $95/185) runs a connecting shuttle service (book at least 24 hours ahead). It also has cars and 4WDs for hire.

If you're visiting without your own wheels, **Shark Bay Coaches & Tours** (☑0429 110 104; www.sharkbaycoaches.com) provides useful transfers between Denham and Monkey Mia ($15), plus links to the airport. The **Monkey Mia Dolphin Resort** (p179) can also arrange airport transfers for its guests.

Overlander Roadhouse to Denham (Shark Bay Road)

It can feel like a long stretch driving the 130km from the North West Coastal Hwy (at Overlander Roadhouse) to Denham, a road known as Shark Bay Rd or, in marketing speak, World Heritage Drive. There are some excellent reasons to stop and break the journey.

Turn-offs lead to great natural attractions, including the 'living fossils' at Hamelin Pool and the stunning Shell Beach. With some preparation and a 4WD, you can explore the Australian mainland's most westerly tip.

⊙ Sights

★ Hamelin Pool   MARINE RESERVE

Twenty-nine kilometres along Shark Bay Rd from the Overlander Roadhouse is the turn-off for Hamelin Pool, a marine reserve with the world's best-known colony of stromatolites. These coral-like formations consist of cyanobacteria almost identical to organisms that existed 3.5 billion years ago; through their use of photosynthesis they are considered largely responsible for creating our current atmosphere, paving the way for more complex life. There's an excellent boardwalk

DIRK HARTOG NATIONAL PARK

The slim, wind-raked island, which runs parallel to the Peron Peninsula, once attracted Dutch, British and French explorers (who left pewter plates nailed to posts as calling cards), but until recently its visitors were mostly fisherfolk and sheep. Now WA's largest island has become a **national park** (https://parks.dpaw.wa.gov.au/park/dirk-hartog-island) and is slowly opening itself up to tourism (although access is not easy, and is very expensive).

Only 20 4WD vehicles are allowed on the island at any one time, so bookings are necessary. The drawcards are isolation, natural beauty, wildlife (from loggerhead turtles to dugongs) and history – a winning combination.

Camping tours, 4WD excursions and scenic flights can be booked in Denham.

with information panels, best seen at low tide.

Steep Point   LANDMARK

The Australian mainland's most westerly point, accessed by 4WD via Useless Loop Rd off Shark Bay Rd.

Shell Beach   BEACH

Inside the vermin-proof fence, and 55km past the Hamelin turn-off, is the road to deserted Shell Beach, where tiny cockle shells, densely compacted over time, were once quarried as building material for places such as the Old Pearler Restaurant in Denham. For swimmers, the water is often warm, but quite salty.

★ Eagle Bluff   VIEWPOINT

About 25km south of Denham, take the turn-off 4km to this brilliant viewpoint, where a boardwalk allows you vistas that meld pinky-orange cliffs with the azure lagoon below. You may spot turtles, sharks or manta rays in the clear waters.

🛏 Sleeping

★ Hamelin Outback Station Stay   FARMSTAY $

(☑08-9948 5145; www.hamelinstationstay.com.au; sites per person $14, d without bathroom from $90; ⊘mid-Mar–Oct) 🌿 Far and away the nicest place to stay along Shark Bay Rd, Hamelin Station is a former pastoral property transformed into a 202,000-hectare conservation reserve by its new owners (since 2015), the NGO Bush Heritage Australia. The rooms in the converted shearers' quarters are lovely and the amenities (including the communal kitchen-dining area) are top-notch; the bush camping sites are all unpowered.

Denham

POP 1000

Beautiful, laid-back Denham, with its aquamarine sea and palm-fringed beachfront, makes a great base for trips to the surrounding Shark Bay Marine Park, nearby Francois Peron and Dirk Hartog Island National Parks, and Monkey Mia, 26km away.

Australia's westernmost town originated as a pearling base, and the streets were once paved with pearl shell.

⊙ Sights

★**Ocean Park**   AQUARIUM
(☑08-9948 1765; www.oceanpark.com.au; Shark Bay Rd; adult/child $25/18; ⊙9am-5pm; 🚗) ✦
On a spectacular headland 8km south of Denham, this family-friendly attraction features an artificial lagoon where you can observe shark feedings, plus tanks filled with turtles, stingrays and fish (many of them being rehabilitated after rescue). It's all revealed on a well-done, 60-minute guided tour. The park also has a range of diving op-

portunities (including diving with the park's sharks), plus 4WD and boat tours (p178). It also has a good restaurant (p178) and there are plans for luxury **accommodation** (☑08-9948 1765; www.oceanpark.com.au; Ocean Park Rd; from around $300; ❋🐾).

★**Little Lagoon**   LAGOON
Idyllic Little Lagoon, 4km from town, has picnic tables and barbecues, and is good for a walk or swim. Don't be surprised if an emu wanders by.

Foreshore   WATERFRONT
(Knight Tce) The recently revamped Denham foreshore (spruced up to host celebrations for Dirk Hartog Island's quadricentenary in 2016) is a lovely place for a barbecue, picnic, stroll or swim. Opposite the visitor centre is a cracker ship-themed playground that children will love.

Shark Bay World Heritage Discovery Centre   MUSEUM
(☑08-9948 1590; www.sharkbayvisit.com; 53 Knight Tce; ⊙9am-5pm Mon-Fri, 10am-4pm Sat & Sun) There are two sides to this centre, which is home to Shark Bay's helpful visitor centre. A gallery (free to enter) that houses stunning aerial photos of the Shark Bay area will have you itching to book a scenic flight. The main part of the centre is dedicated to a museum (adult/child $11/6), which has informative and evocative displays of Shark Bay's ecosystems, marine and animal life,

WORTH A TRIP

FRANCOIS PERON NATIONAL PARK

Covering the whole peninsula north of Denham, this 520-sq-km **national park** (https://parks.dpaw.wa.gov.au/park/francois-peron; admission per car $12) is a spectacular area of low scrub, salt lagoons and sandy dunes, and is home to the rare bilby, mallee fowl and woma python. Rust-red cliffs, white-sand beaches and blue waters all interplay, but you'll need to join a tour in Denham or Monkey Mia, or have a high-clearance 4WD.

Vehicles that are 2WD can only travel as far as the '**Peron Heritage Precinct**' (7km from the main road), where the old **Peron Homestead** houses museum displays. There's a walking trail around the shearing sheds, and a rustic, artesian-bore hot tub for visitors who'd like a soak. Further north, swim, kayak or stand-up paddleboard at the **Big Lagoon**, where there is also an excellent campsite. At the tip of the peninsula, the fantastic **Wanamalu Trail** (3km return) follows the clifftop between Cape Peron and Skipjack Point. Spot marine life in the crystal waters below.

The turn-off to the park is just past **Little Lagoon** on the road to Monkey Mia. Beyond the heritage precinct, the sandy road becomes passable only to high-clearance 4WD vehicles. Near the homestead, there's a tyre station to reduce tyre pressure to 20psi (or reinflate, as you exit). Caravans are not recommended; you'll need an off-road camper trailer.

Indigenous culture, early explorers, settlers and shipwrecks.

Tours

Ocean Park Tours   ADVENTURE
(☑08-9948 1765; www.oceanpark.com.au; Ocean Park Rd) As well as its fun aquarium, Ocean Park (p177) has some great diving excursions (and PADI courses) and boat tours, plus a range of 4WD tours. Dive excursions head west to Steep Point or Dirk Hartog Island (from $275, non-divers welcome at $175). Boat cruises are also available to the same areas, and there are whale-watching trips from August to October ($175).

On land, explore Francois Peron National Park ($190) or Steep Point ($350) with bushwalks and snorkelling. Dirk Hartog Island visits (4WD tows and camping) can be customised.

Shark Bay Scenic Flights   SCENIC FLIGHTS
(☑08-9948 1773; www.sharkbayair.com.au; Shark Bay airport; flights from adult/child $120/60) Flights range from a 15-minute Monkey Mia flyover to a sensational 40-minute trip over Steep Point and the Zuytdorp Cliffs (adult/child $195/98). From the air, the region looks like a piece of art, vibrant with colour. There are also tours available to Dirk Hartog Island, Coral Bay or Mt Augustus.

Sleeping

Expect school-holiday surcharges for accommodation, and possible minimum night stays (two or three nights is the norm). Compared with Monkey Mia, choices are wider and prices are lower.

**Denham Seaside
Tourist Village**   CARAVAN PARK $
(☑08-9948 1242; www.sharkbayfun.com; Knight Tce; sites $33-54, cabins & villas $85-170; ☎) This lovely, shady park on the water's edge is the best of the three parks in Denham, though you will need to borrow the drill for your tent pegs. Accommodation ranges from small five-bed cabins without bathroom through to two-bedroom villas. A handy supermarket is across the road.

Bay Lodge   LODGE $
(☑08-9948 1278; www.baylodge.info; 113 Knight Tce; dm $36, d $80-140; ❄☎☀) Every room (including dorm rooms) at this lodge has its own en suite, kitchenette and TV/DVD, and there are motel-style rooms, family-size

apartments, and beachfront units to choose from. Ideally located across from the beach, it also has a pool and a large common outdoor kitchen. There's a two-night minimum stay during school holidays.

Oceanside Village   APARTMENT $$
(☑08-9948 3003; www.oceanside.com.au; 117 Knight Tce; villas $160-215; ❄☎☀) This complex of neat self-catering cottages is perfectly located opposite the beach. Choose from one- or two-bedroom, beachfront or elevated. Facilities are top-notch.

Eating & Drinking

Ocean Restaurant   CAFE $$
(☑08-9948 1765; www.oceanpark.com.au; Ocean Park Rd; mains $14-34; ◷9am-3pm) The most refined lunch in Denham also comes with the best view. At Ocean Park (p177), overlooking aquamarine waters, breakfast is served until 11am, and you can partner beer and wine with lunches of local seafood and more. The platter for two people ($58) is good value.

Old Pearler Restaurant   SEAFOOD $$$
(☑08-9948 1373; 71 Knight Tce; mains $30-61; ◷from 5pm Mon-Sat) Built from shell bricks, this atmospheric nautical haven serves fantastic seafood. The menu and interior is decidedly old-school and there are no outdoor tables or view, but the fresh fishy fare is great – the hefty seafood platter ($115 for two people) features local snapper, whiting, crayfish, oysters, prawns and squid – all grilled, not fried. BYO drinks; bookings recommended.

Shark Bay Hotel   PUB
(☑08-9948 1203; www.sharkbayhotelwa.com.au; 43 Knight Tce; dinner mains $20-38; ◷10am-late) Sunsets are dynamite from the front beer garden of Australia's most westerly pub, lovingly called 'the Oldie' by locals. It has a decent menu of pub classics (served noon to 2pm, and 6pm to 9pm), plus occasional live music.

ℹ Information

For information, interactive maps and downloadable permits, check out www.sharkbay.org.au. There's more info at www.sharkbayvisit.com.au and www.experiencesharkbay.com.

Department of Parks & Wildlife (☑08-9948 2226; www.parks.dpaw.wa.gov.au; 61 Knight Tce; ◷8am-5pm Mon-Fri) Park passes, maps and information about Edel Land, Dirk Hartog Island and Francois Peron National Park.

Shark Bay Visitor Centre (☐ 08-9948 1590; www.sharkbayvisit.com; 53 Knight Tce; ⊙ 9am-5pm Mon-Fri, 10am-4pm Sat & Sun) Accommodation, tour bookings and bush-camping permits for South Peron. Located inside the Shark Bay World Heritage Discovery Centre.

Monkey Mia

Watching the wild dolphins turning up for a feed each morning in the shallow waters of Monkey Mia, 26km northeast of Denham, is a highlight of every traveller's trip to the region.

There's not much to the place (Monkey Mia is little more than a beach and resort), but you don't need to rush off after the early feeding – the beach is lovely, and there are some excellent tour experiences too.

◉ Sights

★**Monkey Mia Marine Reserve**   BAY
(adult/child/family $12/4.50/28.50; ⊙ feeding at 7.45am; ⏹) 🖉 It's hard not to smile as Indo-Pacific bottlenose dolphins start arriving for a breakfast snack. Note that during feedings, visitors are restricted to the edge of the water, and only a lucky few people per session are selected to wade in and help feed the dolphins. The pier makes a good vantage point for it all. Rangers talk you through the history of the dolphin encounters. It may seem a little touristy, but there's no denying its charm, or the loveliness of the setting.

The first feed is around 7.45am. Stay around after the session, as the dolphins commonly come a second or third time until around noon (and the crowds are usually lighter for these later sessions). The dolphins may spend the day close to the beachfront, too.

You can volunteer to work full time with the dolphins for between four and 14 days – it's popular, so apply several months in advance and specify availability dates, though sometimes there are last-minute openings. Contact the volunteer coordinator (p180).

⌲ Tours

★**Wula Guda Nyinda**
Eco Adventures   ECOTOUR
(☐ 0432 029 436; www.wulaguda.com.au; 2hr sunset tour adult/child $70/35) 🖉 Learn how to let country talk to you on these excellent tours led by local Aboriginal guide Darren 'Capes' Capewell, including the secrets of bush survival and bush tucker. The camp-

fire-at-sunset 'Didgeridoo Dreaming' tours are magical. There are also snorkelling and kayak tours (adult/child $199/145) and exciting 4WD adventures into Francois Peron National Park ($199/140).

Aristocat 2   CRUISE
(☐ 1800 030 427; www.perfectnaturecruises.com. au; 2½hr cruise adult/child $89/49) 🖉 After you've greeted the morning dolphins, step aboard this large catamaran for its 10.30am cruise around Shark Bay, where you might see dugongs, dolphins and loggerhead turtles. You'll also stop off at the Blue Lagoon Pearl Farm. There's an additional afternoon departure in peak times.

Wildsights   ADVENTURE
(☐ 1800 241 481; www.monkeymiawildsights.com. au; 2½hr cruise adult/child $89/45) On the small *Shotover* catamaran you're close to the action for the 2½-hour wildlife cruise. There are also 1½-hour sunset cruises ($49, bring your own drinks and snacks), and a full-day 4WD trip to Francois Peron National Park ($195); discounts are available for multiple trips.

🛏 Sleeping & Eating

Monkey Mia Dolphin Resort   RESORT $$
(☐ 1800 871 570; www.monkeymia.com.au; unpowered/powered sites from $37/54, backpacker dm/d $35/139, d from $267; ❄ 🛜 🎅) With a stunning location, the only accommodation option in Monkey Mia caters to campers, backpackers, package and top-end tourists. The staff are friendly, and the backpacker rooms are good value (two rooms share a bathroom), but the top-end rooms are expensive. It can also get quite crowded. The large grounds are home to a restaurant, bar, pool, store and tour booking office.

★**Boughshed**   MODERN AUSTRALIAN $$
(Monkey Mia Resort; lunch $15-24, dinner mains $27-41; ⊙ 7am-8pm) The setting is fabulous, the views are grand (and the visiting birdlife is prolific – don't leave your food unattended!). The Boughshed has a fresh, stylish interior and plenty of areas in which to nurse a coffee or drink (happy hour is 4pm to 5pm). Menus range from buffet or a la carte breakfast to light lunches and some creative dinner options.

Monkey Bar   BAR
(Monkey Mia Resort; pizzas & meals $16-23; ⊙ 4-10pm) A relaxed and informal option closer to the backpacker section of the resort, the

Monkey Bar has a pool table, happy hour from 5pm to 6pm, and a menu of pizzas and pub-style grub (fish and chips, lasagne, burgers). There are children's options too. It's open from noon during school holidays.

ℹ Information

Monkey Mia Visitor Centre (☑ 08-9948 1366; ☉7am-3.30pm) Information about the area, plus tour bookings. It's on the beach, close to where the dolphin feeding takes place.

Volunteer Coordinator (☑ 08-9948 1366; monkeymiavolunteers@westnet.com.au) Contact for volunteering at Monkey Mia.

GASCOYNE COAST

This wild, rugged, largely unpopulated coastline stretches between two World Heritage-listed areas, Shark Bay and Ningaloo Reef, and offers excellent fishing and waves that attract surfers from around the world.

Subtropical Carnarvon, the region's hub, is an important fruit- and vegetable-growing district, and farms are often looking for seasonal workers. For travellers, it's usually seen as a handy place to restock, but not much more – but with time up your sleeve and a desire to get well off the beaten path, consider the option of heading north from Carnarvon along the Quobba coast.

Carnarvon

POP 6900

On Yinggarda country at the mouth of the Gascoyne River, fertile Carnarvon, with its fruit and vegetable plantations and fishing industry, makes a decent stopover between Denham and Exmouth.

It's a friendly place without the tourist focus of other coastal towns, but it has a few quirky attractions, decent accommodation, well-stocked supermarkets and great local produce. The tree-lined CBD exudes a tropical feel, and the palm-fringed waterfront is a relaxing place to amble. The long picking season from March to January ensures plenty of seasonal work.

◎ Sights

You can walk or cycle 2.5km along the old tramway to the **Carnarvon Heritage Precinct** on Babbage Island, once the city's port. **One Mile Jetty** (off Babbage Island Rd; adult/child $5/free) provides great fishing and

views; walk or take the quirky Coffee Pot Train to the end. The nearby **Lighthouse Keepers Cottage** (off Babbage Island Rd; ☉10am-1pm) FREE has been painstakingly restored; don't miss the view from the top of the creaky water tower in the **Railway Station Museum** (off Babbage Island Rd; ☉9am-5pm). There's a cafe here, housing interpretive displays on the HMAS Sydney shipwreck in 1941.

Carnarvon Space & Technology Museum MUSEUM
(www.carnarvonmuseum.org.au; Mahony Ave; adult/child/family $10/6/25; ☉9am-4pm Apr-Sep, 10am-2pm Oct-Mar; 📷) Established jointly with NASA in 1966, the **OTC Satellite Earth Station** (or OTC Dish) at the edge of town tracked the Gemini and Apollo space missions, as well as Halley's Comet, before closing in 1987. The Space & Technology Museum is here, with its fascinating, family-friendly assortment of space paraphernalia (including handprints from visitors like Buzz Aldrin and Australian astronaut Andy Thomas).

🛏 Sleeping & Eating

A good way to enjoy the local seafood is to cook your own on the free barbecues along the Fascine and at Baxter Park. Self-caterers should check out the produce at the **Gascoyne Arts, Crafts & Growers Market** (www.gascoynefood.com.au/growers-market; Civic Centre car park; ☉8-11.30am Sat late May-early Oct), or stop at various orchards around town.

With a few notable exceptions, the dining scene doesn't exactly shine, but there are takeaways and a handful of pubs.

Coral Coast Tourist Park CARAVAN PARK $
(☑08-9941 1438; www.coralcoasttouristpark.com.au; 108 Robinson St; powered sites $37-43, cabins & units $79-215; ❄️ 🛜 ≋) This pleasant, shady park, with a pool and grassy sites, is close to the town centre. It has a variety of well-appointed cabins, a decent camp kitchen and excellent bathrooms, plus bicycles for hire ($25/75 per day/week).

Fish & Whistle HOSTEL $
(☑08-9941 1704; Beardaj@highway1.com.au; 35 Robinson St; s/d/tw $55/70/70, motel r $120; ❄️ @ 🛜) Travellers love this big, breezy backpackers with its wide verandahs, bunk-free rooms and excellent kitchen. There are aircon motel rooms out the back and the Port Hotel (p181) downstairs. The owners can

MONKEY MIA & THE CENTRAL WEST CARNARVON

help guests find seasonal jobs and provide transport to orchards and farms; there are discounted rates for longer stays.

Best Western Hospitality Inn MOTEL $$
(☑08-9941 1600; www.hospitalityinncarnarvon. com.au; 6 West St; d $159-179; ❉☎❄) Don't mind the dated exterior – this is the best of the motels in town, with fresh, modern rooms and good service. The on-site restaurant, Sails, is highly regarded.

★**Bumbak's** MARKET $
(☑0409 377 934; www.facebook.com/bumbaks; 449 North River Rd; smoothies $8; ☺9am-4pm Mon-Fri, 10am-4pm Sat & Sun) Bumbak's, a working banana and mango plantation about 10km north of town (signposted off the highway), sells a variety of fresh and dried fruit, preserves and delicious homemade ice cream. On the must-try list: mango smoothies, caramelised-fig ice cream and choc-coated bananas.

Sails Restaurant MODERN AUSTRALIAN $$
(☑08-9941 1600; www.hopitalityinncarnarvon. com.au; 6 West St; mains $25-45; ☺6-9pm) Ask a local for a smart food recommendation and this is it: the town's most upmarket choice, at the Hospitality Inn. The kitchen team is led by a bona-fide French chef, and the output is high quality: spicy seafood laksa, honey-glazed spatchcock, parmesan-crusted barramundi and some tropical-minded desserts. Reservations recommended.

Port Hotel CAFE $$
(☑08-9941 1704; 35 Robinson St; meals $14-42; ☺8.30am-2pm Mon-Sat, 6-8.30pm Tue-Sat) There's a relaxed cafe feel to this revamped corner pub on the main drag, and the kitchen's daytime output ranges from eggs Benedict to lunchtime caesar salad and panini (good coffee, too). The evening menu highlights seafood, burgers and tacos.

ℹ Information

Visitor Centre (☑08-9941 1146; www.carnarvon.org.au; Civic Centre, 21 Robinson St; ☺9am-5pm Mon-Fri, to noon Sat) Information, internet, maps and booking service. Open Sunday mornings May to October.

ℹ Getting There & Away

Integrity (www.integritycoachlines.com.au) Runs three times a week to Exmouth ($92, 4¾ hours), Geraldton ($115, six hours) and Perth ($167, 11¾ hours). Buses arrive and depart from the visitor centre.

Quobba Coast

While the North West Coastal Hwy heads inland, the coast north of Carnarvon is wild, rugged and desolate, and a favourite haunt of surfers and fisherfolk. Not many make it this far, but those who do are rewarded by huge winter swells, high summer temperatures, relentless winds, amazing marine life, breath-taking scenery and some truly magical experiences. Red Bluff is the southern point of the majestic Ningaloo Reef.

Two large, remote stations are found along the Quobba coastline, each offering rustic beachside campgrounds and self-contained cottages. The beaches, sunsets, snorkelling, fishing and surfing possibilities are outstanding – as is the feeling that you've really stumbled across a secret, secluded destination.

Blowholes LANDMARK
From the turn-off on the North West Coastal Hwy, it's 49km (on sealed road) to this natural phenomenon. Big swells force sprays of water through sea caves and up out of narrow chimneys in the rocks.

Just south of here (turn left at the 'King Waves Kill' sign and travel a kilometre or two) is Point Quobba, home to a gorgeous sheltered swimming and snorkelling lagoon known locally as the **Aquarium**, plus some beach shacks, excellent fishing and rough campsites.

Gnaraloo Turtle Conservation Program VOLUNTEERING
(GTCP; ☑08-9315 4809; www.gnaraloo.com; Quobba Coast via Carnarvon; ☺Oct-May) ✔ Science graduates (any discipline) prepared to commit for six months can apply to GTCP, where food, accommodation, transport and training are supplied.

Quobba Station Homestead CAMPGROUND, COTTAGE $
(☑08-9948 5098; www.quobba.com.au; unpowered/powered sites per person $13/16, cottages & chalets per person $40-75) ✔ Ten kilometres north of the blowholes is Quobba Station, a huge, ocean-front pastoral property with plenty of rustic self-catering accommodation, campsites (including some generator-powered sites), a small store and legendary fishing. The family-sized chalets are the pick for non-campers.

Quobba Station is also home to Red Bluff Campground (p182), which is some 60km north of the homestead.

Red Bluff
CAMPGROUND $

(☑08-9948 5001; www.quobba.com.au; unpowered sites/shacks per person $15/20, eco-tents from $200) 🖉 On Quobba Station property but 60km north of the homestead, Red Bluff is a spectacular headland with a wicked surf break and excellent fishing, and is the southern boundary of Ningaloo Marine Park. Accommodation comes in all forms, from exposed campsites and palm shelters, to upmarket eco-safari tents with balconies and superb views. It's 10km off the road (4WD recommended).

★ Gnaraloo Station
CAMPGROUND, COTTAGE $$

(☑08-9942 5927; www.gnaraloo.com; unpowered sites per person $18-25, cottage d $70-210; 🛜) 🖉 At the end of the road around 150km from Carnarvon, Gnaraloo Station is the jewel in the crown of the Gascoyne Coast. Surfers from around the world come every winter to ride the notorious **Tombstones**, while summer brings turtle monitoring and windsurfers trying to catch the Carnarvon Doctor, the strong afternoon sea breeze.

You can stay in campsites next to the beach at 3-Mile Camp (there's a small store here), or there's a range of options up at the **homestead** (5km further north of the 3-Mile turn-off). The nicest homestead options are the self-contained stone cabins (bathroom and kitchen) with uninterrupted ocean views – great for spotting migrating whales (between June and November) and sea eagles.

Don't leave without visiting the eye-burningly pristine **Gnaraloo Bay**, 7km from the homestead. Here and around 3-Mile Camp, there's excellent snorkelling close to shore.

Gnaraloo is dedicated to sustainability and has implemented a number of visionary environmental programs. The station is always looking for willing workers. Just be aware that this is a working station in the Australian outback, not a luxury resort.

From the turn-off on the North West Coastal Hwy (about 12km north of the bridge over the Gascoyne River), it's 49km on a sealed road to reach the blowholes. Heading north from here takes you 75km to Gnaraloo Station, passing a couple of coastal sites and campgrounds en route. You'll need to retrace your steps to join the highway again (you can't travel north of Gnaraloo to Coral Bay).

Ask locally for advice about road conditions – north of the blowholes, the road is unsealed and often quite sandy, and a 4WD is recommended. The website www.gnaraloo.com/getting-here has useful info to read before setting out.

Ningaloo Coast & the Pilbara

Best Places to Eat

➡ Whalers Restaurant (p192)

➡ Karijini Eco Retreat Restaurant (p203)

➡ Short Order Local (p191)

➡ Esplanade Hotel (p200)

➡ Empire 6714 (p198)

➡ Fin's Cafe (p187)

Best Places to Swim

➡ Turquoise Bay (p196)

➡ Coral Bay (p186)

➡ Hamersley Gorge (p201)

➡ Fern Pool (p202)

➡ Deep Reach Pool (p204)

Why Go?

Lapping languidly on the edge of the Indian Ocean, the shallow, turquoise waters of the Ningaloo Coast nurture a marine paradise. Lonely bays, deserted beaches and crystal-clear lagoons offer superb snorkelling and diving among myriad forms of sea life, including humpback whales, manta rays and loggerhead turtles. World Heritage–listed Ningaloo Reef is one of the very few places where you can swim with the world's largest fish, the gentle whale shark. Development is low-key, towns few and far between, and seafood and sunsets legendary.

Inland, miners swarm like ants over the high, eroded ranges of the Pilbara, while ore trains snake down to a string of busy ports stretching from Dampier to Port Hedland. But hidden away here are ancient rock-art sites and two beautiful gems – Karijini and Millstream Chichester National Parks, home to spectacular gorges, remote peaks, deep tranquil pools and abundant wildlife.

When to Go
Exmouth

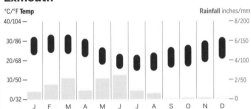

Apr–Jul Whale shark season – don't miss the swim of a lifetime.

Sep & Oct Karijini's gorges warm up and wildflowers blanket the ranges.

Nov–Mar Ningaloo is full of turtle love, eggs and hatchlings. Beware of high temperatures and cyclones.

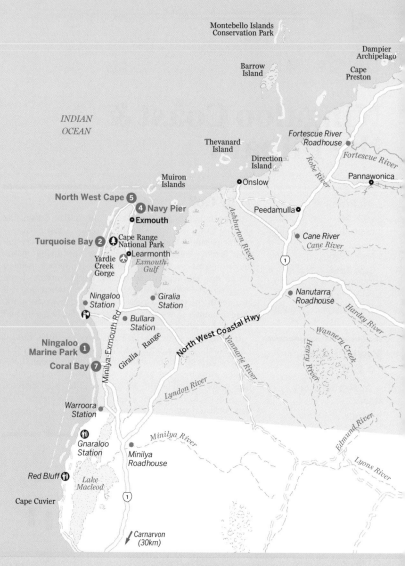

Ningaloo Coast & the Pilbara Highlights

① Swimming with 'gentle giant' whale sharks, manta rays, sea turtles or even humpbacks in **Ningaloo Marine Park** (p195).

② Snorkelling over marine life at **Turquoise Bay** (p196).

③ Descending into the 'centre of the earth' on an adventure tour through the gorges of **Karijini National Park** (p202).

④ Scuba diving off the **Navy Pier** (p193) at Point Murat, one of the world's finest shore dives.

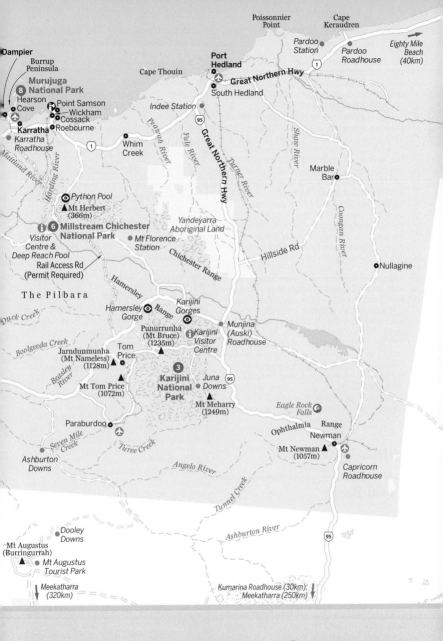

5 Watching the annual humpback whale migration from **North West Cape** (p193).

6 Cooling off in an idyllic waterhole after taking

in spectacular views at **Millstream Chichester National Park** (p204).

7 Spending a few days indulging in beachside R&R in **Coral Bay** (p186).

8 Being welcomed to Country and exploring ancient rock art on an Aboriginal cultural tour at **Murujuga National Park** (p199).

Getting There & Away

AIR

Learmonth airport (south of Exmouth) is the primary hub for Ningaloo, while there are airports enabling the ferrying of workers between Perth and the Pilbara mining towns of Port Hedland, Karratha, Paraburdoo and Newman.

Several airlines service the Ningaloo region and the Pilbara, primarily out of Perth. **Qantas** (☑13 13 13; www.qantas.com.au) covers the biggest network: it flies from Perth to Learmonth, Karratha, Newman, Port Hedland and Paraburdoo. It has codeshare flights from Karratha to Broome and Port Hedland. Qantas also has direct flights from Melbourne and Brisbane to Port Hedland. **Virgin Australia** (☑13 67 89; www.virgin-australia.com) covers some Perth-to-Pilbara routes. **Alliance Airlines** (☑1300 780 970; www.allianceairlines.com.au) is a smaller player, with limited Pilbara destinations.

BUS

Integrity (☑1800 226 339; www.integritycoach-lines.com.au) operates twice-weekly departures from Perth to Broome, stopping at Coral Bay, Exmouth, Karratha, Roebourne and Port Hedland. A weekly departure from Perth runs to Port Hedland via Coral Bay, Exmouth, Paraburdoo and Tom Price. A fourth service runs from Perth to Port Hedland via Meekatharra and Newman.

From April to October, Integrity works with the Flying Sandgroper to offer connections to Karijini National Park.

Integrity's hop-on, hop-off passes are good value: travel 1500/3000km over 12 months for $265/395.

NINGALOO COAST

Coral Bay

POP 255

Beautifully situated just north of the Tropic of Capricorn, the tiny, chilled-out seaside village of Coral Bay is one of the easiest locations from which to access the exquisite Ningaloo Marine Park (p195). Consisting of only one street and a sweeping white-sand beach, the town is small enough to enjoy on foot, making it popular with families.

Coral reefs lie just off the town beach, making it brilliant for snorkelling, swimming and sunbathing. It's also a great base for outer-reef activities such as scuba diving, fishing and whale-watching (June to November), and swimming with whale sharks (April to July) and manta rays.

Development is strictly limited, so expect higher prices for food and accommodation.

Exmouth, 152km away, has more options. The town is busy from April to October.

◉ Sights

★ Bill's Bay   BEACH

Bill's Bay is the perfectly positioned town beach, at the end of Robinson St. Easy access and sheltered waters make this a favourite with everyone, from families to snorkellers. Keep to the southern end when snorkelling; the northern end (Skeleton Bay) is a breeding ground for reef sharks.

Purdy Point   SNORKELLING

Walk 500m south from Bill's Bay along the coast until the 8km/h marker. Snorkelling from this point allows access to some fantastic coral bommies, and you can drift with the current back to the bay. Hire snorkel gear anywhere in town.

☞ Tours

Popular tours from Coral Bay include snorkelling with whale sharks or manta rays (reduced price for observers), boat tours to spot marine life (most with snorkelling offered; diving also possible), coral viewing from glass-bottom boats, and quad-bike trips. Fishing charters and scenic flights are also possible. Book through tour offices at the shopping centre and caravan parks, and check for advance discounts.

Families are catered for with family rates. 'Observers' on whale-shark tours are welcome and pay a reduced rate to swimmers.

Sail Ningaloo   SAILING

(☑1800 197 194; www.sailningaloo.com.au; 4 days per person from $1800; ◉Mar-Dec) ⏏ Sailing from Coral Bay, the *Shore Thing* is a luxury catamaran that offers liveaboard trips sailing the Ningaloo Reef (maximum of 10 passengers). Trips include four-, six- or 10-day options. Guided snorkelling, diving, kayaking and fishing activities are included, as are all meals.

Ningaloo Reef Air   SCENIC FLIGHT

(☑08-9942 5824; www.ningalooreefdive.com/package/scenic-flights; Shopping Centre, Robinson St; per tour from $220) Bookable through Ningaloo Reef Dive & Snorkel (p187), these scenic flights are in a small aircraft primarily used for spotting whale sharks and manta rays, so the pilots know these waters well, and the views from the air (and the wildlife-watching potential) are spectacular. Prices are per flight, not per person; three passengers can be taken. Departures are from the airfield near town.

Coastal Adventure Tours
ADVENTURE

(☑08-9948 5190; www.coralbaytours.com.au; Shopping Centre, Robinson St; quad bike tour $110-130, sunset sail $75) More a booking service than an individual operator, with the prime offering being a combined quad-bike and snorkelling trip (which gets rave reviews). You can also book sailing excursions on the *Coral Breeze* catamaran, glass-bottom boat tours and manta-ray interaction.

Ningaloo Marine Interactions
BOATING, SNORKELLING

(☑08-9948 5190; www.mantaraycoralbay.com.au; Shopping Centre, Robinson St) ◢ Informative and sustainably run tours to the outer reef include two-hour whale-watching (seasonal; $75), half-day manta-ray interaction (year-round; $170) and six-hour wildlife-spotting cruise with snorkelling ($210). Child prices and family deals too.

Coral Coast Tours
ADVENTURE

(☑0427 180 568; www.coralcoasttours.com.au; Shopping Centre, Robinson St) A mixed back of adventure trips: a four-day exploration of Karijini National Park ($685); fun 4x4 buggies for tours over dunes and along beach tracks (can be combined with snorkelling; tours $125 to $145); and snorkelling from the Aqua Rush RIB (rigid-inflatable 12-seater boat). The company also arranges airport transfers ($95) continuing on to Exmouth ($135).

Ningaloo Reef Dive & Snorkel
DIVING, SNORKELLING

(☑08-9942 5824; www.ningalooreefdive.com; Shopping Centre, Robinson St) ◢ This highly regarded PADI and eco-certified dive crew offers snorkelling with whale sharks ($380, March to July) and manta rays ($155, all year), half-day reef dives ($180) and a full range of dive courses (from $300). In 2016 they offered 'humpback whale in-water interaction' tours ($260).

Ningaloo Kayak Adventures
KAYAKING, SNORKELLING

(☑08-9948 5034; www.coralbay.org/kayak.htm; 2/3hr kayaking tour $50/70) From a kiosk by the main beach, you can hire a glass-bottom canoe ($25 per hour), see-through boogie board, wetsuits and snorkelling gear ($15 per day). Kayaking tours with snorkelling are also available, plus one-hour guided snorkelling tours using underwater 'seadoo scooters' for propulsion ($65).

Coral Bay Ecotours
BOATING, SNORKELLING

(☑08-9942 5885; www.coralbayecotours.com.au; Robinson St; 1/2/3hr $41/57/78, full-day tour $175) ◢ Eco-certified and carbon-neutral tours include glass-bottom-boat cruises with snorkelling, and all-day wildlife-spotting trips complete with manta-ray interaction. In season, the company offers snorkelling with whale sharks ($395) and in 2016 it offered humpback-whale interaction ($270). The booking office is next to Fin's Cafe.

🛏 Sleeping & Eating

The town has just four accommodation options and all are in high demand, especially during school holidays (avoid these if you can – they are usually booked out well in advance).

Book well ahead for peak season (April to October). November and February are the town's quietest months.

Consider self-catering, as eating out is expensive and choices are limited. The supermarket in the shopping centre is well stocked (open 7am to 7pm).

Ningaloo Club
HOSTEL $

(☑08-9948 5100; www.ningalooclub.com; Robinson St; dm $29-34, d with/without bathroom $120/95; ❇@≋) Popular with the party crowd, this hostel is a great place to meet people, and boasts a central pool, a well-equipped kitchen and an on-site bar (forget about sleeping before the bar closes). It also sells bus tickets (Integrity coaches stop outside) and discounted tours.

Peoples Park
CARAVAN PARK $

(☑08-9942 5933; www.peoplesparkcoralbay.com; Robinson St; sites $43-61, cabins $225-286, villas $266-330; ❇) This excellent caravan park offers grassy, shaded sites and a variety of self-contained cabins and villas. Friendly staff keep the modern amenities and spacious camp kitchen spotless, and it's the only place with freshwater showers. The hilltop villas have superb views.

Ningaloo Reef Resort
HOTEL $$$

(☑08-9942 5934; www.ningalooreefresort.com.au; 1 Robinson St; r $220-395; ❇🛜≋) New owners have freshened up the dated decor of this small resort. On offer are studios and various apartments (you'll pay more for an ocean view). It's the location that's the winner: directly opposite the beach, in a slightly elevated position, making views from the outdoor areas a treat. There's a restaurant and bar here too.

⭐ Fin's Cafe
SEAFOOD $$

(☑08-9942 5900; www.facebook.com/finscafecb; Robinson St; dinner mains $26-42; ⊗8am-

9.30pm) Out front of Peoples Park, Fin's is a super-casual outdoor place with an ever-changing blackboard menu giving pride of place to local seafood. Menus rove from breakfast eggs benny to a lunchtime king snapper burger, and get interesting at dinner time: crispy soft-shell crab, seared scallops, and seafood fettucine.

Bill's on the
Ningaloo Reef MODERN AUSTRALIAN $$
(📋08-9948 5156; Robinson St; mains $16-40; ⊙11am-late) The interior courtyard at Bill's (with its astroturf carpet and inbuilt fireplaces) is a fine spot to enjoy a menu of classic hits (burgers, steak, catch of the day) prepared with some flair. Try the fabulous fish curry, a selection of tapas or wash down the 'bucket of prawns' with a boutique ale. It has a bar area, too, and a bottleshop out back.

ⓘ Getting There & Away

The closest airport is at **Learmonth** (p192), 116km to the north, en route to Exmouth. Airport transfers can be arranged with **Coral Coast Tours** (📋0427 180 568; www.coralcoasttours.com. au; Shopping Centre, Robinson St; adult/child $95/48). Groups should consider hiring a car.

Three times a week, **Integrity** (📋1800 226 339; www.integritycoachlines.com.au; outside Ningaloo Club) coaches run from Ningaloo Club to Perth ($203, 16 hours) and Exmouth ($47, 90 minutes); twice a week, services head north to Broome ($240, 18½ hours). There are weekly services to Tom Price ($162, 10½ hours), for Karijini National Park. The Flying Sandgroper (www.flyingsandgroper.com.au) offers tours that link with Integrity services and visit Ningaloo and Karijini.

Exmouth

POP 2200

Wandering emus, palm trees laden with screeching cockatoos, and a burning sun all give Exmouth a somewhat surreal, very Australian edge. With World Heritage protection of nearby Ningaloo Reef, Exmouth has become largely a creature of tourism. Many visitors come, not surprisingly, to see and interact with the magnificent and enigmatic whale sharks (from April to July).

Peak season stretches from April to October and sees this laid-back town stretched to epic proportions, but don't be put off: it's still the perfect base to explore nearby Ningaloo Marine and Cape Range National Parks. Alternatively, just relax, wash away the road dust and enjoy the local wildlife.

⊙ Sights & Activities

Ningaloo Centre MUSEUM
(Murat Rd) Due for completion in September 2017, Exmouth's brand-new showpiece is expected to house the expanded visitor centre, the relocated town library, and lots of first-rate interactive displays on the region's history and stunning surrounds, from reef to range. Plans are afoot for an aquarium; expect an admission fee to some displays.

Town Beach BEACH
(end of Warne St) A relatively short walk from town, this beach is popular with kitesurfers when an easterly is blowing. There are barbecues and picnic tables.

Exmouth Boat & Kayak Hire BOATING, FISHING
(📋0438 230 269; www.exmouthboathire.com; 7 Patterson Way) Tinnies (small dinghies) or something larger (including a skipper!) can be hired from $100 per day. You can also hire kayaks (from $50 per day), fishing gear, camping gear and 4WDs, or arrange highly regarded fishing charters.

⌖ Tours

Swim with whale sharks or humpbacks, spot wildlife, dive, snorkel, kayak, surf and fish to your heart's content – the excellent visitor centre (p192) has the full list of tours available, along with all the details and forthcoming availability, and can book everything. Some tours are seasonal. Booking offices for individual operators are primarily found at the shopping centre, with a handful at Exmouth Ningaloo Caravan & Holiday Resort (p191).

Outside whale-shark season (which lasts from around mid-March to August), marine tours focus on humpbacks (August to October) and manta rays (year-round, but in summer these are done out of Coral Bay). To get the most from the tours, you need to be a capable snorkeller and swimmer. Be wary of snorkelling on what may essentially be a dive tour – the action may be too deep. Ask the operators for advice. It's normally 30% cheaper if you don't swim and board a boat as an 'observer'.

Many reef tours depart from **Tantabiddi** on the western cape and include free transfers from Exmouth; some may require you to make your own way to the departure point. Check conditions carefully regarding 'no sighting' policies and cancellations.

Birds Eye View SCENIC FLIGHTS
(📋0427 996 833; www.birdseyeview.net. au; Exmouth Aerodrome; 30/60/90min flight

Exmouth

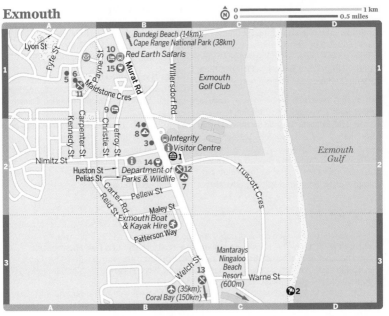

Exmouth

◎ Sights
1 Ningaloo Centre	B2
2 Town Beach	D3

◑ Activities, Courses & Tours
3 Exmouth Adventure Co.	B2
4 Kings Ningaloo Reef Tours	B2
Ningaloo Whaleshark-N-Dive	(see 5)
5 Ocean Eco Adventures	A1
6 Three Islands Whale Shark Dive	A1

▣ Sleeping
7 Exmouth Cape Holiday Park	B2

◎ Eating
8 Exmouth Ningaloo Caravan & Holiday Resort	B2
9 Ningaloo Lodge	B1
10 Potshot Hotel Resort	B1

BBqFather	(see 8)
11 See Salt	A1
12 Short Order Local	B2
13 Whalers Restaurant	C3

◎ Drinking & Nightlife
14 Cadillacs	B2
15 Potshot Hotel	B1

$199/299/399) Don't want to get your feet wet but still after adrenaline? Get some altitude on these incredible microlight flights over the Cape and (longer flights only) Ningaloo Reef.

Ocean Eco Adventures   SNORKELLING
(☏08-9949 1208; www.oceanecoadventures.com. au; Exmouth Shopping Centre; whale-shark swim/ observation $410/200) ◢ A well-set-up operator with luxurious vessel; the rate includes breakfast and tour photographs. The whale-shark swim months are followed by humpback interaction and whale-watching tours.

Dive Ningaloo   DIVING
(☏0456 702 437; www.diveningaloo.com.au; 2 dives from $200) A small, local company garnering a big reputation, Dive Ningaloo offers try dives, PADI courses, snorkelling trips (including with small Sea-Doo scooters), whale-watching cruises and great dive options, including visits to Navy Pier (p193) and the Muiron Islands. You can also sign up for overnight trips.

Three Islands Whale Shark Dive   SNORKELLING
(☏1800 138 501; www.whalesharkdive.com; 1 Kennedy St; whale-shark swim/observation $385/225) ◢ This well-respected outfit consistently wins

awards for its whale-shark tours, which run from mid-March to July. From August to October 2016, it also offered humpback interaction tours ($325). The rest of the year, there are full-day snorkelling tours of the reef or Muiron Islands ($185). From August to October, there are sunset whale-watching cruises ($80).

Exmouth Adventure Co   KAYAKING
(📞0477 685 123; www.exmouthadventureco.com.au; Murat Rd, Exmouth Ningaloo Caravan & Holiday Resort; half-/1-/2-/5-day tour $99/179/665/1650) Newly rebranded (formerly Capricorn Kayak Tours), this company has an expanding range of offerings, including multiday kayaking, snorkelling and hiking adventures (including to Karijini). You can also take surfing and stand-up paddleboarding lessons. Its original offerings are excellent: a half- ($99) or full-day ($199) kayaking and snorkelling in pristine Ningaloo waters.

Kings Ningaloo Reef Tours   SNORKELLING
(📞08-9949 1764; www.kingsningalooreeftours.com.au; Murat Rd, Exmouth Ningaloo Caravan & Holiday Resort; whale-shark swim/observation $395/285) 🐚 Long-time player Kings gets rave reviews for its whale-shark tours. It's renowned for staying out longer than everyone else, and has a 'next available tour' no-sighting policy. In 2016 it also offered humpback interaction.

STATION STAYS

If you're sick of cramped caravan parks and want somewhere a little more relaxed and off the beaten track, consider a station stay. Scattered around the Ningaloo coast are a number of pastoral stations offering a range of rustic accommodation – be it an exquisite slice of empty coast, dusty home paddock, basic shearers' digs or fully self-contained, air-conditioned cottages.

Don't expect top-notch facilities; some sites don't have any at all. Power and water are limited; the more self-sufficient you are, the more enjoyable the stay – remember, you're getting away from it all. You will find loads of wildlife, previously unseen stars, oodles of space and some fair-dinkum outback hospitality.

Some stations offer wilderness camping away from the homestead (usually by the coast) and you'll need a 4WD and chemical toilet. These places tend to cater for fisher-types with boats, and grey nomads who stay by the week.

Certain stations only offer accommodation during the peak season (April to October). It's wise to book ahead for rooms and cottages (usually not necessary for campsites). Check websites for details of what to bring, and how to get there. Also consider the excellent station-stay options along the Quobba coast (p181), north of Carnarvon.

Giralia (📞08-9942 5937; www.giraliastation.com.au; Burkett Rd; camping per person $10-12, economy s $70, cottage $160, homestead s/d $220/300; ❄❄) Popular with fishermen and well set up for travellers. It has a bush camping area with amenities, simple single rooms with shared bathroom, a family-sized cottage, and air-conditioned, en-suite homestead rooms with breakfast and dinner included. The coast is 40 minutes away by 4WD (there's a handful of beachside campsites available). It's 110km northwest of Coral Bay.

Bullara (📞08-9942 5938; www.bullara-station.com.au; Burkett Rd; campsites per person $14, tw/d $110/140, cottage from $220; ⊙Apr-Oct; ❄) A great, friendly, 2WD-accessible set-up that is 65km north of Coral Bay, and 6km east of the Minilya-Exmouth road junction. There are several rooms in the stylishly renovated shearers' quarters (shared kitchen and bathrooms), a couple of self-contained cottages, and powered campsites with amenities (including laundry and open-air showers).

Warroora (📞08-9942 5920; www.warroora.com; Minilya-Exmouth Rd; camping per person per day/week $10/50, budget r per person $35, cottages $150-270) South of Coral Bay, Warroora offers wilderness campsites along the coast (some 2WD accessible), cheap twin-share rooms in the shearers' quarters, as well as a couple of large, self-contained homes. There are two access points off the main road – both are OK for 2WD. Chemical toilets are compulsory for campers, and available for hire.

Ningaloo Station (📞08-9942 5936; www.ningaloostation.com.au; Minilya-Exmouth Rd; sites per week per person $35) Not to be confused with the marine park, the original station offers limited, totally self-sufficient wilderness campsites on pristine coastline. Eco toilets are to be used by all campers (available for hire at the station). A bond of $100 per site is payable. Bookings required. The turn-off is 50km north of Coral Bay.

Ningaloo Whaleshark-N-Dive
SNORKELLING, DIVING

(☎1800 224 060; www.ningaloowhalesharkndive.com.au; Exmouth Shopping Centre; whale-shark swim/observation $399/200) As well as swimming with whale sharks and interaction with humpbacks (snorkelling/observer $349/195), this company arranges dives to Lighthouse Bay and the Muiron Islands.

Ningaloo Ecology Cruises
BOATING

(☑1800 554 062; www.glassbottomboat.com.au; 1/2hr $50/80, full day $170; 🖼) 🌿 Family-friendly operator with well-regarded one-hour glass-bottom-boat trips (April to October) and longer trips (all year) including snorkelling. It also offers a full-day snorkelling option, and whale-watching cruises in season (adult/child $80/40).

🛏 Sleeping

Accommodation is limited, so book ahead, especially for the peak season (April to October).

Exmouth Cape Holiday Park
CARAVAN PARK $

(☎1800 871 570; www.parksandresorts.rac.com.au/park/exmouth/; 3 Truscott Cres; unpowered/powered sites $39/53, dm/d $34/105, cabins from $135; ❄️🎧🏊🐾) Under new ownership, this large park is getting a spruce-up and offers good facilities for campers, backpackers (its rooms are known as Blue Reef Backpackers), families and more. Lots of cabin options, too, from simple (some kitchen facilities, no bathroom) to deluxe family-sized units. Bike hire available.

Exmouth Ningaloo Caravan & Holiday Resort
CARAVAN PARK $

(☎08-9949 2377; www.exmouthresort.com; Murat Rd; unpowered/powered sites $40/50, dm/d $40/84, chalets from $205; ❄️🎧🏊🐾) Across from the visitor centre, this friendly, spacious park has grassy sites, self-contained chalets, backpacker dorms and doubles (shared bathrooms; known as Winston's Backpackers), an on-site restaurant and even a pet section.

Potshot Hotel Resort
RESORT $

(Excape Backpackers YHA; ☑08-9949 1200; www.potshotresort.com; Murat Rd; dm/d $36/88, motel d $145-245, apt $195-340; ❄️@🎧🏊) A town within a town, this sprawling resort has six-bed dorms and double rooms – all with en suite and air-con – which are good value if a little scruffy. Aside from backpacker accommodation, there are standard motel rooms, self-contained apartments, several bars and a pub-style bistro, spread across grounds that need a little TLC.

Ningaloo Lodge
GUESTHOUSE $$

(☎08-9949 4949; www.ningaloolodge.com.au; Lefroy St; d $160; ❄️🎧🏊) One of the better deals in town. Rooms at this lodge are compact but clean and well-appointed, and the bathrooms are somewhat dated, but the extras are great: a modern communal kitchen and laundry, barbecue, shady pool and courtyard, and quite possibly the best wi-fi in town.

★ Mantarays Ningaloo Beach Resort
RESORT $$$

(☎08-9949 0000; www.mantaraysningalooresort.com.au; Madaffari Dr; d/apt from $325/377; ❄️@🎧🏊) At the marina, this newly re-branded resort (formerly a Novotel) is at the pointy end of sophistication (and expense) in Exmouth. The tastefully designed rooms are spacious and well-equipped and all have balconies. They range from standard rooms to two-bedroom self-contained bungalows with ocean views. Grounds, pool, beach access and restaurant are all top-notch.

🍴 Eating

★ Short Order Local
CAFE $

(☎0421 777 864; www.facebook.com/theshortorderlocal; 3 Truscott Cres; snacks $5-10; ⏰6.30-11.30am Mon-Sat) Cute as a button, this pastel-striped food van is parked at the entry to Exmouth Cape Holiday Park and rewards early risers with great coffee, toasties and fresh muffins to early risers. It has a sweet array of timber tables and chairs scattered around, and occasional emu visitors dropping by.

BBqFather
BARBECUE, ITALIAN $$

(Pinocchio's; ☎08-9949 4905; www.thebbqfather.com.au; Murat Rd, Exmouth Ningaloo Caravan & Holiday Resort; mains $18-40; ⏰6-9pm Mon-Sat; 🖼) This popular, licensed alfresco *ristorante* changed its name and went barbecue crazy, serving up huge, succulent, smoky slabs of meat. After local outcry, the Italian owners returned their much-loved pizzas and homemade pastas to the menu – so these days, the options are wide, and crowd-pleasing. The servings are as legendary as ever. Locals still call it Pinocchio's. BYO wine.

Mantaray's
MODERN AUSTRALIAN $$

(☎08-9949 0000; www.mantaraysningalooresort.com.au; Madaffari Dr; lunch $17-30, dinner mains $28-43; ⏰6.30am-late) At Mantarays Ningaloo Beach Resort, this brasserie offers a postcard-pretty alfresco area, tropical-fruit cocktails and light lunches of crab sandwiches or sushi rolls. At dinner, the kitchen borrows global influences to play with local seafood – try French bouilla-baisse or Thai red prawn curry.

See Salt CAFE $$

(☑08-9949 1400; www.seesalt.com.au; 3 Thew St; meals $9-30; ⊙7am-4pm daily, plus 6-8.30pm Thu-Sun Apr-Oct; 🖭🎵) Easy-breezy daytime options, expanding to dinners later in the week during the peak season. Kickstart your morning with chilli eggs or a bowl of Viet-namese *pho* (beef and rice-noodle soup), or keep it sweet with banana pikelets. Lunch might roam from Mexican fish burrito to Sri Lankan chicken curry. Joy for vegetarians, and decent coffee and smoothies too.

★ **Whalers Restaurant** SEAFOOD $$$

(☑08-9949 2416; whalersrestaurant.com.au; 27 Murat Rd, inside Exmouth Escape; mains $30-40; ⊙5.30pm-late; 🎵) This Exmouth institution has a pretty poolside location, smart service and a mega-seafood menu (but vegetarians and vegans get some loving too). Don't miss the signature New Orleans gumbo, or spread your wings to the blackened fish tacos or In-dian seafood curry. Die-hard bug aficiona-dos need look no further than the towering seafood medley. Bookings recommended.

🍷 Drinking & Nightlife

Cadillacs (Grace's Tavern; ☑08-9949 1000; www.cadillacsbar.com.au; cnr Murat Rd & Pelias St; ⊙8am-10pm), at Grace's Tavern, and the bars of **Potshot Hotel** (☑08-9949 1200; www.pot-shotresort.com; Murat Rd; ⊙10am-late) are your drinking options, and both serve decent pub meals. Mantaray's (p191) at Mantarays Ningaloo Beach Resort is a great spot for a sundowner cocktail.

Rumour has it that a new microbrewery will be opening on Kennedy St, behind the shopping centre.

ℹ️ Information

For information on environmental projects around the cape, check out the Cape Conserva-tion Group's Facebook page.

Department of Parks & Wildlife (DPaW; ☑08-9947 8000; www.dpaw.wa.gov.au; 20 Nimitz St; ⊙8am-5pm Mon-Fri) Supplies maps, bro-chures and permits for Ningaloo, Cape Range and Muiron Islands, including excellent wildlife guides. Can advise on turtle volunteering.

Visitor Centre (☑08-9949 1176; www.visitningaloo.com.au; Murat Rd; ⊙9am-5pm Apr-Oct, 9am-5pm Mon-Fri, to 1pm Sat & Sun Oct-Mar; 🎵) Tour bookings, bus tickets, accommodation service and parks information. It's a great first-port-of-call, with boards and

folders outlining all the tour options in the area, and friendly helpful staff. You can hire snorkel gear here too.

ℹ️ Getting There & Away

Learmonth Airport (www.exmouth.wa.gov.au) is 36km south of town and has regular links with Perth courtesy of Qantas.

The **airport shuttle bus** (☑08-9949 4623) must be prebooked; it costs adult/child $35/25 between Learmonth and Exmouth town.

Three times a week, **Integrity** (☑1800 226 339; www.integritycoachlines.com.au) coaches run from the visitors centre to Perth ($240, 17½ hours) and Coral Bay ($47, 90 minutes); twice a week, services head north to Broome ($240, 16¾ hours). There are weekly services to Tom Price ($146, 8½ hours), for Karijini National Park. The **Flying Sand-groper** (p202) offers tours that link with Integrity services and visit Ningaloo and Karijini.

Red Earth Safaris (☑1800 827 879; www.redearthsafaris.com.au) operates a weekly tour out of Perth, which reaches Exmouth over six days ($785, including dorm accommodation and most meals). On Sundays it departs Exmouth from the Potshot Hotel Resort at 7am, returning to Perth over two days ($200, 30 hours; price includes meals and an overnight stop).

ℹ️ Getting Around

Budget, Avis and Europcar have agents around town, with car rental starting at around $90 per day. They can arrange car rental from the airport. **Allens** (☑08-9949 2403; alscarhire@bigpond.com; 24 Nimitz St; per day from $45) is a cheaper local option, with older cars; 4WDs and airport transfers also available. **Exmouth Camper Hire** (☑08-9949 4050; www.ningalooexcape.com.au; 16 Nimitz St; 4 nights from $575) has campervans and motor homes with everything you need to spend time in Cape Range National Park, including solar panels. There's a minimum four-night hire.

You only need a car licence for the 50cc scooters hired out by **Ningaloo Salty's Scooters** (☑0448 997 906; www.ningaloosaltyscooters.com.au; 77 Maidstone Cres; 1/3/7 days $70/150/240). They're considerably cheaper by the week. Its base is behind the Caltex petrol station.

Bikes can be hired from **Exmouth Cape Holi-day Park** (p191).

For a taxi, contact **Cabs on Call** (☑0408 449 944). Airport transfers are possible, but must be booked.

Around Exmouth

North of Exmouth, the main road skirts the top of the **North West Cape** before turning and running south, passing glorious beaches until it reaches the entry to Cape Range Na-tional Park (p196).

NINGA TURTLE TRACKERS

Along the northwest coast each year between October and March, volunteer turtle-monitoring programs provide exciting opportunities for active involvement in local conservation. Expect strange hours, some uncomfortable conditions and immense satisfaction. Applications usually open around August, but check individual programs.

Ningaloo Turtle Program (NTP; www.ningalooturtles.org.au; Exmouth; 5 weeks $1300; ☺Dec-Jan) Volunteers must commit to a five-week period, and some of that time is spent camping at a remote Ningaloo base (some is in Exmouth). Work from sunrise for five hours collecting data on turtle nesting, habitat and predation, then the rest of the day is free. Your fee covers all training and equipment, some meals, accommodation and transport from Exmouth.

Pendoley Environmental (☑08-9330 6200; www.penv.com.au; ☺Nov-Jan) Pendoley is a marine conservation consultancy working with the oil and gas industry at Pilbara sites such as Barrow Island, offshore from Onslow. Typical program placements are for 17 days with all expenses covered; there's a strict selection process.

Care for Hedland (☑0447 907 661; www.careforhedland.org.au; Port Hedland; ☺Oct-Mar) Grass-roots environmental group runs volunteer monitoring programs of flatback turtles on Port Hedland beaches from October to March.

Gnaraloo Turtle Conservation Program (p181) Science graduates (any discipline) prepared to commit for six months can apply to GTCP, which supplies food, accommodation, transport and training. The base is remote Gnaraloo Station, 150km north of Carnarvon.

Head north past Harold E Holt Naval Communication Station to an intersection before the VLF antenna array. Continue straight on for Bundegi Beach or turn left onto Yardie Creek Rd for the magnificent beaches and bays of the western cape and Ningaloo Reef.

◉ Sights & Activities

Bundegi Beach   BEACH
(Murat Rd) In the shadow of the VLF antenna array, and within cycling range of Exmouth (which is 13km to the south), the calm, sheltered waters of Bundegi Beach and accompanying reef provide pleasant swimming, snorkelling, diving, kayaking and fishing.

SS Mildura Wreck   SHIPWRECK
(Mildura Wreck Rd) Follow the signpost from Yardie Creek Rd to find the 1907 cattle steamer shipwreck that ran aground on the reef. It's visible from shore.

**★Vlamingh Head
Lighthouse**   LIGHTHOUSE, VIEWPOINT
(off Yardie Creek Rd) It's hard to miss this hilltop lighthouse built in 1912. Spectacular views of the entire cape make it a great place for whale spotting and sunset watching, and info panels give you excellent overviews of what makes the area special.

Jurabi Turtle Centre   VISITOR CENTRE
(JTC; www.ningalooturtles.org.au/jurabi.html; Yardie Creek Rd; ☺24hr) 🖉FREE Visit this un-

manned interpretive centre by day to study turtle life cycles and obtain the Department of Parks and Wildlife pamphlet *Marine Turtles in Ningaloo Marine Park*. Return at night to observe nesting turtles and hatchlings (December to March), remembering to keep the correct distance and to never shine a light or camera flash directly at any animal. Guided evening **turtle-viewing tours** (www.ningalooturtles.org.au/datesjurabi.html; Jurabi Turtle Centre, Yardie Creek Rd; adult/child $20/10; ☺6.30pm Mon, Wed & Fri Dec-Feb) available.

★Navy Pier   DIVING
(☑0456 702 437; www.diveningaloo.com.au; Point Murat; 1-/2-dive tours $130/200) Point Murat, named after Napoleon's brother-in-law, is home to one of the world's very best shore dives, under the Navy Pier. There's a fantastic array of marine life including nudibranchs, scorpion fish, moray eels and reef sharks. As it's on Defence territory, there are strict visitation rules and you'll need to join a tour operated by Dive Ningaloo (p189).

Exmouth Kite Centre   KITESURFING
(☑0467 906 091; www.exmouthkitecentre.com.au; Yardie Creek Rd, Ningaloo Lighthouse Caravan Park; 1/3hr kitesurf lessons $100/290) Learn to kitesurf, surf or stand-up paddleboard (SUP) with this fun, expert crew based at the Ningaloo Lighthouse Caravan Park. You can take various lessons, SUP sunset tours or just rent the gear. Locations for lessons

North West Cape

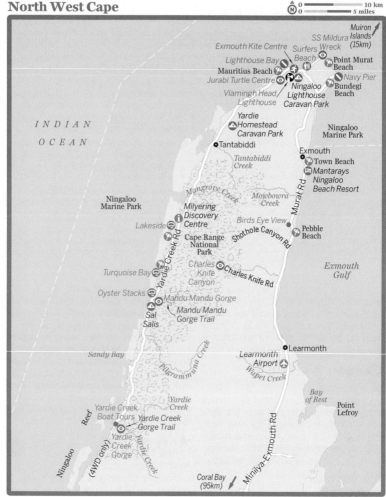

are determined based on weather and wind conditions.

🛏 Sleeping

Yardie Homestead
Caravan Park   CARAVAN PARK $

(☑08-9949 1389; www.yardie.com.au; Yardie Creek Rd; unpowered/powered sites $32/38, cabins & chalets d $150-180; ❋ ❡ ❄ ❄) Located just outside the entrance to Cape Range National Park, this former sheep station has some nice grassy tent sites. There's a range of cabins plus a pool, shop and camp kitchen. It's about 35km from Exmouth.

Ningaloo Lighthouse
Caravan Park   CARAVAN PARK $

(☑08-9949 1478; www.ningaloolighthouse.com; Yardie Creek Rd; unpowered/powered sites $35/45, budget cabins $120, chalets d $165-245; ❋ ❄) Superbly located on the western cape under Vlamingh Head Lighthouse, this park has lots of options (and resident wildlife): the clifftop chalets have fantastic views, there are plenty of shady tent sites for lesser mortals, and a cafe opens during peak season (May to September). Sells fuel and some supplies. It's about 20km from Exmouth.

ⓘ Getting There & Away

The Cape Range National Park (p196) entrance station is 40km from Exmouth, and the road south is navigable by all vehicles as far as Yardie Creek (a further 50km from the entrance station).

For exploration, cars, scooters and boats can be hired out of Exmouth.

Ningaloo Marine Park

You'll be hard-pressed to find words that do justice to the pristine, aquarium-like waters and pure sands of Ningaloo, Australia's largest fringing reef. The fact that it abuts the arid, rugged Cape Range National Park for much of its length simply adds to the appeal. Quite simply, this is bucket-list-worthy stuff.

World Heritage-listed Ningaloo Marine Park protects the full 300km length of Ningaloo Reef, from Bundegi on the eastern tip of the North West Cape to Red Bluff on Quobba Station far to the south. It's home to a staggering array of marine life – sharks, manta rays, humpback whales, turtles, dugongs, dolphins and more than 200 coral species and 500 fish species – and it's also easily accessible; in places it's only 100m offshore.

When to Go

December to March Turtles – three endangered species nest and hatch in the dunes. Best seen outside Exmouth.

March & April Coral spawning – an amazing event occurring seven days after the full moon.

Mid-March to mid-August Whale sharks – the biggest fish on the planet arrive for the coral spawning. Tours out of Exmouth and Coral Bay.

May to November Manta rays – present year-round; their numbers increase dramatically over winter and spring. Snorkelling and diving tours that interact with manta rays (ie, swim above them) leave from Exmouth and Coral Bay in winter, and from Coral Bay in summer.

June to November Humpback whales – breed in the warm tropics then head back south to feed in the Antarctic. Tours out of Exmouth and Coral Bay (whale watching, and also new interaction tours).

September to February Reef sharks – large numbers of harmless black tip reef sharks can be found inhabiting the shallow lagoons. Skeleton Bay near Coral Bay is a well-known nursery.

Aside from marine encounters, factors to consider: school holidays (avoid if you can, as you'll pay more, and have strong competition for accommodation) and weather. The region is dry and warm all year, but temperatures are high in summer (mid-30s to low 40s Celsius from November to March), and there is also moderate risk at this time of a tropical cyclone.

Hint: bring polarised sunglasses, which make it easier to spot marine life in the water.

Wildlife

Over 220 species of hard coral have been recorded in Ningaloo, ranging from bulbous brain corals found on bommies (submerged offshore reefs), to delicate branching staghorns and the slow-growing massive coral. While less colourful than soft corals (which are normally found in deeper water on the outer reef), the hard corals have incredible formations. Spawning, where branches of hermaphroditic coral simultaneously eject eggs and sperm into the water, occurs after full and new moons between February and May, but the peak action is usually seven to 10 days after the March and April full moon.

It's this spawning that attracts the park's biggest drawcard, the solitary speckled whale shark *(Rhiniodon typus)*. Ningaloo is one of the few places in the world where these gentle giants arrive like clockwork each year to feed on plankton and small fish, making it a mecca for marine biologists and visitors alike. The largest fish in the world, whale sharks can reach up to 18m long, and are believed to live for 70 to 100 years. Whale sharks encountered at Ningaloo are mostly between 3m and 12m (a 12m whale shark may weigh as much as 11 tonnes and have a mouth more than 1m wide).

Upload your amazing whale-shark pics to Wildbook for Whale Sharks (www.whaleshark.org), which will identify and track your whale shark.

🏃 Activities

Snorkelling & Diving

Most travellers visit Ningaloo Marine Park to snorkel. Always stop first at Milyering Discovery Centre (p197) for maps and information on the best spots and conditions. Check the tide chart and know your limits: currents can be dangerous, the area is remote, and there's no phone coverage or lifeguards. While not common, unseasonal conditions can bring dangerous 'smacks' of irukandji jellyfish. Milyering also rents and sells snorkelling equipment (as do many other places around Exmouth and Coral Bay).

Add a new dimension to your snorkelling or diving by collecting marine data in your own time, or volunteering for reef monitoring (courses available). Visit www.reefcheck-australia.org for more information.

★ Turquoise Bay   SNORKELLING
(Yardie Creek Rd) Some 63km from Exmouth, this beautiful bay lives up to its name. The **Bay Snorkel Area** is suitable for all skill levels with myriad fish and corals just off the beach. The **Drift Snorkel Area** attracts stronger swimmers where the current carries you over coral bommies. Don't miss the exit point or you'll be carried out through the gap in the reef.

The Drift Snorkel Area is 300m south along the beach from the Drift car park; swim out for about 40m then float face down in the current. Get out before the sandy point where the current strengthens, then run back along the beach and start all over!

Yardie Creek Boat Tours (p197) offers a bus service between Exmouth and Turquoise Bay ($35 per person return, including national park entry) in peak season. Pick-up in Exmouth is around 9am, and you return around 3pm, giving you four hours at the beach. Bookings are essential.

Oyster Stacks   SNORKELLING
(Yardie Creek Rd) These spectacular bommies (submerged offshore reefs) are just metres offshore, but you need a tide of at least 1.2m, and sharp rocks make entry/exit difficult. If you tire, don't stand on the bommies; look for some sand. The car park is 69km from Exmouth.

Lakeside   SNORKELLING
(Yardie Creek Rd) Lakeside is accessed from the road by Milyering Visitor Centre; it's 56km from Exmouth. Walk 500m south along the beach from the car park then snorkel out with the current before returning close to your original point.

Lighthouse Bay   DIVING
(Yardie Creek Rd) There's great scuba diving at Lighthouse Bay (at the northern tip of the cape) at sites such as the Labyrinth, Blizzard Reef and Helga's Tunnels. Check out the DPaW book *Dive and Snorkel Sites in Western Australia* for other ideas. Dive operators in Exmouth can set you up and take you out.

Kayaking
Kayak moorings are installed at some of Ningaloo's best snorkelling sites. Tether your craft and snorkel at Bundegi, Tantabiddi and Osprey in the north, and Maud in the south (close to Coral Bay). Kayaks can be hired off the beach in Coral Bay or in Exmouth town, or you can join a tour from either destination.

Cape Range National Park

It's the coastline of **Cape Range National Park** (https://parks.dpaw.wa.gov.au/park/cape-range; admission per car $12) that gets most of the attention – after all, these are the spectacular beaches that give access to the pristine Ningaloo Marine Park (p195).

Still, the jagged limestone peaks and gorges of the rugged 510-sq-km park deserve some acclaim of their own – they offer relief from the otherwise flat, arid expanse of North West Cape, and are rich in wildlife, including the rare black-flanked rock wallaby, five types of bat and over 200 species of bird. Spectacular deep canyons cut dramatically into the range, before emptying out onto the wind-blown coastal dunes and turquoise waters of Ningaloo Reef.

◉ Sights & Activities

Charles Knife Canyon   GORGE
(Charles Knife Rd) On the east coast, an incredibly scenic and at times dramatic road (11km in length) ascends a knife-edge ridge via rickety corners, necessitating frequent stops to make the most of the breathtaking views. A rough track continues to **Thomas Carter lookout** (at 311m, with great views). From the lookout area, in the cooler months you can walk the 8km **Badjirrajirra loop trail** through spinifex and rocky gullies; there's no shade or water. Under no circumstances attempt this during summer.

The signposted canyon road is 22km south of Exmouth (it's not suitable for caravans).

Yardie Creek Gorge   GORGE
(end of Yardie Creek Rd) A couple of walking trails give access to excellent views above this water-filled gorge: the gentle Nature Walk is 1.2km return, or the longer trail is 2km return and takes you high above the creek. There's also the option of a more relaxing boat tour (p197).

Yardie Creek is 50km from the park entry (and accessible to all vehicles).

ℹ CAMPING IN CAPE RANGE NATIONAL PARK

The campgrounds (adult/child $10/2.20) are run by the Department of Parks & Wildlife, and from April to October sites must be prebooked (up to 180 days before arrival). All peak-season bookings are done online, where you can also see the location and facilities of each campground: https://parkstay.dpaw.wa.gov.au.

Off-peak, sites operate on a first-come, first-served basis, and info is available at the park's entrance station as well as the visitor centre.

The park campgrounds stretch from Neds Camp in the north to Yardie Creek in the south (note: there is no campground at Turquoise Bay).

Facilities and shade are minimal at the sandy grounds, though most have eco-toilets (no showers, no water) and some shelter from prevailing winds, plus possibly a picnic shelter or two. No campfires are allowed; bring your own camp stove. There are no powered sites; seek a generator-free area if you're after peace and quiet. Most camps have resident caretakers during peak season. Our pick: the redeveloped grounds at Osprey Bay, or beachside North Kurrajong.

Mandu Mandu Gorge GORGE

(Yardie Creek Rd) There's a small car park off the main road 14km south of the Milyering Discovery Centre, and from here there's a pleasant, occasionally steep 3km return walk onto the gorge rim.

Yardie Creek Boat Tours BOATING

(☑08-9949 2920; www.yardiecreekboattours.com.au; adult/child/family $35/15/80; ⊗11am & 12.30pm on scheduled days; 🚻) A relaxing one-hour cruise up the short, sheer Yardie Creek Gorge, where you might spot rare black-flanked rock wallabies. It's worth checking operating days – with the company, or with Exmouth visitor centre (p192) – as these vary with season. There are no cruises from early January to late March.

🛏 Sleeping

Sal Salis TENTED CAMP $$$

(☑08-9949 1776; www.salsalis.com; South Mandu, off Yardie Creek Rd; per person per night $750–1080; ⊗mid-Mar–Oct) 🌱 Want to watch that crimson Indian Ocean sunset from between 500-threadcount sheets? Pass the chablis! For those who want their camp without the cramp, this exclusive tented camp has a minimum two-night stay, 16 en-suite tents, three gourmet meals a day, a free bar (!) and the same things to do as the folks staying over the dune in the pop-up camper.

ℹ Information

Milyering Discovery Centre (☑08-9949 2808; Yardie Creek Rd; ⊗9am-3.45pm; 🚻) Serving both Ningaloo Marine Park and Cape Range National Park, this visitor centre has informative natural and cultural displays, maps, tide charts, campsite photos and publications. Check here for road and water conditions.

It rents out snorkelling gear (day/overnight $10/15), and sells drinks and ice creams.

THE PILBARA

Karratha

POP 19,250

In the past, most travellers to Karratha ran their errands – banking, restocking, repairing stuff etc – and then got out of town before their wallet ignited. That did the town a small disservice. It's the primary base for mining and industry in the region, and while it won't win any awards for prettiest town, it certainly has a few things worth sticking around to investigate – from tours to ancient rock art to cafes that wouldn't look out of place in the coolest parts of Perth.

◉ Sights & Activities

Miaree Pool LAKE

(North West Coastal Hwy) Yeah, it gets hot up here. You might have noticed. Cool off at this shady waterhole, popular with locals for picnicking and swimming. It's 30km southwest of the Karratha turn-off, on the North West Coastal Hwy (Hwy 1).

Yaburara Heritage Trail WALKING

From behind the visitor centre, a series of trails (the longest of which is 3.5km one way) wind through significant traditional sites, detailing the displacement and eventual extinction of the Yaburara people. Sites include rock art, stone quarries and shell middens, plus excellent lookout points. Bring plenty of water and start your walks early.

⚐ Tours

★ **Ngurrangga Tours** CULTURAL
(☑ 08-9182 1777; www.ngurrangga.com.au; half-day adult/child $132/66; ⊗ Feb-Nov) Clinton Walker, Ngarluma man, runs cultural tours that garner rave reviews from travellers. His half-day Murujuga National Park tour explores rock-art petroglyphs on the Burrup Peninsula near Dampier, while longer day tours explore the culturally significant areas of Millstream Chichester National Park (adult/child $300/150). Three-day Millstream camping tours are also available ($800/400). Departures are from the Karratha visitor centre (p199).

☆ Festivals & Events

Red Earth Arts Festival CULTURAL
(www.reaf.com.au; ⊗ Sep) Over 10 days in mid-September, Karratha and the surrounding coastal Pilbara towns come alive for this festival, an eclectic mix of live music (all genres), theatre, comedy, visual arts and storytelling.

⊨ Sleeping & Eating

The Ranges APARTMENT $$
(☑ 1300 639 320; www.therangeskarratha.com.au; De Witt Rd; d $195-285; ☎ ☒) This swank complex of deluxe self-contained apartments offers a surprising level of sophistication, with king-sized beds and smart kitchen appliances. Outside are manicured grounds and a big pool and barbecue area. Service is first-rate. It's about 1km south of the visitor centre, on the road into town.

★ **Empire 6714** CAFE $$
(☑ 0427 654 045; www.empire6714.com.au; Warambie Rd; meals $13-28; ⊗ 6am-4pm; ☒) Sure, you can get your standard bacon and eggs here, but why wouldn't you go for coconut flour pancakes with berries or fig and fennel fruit loaf? There's lots of organic, hard-to-source goodness on the menu, but we like how it's not one-sided (raw pizza is on the lunch menu, alongside steak sandwich). There are also impeccable smoothies, cold-pressed juices, coffee and kombucha (fermented tea drink).

Soul CAFE, BAR $$
(☑ 08-9183 8278; www.facebook.com/soulkarratha; Warambie Rd, Pelago Centre; dishes $10-33; ⊗ 6am-10pm Mon-Sat, 7am-3pm Sun) City-style sophisticated breakfasts (until 11am) are followed by an all-day menu of crowd-pleasers, from gourmet burgers to tempting share plates (sliders, quesadillas, antipasto platters). It delivers top-notch coffee, too, from its cute, bright-blue Elektra coffee machine.

INTERACTIVE TOURS WITH HUMPBACK WHALES

In August 2016, under the directive of the Department of Parks & Wildlife, operators in Ningaloo began trialling 'in-water humpback whale interaction'. The trial has been extended to 2017. Ningaloo becomes only one of a handful of places in the world where it's possible to interact in this way with humpbacks (the others being Tonga, the Dominican Republic and Queensland's Sunshine Coast).

Humpback whales make their annual migration up the WA coastline around late April to May, when they mate and calve in warmer waters. From about August, they begin travelling south again to their Antarctic feeding grounds. An estimated 30,000 whales travel through the area; the interactive tour season in 2016 was from August to October, nicely dovetailing with the whale-shark period (generally running about mid-March to August). Existing whale-shark tour operators in Exmouth and Coral Bay were given the opportunity to participate in the 2016 trial, given they have the correct set-up for such encounters.

Keen participants do need to be aware that the humpback interactions are a different beast (so to speak) to whale-shark swims. Humpbacks are not nearly as docile and predictable as whale sharks and there are more rules around when you can get in the water with humpbacks (not if there are calves present – which is common; not if it's a group of male juveniles, as they're too unpredictable; not if there is any tail-slapping and/or breaching behaviour, etc). Operators are still fine-tuning how to sell the interaction, and signing up for a 'swim with humpbacks' tour is not straightforward (it may just be a successful whale-watching trip). Overall, there was a 70% success rate for tours in 2016 (with 'success' defined as swimmers in the water near whales).

It's worth reading up on the prices and conditions surrounding these humpback interaction tours so that you know what to expect and don't feel disappointed if you head out on a boat but don't end up in the water.

ⓘ Information

Karratha Visitor Centre (☏08-9144 4600; www.karrathavisitorcentre.com.au; De Witt Rd; ◷8.30am-5pm Mon-Fri, 9am-2pm Sat & Sun Apr-Sep, 9am-4pm Mon-Fri, 10am-1pm Sat Oct-Mar; ☎) Has excellent local maps and info, supplies rail access road permits (for the most direct route to Tom Price), books tours (including to mining infrastructure) and may find you a room.

ⓘ Getting There & Away

Karratha Airport (www.karrathaairport.com.au), located halfway between Karratha and Dampier, is well connected to Perth courtesy of Virgin Airlines, Qantas and Alliance Airlines.

Integrity (☏1800 226 339; www.integritycoachlines.com.au) operates twice-weekly bus services from Perth to Broome, stopping at Coral Bay, Exmouth, Karratha, Roebourne and Port Hedland.

Fares from Karratha include Perth ($282, 24 hours), Exmouth ($164, 6½ hours), Port Hedland ($89, 3½ hours) and Broome ($187, 10 hours).

Buses arrive and depart from the bus stop on Welcome Rd (opposite the church) in the centre of the shopping area.

Around Karratha

Practically a suburb of Karratha, Dampier is the region's main port and is home to heavy industry. It's spread around King Bay 20km northwest of Karratha. Its most famous resident is Red Dog (who has had books written about him, and movies made), a much-loved dog that roved the town and surrounds in the 1970s. A statue of him is at the entry to town.

Sitting on Ngaluma country, 40km east of Karratha, Roebourne is the oldest (1866) Pilbara town still functioning. It's home to a large Aboriginal community; Yindjibarndi is the dominant language group. There are some beautiful old buildings and a thriving indigenous art scene (www.roebourneart.com.au). The **Yinjaa-Barni** (☏08-9182 1959; www.yinjaa-barni.com.au; Lot 3 Roe St; ◷vary) Indigenous-run gallery showcases gifted Millstream artists.

In good news for the town, the old Victoria Hotel (built in 1866, but shuttered since 2006) is slated for restoration, to return it to its architectural glory. Once restored, the plan is to make it a tourism and cultural hub for the local community.

★**Murujuga National Park** NATIONAL PARK (parks.dpaw.wa.gov.au/park/murujuga; Burrup Peninsula Rd) FREE Murujuga is home to the world's largest concentration of rock art (dating back more than 30,000 years), stretched out along the rocky hills of the heavily industrialised Burrup Peninsula. The most accessible are at **Deep Gorge**, near Hearson's Cove. Devastatingly, some sites have been vandalised. The engravings depict fish, turtles, kangaroos and even a Tasmanian tiger.

The best way to see and appreciate the importance of this art is through a half-day tour out of Karratha with Ngurrangga Tours (p198).

Dampier Archipelago NATURE RESERVE (https://parks.dpaw.wa.gov.au/park/dampier-archipelago) Offshore from Dampier, the coral waters and pristine islands of the Dampier Archipelago support a wealth of marine life and endangered marsupials (25 of the 42 islands are nature reserves). It's a recreational fishing and boating mecca, and plenty of boat-owning locals head here for R&R. Enquire at Karratha visitor centre about fishing charters and cruises.

Hearson's Cove BEACH (Hearson Cove Rd) A fine swimming beach and picnic spot, providing Staircase to the Moon viewing (March to October) and great mudflat exploring at low tide.

Port Hedland

POP 16,000

Port Hedland ain't the prettiest place. A high-visibility dystopia of railway yards, iron-ore stockpiles, salt mountains, furnaces and a massive deep-water port confront the passing traveller. Yet under that red dust lurks a colourful 130-year history of mining booms and busts, cyclones, pearling and WWII action. Several pleasant hours may be spent exploring Hedland's thriving art and cafe (real coffee!) scene, historic CBD and scenic foreshore.

◉ Sights & Activities

Collect the brochure entitled *Adventure Awaits: Your Guide to Port Hedland* from the visitor centre and take a self-guided tour around the CBD and foreshore.

Goode St, near Pretty Pool, is handy to observe Port Hedland's **Staircase to the Moon** (on full-moon nights from March to October), where water caught in sand ripples reflects the moonlight, creating the effect of a staircase to the moon.

★ **Courthouse Gallery**   GALLERY
(☑ 08-9173 1064; www.courthousegallery.com.au; 16 Edgar St; ⊙ 9am-4.30pm Mon-Fri, 9am-3pm Sat) More than a gallery, this leafy arts HQ is the centre of all goodness in Port Hedland. Inside are stunning, curated local contemporary and Indigenous exhibitions, while the shady surrounds host sporadic craft markets. If something is happening, these folks will know about it.

Spinifex Hill Studios   GALLERY
(☑ 08-9172 1699; www.spinifexhillstudio.com.au; 18 Hedditch St, South Hedland; ⊙ 9am-5pm Tue-Fri, 10am-2pm Sun) A great new initiative showcasing Aboriginal artists from Port Hedland and across the Pilbara. Saturday is the best time to visit, with artists at work and coffee offered (a kind of 'open house'). It's generally open at other times, but it's a good idea to call before visiting.

Pretty Pool   SWIMMING
(off Matheson Dr) A popular picnicking and swimming spot (beware of stonefish and backpackers), 7km east of the town centre. The best swimming spots depend on the tides – follow the locals' lead.

☞ Tours

Harbour Tour   TOURS
(☑ 08-9173 1315; www.phseafarers.org; cnr Wedge & Wilson Sts; adult/child $55/30; ⊙ 9.30am Mon-Sat, 1.30pm Sun) Run by the Seafarers Centre, this hour-long tour covers the facts and figures of the port, and includes a boat tour around the harbour. Tour times may vary, so it pays to check.

BHP Billiton Iron Ore Tour   TOURS
(adult/child $45/30; ⊙ 1pm Tue & Thu) Popular one-hour guided tour of an iron-ore plant. Book through the visitor centre, from which the tour departs. It's free for kids under 10 years.

🛏 Sleeping & Eating

The visitor centre (p200) can help with information or bookings.

If you prefer somewhere on the beach, away from town and mines, better to plan a stay at Eighty Mile Beach en route north, or Point Samson south.

Discovery Parks Port Hedland   CARAVAN PARK $
(☑ 08-9173 1271; www.big4.com.au; cnr Athol & Taylor Sts; powered sites $38-55, backpacker d $60, unit d from $119; ❈ ☎ ⊠) At the town's eastern

end, this park offers lots of cabin options, backpacker rooms (with shared kitchen and bathroom) and well-maintained amenities. There's a nice view over the mangroves.

Esplanade Hotel   HOTEL $$
(☑ 08-9173 9700; www.theesplanadeporthedland. com.au; 2-4 Anderson St; d incl breakfast weekend/ weekday from $165/215; ❈ @ ☎) Previously one of the roughest pubs in Port Hedland, the 'Nard' is now an exclusive 4½-star resort with 98 smart, well-equipped guest rooms (though they're petite and quite pricey). It's a favourite with business travellers, making the weekend rates considerably cheaper. It has good food and drink on-site.

★ **Esplanade Hotel**   MODERN AUSTRALIAN $$
(☑ 08-9173 9700; www.theesplanadeporthedland. com.au; 2-4 Anderson St; bar mains $20-30, restaurant mains $20-45; ⊙ 5.30am-midnight) There's a surprising air of sophistication about this old hotel. Breakfast until 11.30am is good value, then the Empire Bar's all-day menu blends old classics with new (Vietnamese poached chicken salad, scotch fillet steak). There's an evening restaurant too, with surprises like jerk chicken with wild rice or goat vindaloo.

Our favourite feature: the big courtyard and various bar events throughout the week.

ⓘ Information

Visitor Centre (☑ 08-9173 1711; www.visitporthedland.com; 13 Wedge St; ⊙ 9am-5pm Mon-Fri & to 2pm Sat; ☎) This excellent centre sells travel books, publishes shipping times, arranges iron-ore plant tours, and helps with accommodation and turtle monitoring (November to February). Open Sundays (9am to 2pm) April to September.

ⓘ Getting There & Away

Port Hedland International Airport (www. porthedlandairport.com.au) is about 12km south of town and has good connections. Virgin and Qantas both fly to Perth daily, and Qantas also has a weekly direct flight to Brisbane and Melbourne. Virgin has handy weekend flights to Bali.

The large car-hire companies (Hertz, Avis, Budget etc) offer car rental from the airport. A **taxi** (☑ 08-9173 1010; www.hedlandtaxis.com. au) to the town centre costs $35 to $40.

Integrity (☑ 1800 226 339; www.integritycoachlines.com.au) operates two weekly bus services north to Broome ($129, 6½ hours). There are four services south to/from Perth ($274 to $293, 21¼ to 28¼ hours) taking various routes, coastal and inland. The quickest journey runs from Port Hedland on Thursdays via Newman and Meekatharra.

Buses arrive and depart from the Port Hedland visitor centre and South Hedland shopping centre.

MARBLE BAR
....

Marble Bar, a long way off everybody's beaten track, burnt itself into the Australian psyche as the country's hottest town when, back in summer of 1923–24, the mercury reached 37.8°C (100°F) for 160 consecutive days. The town was (mistakenly) named after a bar of jasper beside a pool on the Coongan River, 5km southwest of the town centre.

Most days there's not much to do. Pore over the minerals at the **Comet Gold Mine,** (⏺08-9176 1015; Hillside Rd; $3; ⊙9am-4pm) 8km out of town, or prop yourself up at the bar and have a yarn with Foxie at the **Ironclad Hotel** (⏺08-9176 1066; 15 Francis St; mains $17-45; ⊙noon-close). This classic outback pub offers comfy rooms, decent meals, and a warm welcome. If the temperature's climbing, head for the town's swimming pool.

Come the first weekend in July, the sleepy town swells to 10 times its normal size for a weekend of drinking, gambling, fashion crime, country music, nudie runs and horse racing known as the **Marble Bar Cup** (www.marblebarraces.com; ⊙early Jul). The **holiday park** (⏺08-9176 1569; Contest St; unpowered/powered sites $20/38) overflows and the Ironclad is besieged as punters from far and wide come for a bit of an outback knees-up.

Marble Bar is 200km from Port Hedland via Rte 138 (a sealed road). To carry on to Newman is 300km on an unsealed road that sees little traffic, but is usually OK for 2WDs (check locally; carry plenty of water).

The East Pilbara shire runs a bus between Port Hedland and Marble Bar ($29, 3¼ hours) a couple of times a week (twice in either direction). See www.eastpilbara.wa.gov.au for details.

Karijini National Park

The narrow, breathtaking gorges, hidden pools and spectacular waterfalls of Karijini National Park (https://parks.dpaw.wa.gov.au/park/karijini; admission per car $12) form one of WA's most impressive attractions. Adventurers and nature lovers flock to the rocky red ranges and deep, dark chasms, home to abundant wildlife and over 800 different plant species.

Kangaroos, snappy gums and wildflowers dot the spinifex plains, rock wallabies cling to sheer cliffs and endangered olive pythons lurk in giant figs above quiet pools. The park also contains WA's three highest peaks: Mt Meharry, Punurrunha (Mt Bruce) and Mt Frederick.

Summer temperatures reach extremes in the park (frequently over 40°C), so carry plenty of water. Winter nights are cold. At any time of year, choose walks wisely, dress appropriately and never enter a restricted area without a certified guide. Avoid the gorges during and after rain, as flash flooding does occur.

◉ Sights & Activities

Generally, within the park, roads lead to car parks from where there are short, relatively easy walks to scenic lookouts that peer into a gorge. There are a few flat walking trails along gorge-rim paths, plus longer and more difficult trails (some via steps or ladders) that descend to gorge floors and pools.

The best swimming is at Fortescue Falls and Fern Pool (in Dales Gorge in the park's east), and at Hamersley Gorge (tucked away in the park's northwest). Other gorge pools are beautiful, but many are sheltered from the sun and the water is often chilly.

★ Dales Gorge   GORGE
(accessed from Banjima Dr East; ⓓ) From the Fortescue Falls car park (just south of Dales Campground), a trail descends steeply via a long staircase to stunning **Fortescue Falls** (the park's only permanent waterfall) and a photogenic swimming hole, behind which a leafy 300m stroll upstream reveals beautiful **Fern Pool**.

You can enjoy a 2km **gorge-rim trail** from the start of the Fortescue Falls track to Circular Pool lookout, with great views into Dales Gorge. The Circular Pool lookout is also connected to Dales Campground by an easy walking trail.

For a lengthier walk (for more experienced bushwalkers), head 1km downstream, along the gorge floor, from Fortescue Falls to picturesque Circular Pool; ascend to Three Ways Lookout and return to the car park along the gorge rim.

★ Hamersley Gorge   GORGE
(off Nanutarra-Munjina Rd; ⓓ) Away in Karijini's northwest corner, this idyllic swimming hole makes a lovely stop if you're heading north towards the coast or Millstream (it can't be accessed from Banjima Dr). It's about 67km from Tom Price: head north on Bingarn Rd for 26km, and turn right at the T-junction,

carrying on another 41km (unsealed). Turn at the sign for Hamersley Gorge, not Hamersley Range.

★ Fern Pool
LAKE

(Jubura) Swim quietly and with respect at this lovely, shady pool – it has special significance to the local Indigenous people. It's a 300m walk upstream from Fortescue Falls.

Hancock Gorge
GORGE

(Weano Rd, accessed from Banjima Dr West) At Hancock Gorge, a steep descent (partly on ladders) brings you to the sunny **Amphitheatre**. Follow the slippery **Spider Walk** to sublime **Kermits Pool**.

Oxer Lookout
VIEWPOINT

(Weano Rd, accessed from Banjima Dr West) The final 13km drive (past the Karijini Eco Retreat) to the breathtaking Oxer Lookout can be rough, but it's worth it for the magnificent views of the junction of the Red, Weano, Joffre and Hancock Gorges some 130m below. The lookout is a short walk from the car park.

Joffre Gorge
GORGE

(Joffre Falls Rd, accessed from Banjima Dr West) When not trickling, **Joffre Falls** are spectacular, but the frigid pools below are perennially shaded. The gorge lookout is 10 minutes' walk from the parking area; there's a 1.3km-return trail down to the pool. There's also a walking track to the falls from the nearby Karijini Eco Retreat (p202).

Weano Gorge
GORGE

(Weano Rd, accessed from Banjima Rd West) The upper gorge is dry, but the steep track winding down from the car park to the lower gorge narrows until you reach the perfect, surreal bowl of **Handrail Pool**.

Kalamina Gorge
GORGE

(Kalamina Gorge Rd, accessed from Banjima Dr North; 🚻) Wide, easy gorge with a small, tranquil pool and falls. You'll need a 4WD to access it, as it lies north of Banjima Dr North.

Punurrunha (Mt Bruce)
HIKING

Gorged out? Go and grab some altitude on WA's second-highest mountain (1235m), a superb ridge walk with fantastic views all the way to the summit. Start early, carry lots of water and allow six hours (9km return). The access road is off Karijini Dr opposite Banjima Dr West.

There are shorter walks from the car park, including the three-hour (4.6km return) Honey Hakea Track to a vantage point.

🎫 Tours

★ West Oz Active
Adventure Tours
ADVENTURE

(☑ 0438 913 713; www.westozactive.com.au; Karijini Eco Retreat; tour $285; ☺ Apr-Oct) Based at Karijini Eco Retreat, this highly regarded company offers action-packed day trips through the restricted gorges of the park and combines hiking, swimming, floating on inner tubes, climbing, sliding off waterfalls and abseiling. All equipment and lunch provided. The minimum age for tours is 14.

★ Flying Sandgroper
TOURS

(☑ 0438 913 713; www.flyingsandgroper.com.au; ☺ Apr-Oct) The Flying Sandgroper's aim is to overcome the huge distances and costs of visiting the northwest, so it is set up to offer multi-day tours that take in Karijini (and Ningaloo too), with the choice of bus-in bus-out and fly-in-fly-out packages, depending on your budget. It's affiliated with the excellent West Oz Active Adventure Tours, and based at Karijini Eco Retreat.

Working with Integrity bus services, the two-day no-frills Karijini package ($385) offers pick-up from Tom Price, two nights camping, most meals and park exploration. A six-day 'Reef to Range' takes in the best of Karijini and Ningaloo ($1585).

Lestok Tours
BUS

(☑ 08-9189 2032; www.lestoktours.com.au; adult/child $180/90; ☺ Apr-Oct) Full-day outings to Karijini departing from Tom Price (also able to pick up from Karijini Eco Retreat). Useful if you don't have your own transport to explore, but doesn't take you anywhere you can't visit on your own. Price includes lunch.

🛏 Sleeping & Eating

Dales Gorge Campground
CAMPGROUND $

(sites adult/child $10/2.20) Though somewhat dusty, this large Department of Parks and Wildlife campground offers shady, spacious sites with nearby toilets, gas barbecues and picnic tables. Forget tent pegs – you'll be using rocks as anchors. It's first come, first served (no bookings). The camping ground is 17km on sealed road from the eastern entrance station.

★ Karijini Eco Retreat
RESORT $$$

(☑ 08-9425 5591; www.karijiniecoretreat.com; Weano Rd, accessed from Banjima Dr West; sites per person $20, deluxe tent d low/high season $189/349) 🌱 This 100% Indigenous-owned retreat is a model for sustainable tourism,

Karijini National Park

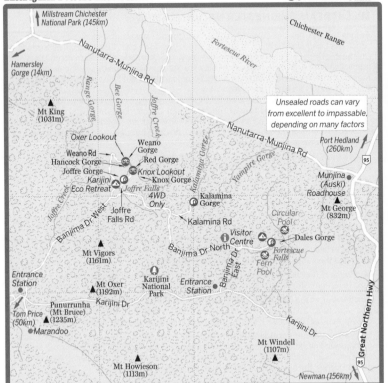

and the on-site restaurant (p203) has fantastic food. The deluxe eco-tents have en suites; there are also cheaper tents and cabins with shared bathrooms. Campers get access to hot showers and the same rocks as elsewhere in the park. The setting, close to Joffre Gorge, is beautiful.

★ Karijini Eco Retreat Restaurant
MODERN AUSTRALIAN $$
(www.karijiniecoretreat.com.au; Weano Rd, off Banjima Dr West; dinner mains $18-39; ⊗7am-8pm) The restaurant at Karijini Eco Retreat has fantastic food, with the chefs offering high-quality dishes that are often accented by bush-tucker ingredients (bush tomatoes, wild herbs, wattleseed). To be this far from 'civilisation' but able to dine on salmon on soba noodles or scotch fillet steak is pretty wondrous. Breakfast and lunch are also served.

🛈 Orientation

ACCESS TOWNS FOR THE PARK
Bookending Karijini National Park are the neat, company-built mining towns of **Tom Price** and **Newman**. Newman, to the east on the Great Northern Hwy, is larger though more distant, with better transport and accommodation. Both have good supermarkets, petrol stations and visitor centres, where you can book mine tours if huge holes are your thing. There are also decent camping and eating spots.

In Newman, don't miss the brilliant new **East Pilbara Arts Centre** (p257). Opened in 2016, this beautiful gallery is home to **Martumili Artists**, one of the state's most successful art collectives. The Martu people live in remote desert communities in the East Pilbara region, and are the traditional custodians of vast stretches of WA deserts. For sale are authentic Aboriginal paintings, artifacts and woodcarvings.

INSIDE THE PARK
Karijini Dr is a sealed road stretching about 115km between Tom Price in the west, and the Great Northern Hwy (Rte 95) in the east. The

WORTH A TRIP

MILLSTREAM CHICHESTER NATIONAL PARK

Among the arid, spinifex-covered plateaus and basalt ranges between Karijini and the coast, the tranquil waterholes of the Fortescue River form cool, lush oases in Millstream Chichester National Park (https://parks.dpaw.wa.gov.au/park/millstream-chichester; admission per car $12). In the park's north are the stunning breakaways and eroded mesas of the Chichester Range. As a lifeline for local flora and fauna, the park is one of the most important Aboriginal sites in WA.

There are two main areas of the park: **Millstream** sits west of the Karratha-Tom Price Rd, and is home to the unmanned visitor centre, the park campgrounds and Deep Reach pool.

In the park's north, east off the Karratha-Tom Price Rd, are the rolling hills, rocky peaks and escarpments of the **Chichester Range**. The drive through the range (along the Roebourne-Wittenoom Rd) is superbly scenic.

Millstream Homestead Visitor Centre (Millstream; ⊘8am-4pm) Once the station homestead, the unmanned visitor centre houses historical, ecological and cultural displays. It's 22km west of the Karratha-Tom Price Rd.

Python Pool (Chichester Range) Just off the road that traverses the Chichester Range (19km east of the Karratha-Tom Price Rd), this plunge pool sits photogenically at the base of a cliff. The water is normally fine for swimming, though check for algae bloom before sliding in.

Deep Reach Pool (Millstream; 🏊) Some 4km from the visitor centre, shady picnic tables and barbecues back onto a perfect swimming hole (Nhangganggunha in the local language) believed to be the resting place of the Warlu (creation serpent). The water is deep and the banks can be steep, so use the steps here.

Mt Herbert (Chichester Range) A 10-minute climb from the car park (arrowed off the road to Roebourne) reveals a fantastic panorama of the ragged Chichester Range.

Jirndarwurrunha Pool (Millstream) A short stroll from the visitor centre, beautiful lily- and palm-fringed Jirndarwurrunha is deeply significant to the traditional Yindjibarndi owners. An easy half-hour walk leads through the wetlands area; swimming is not permitted.

Miliyanha Campground (Millstream; sites adult/child $10/2.20) A nicely shaded, circular campground near the visitor centre with a kitchen in the middle. If full, there's a second (seasonal) campground, the sparse Stargazers. Camp hosts are stationed at the campground during the busy season (from April to September).

turn-off on Rte 95 is 160km northwest of Newman, and 300km south of Port Hedland.

Banjima Dr, the park's main thoroughfare, connects with Karijini Dr at two entrance stations. The eastern access is closest to the visitor centre and Dales Gorge; the western access is closest to Karijini Eco Retreat.

(Note that Hamersley Gorge is in a third, less-visited part of the park, and is inaccessible from the east or west entrances.)

The east and west access roads are sealed, but Banjima Dr North is unsealed for most of its 29km length, and is recommended for 4WDs only. If you're in a 2WD, keep to the asphalt and use Karijini Dr to move between the park's east and west sections (it's longer, but far safer).

From Banjima Dr West, Weano Rd heads north to Karijini Eco Retreat and an area of gorge lookouts and trails. This road is unsealed and can be rough going – take it slowly.

Take extra care driving, and avoid driving at night.

ⓘ Information

Visitor Centre (☏08-9189 8121; https://parks.dpaw.wa.gov.au/park/karijini; Banjima Dr North; ⊘9am-4pm mid-Feb–mid-Dec) An Indigenous-managed centre with excellent interpretive displays highlighting Banyjima, Yinhawangka and Kurrama culture, as well as displays on park wildlife, good maps and walks information, a public phone, cold drinks and souvenirs for sale, and really great air-con. In a separate building are toilets, plus showers ($4).

It's accessible on a sealed road, 10km from the eastern entrance. West of here, the road is unsealed.

ⓘ Getting There & Away

Bring your own vehicle or join a tour. Check out the excellent options from the **Flying Sandgroper** (p202) to make a visit more accessible.

The closest airports are Paraburdoo (101km) and Newman (201km).

Integrity (☏1800 226 339; www.integritycoachlines.com.au) operates a weekly bus service between Perth and Port Hedland along the coast, heading inland from Exmouth on Rte 136 and stopping at Paraburdoo and Tom Price, where you can pick up a tour to the park.

Broome & the Kimberley

POP 32,000

Best Places to Eat

➡ Whale Song Cafe (p218)
➡ 18 Degrees (p215)
➡ Neaps Bistro (p222)
➡ Pumphouse (p230)
➡ Good Cartel (p216)

Best Off the Beaten Track Locations

➡ Mornington Wilderness Camp (p225)
➡ Mitchell Falls (p227)
➡ Pender Bay (p218)
➡ Kalumburu (p225)

Why Go?

Australia's last frontier is a wild land of remote, spectacular scenery spread over huge distances, with a severe climate, a sparse population and minimal infrastructure. Larger than 75% of the world's countries, the Kimberley is hemmed by impenetrable coastline and unforgiving deserts. In between lie vast boab-studded spinifex plains, palm-fringed gorges, desolate mountains and magnificent waterfalls. Travelling here is a true adventure, and each dry season a steady flow of explorers search for the real outback along the legendary Gibb River Road.

Aboriginal culture runs deep across the region, from the Dampier Peninsula, where neat communities welcome travellers to Country, to distant Mitchell Plateau, where ancient Wandjina and Gwion Gwion stand vigil over sacred waterholes.

Swashbuckling Broome (home to iconic Cable Beach, camel-tinged sunsets and amber-hued watering holes) and practical Kununurra (with its irrigation miracle) bookend the region. Both are great places to unwind, find a job and meet other travellers.

When to Go

Broome

Apr Fly over thundering Mitchell and King George Falls.

May Broome's at its greenest right before the tourist tide.

Sep & Oct Hit Purnululu and the Gibb River Road as the season winds down.

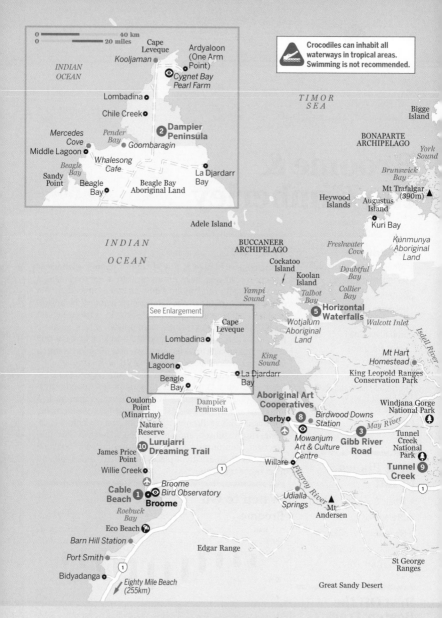

Crocodiles can inhabit all waterways in tropical areas. Swimming is not recommended.

Broome & the Kimberley Highlights

1 Taking a camel ride at sunset along Broome's **Cable Beach** (p209).

2 Learning about traditional culture with Aboriginal communities on the pristine **Dampier Peninsula** (p217).

3 Tackling the notorious **Gibb River Road** (p223) on a 4WD adventure.

4 Flying over the stunning **Mitchell & King George Falls** (p229) after the Wet.

5 Riding the wild **Horizontal Waterfalls** (p220).

ⓘ Getting There & Around

AIR

A number of airlines service Broome and the Kimberley:

Airnorth (☑1800 627 474; www.airnorth.com.au) Broome and Kununurra to Darwin.

Qantas (☑13 13 13; www.qantas.com.au) Perth daily and east-coast cities direct in season.

Skippers (☑1300 729 924; www.skippers.com. au) Flies between Broome, Halls Creek and Fitzroy Crossing.

Virgin Australia (☑13 67 89; www.virginaustralia. com.au) From Perth to Broome and Kununurra.

BUS

Integrity (p220) Perth to Broome twice a week.

Greyhound (p217) Broome to Darwin daily (except Sunday).

THE KIMBERLEY

Port Hedland to Broome

The Big Empty stretches from Port Hedland to Broome, as the Great Northern Highway skirts the Great Sandy Desert. It's 609km of willy-willies (mini dust whirlwinds) and sand and not much else. There are only two roadhouses, **Pardoo** (☑08-9176 4916; www.pardoo.com.au; Great Northern Hwy; unpowered/powered sites $24/30, s/d/f $80/100/120; ⊘24hr; P⛅☕) 148km from Portland, and **Sandfire** (☑08-9176 5944; www.facebook.com/sandfire.rh; Great Northern Hwy; unpowered/powered sites $20/30, dongas from $50; ⊘7am-7pm; P), 288km, so keep the tank full. The coast, wild and unspoilt, is never far away.

◉ Sights

Bidyadanga Community
Art Centre   GALLERY
(☑08-9192 4885; http://desertriversea.com.au/art-centres/bidyadanga-community-art-centre; Bidyadanga Rd, Bidyadanga; ⊘9am-1pm Mon-Thu) Bringing together inspiration from the desert to the coast, this art centre, in WA's largest Indigenous remote community, is a focus for five different language groups. Ring first.

🛏 Sleeping & Eating

Places along the Great Northern Highway can be packed from May to September.

If you can't do 600 klicks without seared scallops and a decent chardy, then Jack's Bar (p208) at Eco Beach is your only hope. Otherwise, it's steak sangers and coffee-flavoured milk at the roadhouses.

Eighty Mile Beach
Caravan Park   CARAVAN PARK $
(☑08-9176 5941; www.eightymilebeach.com.au; unpowered/powered sites $35/45, cabins $190) Popular with fishers, this shady, laid-back park 250km from Port Hedland backs onto a beautiful white-sand beach. Turtles nest from November to March.

Port Smith Caravan Park   CARAVAN PARK $
(☑08-9192 4983; www.portsmithcaravanpark.com. au; unpowered/powered sites $38/42, dongas d $110, cabins $220; P⛅☕) There's loads of wildlife at this park on a tidal lagoon, 160km south of Broome and 487km from Port Hedland.

Barn Hill Station   FARMSTAY $
(☑08-9192 4975; www.barnhill.com.au; unpowered/powered sites $25/32, cabins from $100; ⊘Apr-Nov; P✳☕☕) Barn Hill, 490km from Port Hedland and 130km south of Broome, is a working cattle station with its own 'mini Pinnacles'. It's especially popular among adventurous grey nomads (but all are welcome!).

Eco Beach   RESORT $$$
(☑08-9193 8015; www.ecobeach.com.au; Thangoo Station, Great Northern Hwy; safari tents from $225, villa d from $345; ✳☕☕) ⚲ This award-winning luxury eco-resort is set on secluded coastline 120km southwest of Broome. There's a choice of safari tents (no air-con) or villas, a top-notch restaurant (p208) (mains $38 to $45) and a host of tours and activities.

Jack's Bar
& Restaurant   MODERN AUSTRALIAN $$$
(☑08-9193 8015; www.ecobeach.com.au; Eco Beach Resort; mains $38-45; ⊘7-10am, noon-2pm & 6-8pm Apr-Nov, weekends only Dec-Mar) Is that the Indian Ocean or your glass of pinot gris? You're so close it's hard to tell. The succulent (though pricey) morsels that wash up onto your plate will mainly suit carnivores. Ring first to book.

Broome

POP 16,500

Like a paste jewel set in a tiara of natural splendours, Broome clings to a narrow strip of red pindan on the Kimberley's far-western edge, at the base of the pristine Dampier Peninsula. Surrounded by the aquamarine waters of the Indian Ocean and the creeks, mangroves and mudflats of Roebuck Bay,

GETTING AS FAR AWAY AS POSSIBLE

Suddenly come into a small fortune? Only got three days leave from your film set, board-room or personal fiefdom? Then consider one of the *exotique* luxury wilderness camps hidden away along the rugged, inhospitable Kimberley coastline. Far from any road, access is only by air or boat so rest assured, there won't be any peasant backpackers, paparazzi or grey nomads in sight. With guest numbers kept to an absolute minimum, you should expect full five-star service, all the freshly caught seafood and champagne you can guzzle, sensational views, searing sunsets, lots of wildlife and inclusive activities like bushwalking, rock-art tours and boat cruises. There's usually a minimum stay, and check carefully if air transfers from Kununurra are included before booking. Needless to say, prices will dip during the Wet.

Faraway Bay (☑0419 918 953; www.farawaybay.com.au; per person $1000; ☺Mar-Oct; ☒) Faraway by name and location, all meals and activities are included at this bush camp on the wild Kimberley coast. En-suite cabins with stunning views and private outdoor show-ers sit above a remote bay. Includes a free cruise to the nearby, spectacular W-shaped King George Falls. Unless you're coming by boat, slap on another $1700 per person for air transfers from Kununurra.

Kimberley Coastal Camp (☑0417 902 006; www.kimberleycoastalcamp.com.au; Admiralty Gulf; per person from $695) Pick (and pay for) activities such as fishing, yoga, rock-art tours and cooking lessons at this exclusive camp on the eastern side of Admiralty Gulf near Mitchell Falls. Getting there (by float-plane or helicopter) is not included.

Berkeley River Lodge (☑08-9169 1330; www.berkeleyriver.com.au; Berkeley River; villa s/d $1320/1750; ✳☎☒) Twenty luxury air-con villas sit on top of a dune above the pristine coastline of Joseph Bonaparte Gulf. Transfer by air from Kununurra costs $900 per person.

El Questro Homestead (☑08-9169 1777; www.elquestro.com.au; ☺r $2000-3000; ✳☎☒) Not on the coast, but perched literally on the cliff-edge of Chamberlain Gorge on El Questro Station, these luxury rooms come with incredible views, gourmet meals and guided tours around the property.

this Yawuru country is a good 2000km from the nearest capital city.

Cable Beach, with its luxury resorts, hauls in the tourists during high (dry) season (April to October), with romantic notions of camels, surf and sunsets. Magnificent, sure, but there's a lot more to Broome than post-cards, and tourists are sometimes surprised when they scratch the surface and find pin-dan just below.

The Dry is a great time to find casual work, while in the Wet (low season) prices plummet.

Each evening, the whole town collective-ly pauses, drinks in mid-air, while the sun slinks slowly towards Madagascar.

⊙ Sights

Cable Beach Area

★**Cable Beach**   BEACH
(🅿️♿) Western Australia's most famous landmark offers turquoise waters and beau-tiful white sand curving away to the sunset. Clothing is optional north of the rocks, while south of them, walking trails lead through the red dunes of **Minyirr Park**, a spiritual place for the Yawuru people. Cable Beach is synonymous with camels, and an evening ride along the sand is a highlight for many visitors. Locals in their 4WDs swarm north of the rocks for sunset drinks. Stingers are common in the Wet.

**Gantheaume Point
& Dinosaur Prints**   VIEWPOINT
(🅿️♿) Beautiful at dawn or sunset when the pindan cliffs turn scarlet and the Indi-an Ocean brilliant turquoise, this peaceful lookout holds a 135-million-year-old secret. Nearby lies one of the world's most varied collections of dinosaur footprints, impos-sible to find except at very low tides. Grab the map from the visitor centre (p217) and beware of slippery rocks. Look out for the ospreys returning with fish to their nests on the lighthouse.

Broome

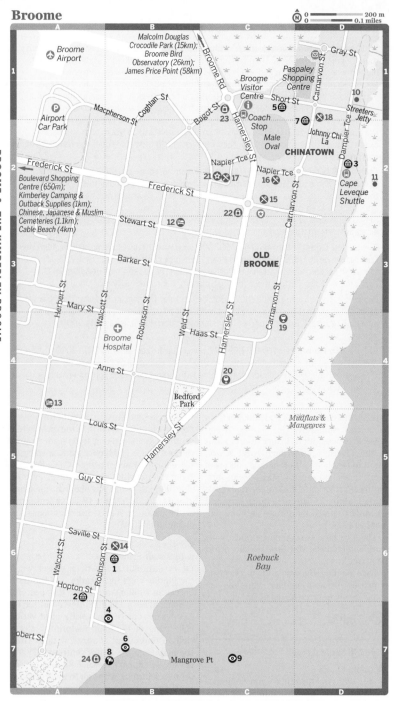

N

0 ——————— 200 m
0 ——————— 0.1 miles

Broome Airport

Malcolm Douglas
Crocodile Park (15km);
Broome Bird
Observatory (26km);
James Price Point (58km)

Broome Rd

Gray St

Paspaley Shopping Centre

Carnarvon St

10

Streeters Jetty

Airport Car Park

Macpherson St

Coghlan St

Bagot St

Broome Visitor Centre

23

Short St

Coach Stop

Male Oval

5

7

18

Johnny Chi La

Dampier Tce

CHINATOWN

3

Frederick St

Boulevard Shopping Centre (650m);
Kimberley Camping & Outback Supplies (1km);
Chinese, Japanese & Muslim Cemeteries (1.1km);
Cable Beach (4km)

Frederick St

Napier Tce

21 17

Napier Tce

16

15

22

11

Cape Leveque Shuttle

Stewart St

12

OLD BROOME

Barker St

Herbert St

Mary St

Walcott St

Robinson St

Weld St

Haas St

Carnarvon St

19

Broome Hospital

Anne St

20

13

Bedford Park

Louis St

Hamersley St

Mudflats & Mangroves

Guy St

Saville St

14

Roebuck Bay

1

Hopton St

2

4

obert St

6

24

8

Mangrove Pt

9

Broome

⊙ Sights
1 Broome Museum	B6
2 Bungalow	A6
3 Pearl Luggers	D2
4 Pioneer Cemetery	B7
5 Short Street Gallery	C1
6 Staircase to the Moon	B7
7 Sun Pictures	D2
8 Town Beach	B7
9 WWII Flying Boat Wrecks	C7

⊙ Activities, Courses & Tours
10 Jetty to Jetty	D1
11 Narlijia Cultural Tours	D2

⊕ Sleeping
12 Broome Town B&B	B3
13 McAlpine House	A4

⊗ Eating
14 18 Degrees	B6
15 Aarli	C2
16 Azuki	C2
17 Good Cartel	C2
18 Yuen Wing	D1

⊙ Drinking & Nightlife
19 Bay Club	C4
20 Matso's Broome Brewery	C4

⊕ Entertainment
21 Twin Cinema	C2

⊕ Shopping
22 Courthouse Markets	C2
23 Magabala Books	C1
24 Town Beach Markets	A7

Reddell Beach   BEACH
(Ⓟ🐪) For a blistering sunset without tourists, camels or 4WDs, pull into any of the turn-offs along Kavite Rd between Gantheaume Point (p209) and the **port** (Ⓟ🐪) and watch the pindan cliffs turn into molten lava.

Chinatown

Sun Pictures   HISTORIC BUILDING
(🖉08-9192 1077; www.sunpictures.com.au; 27 Carnarvon St; movies adult/child $17/12, history tour $5; ⊙history tour 10.30am & 1pm; 🚻) Sink back in a canvas deck chair in the world's oldest operating picture gardens, dating from 1916. The history of the Sun building is the history of Broome itself; it has witnessed war, floods, low-flying aircraft (it's still on the airport flight path) and racial segregation. There's a short 15-minute history tour during the Dry.

Short Street Gallery   GALLERY
(🖉08-9192 6118; www.shortstgallery.com.au; 7 Short St; ⊙10am-3pm Mon-Fri, 11am-3pm Sat) This original Chinatown building houses back-to-back exhibitions of contemporary Indigenous artworks.

Pearl Luggers   MUSEUM
(🖉08-9192 0000; www.pearlluggers.com. au; 31 Dampier Tce; 1hr tour adult/child/family $25/12.50/60; ⊙tours 11.30am & 3pm) FREE This compact museum provides an insight into Broome's tragic pearling past, evoking the diver experience with genuine artefacts. You can also wander over two of the last

surviving luggers, named *Sam Male* and *DMcD*.

Old Broome

Broome Museum   MUSEUM
(🖉08-9192 2075; www.broomemuseum.org.au; 67 Robinson St; adult/child $6/1; ⊙10am-4pm Mon-Fri, to 1pm Sat & Sun dry season, to 1pm daily wet season; Ⓟ) Discover Cable Beach and Chinatown's origins through exhibits devoted to the area's pearling history and WWII bombing in this quirky museum, occupying the former Customs House.

Cemeteries
A number of cemeteries testify to Broome's multicultural past. The most striking is the **Japanese Cemetery** (Port Dr) with 919 graves (mostly pearl divers). Next to this, the **Chinese Cemetery** (Frederick St) has over 90 graves and monuments. The small **Muslim Cemetery** (Frederick St) honours Malay pearl-divers and Afghan cameleers.

A couple of kilometres southeast, the small **Pioneer Cemetery** overlooks Roebuck Bay at Town Beach.

Around Town Beach

WWII Flying Boat Wrecks   HISTORIC SITE
On a very low tide it's possible to walk out across the mudflats from **Town Beach** (Ⓟ) to the wrecks of Catalina and Dornier flying boats attacked by Japanese 'Zeroes' during WWII. The planes had been evacuating refugees from Java and many still had passengers aboard. Over 60 people and 15 flying

Cable Beach

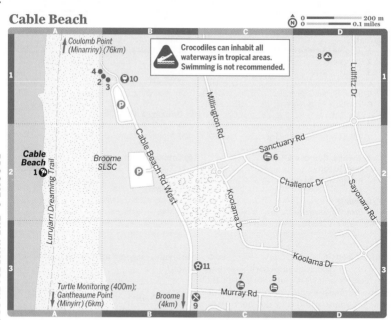

Crocodiles can inhabit all waterways in tropical areas. Swimming is not recommended.

Cable Beach

---

boats (mostly Dutch and British) were lost. Only six wrecks are visible, with the rest in deep water.

Start walking an hour before low tide, and head roughly southeast for 1.5km (about 30 minutes). Wear appropriate footwear – the mud's sticky and can hide sharp objects, not all of them inanimate. Watch out for other marine hazards like jellyfish and check with the visitor centre (p217) for tide times. The museum (p211) also has a handy brochure. Or just take the **hovercraft** (☑08-9193 5025; www.broomehovercraft.com.au; adult/child dinosaur $128/91, sunset $185/117, flying boats $205/137).

Bungalow GALLERY
(☑08-9192 6118; www.shortstgallery.com; 3 Hopton St, Town Beach; ☉10am-3pm Mon-Sat, shorter hours wet season) Short St Gallery's Hopton St stock room at Town Beach holds a stunning collection of canvasses from across the Kimberley and beyond.

Nagula Jarndu
Women's Resource Centre ARTS CENTRE
(☑0499 330 708; www.nagulajarndu.com.au; 3/12 Gregory St; ☉9.30am-4pm Mon-Fri) Beautiful screen- and block-printed textiles and other crafts are on show (and sale!) at this studio/gallery run by Yawuru women. Enter via Pembroke Rd.

Around Broome

Broome Bird Observatory NATURE RESERVE
(✆08-9193 5600; www.broomebirdobservatory.com; Crab Creek Rd; by donation, camping per person $18, unit with shared bathroom s/d/f $45/60/85, chalets $165; ⊙8am-4pm; P) ✐ The tidal mudflats of Roebuck Bay are a vital staging post for thousands of migratory birds, some coming from as far away as Siberia. In a peaceful coastal setting 25km from Broome, the 'Bird Obbie' offers quiet walking trails, secluded bush camp sites and a choice of low-key rooms. There's a number of tours ($70, 2½ hours) and courses ($1400, five days) available as well as volunteering opportunities.

Hard-core twitchers shouldn't miss the daily 6pm bird count.

Malcolm Douglas
Wilderness Park WILDLIFE RESERVE
(✆08-9193 6580; www.malcolmdouglas.com.au; Broome Hwy; adult/child/family $35/20/90; ⊙2-5pm; P ⊞) Visitors enter through the jaws of a giant crocodile at this 30-hectare animal refuge 16km northeast of Broome. The park is home to dozens of crocs (don't miss the 3pm feeding), as well as kangaroos, cassowaries, emus, dingoes, jabirus and numerous other birds.

🏃 Activities

Scenic flights taking in Cape Leveque, the Horizontal Falls and the Devonian Reef National Park are popular.

Odyssey Expeditions DIVING
(www.odysseyexpeditions.com.au; 8-day tour from $3495; ⊙Sep-Oct) Runs several eight-day, liveaboard diving tours from Broome each spring to the **Rowley Shoals Marine Park**. You need to be an experienced diver with your own gear (though some gear may be hired in Broome).

Turtle Monitoring WILDLIFE
(✆08-9195 5500; Yawuru.Rangers@dpaw.wa.gov.au; Cable Beach; ⊙Nov-Feb; ⊞) ✐ FREE Stuck in Broome over the Wet? Volunteers walk 4km along Cable Beach (p209) in the morning and record the previous night's turtle activity. Free training provided.

Broome Aviation SCENIC FLIGHTS
(✆08-9192 1369; www.broomeaviation.com.au; half-/full-day flights from $640/1090) Half-day flights to Cape Leveque and the Horizontal Falls (p220) from Broome. Full-day tours

add-on the Devonian Reef National Parks, Bell Gorge (p224) and Mt Hart or Mitchell Falls.

King Leopold Air SCENIC FLIGHTS
(✆08-9193 7155; www.kingleopoldair.com.au; half-/full-day tours from $595/1060) Flights over the Dampier Peninsula (half-day) and to Mitchell Falls or Devonian Reef National Parks (full day). Also has a 30-minute flight over Broome's beaches (per person two passengers/three to five passengers $240/150).

Kimberley Aviation SCENIC FLIGHTS
(✆0429 112 407; www.kimberleyaviation.com.au; half-/full-day tours from $595/1090) The usual half-day tour to Cape Leveque and Horizontal Falls (p220) and full-day tour onto Mitchell Falls. Also has a tie-in with Cygnet Bay's King Sound tours ($845).

👉 Tours

Camel Tours

Broome Camel Safaris OUTDOORS
(✆0419 916 101; www.broomecamelsafaris.com.au; Cable Beach; adult/child morning $65/45, afternoon $45/30, sunset $85/65; ⊞) Run by Alison 'the Camel Lady', Broome Camel Safaris (with animals sporting blue camel blankets) offers 45-minute morning, 30-minute afternoon (3pm) and one-hour sunset camel rides along Cable Beach (p209).

Red Sun Camels OUTDOORS
(✆1800 184 488; www.redsuncamels.com.au; Cable Beach; adult/child morning $65/45, afternoon $45/30, sunset $90/65) Morning (40-minute), afternoon (30-minute) and sunset (one-hour) camel rides along Cable Beach (p209) on red-blanketed camels.

Sundowner Camel Tours OUTDOORS
(✆0477 774 297; www.sundownercameltours.com.au; Cable Beach; adult/child afternoon $40/30, sunset $90/60) Yellow-blanketed camels hit Cable Beach (p209) in the afternoon (3pm) and at sunset.

Non-camel Tours

Other options around Broome include kayaking, stargazing, birdwatching, historical walking tours, dolphin and marine wildlife spotting, and hovercraft tours.

★Lurujarri Dreaming Trail WALKING
(✆Frans 0423 817 925; www.goolarabooloo.org.au; adult/student $1600/900; ⊙May-Jul but can vary; ⊞) This incredible 82km walk follows a section of ancient songline north along

ROWLEY SHOALS MARINE PARK

These three coral atolls lie approximately 300km from Broome in the Indian Ocean, on the edge of Australia's continental shelf, and have a reputation for some of the best diving in the country. Protected by a marine park, there are over 600 species of fish and 200-plus different varieties of coral. At a good 12-hour cruise from land, the shoals only see a minute number of visitors each year. Several Broome operators offer multinight cruises for experienced divers.

the coast from Gantheaume Point (p209) (Minyirr) to Coulomb Point (Minarriny). The Goolarabooloo organise several guided nine-day walking trips each dry season, staying at traditional camp sites. There is a strong emphasis on sharing Indigenous culture with activities like spear-making, bush-tucker hunting, fishing, mud-crabbing and native jewellery making.

★ **Jetty to Jetty** WALKING
(www.yawuru.com; 🚻📷) FREE This self-guided walking tour from the local Yawuru people comes with a fantastic audio accompaniment (download the free Jetty to Jetty smartphone app), taking you past 13 points of historical and cultural significance between Chinatown's Streeter's Jetty and the Old Jetty at Town Beach (p211). The 2.8km walk (with stops) should take around two hours.

Narlijia Cultural Tours CULTURAL
(☑08-9195 0232; www.narlijiaculturaltours.com.au; Chinatown; adult/child mangroves $75/35, history $55/25; ⊙May–mid-Oct; 🚻) Yawuru local Bart Pigram runs short (two-hour) informative cultural tours around the mangroves and historical buildings of Chinatown.

🎊 Festivals & Events

Festival timings vary from year to year so check with the visitor centre (p217).

Sea Grass Monitoring ENVIRONMENTAL
(☑08-9192 1922; www.facebook.com/broome.seagrass; Roebuck Bay; ⊙hours vary Mar, Jun, Aug & Dec; 🚻) 🖋FREE Every three months or so volunteers walk out onto the mudflats

of Roebuck Bay to monitor the sea grass that marine creatures such as dugongs and turtles depend on. All are welcome and no experience is necessary. Bring a hat, water bottle and closed shoes.

A Taste of Broome FOOD & DRINK
(www.goolarri.com; Goolarri Amphitheatre, Blackman St, Old Broome) Indigenous flavours, dance and music caress the senses at this ticket-only event held monthly during the Wet.

Kullarri Naidoc Week CULTURAL
(www.goolarri.com; ⊙late Jun–mid-Jul) Celebration of Aboriginal and Torres Strait Islander culture.

Broome Race Round SPORTS
(www.broometurfclub.com.au; Broome Racecourse; ⊙Jul/Aug) Locals and tourists frock up and party hard for the Kimberley Cup, Ladies' Day and Broome Cup horse races.

Corrugated Lines LITERATURE
(www.facebook.com/corrugatedlines; ⊙Aug) Three-day festival of the written (and spoken) word with various workshops and talks around town.

Shinju Matsuri Festival of the Pearl CULTURAL
(www.shinjumatsuri.com.au; ⊙Aug/Sep; 🚻) Broome's homage to the pearl includes a week of parades, food, art, concerts, fireworks and dragon-boat races.

🛏 Sleeping

Accommodation is plentiful, but either book ahead or be flexible. If you're travelling in a group, consider renting an apartment. Prices plummet in the Wet.

★ **Beaches of Broome** HOSTEL $
(☑1300 881 031; www.beachesofbroome.com.au; 4 Sanctuary Rd, Cable Beach; dm $32-45, motel d without/with bathroom $140/180; 🅿❄@🛜🏊) More resort than hostel, spotless, air-conditioned rooms are complemented by shady common areas, a poolside bar and a modern self-catering kitchen. Dorms come in a variety of sizes (and include female-only rooms), and the motel rooms are beautifully appointed. Both the continental breakfast and wi-fi are free. Scooter and bike hire available.

Tarangau Caravan Park CARAVAN PARK $
(☑08-9193 5084; www.tarangaucaravanpark.com; 16 Millington Rd, Cable Beach; unpowered/powered

sites $38/48; P 🐾) A quieter alternative to the often noisy Cable Beach caravan parks, Tarangau has pleasant, grassy sites 1km from the beach.

★ **McAlpine House** B&B $$$
(☎08-9192 0588; http://mcalpinehouse.com.au; 55 Herbert St; d $185-420; P ❄ 🐾 🛜 🐾) Lord McAlpine made this stunning house, a former pearl master's lodge, his Broome residence during the '80s. Now renovated to its former glory, there are lovely airy rooms, open communal areas, shady tropical verandahs and a lush canopy of mango trees, tamarind and frangipanis. Escape from the heat by the pool, or travel back through time in the library.

Bali Hai Resort & Spa SPA HOTEL $$$
(☎08-9191 3100; www.balihairesort.com; 6 Murray Rd, Cable Beach; r from $228, cafe mains $29-42; ❂cafe 3.30pm-late Wed-Sun; P ❄ ❄ 🛜 🐾) Lush and tranquil, this beautiful small resort has gorgeously decorated studios and villas, each with individual outside dining areas and open-roofed bathrooms. The emphasis is on relaxation, and the on-site spa offers a range of exotic therapies. There's also an Asian-themed cafe showcasing fresh WA produce. The off-season prices are a bargain.

Broome Town B&B B&B $$$
(☎08-9192 2006; www.broometown.com.au; 15 Stewart St, Old Broome; r $285; P ❄ 🛜 🐾) This delightful, boutique-style B&B epitomises Broome-style architecture, with high-pitched roofs, wooden louvres, jarrah floors, tasteful rooms, an open communal guest lounge and lots of tropical shade.

Broome Beach Resort APARTMENT $$$
(☎08-9158 3300; www.broomebeachresort.com; 4 Murray Rd, Cable Beach; 1-/2-/3-bedroom apt $305/345/375; P ❄ 🛜 🐾) Great for families and groups, these large, modest apartments surround a central pool and are within easy walking distance of Cable Beach (p209). Much cheaper if you stay three-plus days.

✘ Eating

Be prepared for 'Broome prices' (exorbitant), 'Broome time' (should be open but it's closed) and surcharges (credit cards, public holidays, bad karma). Service fluctuates wildly, as most staff are just passing through. Most places close in low season.

You'll find cafes along Carnarvon St in Chinatown, while many resorts have in-house restaurants, though often you're just paying for the view.

Cable Beach General Store & Cafe CAFE $
(☎08-9192 5572; www.cablebeachstore.com.au; cnr Cable Beach & Murray Rds; snacks $6-19; ❂6am-8pm; P 🛜 🐾) Cable Beach unplugged – a typical Aussie corner shop with egg breakfasts, barramundi burgers, pies, internet and no hidden charges. You can even play a round of minigolf (adult/child/family $12/8/20).

Yuen Wing MARKET $
(☎08-9192 1267; 19 Carnarvon St; ❂8.30am-5.30pm Mon-Fri, to 2pm Sat & Sun) This friendly grocery is your best bet for spices, noodles and all things Asian. Also stocks beach and camping gear.

★ **18 Degrees** MODERN AUSTRALIAN $$
(☎08-9192 7915; www.18degrees.com.au; Shop 4, 63 Robinson St; share plates $8-34; ❂meals 4-9pm Tue-Sat, snacks 9-11pm Thu-Sat; P) Exquisite share plates (serving two) and the best cocktails in town await you at Broome's newest, hippest nightspot. The more daring can try the squid ink, tentacles and chorizo with beetroot aioli, while the meeker can safely opt for grapefruit-glazed chicken

---

STAIRCASE TO THE MOON

The reflections of a rising full moon rippling over exposed mudflats at low tide create the optical illusion of a **golden stairway** (Town Beach; ❂Mar-Oct; 🚻🐾) leading to the moon. Between March and October Broome buzzes around the full moon, with everyone eager to see the spectacle. At **Town Beach** (p211) there's a lively **evening market** (❂Mar-Oct) with food stalls, and people bring fold-up chairs, although the small headland at the end of Hamersley St has a better view.

While Roebuck Bay parties like nowhere else, this phenomenon happens across the Kimberley and Pilbara coasts – anywhere with some east-facing mudflats. Other good viewing spots are **One Arm Point** at Cape Leveque, **Cooke Point** in Port Hedland, **Sunrise Beach** at Onslow, **Hearson Cove** near Dampier and the lookout at **Cossack**. Most visitor centres publish the dates on their websites.

breast. The desserts are brilliant, and the bar list runs for nine pages.

★ Good Cartel
CAFE $$

(☑ 0499 335 949; 3 Weld St; breakfast $7-19, burgers $15-20; ☺ 5am-noon Mon-Fri, to 2pm Sat & Sun; P 🖘 🐾) 🍴 What started as a pop-up cafe is now *the* place in town to grab a great coffee, healthy juice and Mexican-themed breakfasts. Burgers appear weekend lunchtimes and Friday nights (5pm to 9pm). Follow the line of cars behind the Twin Cinema (☑ 08-9192 3199; http://broomemovies.com.au; 3 Weld St; adult/child/family $17/12/55; ☺ 10am-midnight or end of last movie; 🖘) in the business park. Doggies more than welcome as the cafe is active in rehabilitating strays.

★ Aarli
TAPAS $$

(☑ 08-9192 5529; www.facebook.com/theaarli; Frederick St; share plates $11.50-21.50, breakfast $5-17.50; ☺ 8am-late; P) Aarli offers the wonderful outdoor relaxed dining that Broome does so well. Drop in for some quick tapas share plates (Med-Asian fusion) or while away the afternoon working your way through the excellent wine list. Also open for breakfast (8am to noon).

Azuki
JAPANESE $$

(☑ 08-9193 7211; www.facebook.com/azukijapanesefusion; 1/15 Napier Tce; sushi $14-18, bentos $25-30; ☺ 11am-2.30pm Mon-Fri; 🖘) Enjoy the exquisite subtlety of authentic Japanese cuisine at this tiny BYO restaurant, from the takeaway fresh sushi rolls to the wonderfully tasty bento boxes. It also has a food truck that pops up around town at special events.

Wharf Restaurant
SEAFOOD $$$

(☑ 08-9192 5800; 401 Port Dr, Port; mains $31-120; ☺ 10am-late; P) Settle back for a long, lazy seafood lunch with waterside ambience and the chance of a whale sighting. OK, it's pricey, but the wine's cold, the sea stunning and the chilli blue swimmer crab sensational. Just wait until after 2pm to order oysters (when they become half-price).

🍷 Drinking & Entertainment

Choices are split between Old Broome and Cable Beach. Both of the town's pubs regularly host bands, while those with outdoor areas like the Bay Club (p216) and Matso's (p216) are more family friendly.

Matso's Broome Brewery
PUB

(☑ 08-9193 5811; www.matsos.com.au; 60 Hamersley St; share plates $6-35, mains $20-39;

☺ 7am-midnight; 🖘) Get yourself a 50/50 chilli/ginger beer combo and a half-kilogram bucket of prawns then kick back to the lazy afternoon music on the shady verandah of Broome's finest brewery.

Bay Club
BAR

(Mangrove Hotel; ☑ 08-9192 1303; www.mangrovehotel.com.au; 47 Carnarvon St; mains $19-38; ☺ 11am-10pm) The Mangrove Hotel's casual outdoor bar is perfect for a few early bevvies while contemplating Roebuck Bay. Decent bistro meals and live music complement excellent Staircase to the Moon (p215) viewing. On Sundays, parents can drop their kids at the bouncing castle.

Sunset Bar & Grill
BAR

(☑ 08-9192 0470; www.cablebeachclub.com; Cable Beach Club Resort, Cable Beach Rd; ☺ breakfast 6.30-10.30am, bar 4-9pm, dinner 5.30-9pm) Arrive around 4.45pm, grab a front-row seat, order a drink and watch the show – backpackers, package tourists, locals, camels and a searing Indian Ocean sunset shaded by imported coconut palms.

Diver's Tavern
LIVE MUSIC

(☑ 08-9193 6066; www.diverstavern.com.au; Cable Beach Rd; ☺ 11am-midnight) Diver's pumps most nights, and if you're camped anywhere nearby, you'll know it. The Sunday Session jams are legendary.

🛍 Shopping

The old tin shanties of Short St and Dampier Tce are chock-full of Indigenous art, pearl jewellery and cheap, tacky souvenirs.

Magabala Books
BOOKS

(☑ 08-9192 1991; www.magabala.com; 1 Bagot St; ☺ 9am-4.30pm Mon-Fri; 🖘) Brilliant Indigenous publishers showcasing Kimberley storytelling with a selection of novels, social history books, biographies and children's literature.

Courthouse Markets
MARKET

(Hamersley St; ☺ 8am-1pm Sat year-round, Sun Apr-Oct; 🖘) Local arts, crafts, music, hawker food and general hippie gear.

Boulevard Shopping Centre
SHOPPING CENTRE

(106 Frederick St) Supermarket, health food, bottle shop (liquor store) and service station.

Kimberley Camping & Outback Supplies
SPORTS & OUTDOORS

(☑ 08-9193 5909; www.kimberleycamping.com.au; cnr Frederick St & Cable Beach Rd; ☺ 8.30am-5pm

Mon-Fri, to 1.30pm Sat, 9am-1pm Sun) Jerrycans, Akubra hats, tent pegs and everything else you need for a Kimberley expedition.

ⓘ Information

Broome Visitor Centre (☑08-9195 2200; www.visitbroome.com.au; ⊙8.30am-5pm Mon-Fri, to 4.30pm Sat & Sun, shorter hours during wet season) Great for info on road conditions, **Staircase to the Moon** (p215), **dinosaur footprints** (p209), **WWII wrecks** (p211), tide times and souvenirs. Books accommodation and tours for businesses registered with it, and is also the long-haul coach stop. It's on the roundabout entering town, opposite Male Oval.

Broome Community Resource Centre (CRC; ☑ 08-9193 7153; www.broome.crc.net.au; 40 Dampier Tce; per hr $7.50; ⊙ 8.30am-4.30pm Mon-Fri; ⓐ) Cheap printing, wi-fi and internet.

ⓘ Getting There & Away

Unless you're on a long-haul road trip, the easiest way into Broome is by air. **Broome Airport** (☑ 08-9194 0600; www.broomeair.com.au; Macpherson St) is centrally located and serviced by **Qantas** (☑ 13 13 13; www.qantas.com.au), Skippers (p272), **Virgin** (☑ 13 67 89; www.virginaustralia.com) and **Airnorth** (☑ 08-8920 4001; www.airnorth.com.au). A **shuttle** (Airport Shuttle; ☑ 08-9192 5252; www.broometaxis.com; Broome/Cable Beach hotels $7/11) service meets flights and drops off passengers at most Broome hotels and Cable Beach resorts.

Long-distance **Integrity** (☑ 08-9274 7464; www.integritycoachlines.com.au) buses run to Perth and **Greyhound** (☑1300 473 946; www.greyhound.com.au) to Darwin. A local **bus** (p222) goes to Derby and there's a daily **shuttle** (p220) to Cape Leveque as well as the thrice-weekly **mail run** (p220).

Britz (☑ 08-9192 2647; www.britz.com; 10 Livingston St; minimum 5-day hire van/4WD from $1000/1600) hires campervans, motorhomes and rugged 4WDs, the latter being essential for the Gibb River Road.

ⓘ Getting Around

Broome's attractions are fairly spread out; don't underestimate distances or the heat. Most hostels will rent out bicycles and/or scooters.

Town Bus Service (☑ 08-9193 6585; www.broomebus.com.au; adult $4, day pass $10; ⊙7.23am-6.23pm dry season, 8.53am-5.53pm Mon-Sat, from 10.53am Sun wet season; ⓐ) links Town Beach, Chinatown and Cable Beach every 30 minutes during the Dry and every hour during the Wet.

Broome Broome (☑ 08-9192 2210; www.broomebroome.com.au; 3/15 Napier Tce;

car/4WD/scooter per day from $65/155/35) is the only rental car company that can offer unlimited kilometres. Scooter hire is $35 per day.

Broome Cycles (☑08-9192 1871; www.broomecycles.com.au; 2 Hamersley St; per day/week $30/100, deposit $150; ⊙8.30am-5pm Mon-Fri, to 2pm Sat) hires mountain bikes out by the day ($30) or week ($100) from Chinatown, and from a trailer at **Cable Beach** (☑0409 192 289; cnr Cable Beach & Sanctuary Rds, Cable Beach; ⊙9am-noon May-Oct) when in season.

For a taxi, try **Broome Taxis** (☑13 10 08), **Chinatown Taxis** (☑1800 811 772) or **Pearl Town Taxis** (☑13 13 30).

Dampier Peninsula

Stretching north from Broome, the red pindan of the Dampier Peninsula ends abruptly above deserted beaches, secluded mangrove bays and cliffs burnished crimson by the setting sun. This remote and stunning country is home to thriving Indigenous settlements of the Ngumbarl, Jabirr Jabirr, Nyul Nyul, Nimanburu, Bardi Jawi and Goolarabooloo peoples. Access is by 4WD, along the largely unsealed 215km-long Cape Leveque Rd.

The Manari Road (p219) turn-off, home to Broome's northern beaches and bush camp sites, is reached after 15km.

If you wish to visit Aboriginal communities, you must *always* book ahead (ideally directly with your community hosts, though the Broome Visitor Centre (p217) may help); check if permits and/or payments are required. Look for the informative booklet *Ardi–Dampier Peninsula Travellers Guide* ($5). You need to be self-sufficient, though limited supplies are available.

Beagle Bay

Beagle Bay Church　　　　CHURCH
(☑08-9192 4913; by donation) Around 110km from Broome, Beagle Bay is notable for the extraordinarily beautiful mother-of-pearl altar at Beagle Bay church, built by Pallottine monks in 1918. Fuel is available at the community store (weekdays only).

Banana Well Getaway　　　CAMPGROUND $
(☑08-9192 4040; www.bananawellgetaway.com.au; Banana Wells, Beagle Bay; ⊙unpowered/powered sites $35/40, cabins from $110; ⓐ) Quiet, friendly and relaxed, near the southern shore of Beagle Bay; there's not much to do here other than fish.

Ngarlan Yarnin' HISTORY

(☑0438 118 578; Beagle Bay; 2 people/family $25/40; ☺tours 9am, 10.30am, noon, 1.50pm & 5pm Mon-Sat) Mena Lewis, a local Nyul Nyul and Bardi woman, holds fascinating one-hour story tellings on the history of the Sacred Heart Church, Beagle Bay and the community itself. Cash only.

Middle Lagoon & Around

Middle Lagoon CAMPGROUND $

(Nature's Hideaway; ☑08-9192 4002; www.middlelagoon.com.au; sites per person $20-22, cabins $150-250, day use $10; ☒) Middle Lagoon, 180km from Broome and surrounded by empty beaches, is superb for swimming, snorkelling, fishing and, well, doing nothing. There's plenty of shade and bird life, and the cabins (available April to September) will take up to five people.

Mercedes Cove CABIN $$

(☑08-9192 4687; www.mercedescove.com.au; Pender Bay; eco-tents/cabins $150/300; ☺Apr-Sep; ✿☒) 🏄 On a stunning, secluded cove near Middle Lagoon (p218), Mercedes offers a chilled glamping experience with beautifully appointed eco-tents and air-con cabins, all with amazing Indian Ocean views. It's the perfect spot for whale watching, beachcombing, fishing and birdwatching. A minimum stay (two/three nights) applies for weekends/long weekends.

Gnylmarung Retreat CAMPGROUND $

(☑0429 411 241; www.gnylmarung.org.au; near Middle Lagoon; sites per person $20, children under 12 free; ☒☺) This small, low-key community near Middle Lagoon offers a limited number of secluded camp sites and is popular with fishers.

Pender Bay

Pender Bay BAY

(☑0429 845 707; day use/camp sites per person $10/15; ☒) Exquisitely remote, this pristine bay is an important calving ground for humpback whales and many can be seen offshore from May to November. The easiest access is from either Whale Song Cafe (p218), if open, or via the small Pender Bay camping ground (between Mercedes Cove and Whale Song), where clifftop vantage points provide exceptional viewing. Simple bush camp sites (and an amenity block) are available.

Goombaragin Eco Retreat CAMPGROUND $$

(☑0429 505 347; www.goombaragin.com.au; Pender Bay; site per person $18, tent with/without bathroom $175/80, chalets $220; ☺Apr-Oct; ☎) 🏄 With a superb location overlooking the scarlet pindan cliffs and turquoise waters of Pender Bay, this eco-retreat offers several unpowered camp sites, a range of safari tents and a self-contained chalet. There's a nightly communal get-together around the fire.

★**Whale Song Cafe** CAFE $$

(☑08-9192 4000; www.whalesongcafe.com.au; Munget, Pender Bay; light meals $11-29; ☺9am-2pm Jun-Aug; ☒) 🏄 This exquisitely located eco-cafe overlooking Pender Bay serves fabulous organic mango smoothies, homemade gourmet pizzas and the best coffee on the peninsula. There's a tiny bush camping ground (camp sites per person $20) with stunning views, a funky outdoor shower and not a caravan in sight. Telstra mobile reception available.

Lombadina & Around

Lombadina INDIGENOUS COMMUNITY

(☑08-9192 4936; www.lombadina.com; entry per car $10; ☺office 8am-noon & 1-4pm Mon-Fri) Between Middle Lagoon and Cape Leveque, Lombadina is 200km from Broome. This beautiful tree-fringed Indigenous community offers various tours (minimum three people), including fishing, whale watching, 4WD tours, mud-crabbing, kayaking and walking, which can be booked through the office. Accommodation is in backpacker-style rooms and self-contained cabins ($220 to $280 for four people), but there's no camping. Fuel is available on weekdays and there are lovely pieces for sale at the Arts Centre (open weekdays). Don't miss the paperbark church.

Ardi Festival CULTURAL

(www.visitbroome.com.au; Lombadina; adult $20, under 15 free; ☺varies Jun-Sep) Annual celebration of Ardi culture featuring music, food and art at Lombadina (p218) community. Check the dates with the Broome Visitor Centre (p217) as the timing of this fledgling festival varies each year. Drug and alcohol free.

Chile Creek CAMPGROUND $

(☑08-9192 4141; www.chilecreek.com.au; Chile Creek, Lombadina; sites per adult/child $16.50/10, bungalows $95, family safari tents $185) Tiny

MANARI ROAD: BROOME'S NORTHERN BEACHES

The beaches, headlands and red pindan cliffs along Manari Rd are one of Broome's best-kept secrets, frequented mainly by anglers, locals and adventurous travellers looking for something more than just Broome-time. Leaving the Cape Leveque Rd just 15km from the Great Northern Hwy, unsealed, sandy and sometimes corrugated Manari Rd runs roughly northwest through **Goolarabooloo Country**, parallel to the coastal **Lurujarri Songline** (an oral memory map of stories, song and dance that describes the landscape and is handed down from generation to generation).

Just 5km along you'll reach the turn-off to **Willie Creek** where there's a **pearl farm** (Wirrkinymirri; ☑08-9192 0000; www.thebroomeexperience.com.au; Willie Creek Rd; tours adult/child/family from $65/35/165; ☺cafe 11am-3pm Apr-Sep; 🅿) in a stunning location on a mangrove-lined inlet; the 7.5km sandy access track feels quite remote as you skirt a wide salt lake. Various tours are available and there's a cafe for lunch, but don't swim, as there are salties (saltwater crocodiles) in the creek.

Back on Manari Rd, there are bush camp sites (no facilities, maximum three-night stay) at **Barred Creek** (Nuwirrar; Manari Rd; 🅿🐕) 🐾 FREE, **Quandong Point** (Kardila-kan; Manari Rd; 🚐🐕) FREE, **James Price Point** (Walmadan; Manari Rd; 🚐🐕) 🐾 FREE and **Coulomb Point** (Minarinny; Manari Rd; 🚐🐕) 🐾 FREE, where there is a nature reserve. You can swim at the beaches here, fish off the reefs and wander the rock platforms at low tide looking for dinosaur footprints and plant fossils, but don't take anything away other than rubbish.

Conventional vehicles should make it to James Price Point, in the middle of the Songline. Its crumbling, crimson pindan cliffs, once home to the proud warrior **Walmadan**, have in more recent years become both an icon and the frontline of the Kimberley's environmental movement. Whether or not you plan on camping, don't miss this spectacular location. Especially at sunset!

For more information about the area, see www.goolarabooloo.org.au and www.environskimberley.org.au.

mangrove-fringed Chile Creek, 10km from Lombadina (p218) down an eroded sandy track, offers basic bush camp sites, bungalows (shared bathroom) and en-suite safari tents (minimum two-night stay). There's great bird life and plenty of mud crabs, but BYO food (unless you plan to catch it!).

Cape Leveque & Around

👁 Sights

Cape Leveque (Kooljaman)　　　BEACH
(day access per person $5; ♿) 🐾 Spectacular Cape Leveque, right on the tip of the Dampier Peninsula, has stunning red cliffs and gorgeous white beaches perfect for swimming and snorkelling. Access is via Kooljaman (p220) resort where there are plenty of accommodation options.

Ardyaloon
(One Arm Point)　　INDIGENOUS COMMUNITY
(Bardi; ☑08-9192 4930; http://ardyaloon.org.au; per person $15, child free; ☺office 8am-noon & 1.30-4pm Mon-Thu, 8am-noon & 1.30-3pm Fri)

The neat Indigenous community of Ardyaloon (One Arm Point) has a well-stocked store (open 8am to 5pm Monday to Friday), 24-hour fuel, great fishing, and swimming with views of the Buccaneer Archipelago. Your day entry permit (payable at the office) includes admission to the trochus shell hatchery out on the point. There's no accommodation or camping.

👣 Tours

Brian Lee Tagalong Tours　　TOURS
(☑08-9192 4970; www.brianleetagalong.com.au; Kooljaman; adult/child $98/45) Tag-along (in your own 4WD) with Bardi traditional owner Brian Lee as he reveals the culture and history surrounding Hunters Creek, where you'll get a chance to fish and hunt for mud crabs.

Bundy's Tours　　CULTURAL
(☑09-9192 4970; www.bundysculturaltours.com.au; Kooljaman; adult $45-80, child $25-40) Bardi custodian Bundy offers a range of cultural tours providing an amazing insight into traditional customs, including bush tucker, night fishing and spear-making.

🛏 Sleeping & Eating

Gumbanan CAMPGROUND $
(☑0499 330 169; www.kimberleyoutbackxposure. com.au; near One Arm Point; site per adult $15, child under 10 free, safari tent d/f $120/140) On a beautifully unspoiled mangrove coast, this small outstation between Cape Leveque and Ardyaloon (p219) offers quiet, unpowered sites and simple safari tents. Immerse yourself in traditional culture with spear-making ($85) or mud-crabbing ($95) courses, or jump on a quad bike and see the Joowon marshes ($130).

Kooljaman RESORT $$
(☑08-9192 4970; www.kooljaman.com.au; entry per adult $5, unpowered/powered sites $45/50, dome tents $85, beach shelters $120, cabin with/ without bathroom $200/155, safari tents from $275; P 🐾) Ecotourism award-winner Kooljaman offers a range of accommodation from grassy camp sites and budget dome tents to driftwood beach shelters, cabins with or without bathrooms, and hilltop safari tents with superb views. On-site restaurant Raugis (p220) overlooks Western Beach and the smaller Dinkas Cafe (open March to September) is on the eastern side, or you can order takeaway BBQ packs.

Cygnet Bay Pearl Farm RESORT $$
(☑08-9192 4283; www.cygnetbaypearls.com.au; Cygnet Bay; powered sites/safari tents/pearlers' shacks from $60/195/350; P ❄ 🐾) In Bardi Jawi Country, and overlooking incredible Cygnet Bay, this historic pastoral lease and pearl farm offers a range of accommodation, from camping (up to six people) and safari tents to air-conditioned pearlers' shacks. There are also two-hour cruises (from $170) among the legendary tides of King Sound,

and an on-site restaurant (lunch $18 to $32, buffet dinner $37.50).

Raugis MODERN AUSTRALIAN $$
(☑08-9192 4970; Kooljaman Resort; mains $27-39, BBQ packs $25; ⊙7.30-10am, 11.30am-2pm & 6-10pm Apr-Oct, 11.30am-2pm Nov-Mar; 🍴) Overlooking the red pindan cliffs of Cape Leveque's Western Beach, this BYO restaurant at Kooljaman (p220) resort opens for all meals (April to October) and serves up tasty, stylish fare. Or you can order a takeaway BBQ pack.

ℹ Getting There & Away

The **Cape Leveque Shuttle** (Broome Transit; ☑08-9192 5252; www.broometaxis.com; ⊙one way/day return $70/120) runs daily (dependent on passenger numbers) from Broome to Beagle Bay, Cape Leveque (Kooljaman) and Cygnet Bay and back.

The **Cape Leveque Mail Run** (☑08-9193 7650; http://ahoybuccaneers.com.au; one way/ return $70/140; ⊙5am Mon, Wed & Fri) postie can drop off and pick up passengers from Beagle Bay, Lombadina, Djarindjin, Gambanan (June to September only), Cape Leveque (Kooljaman) and Cygnet Bay on Monday, Wednesday and Friday.

Greyhound (p217)

Integrity (☑08-9274 7464; www. integritycoachlines.com.au)
A high-clearance 4WD is best, as the roads can become severely corrugated and washed out after rain.

Derby

POP 4000

Late at night while Derby sleeps, the boabs cut loose and wander around town, maraud-

---

HORIZONTAL WATERFALLS

One of the most intriguing features of the Kimberley coastline is the phenomenon known as 'horizontal waterfalls'. Despite the name, the falls are simply tides gushing through narrow coastal gorges in the Buccaneer Archipelago, north of Derby. What creates such a spectacle are the huge tides, often varying up to 11m. The water flow reaches an astonishing 30 knots as it's forced through two narrow gaps 20m and 10m wide – resulting in a 'waterfall' reaching 4m in height.

Many tours leave Derby (and some Broome) each Dry, by air, sea or a combination of both. It's become de rigueur to 'ride' the tide change through the gorges on a high-powered speedboat. There is a risk element involved, and accidents have occurred. Scenic flights are the quickest and cheapest option, and some seaplanes will land and transfer passengers to a waiting speedboat for the adrenalin hit. If you prefer to be stirred, not shaken, then consider seeing the falls as part of a longer cruise through the archipelago. Book tours at the Derby and Broome visitor centres.

ing mobs flailing their many limbs in battle against an army of giant, killer croc-people emerging from the encircling mudflats... If only.

There *are* crocs hiding in the mangroves, but you're more likely to see birds, over 200 different varieties, while the boabs are firmly rooted along the two main parallel drags, Loch and Clarendon Sts. Derby, sitting on King Sound, is the departure point for tours to the Horizontal Waterfalls (p220) and Buccaneer Archipelago, and the western terminus of the Gibb River Road (GRR).

Derby is West Kimberley's administrative centre, though the closure of the asylum seeker detention facility at nearby RAAF Curtin has seen an outflux of contract workers, freeing up stretched accommodation resources.

⊙ Sights

★ Norval Gallery GALLERY
(☑ 0458 110 816; www.facebook.com/norval-gallery-676996675735315; 1 Sutherland St; ⊙varies) Kimberley art legends Mark and Mary Norval have set up an exciting gallery-cafe in an old tin shed on the edge of town. Featuring striking artworks, exquisite jewellery, decent coffee and 5000 vinyl records (brought out on themed nights), a visit here is a delight to the senses.

There's always a chance to see visiting Indigenous artists in action at one of the many workshops.

Wharefinger Museum MUSEUM
(cnr Elder & Loch Sts; by donation) Grab the key from the visitor centre (p222) and have a peek inside the nearby museum, with its atmospheric shipping and aviation displays.

Jetty LANDMARK
Check out King Sound's colossal 11.5m tides from the circular jetty, 1km north of town, a popular fishing, crabbing, bird-spotting and staring-into-the-distance haunt. Yep, there are crocs in the mangroves.

Kimberley School of the Air SCHOOL
(Marmion St; $10) Fascinating look at how school is conducted over the radio for children on remote stations. Opening times vary, so check with the visitor centre (p222) first.

☆ Activities

The Horizontal Waterfalls (p220) are Derby's top draw and most cruises also include the natural splendours of remote King Sound and the Buccaneer Archipelago. There are many operators to choose from; ask at the visitor centre (p222) for a full list. Most tours only operate during peak season.

★ Horizontal Falls
Seaplane Adventures SCENIC FLIGHTS
(☑ 08-9192 1172; www.horizontalfallsadventures.com.au; 6hr tours from Derby/Broome $745/795) If you do one tour in the Kimberley, make sure it's this one. Flights to Horizontal Waterfalls (p220) land on Talbot Bay before transferring to high-powered speedboats for an adrenalin-packed ride through both sets of falls. There's also an overnight-stay option (ex-Derby) from $895.

Depending on the tide, several runs are made through the falls, before a barramundi lunch is served on the base pontoon. For a different perspective, try the 10-minute chopper ride ($100). After lunch, there are a few more runs as the tide changes direction, before flying back over the Buccaneer Archipelago.

North West Bush Pilots SCENIC FLIGHTS
(☑ 08-9193 2680; www.northwestbushpilots.com.au; flights from $370) Horizontal Waterfalls (p220), Buccaneer Archipelago and Walcott Inlet – you can look but not touch.

☞ Tours

Kimberley Dreamtime
Adventure Tours CULTURAL
(☑ 08-9191 7280; www.kdat.com.au; adult/child 2-day $492/350, 3-day $710/565; ⊙Mon & Wed Apr-Oct) Indigenous-owned and -operated cultural tours based in Nyikina Mangala country on Mt Anderson Station, 126km southeast of Derby. Camp under the stars, ride camels, fish, hunt, walk and learn about Aboriginal culture. Pick-ups from Broome, Willare or Derby.

Wandjina Tours CULTURAL
(☑ 1800 111 163; www.wandjinatours.com.au; Freshwater Cove; 2-/4-day tour $2600/3800) Immerse yourself in Worrorra culture at Freshwater Cove, a remote beach camp 200km north of Derby on the pristine West Kimberley coast. Experience rock art, sacred beaches, traditional artists and amazing seafood. Return over the Horizontal Waterfalls (p220). Access is by air from Derby.

Uptuyu CULTURAL
(☑ 0400 878 898; www.uptuyu.com.au; Oongkalkada Wilderness Camp, Udialla Springs; per day

BROOME & THE KIMBERLEY DERBY

from $450) Down in Nyikina country on the Fitzroy River, 50km from the Great Northern Hwy, Neville and Jo run 'designer' cultural tours taking in wetlands, rock art, fishing and Indigenous communities along the Fitzroy and further afield.

Windjana Tours CULTURAL
(☑0499 336 967; www.windjana.com.au; adult/child $195/95; ⊘Tue, Thu & Sun May-Sep, also Fri Jun-Aug) Full, all-day cultural tours to Windjana Gorge (p223) and Tunnel Creek (p222) National Parks from Derby. Lunch and refreshments are included. May still run during the Wet (dependent on numbers and road conditions).

★✿ Festivals & Events

Boab Festival MUSIC, CULTURAL
(www.derbyboabfestival.org.au; ⊘Jul) Concerts, mud footy, horse and mud-crab races, poetry readings, art exhibitions and street parades. Try to catch the Long Table dinner out on the mudflats.

🛏 Sleeping & Eating

Kimberley Entrance
Caravan Park CARAVAN PARK $
(☑08-9193 1055; www.kimberleyentrancecaravanpark.com; 2 Rowan St; unpowered/powered sites $34/40; P 🐾) Not all sites are shaded, though there's always room. Expect lots of insects this close to the mudflats.

Desert Rose B&B $$
(☑08-9193 2813; 4 Marmion St; d $225; ❄) It's worth booking ahead for the best sleep in town, with spacious, individually styled rooms, a nice shady pool, lead-light windows and a sumptuous breakfast. Host Anne is a fount of local information.

Spinifex Hotel RESORT $$
(☑08-91911233; www.spinifexhotel.com.au; 6 Clarendon St; donga/motel r $120/225; P ❄ @ 🛜 ❄) Rising phoenix-like from the ashes of the old Spini, this sleek resort has corporate-class rooms (some with kitchenettes) and an on-site restaurant (mains $22-42). Peak season brings outdoor live music.

★ Neaps Bistro MODERN AUSTRALIAN $$
(☑08-9193 2924; www.facebook.com/neapsbistro; Derby Lodge, 15-19 Clarendon St; mains $19-39; ⊘7-11am daily, 6-9pm Mon-Sat; ❄) The new favourite among Derby locals, with a chef direct from the Barossa Valley. Dinners are succulent and draw from a wide palette, while

the breakfasts ($7 to $23) are outstanding, showing a level of refinement rarely seen outside of capital cities.

Jila Gallery ITALIAN $$
(☑08-9193 2560; www.facebook.com/jilagallery; 18 Clarendon St; pizzas $20-28, mains $24-34; ⊘10.30am-2pm & 6pm-late Tue-Fri, 6pm-late Sat) Jila's fortunes fluctuate with its chefs, who turn out wood-fired pizzas, homemade pastas and wonderful cakes, all in a shady, alfresco setting.

ℹ Information

Derby Visitor Centre (☑08-9191 1426; www.derbytourism.com.au; 30 Loch St; ⊘8.30am-4.30pm Mon-Fri, 9am-3pm Sat & Sun dry season) Helpful centre with the low-down on road conditions, accommodation, transport and tour bookings.

ℹ Getting There & Away

Charter and sightseeing flights use Derby Airport (DRB), just past the Gibb turn-off. There are currently no scheduled commercial services, but if Perth flights are ever reinstated, they will leave from Curtin Airport (DCN), 40km away.

All buses depart from the **visitor centre**.

Derby Bus Service (☑08-9193 1550; www.derbybus.com.au; one way/return $50/90; ⊘Mon, Wed & Fri) Leaves early for Broome (2½ hours), stopping at Willare Roadhouse (and basically anywhere else you ask the driver to stop along the way), and returning the same day.

Greyhound (☑1300 473 946; www.greyhound.com.au) Broome ($52, 2½ hours), Darwin ($261, 23 hours) and Kununurra ($134, 11 hours) daily (except Sundays).

Devonian Reef National Parks

Three national parks with three stunning gorges were once part of a western 'great barrier reef' in the Devonian era, 350 million years ago. Windjana Gorge (p223) and Tunnel Creek National Parks are accessed via the unsealed Fairfield-Leopold Downs Rd (linking the Great Northern Hwy with the Gibb River Road), while Geikie Gorge (p223) National Park is 22km northeast of Fitzroy Crossing.

◉ Sights

★ Tunnel Creek NATIONAL PARK
(per car $12; ⊘dry season; P) Sick of the sun? Then cool down underground at Tunnel

Creek, which cuts through a spur of the Napier Range for almost 1km. It was famously the hideout of Jandamarra (an Indigenous Bunuba man who waged an armed guerrilla war against the police and white settlers for three years before he was killed). In the Dry, the full length is walkable by wading partly through knee-deep water; watch out for bats and bring good footwear and a strong torch.

There's rock art in the area around the far entrance. Camping not permitted.

Geikie Gorge   NATIONAL PARK

(Darngku; ⊘ Apr-Dec; P) Don't miss this magnificent gorge near Fitzroy Crossing. The self-guided trails are sandy and hot, so take one of the informative boat cruises run by either the **Department of Parks & Wildlife** (☑ 08-9191 5121; 1hr tour adult/child $45/12; ⊘ cruises from 8am May-Oct) or local Bunuba guides (p223).

Windjana Gorge   NATIONAL PARK

(entry per car $12, camping adult/child $12/2.20; ⊘ dry season; P ⚁) The walls of this gorge soar 100m above the Lennard River, which surges in the Wet but is a series of pools in the Dry. Scores of freshwater crocodiles lurk along the banks. Bring plenty of water for the 7km return walk from the camping ground. Swimming is not recommended due to croc numbers.

☞ Tours

Darngku Heritage Tours   CRUISE

(☑ 0417 907 609; www.darngku.com.au; adult/child 2hr tour $70/60, 3hr $90/75, half-day $175/138; ⊘ Apr-Dec; ⚁) Local Bunuba guides introduce Indigenous culture and bush tucker on these amazingly informative cruises through Geikie (Darngku) Gorge (p223). A shorter one-hour cruise (adult/child $35/7.50) operates during the shoulder seasons (April and October to December).

Bungoolee Tours   CULTURAL

(☑ 08-9191 5355; www.bungoolee.com.au; 2hr tour adult/child $60/20; ⊘ 9am & 2pm Mon, Wed & Fri dry season) Bunuba lawman Dillon Andrews runs informative two-hour Tunnel Creek (p222) tours explaining the story of Jandamarra. Book through Fitzroy Crossing visitor centre (p227).

❶ Getting There & Away

You'll need your own vehicle to visit the three parks. **Geikie Gorge** (p223) is easily accessed from Fitzroy Crossing, but if you only have a 2WD, check the condition of Fairfield-Leopold Downs Rd first (for **Windjana Gorge** and **Tunnel Creek**); there's at least one permanent creek crossing. Otherwise, consider taking a **day tour** from Derby.

Gibb River Road

Cutting a brown swath through the scorched heart of the Kimberley, the legendary Gibb River Road ('the Gibb' or GRR) provides one of Australia's wildest outback experiences. Stretching some 660km between Derby and Kununurra, the largely unpaved road is an endless sea of red dirt, big open skies and dramatic terrain. Rough, sometimes deeply corrugated side roads lead to remote gorges, shady pools, distant waterfalls and million-acre cattle stations. Rain can close the road any time, and it's permanently closed during the Wet. This is true wilderness with minimal services, so good planning and self-sufficiency are vital.

A high-clearance 4WD (eg Toyota Land Cruiser) is mandatory, with two spare tyres, tools, emergency water (20L minimum) and several days' food in case of breakdown. Britz (p217) in Broome is a reputable hire outfit. Fuel is limited and expensive, most mobile phones won't work, and temperatures can be life-threatening.

☞ Tours

Adventure Tours   DRIVING

(☑ 03-8102 7800; www.adventuretours.com.au; from $1995) Nine-day Gibb River Road camping tours catering for a younger crowd.

Wundargoodie Aboriginal Safaris CULTURAL

(☑ 0429 928 088; www.wundargoodie.com.au; tag-along per vehicle per day $250, women-only 11-day tour $3500; ⊘ Apr-Sep; ⚁) These insightful Indigenous-run 4WD tag-along tours (ie you bring your own vehicle) showcase local culture and rock art in the remote West Kimberley. The women-only tour is all-inclusive, camping at special sites and sharing experiences with Aboriginal women from various communities.

Kimberley Adventure Tours   DRIVING

(☑ 1800 171 616; www.kimberleyadventures.com.au; 9-day tour $1995) Small-group camping tours from Broome up the Gibb, with the nine-day tour continuing to Purnululu and Darwin. Also offers the reverse direction, starting in Darwin.

Kimberley Wild Expeditions DRIVING
(☑1300 738 870; www.kimberleywild.com.au) Consistent award winner. Tours from Broome range from one ($239) to 14 days ($3995) on the Gibb River Road.

ⓘ Information

Check out www.kimberleyaustralia.com or visit the **Derby** (p222) and **Kununurra** (p232) visitor centre websites. The visitor centres also sell *The Gibb River & Kalumburu Road Guide* ($5).
Mainroads Western Australia (MRWA; ☑13 81 38; www.mainroads.wa.gov.au; ☻24hr) Highway and Gibb River Road conditions.
Parks & Wildlife (www.dpaw.wa.gov.au) Park permits, camping fees and information. Consider a Holiday Pass ($44) if visiting more than three parks in one month.
Shire of Derby/West Kimberley (☑08-9191 0999; www.sdwk.wa.gov.au) Side-road conditions and closures for the Western and Central Gibb.
Shire of Wyndham/East Kimberley (☑08-9168 4100; www.swek.wa.gov.au) Kalumburu/Mitchell Falls road conditions.

Derby to Imintji

Heading east from Derby, the first 100-odd kilometres of the Gibb River Road are now sealed. Don't miss Mowanjum Art & Culture Centre (☑08-9191 1008; www.mowanjumarts.com; Gibb River Rd, Derby; ☻9am-5pm daily dry season, closed Sat & Sun wet season, closed Jan; ☑) FREE, only 4km along.

The Windjana Gorge (p223) turn-off at 119km is your last chance to head back to the Great Northern Highway. Windjana is an easy 22km off the Gibb and is a popular camp side. Back on the GRR, the scenery improves after crossing the **Lennard River** into Napier Downs Station as the **King Leopold Ranges** loom ahead. Just after **Inglis Gap** is the Mt Hart Homestead turn-off and another 7km brings the narrow **Lennard River Gorge** (☑).

Despite its name, **March Fly Glen**, 204km from Derby, is a pleasant, shady picnic area ringed by pandanus and frequented by blue-faced honeyeaters. Don't miss stunning **Bell Gorge** (per car $12; ☑☴), with its waterfall and plunge pool. Refuel (diesel only), grab an ice cream and check your email at **Imintji Store** (☑08-9191 7227; www.imintji.com; ☻9am-5pm dry season, shorter hours wet season; ☎).

Mt Hart Homestead CAMPGROUND $
(☑08-9191 4645; www.kimberleyoutbacktours.com; sites per person $18, s/d incl dinner & break-

fast $430/590, safari tents $590; ☻dry season) Below Inglis Gap a rough 50km track leads to the remote Mt Hart Homestead with grassy camp sites, pleasant gorges, and swimming and fishing holes.

Full board is available in lovely restored rooms or modern safari tents, and campers may eat in the restaurant (breakfast/lunch/dinner $25/25/40). Diesel is available at Imintji prices and there's an on-site bar, though nearby Sunset Hill across the airstrip is the appropriate venue for sundowners.

Birdwood Downs Station FARMSTAY $
(☑08-9191 1275; www.birdwooddowns.com; camping $14.50, huts per person $86; ☑) About 20km from Derby, 2000-hectare Birdwood Downs offers rustic savannah huts, butterflies and basic camping. WWOOFers are welcome and it's also the home of the Kimberley School of Horsemanship, with lessons, riding camps and trail rides ($60 per hour).

There's also a 90-minute sunset ride ($105) complete with bubbly, and, for the more experienced rider, a three-hour journey across the marshes of King Sound ($180). If you prefer your horsepower under the hood, try the Savannah Eco Tour ($60), an informative 90-minute 4WD cruise around the property.

Imintji to Mt Elizabeth Station

Heading east from Imintji, it's only 25km to the Mornington turn-off and another 5km further to the entrance of **Charnley River Station** (☑08-9191 4646; www.australianwildlife.org; sites per person $20, entry per vehicle $25; ☑☴). If heading across the wild, lonely savannah to exquisite Mornington Wilderness Camp (p225), call first using the radio at the Gibb. Back on the GRR, most of the cattle you pass are from **Mount House Station**. Cross the **Adcock**, wave to Nev and Leonie as you pass Over the Range Repairs (p225), then drop down to **Galvans Gorge** (Gibb River Rd; ☑☴) at the 286km mark.

Fuel up at Mt Barnett Roadhouse (p225), 300km from Derby, and get your camping permit if choosing to stay at nearby **Manning River Gorge** (7km behind Mt Barnett Roadhouse; camp site per person $22.50; ☑☴), though there are better options further east. There's free camping on the **Barnett River** (29km east of Mt Barnett Roadhouse) FREE at the 329km mark, and if you've still got daylight, consider pushing on to historic **Mt Elizabeth Station** (☑08-9191 4644; sites per person

$22, s/d incl breakfast & dinner $195/390; ☺dry season), turn-off 338km mark.

★Mornington
Wilderness Camp   WILDLIFE RESERVE

(☑08-9191 7406; www.awc.org.au; entry per vehicle $25, camp sites per adult/child $20/10, full-board safari tents s/d $335/600; ☺May–mid-Oct; P★) ✒ Part of the Australian Wildlife Conservancy, the superb Mornington Wilderness Camp is as remote as it gets, lying on the Fitzroy River, an incredibly scenic 95km drive across the savannah from the Gibb's 247km mark. Nearly 400,000 hectares are devoted to conserving the Kimberley's endangered fauna and there's excellent canoeing, swimming, birdwatching and bushwalking.

Choose from shady camp sites with gas BBQs or spacious raised tents (including full board) with verandahs and bathrooms. The bar and restaurant offer full dinner ($60), BBQ packs ($25) and the best cheese platter ($25) this side of Margaret River. **Sir John Gorge** in the late afternoon sun is sublime. Call ahead using the radio provided at the Gibb turn-off.

Over the Range Repairs   MECHANIC

(☑08-9191 7887; ☺8am-5pm dry season) Between Adcock and Galvans gorges, Nev and Leonie are your best – if not only – hope of mechanical salvation on the whole Gibb.

Mt Barnett Roadhouse   PETROL STATION

(☑08-9191 7007; ☺8am-5pm dry season, shorter hours wet season) Groceries, diesel and unleaded petrol (most expensive on the Gibb). Also camping permits for Manning River Gorge (p224), 7km behind the roadhouse.

Kalumburu Rd to Wyndham/ Kununurra

Four-hundred-and-six kilometres from Derby you reach the Kalumburu turn-off. Head right on the Gibb River Road, and continue through spectacular country, crossing the mighty **Durack River** then climbing though the **Pentecost Ranges** to 579km where there are panoramic views of the Cockburn Ranges, Cambridge Gulf and Pentecost River. Shortly after is the turn-off to the lovely Home Valley Station (p226).

Soon after Home Valley, at 589km from Derby, you'll cross the infamous **Pentecost River** – take care as water levels are unpredictable and saltwater crocs lurk nearby. El Questro Wilderness Park (p226) looms on the right. The last section of the Gibb River Road is sealed. The turn-off to beautiful **Emma Gorge** (☺Apr-Sep; P) is 10km past El Questro. You'll cross **King River** 630km from Derby and, at 647km, you'll finally hit the Great Northern Highway – turn left for Wyndham (48km) and right to Kununurra (53km).

OFF THE BEATEN TRACK

KALUMBURU

Kalumburu is a picturesque mission nestled beneath giant mango trees and coconut palms with two shops and fuel. There's some interesting rock art nearby, and the odd WWII bomber wreck. You can stay at the **Kalumburu Mission** (☑08-9161 4333; www. kalumburumission.org.au; sites per adult/child $20/8, donga s/d $125/175; P), which has a small **museum** (Fr Thomas Gill Museum; ☑08-9161 4333; www.kalumburumission.org.au; $10; ☺11am-1pm), or obtain a permit from the Kalumburu Aboriginal Community (KAC) office to camp at **Honeymoon Bay** (☑08-9161 4378; www.facebook.com/honeymoonbaywa; sites $20) or **McGowan Island** (☑08-9161 4748; www.facebook.com/pages/McGowan-Island/194876760642959; sites $20), 20km further out on the coast – the end of the road. Alcohol is banned at Kalumburu.

The road to Kalumburu deteriorates quickly after the Mitchell Plateau turn-off and eventually becomes very rocky.

Fuel (☑08-9161 4333; www.kalumburumission.org.au; ☺7-11.30am & 1.30-4pm Mon-Fri, 9-11am Sat) is available from the yard next to the mission store.

You'll need a permit from the **Department of Aboriginal Affairs** (DAA; ☑1300 651 077; www.daa.wa.gov.au) in Broome to visit Kalumburu and a Kalumburu Aboriginal Community (08-9161 4300, www.kalumburu.org) visitors' permit ($50 per vehicle, valid for seven days) upon entry, available from the **Community Resource Centre** (CRC, Visitor Centre; ☑08-9161 4627; www.kalumburu.org; ☺varies; 🛜).

El Questro Wilderness Park   PARK

(☑08-9169 1777; www.elquestro.com.au; adult permit per day/week $12/20; ☉dry season; P⛟) This vast 400,000-hectare former cattle station turned international resort incorporates scenic gorges (Amelia, **El Questro**) and **Zebedee Springs** (El Questro Wilderness Park; ☉7am-noon; P) (mornings only). Boat tours (p226) explore Chamberlain Gorge or you can hire your own boat ($100). There are shady camp sites and air-con bungalows at **El Questro Station Township** (☑08-9169 1777; www.elquestro.com.au; sites per person $20-28, station tent d $164, bungalow d from $329; ✳☎☲) and also an outdoor bar and upmarket steakhouse (mains $28 to $44).

Chamberlain Gorge Boat Tours   CRUISE

(adult/child $62/32; ☉3pm) Departing from El Questro Wilderness Park (p226), boat tours explore massive Chamberlain Gorge.

★Home Valley Station   FARMSTAY $

(☑08-9161 4322; www.homevalley.com.au; camp sites adult/child $19.50/5, eco-tent d from $165, homestead d from $295; ☉May-Oct; P✳@ ☎☲) The privations of the Gibb are left behind after pulling into amazing Home Valley Station, an Indigenous hospitality training resort with a superb range of luxurious accommodation. There are excellent grassy camp sites and motel-style rooms, a fantastic open-air bistro (mains $28 to $45), tyre repairs and activities including trail rides, bushwalks, fishing and cattle mustering.

Great Northern Highway

One of the Kimberley's best-kept secrets is the vast subterranean labyrinth of Mimbi Caves (p226), 90km southeast of Fitzroy Crossing, located within Mt Pierre Station on Gooniyandi land. Nearby **Larrawa Station** (Bush Camp; ☑08-9191 7025; www.larrawabushcamp. com; Great Northern Hwy; camp sites per person $10; ☉Apr-Sep; @☲) makes a pleasant overnight stop, with hot showers, basic camp sites and shearers' rooms. Another 30km towards Halls Creek is tiny Yiyili with its Laarri Gallery.

Pushing on from Halls, the scenery becomes progressively more interesting and just after the **Ord River** bridge you'll pass the Purnululu National Park (p232) turn-off at 108km. Warmun (162km) has a roadhouse and an amazing gallery (p226) in the nearby community. **Doon Doon Roadhouse** (☑08-9167 8004; Doon Doon; ☉7am-5.30pm), 91km from Warmun and 60km from the Victoria

Hwy junction, is the only other blip on the landscape and your last chance to refuel before Kununurra or Wyndham. If heading to **Wuggubun** (☑08-9161 4040; http://wuggubuntourism.com; ☉Apr-Sep; ⛟), the signposted turn-off is 4km south of the highway junction, just before Card Creek (if heading north).

◉ Sights

★Mimbi Caves   CAVE

(Mt Pierre Station) One of the Kimberley's best-kept secrets, this vast subterranean labyrinth, 90km southeast of Fitzroy Crossing, on Gooniyandi land, houses a significant collection of Aboriginal rock art and some of the most impressive fish fossils in the southern hemisphere. Indigenous-owned Girloorloo Tours (p226) runs trips here.

Warmun Arts   GALLERY

(☑08-9168 7496; www.warmunart.com; Great Northern Hwy, Warmun; ☉9am-4pm Mon-Fri; P) Between Kununurra and Halls Creek, Warmun artists create abstract works using ochres to explore Gija identity.

Laarri Gallery   GALLERY

(☑08-9191 7195; www.laarrigallery.com; Yiyili; ☉8am-4pm school days; P⛟) This tiny not-for-profit gallery in the back of the community school has interesting contemporary-style and traditional art and crafts detailing local history. It's 120km west of Halls Creek and 5km from the Great Northern Highway. Phone ahead.

☞ Tours

Girloorloo Tours   CULTURAL

(☑08-9191 5468; www.mimbicaves.com.au; 3hr tour adult/child $80/40; ☉10am & 2pm Mon-Thu & Sat Apr-Sep) Aboriginal-owned Girloorloo Tours runs trips to the remarkable Mimbi Caves, a vast subterranean labyrinth housing Aboriginal rock art and impressive fish fossils. The tours include an introduction to local Dreaming stories, bush tucker and traditional medicines. Book through Fitzroy Crossing (p227) or Halls Creek (p228) visitor centres.

Luridgii Tours   DRIVING

(Junama; ☑0438 080 291; http://luridgiitours. com.au; Doon Doon; per vehicle $150; ☉Sat & Sun; ⛟) Be personally guided through Miriuwung country by the traditional owners on these weekend 4WD cultural tag-alongs (ie you follow the guide in your own vehicle). Gorges, thermal pools and Dreaming stories abound, and you have the option of camping overnight. BYO food. Tours depart from Doon Doon Roadhouse (p226) on the Great Northern Highway.

Fitzroy Crossing

POP 1300

Gooniyandi, Bunuba, Walmajarri, Nyikina and Wangkajungka peoples populate the small settlement of Fitzroy Crossing where the Great Northern Highway crosses the mighty Fitzroy River. There's little reason to stay other than that it's a good access point for the Devonian Reef National Parks and has some fine art galleries.

Mangkaja Arts GALLERY
(☑08-9191 5833; www.mangkaja.com; 8 Bell Rd; ⊙11am-4pm Mon-Fri) This Fitzroy Crossing gallery is where desert and river tribes interact, producing unique acrylics, prints and baskets.

Marnin Studio ARTS CENTRE
(Marninwarntikura Women's Resource Centre; ☑ 08-9191 5284; www.mwrc.com.au; Lot 284, Balanijangarri Rd; ⊙ 8.30am-4.30pm Mon-Fri) Marnin is the Walmajarri word for women, and this studio uses crafts such as boab-nut painting, textile printing and bush-nut jewellery-making to bind together the women of the various local language groups.

Crossing Inn CAMPGROUND $
(☑08-9191 5080; www.crossinginn.com.au; Skuthorpe Rd; unpowered/powered sites $32/39, r from $179; ❀@) The oldest pub in the Kimberley also has tidy rooms with views (continental breakfast included) and a small camping area. A true outback beer experience.

Fitzroy River Lodge RESORT $$
(☑08-9191 5141; www.fitzroyriverlodge.com.au; Great Northern Hwy; camping per person $17, tent d $180, motel d $230, studio $340-460; ᴘ❀@ ⬤⬤) Across the river from town, Fitzroy River Lodge has comfortable motel rooms, safari tents, exclusive Riverview studios and grassy camp sites. The friendly bar (open for lunch from noon to 2pm and dinner 5pm to 8.30pm) has decent counter meals ($22 to $42).

Grungaja Shop CLOTHING
(☑08-9191 5316; www.facebook.com/grungaja-shop-fitzroy-crossing-173685496325481; 1 Emmanuel Way; ⊙10am-4.30pm Mon-Fri) If rodeo clothing is your thing, Grungaja stocks everything you need to ride a bull. You won't find better hats or boots. Opening hours vary so call ahead.

WORTH A TRIP

MITCHELL FALLS & DRYSDALE RIVER

In the Dry, Kalumburu Rd is normally navigable as far as **Drysdale River Station** (☑08-9161 4326; www.drysdale-river.com.au; camp sites per person $12-16, d from $150; ⊙8am-5pm Apr-Oct; ᴘ❀), 59km from the Gibb River Road.

The **Mitchell Plateau** (Ngauwudu) turn-off is 160km from the Gibb, and within 6km a deep, rocky ford crosses the **King Edward River**, formidable early in the season. The turn-off to **Munurru Campground** (adult/child $7.50/2.20) is on the right, soon after the crossing.

From the Kalumburu Rd it's a rough 87km, past lookouts and forests of *Livistona* palms to the dusty camping ground at **Mitchell River National Park** (entry per vehicle $12, camping adult/child $10/2.20; ⊙dry season; ᴘ⛺). The park contains the stunning, multi-tiered **Mitchell Falls** (Punamii-unpuu), which can be seen on a lovely three-hour return walk passing inviting, shady waterholes and incredible Aboriginal rock art.

ⓘ Information

Visitor Centre (☑08-9191 5355; www.sdwk.wa.gov.au; ⊙8.30am-4.30pm Mon-Fri year-round, 9am-1pm Sat dry season) For tours (including Mimbi Caves), accommodation and bus tickets. Greyhound stops here.

ⓘ Getting There & Away

Greyhound (☑1300 473 946; www.greyhound.com.au) Broome ($92, five hours), Derby ($62, 2½ hours), Halls Creek ($78, three hours), Kununurra ($120, 7½ hours) and Darwin ($257, 20 hours) Monday to Saturday.
Skippers (p272) flies to Broome and Halls Creek three times weekly.

Halls Creek

POP 1700

On the edge of the Great Sandy Desert, Halls Creek is a small town with communities of Kija, Jaru and Gooniyandi peoples. The excellent visitor centre (p228) can book tours to the Bungles and tickets for Mimbi Caves (p226). Across the highway, **Yarliyil Gallery** (☑08-9168 6723; http://yarliyil.com.au; Great Northern Hwy; ⊙8am-4pm Mon-Fri; ᴘ) is

OFF THE BEATEN TRACK

THE DUNCAN ROAD

The first 50km from Halls Creek is usually the roughest as you cross the Albert Edward Range and **Caroline Pool** (Duncan Rd) FREE at 15km, Palm Springs (p228) at 45km and Sawpit Gorge (p228) at 50km have some nice campsites. Nicholson Station no longer grants permission to camp at Morella Gorge. At Nicholson (174km) turn north and follow the ridges behind Purnululu and Lake Argyle (271km) to the Victoria Hwy. Kununurra is another 56km.

The latest conditions can be checked online at www.hallscreek.wa.gov.au (WA) and www.ntlis.nt.gov.au/roadreport (NT).

The only formal accommodation on Duncan Rd is **Zebra Rock Mine** (Wetland Safaris; ☑0400 767 650; www.zebrarockmine.com.au; Duncan Rd, NT; sites per adult $10; ☉Apr-Sep; ☀) 10km from the Victoria Hwy and technically in the Northern Territory. Travellers love the rustic vibe, and the sunset birdwatching tour ($100) is not to be missed. There's also a small cafe and gift shop.

definitely worth a look. The town regularly suffers water shortages.

Sawpit Gorge GORGE
(Duncan Rd; ℗🚻☀) FREE Great bushwalking, swimming and secluded camp sites await the traveller prepared to cross the rocky Albert Edward Range in this gorge 50km from Halls Creek.

Palm Springs OASIS
(Lugangarna; Duncan Rd; 🚻☀) FREE Soak your weary, corrugations-bashed body in this beautiful, permanent pool on the Black Elvire River, 45km from Halls Creek. Free, 24-hour camping allowed.

Northwest Regional Airlines SCENIC FLIGHTS
(☑08-9168 5211; www.northwestregional.com.au; Halls Creek Airport; flights per person 2/3/4 passengers from $535/360/275) Scenic flights from Halls Creek over **Wolfe Creek Meteorite Crater** (Kandimalal; Tanami) FREE and the Bungle Bungles.

Kimberley Hotel HOTEL $$
(☑08-9168 6101; www.kimberleyhotel.com.au; Roberta Ave; r from $220; ℗❄☎☀) Comfortable rooms are complemented by a lovely pool,

shady terrace bar and a kitchen open for breakfast, lunch ($14 to $20, noon to 2pm) and dinner ($18 to $46, 5.30pm to 8.30pm).

Russian Jack's BISTRO $$$
(☑08-9168 9600; www.hallscreekmotel.com.au; Halls Creek Motel; mains $26-45; ☉5-8.30pm) Probably the best food in Halls Creek with miner-sized helpings of bistro tucker. It's at the **Halls Creek Motel** (☑08-9168 9600; www.hallscreekmotel.com.au; s/d $165/225; ❄☎☀).

ⓘ Information

Visitor Centre (☑08-9168 6262; www.hallscreektourism.com.au; Great Northern Hwy; ☉8am-4pm; ☎) Can book tours (including Mimbi Caves) and arrange art-gallery visits.

ⓘ Getting There & Away

Greyhound (Poinciana Roadhouse) leaves from the roadhouse. Buses go to Broome ($120, nine hours), Derby ($95, six hours) and Fitzroy Crossing ($80, three hours) Sunday to Friday, and Kununurra ($104, four hours), Katherine ($198, 11 hours) and Darwin ($236, 16 hours) Tuesday to Sunday.
Skippers (☑1300 729 924; www.skippers.com.au) flies to Broome and Fitzroy Crossing.
Aviair (☑08-9166 9300; www.aviair.com.au) flies to Kununurra three times weekly.

Kununurra
POP 6000

Kununurra, on Miriwoong country, is a relaxed town set in an oasis of lush farmland and tropical fruit and sandalwood plantations, thanks to the Ord River irrigation scheme. With good transport and communications, excellent services and well-stocked supermarkets, it's every traveller's favourite slice of civilisation between Broome and Darwin.

Kununurra is also the departure point for most of the tours in the East Kimberley, and with all that fruit, there's plenty of seasonal work. Note the Northern Territory is in the Australian Central time zone, which is 90 minutes ahead of Australian Western Standard Time.

⊙ Sights

Waringarri Aboriginal Arts Centre GALLERY
(☑08-9168 2212; www.waringarriarts.com.au; 16 Speargrass Rd; ☉8.30am-4.30pm Mon-Fri, 10am-2pm Sat dry season, weekdays only wet season; ℗) This excellent Kununurra gallery-studio hosts local artists working with ochres in a

unique abstract style. It also represents artists from Kalumburu.

Kelly's Knob · VIEWPOINT
(Kelly Rd; P🐾) FREE The best view in Kununurra is from this rock outcrop on the town's northern edge. Great for sunrise or sunset.

Lily Creek Lagoon · LAKE
(🚣) Across the highway from the township, Lily Creek Lagoon is a mini-wetlands with amazing bird life, boating and freshwater crocs.

Lake Kununurra · LAKE
(Diversion Dam; P🚣) Lake Kununurra has pleasant picnic spots, a swimming beach at the end of Millington Dr, and great fishing.

Kununurra Historical Society Museum · MUSEUM
(www.kununurra.org.au; Coolibah Dr; gold coin donation; ⏲10am-3pm; P) Old photographs and newspaper articles document Kununurra's history, including the story of a wartime Wirraway aircraft crash and the subsequent recovery mission. The museum is opposite the country club exit.

Mirima National Park · NATIONAL PARK
(per car $12; P🚣) Like a mini–Bungle Bungles, the eroded gorges of Hidden Valley are home to brittle red peaks, spinifex, boab trees and abundant wildlife. Several walking trails lead to lookouts, and early morning or dusk are the best times for sighting fauna.

🏃 Activities

Helispirit · SCENIC FLIGHTS
(📞1800 180 085; www.helispirit.com.au; 18/30/42min flights ex Bellbird $269/379/499) The Kimberley's largest chopper outfit offers scenic flights over the Bungles from Bellbird (inside the park) and Warmun (45 minutes $399). It also arranges flights over Mitchell Falls, Kununurra, King George Falls, Lake Argyle and anywhere else in the Kimberley.

Yeehaa Trail Rides · HORSE RIDING
(📞0417 957 607; www.yeehaatrailrides.com; Boab Park; 1-6½hr rides $70/220) Trail rides and tuition to suit all skill levels, 8km from Kununurra. The sunset ride to Elephant Rock ($120, 2½ hours) is the perfect introduction to the Kimberley.

Kimberley Air Tours · SCENIC FLIGHTS
(📞08-9168 2653; www.kimberleyairtours.com.au; half-/full-day $495/995) There's a choice of a full-day flight along the coast to Mitchell Falls and back to Kununurra, or a half-day float-plane tour to Lake Argyle and the Bungle Bungles. Also runs flights out of Broome.

Go Wild · ADVENTURE SPORTS
(📞1300 663 369; www.gowild.com.au; 3-day canoe trips $220) Self-guided multiday canoe trips from Lake Argyle along the Ord River, overnighting at riverside camp sites. Canoes, camping equipment and transport are provided; BYO food and sleeping bag. It also runs group caving, abseiling and bushwalking trips.

Kingfisher Tours · SCENIC FLIGHTS
(📞08-9168 1333; www.kingfishertours.net; per person from $290) Various flights around the Bungles, Cambridge Gulf, Kalumburu and majestic Mitchell and King George Falls.

Kununurra Self Drive Hire Boats · BOATING
(Lakeside Resort; 📞0409 291 959; Lakeside Resort, Casuarina Way; from $174) Groups could consider hiring their own 'barbie' boat from **Lakeside Resort** (📞08-9169 1092; www.lakeside.com.au; Casuarina Way; unpowered/powered sites $35/40, r from $205; ❄@🛜🏊).

East Kimberley · SCENIC FLIGHTS
(📞08-9168 2213; www.eastkimberleytours.com.au; 1-/2-/3-day tours ex Kununurra $790/1855/2150, 1-day tour ex Warmun $1295) Several fly/drive/walk tours of the Bungle Bungles departing Kununurra (fixed-wing) and Warmun (helicopter). Also offers accommodation (with meal options; cabins from $250) inside the park.

👉 Tours

Kimberley Outback Tours · BOATING
(Sunset Tour; 📞1300 286 453; www.kimberleyoutbacktours.com; $130; ⏲11am) Half-day sailing tour on Lake Argyle culminating in sunset viewing and a swim. Lunch, refreshments and bus transfers to/from Kununurra all included.

Sunset BBQ Cruises · CRUISE
(Kununurra Cruises; 📞08-9168 2882; www.kununurracruises.com.au; adult/child $85/55) Popular sunset BBQ dinner cruises on Lily Creek Lagoon (p229) and the Ord River. Complimentary drinks included.

Triple J Tours · CRUISE
(📞08-9168 2682; www.triplejtours.com.au; adult/child $180/140; ⏲Apr-Oct) Triple J cruises the 55km Ord River between Kununurra and Lake Argyle Dam (dry season only).

✺ Festivals & Events

Ord Valley Muster
CULTURAL

(☑ 08-9168 1177; www.ordvalleymuster.com.au; ☺ May; 🎪) For 10 days each May, Kununurra hits overdrive with a collection of sporting, charity and cultural events culminating in a large outdoor concert under the full moon on the banks of the Ord River.

🛏 Sleeping

★ Wunan House
B&B $

(☑ 08-9168 2436; www.wunanhouse.com; 167 Coolibah Dr; r from $125; P ⊖ ❄ 🔊) Indigenous-owned and -run, this immaculate B&B offers light, airy rooms, all with en suites and TVs. There's free wi-fi, off-street parking and an ample continental breakfast.

Hidden Valley Tourist Park
CARAVAN PARK $

(☑ 08-9168 1790; www.hiddenvalleytouristpark. com; 110 Weaber Plains Rd; unpowered/powered sites $30/40, cabin d $135; @ 🔊🔊) Under the looming crags of Mirima National Park (p229), this excellent little spot has nice grassy sites and is popular with seasonal workers and road-trippers. The self-contained cabins are good value.

Kimberley Croc Backpackers
HOSTEL $

(☑ 08-9168 2702; www.kimberleycroc.com; 120 Konkerberry Dr; dm $28-33, d $99-110; ❄ @ 🔊🔊) You might be able to get a bed at this YHA close to the action, though it's usually full of long-term residents and looking a bit tatty these days. There's a large pool, barbecue area and functional kitchen.

Freshwater
APARTMENT $$

(☑ 08-9169 2010; www.freshwaterapartments.net. au; 19 Victoria Hwy; studio $224, 1-/2-/3-bedroom apt $255/339/399; P ❄ 🔊🔊) Exquisite, fully self-contained units with exotic open-roofed showers.

Kimberley Croc Motel
MOTEL $$

(☑ 08-9168 1411; www.kimberleycrocmotel.com. au; 2 River Fig Ave; budget/standard/deluxe d from $119/149/179; P ❄ 🔊🔊) Taken over by Gulliver's (p231), the old Croc lodge has reinvented itself as a sleek motel, offering a variety of newly renovated budget (basically four-bed dorms), standard and deluxe rooms, all with en suites and kitchenettes. Add on the central location, mandatory pool, guests' kitchen and free wi-fi and you have a winner.

The rooms get cheaper if you stay three or more nights.

Lakeview Apartments
APARTMENT $$

(☑ 08-9168 0000; www.lakeviewapartments. net; 31 Victoria Hwy; 1-/2-/3-bedroom apt $230/280/380; P ⊖ ❄ 🔊🔊) These spacious, self-contained apartments across from Lily Creek Lagoon (p229) have all the mod cons, fully equipped kitchens, free wi-fi and cable TV. There's a weekend minimum two-night stay.

🍴 Eating & Drinking

Like other Kimberley and Top End towns, there are restrictions on where and when you can buy and consume takeaway alcohol. Kununurra and Wyndham have been trialling a Takeaway Alcohol Management System (TAMS), so if you're stocking up for the Gibb River Road, check the rules first.

★ Wild Mango
CAFE $$

(☑ 08-9169 2810; www.wildmangocafe.com.au; 20 Messmate Way; breakfast $9-23, lunch $15-19; ☺ 7am-4pm Mon-Fri, to 1pm Sat & Sun; P ❄) 🍃 The hippest, healthiest feed in town with breakfast burritos, succulent salads, mouth-watering pancakes, chai smoothies, real coffee and homemade gelato. The entrance is on Konkerberry Dr.

Ivanhoe Cafe
CAFE $$

(☑ 0427 692 775; www.facebook.com/ivanhoe-cafe-549293358437140; Ivanhoe Rd; breakfast $9-23, lunch $11-22; ☺ 8am-2pm Wed-Mon Apr-Sep; P 🍴) Grab a table under the leafy mango trees and tuck into tasty wraps, salads and burgers, all made from fresh, local produce. Don't miss the signature mango smoothie.

★ PumpHouse
MODERN AUSTRALIAN $$$

(☑ 08-9169 3222; www.thepumphouserestaurant. com; Lakeview Dr; mains lunch $18-27, dinner $32-42; ☺ 4.30pm-late Tue-Fri, 8am-late Sat & Sun; P) Idyllically situated on Lake Kununurra (p229), the PumpHouse creates succulent dishes featuring quality local ingredients. Watch the catfish swarm should a morsel slip off the verandah, or just have a beer and watch the sunset. There's also an excellent wine list.

Kelly's Bar & Grill
AUSTRALIAN $$$

(Country Club; ☑ 08-9168 1024; www.kununurra-countryclub.com.au; 47 Coolibah Dr; mains $29-46, burgers $17; ☺ from 6am) Inside the Country Club, you'll find the usual, rather pricey bistro nosh. If you haven't booked or can't face the thought of wearing shoes, stay outside around the pool. The lunchtime burgers are better value.

THE KIMBERLEY'S ART SCENE

The Indigenous art of the Kimberley is unique. Encompassing powerful and strongly guarded Wandjina, prolific and enigmatic Gwion Gwion (Bradshaws), bright tropical coastal X-rays, subtle and sombre bush ochres and topographical dots of the western desert, every work sings a story about Country.

To experience it firsthand, visit some of these Aboriginal-owned cooperatives; most are accessible by 2WD.

Mowanjum Art & Culture Centre (p224) This incredible gallery, shaped like a Wandjina image, features work by Mowanjum artists. Just 4km along the Gibb River Road from Derby.

Waringarri Aboriginal Arts Centre (p228) This excellent Kununurra gallery-studio hosts local artists working with ochres in a unique abstract style. It also represents artists from Kalumburu.

Warmun Arts (p226) Between Kununurra and Halls Creek, Warmun artists create beautiful works using ochres to explore Gija identity.

Laarri Gallery (p226) This tiny not-for-profit gallery located in the back of the Yiyili community school depicts local history through interesting contemporary-style art. It's 120km west of Halls Creek and 5km from the Great Northern Highway. Phone ahead.

Mangkaja Arts (p227) Respected Fitzroy Crossing gallery where desert and river tribes interact, producing unique acrylics, prints and baskets.

Yarliyil Gallery (p227) Great Halls Creek gallery showcasing talented local artists as well as some of the Kundat Djaru (Ringer Soak) mob.

Warlayirti Artists Centre (☑08-9168 8960; www.balgoart.org.au; Balgo; ⊙9am-4pm Mon-Fri) This Balgo centre, 255km down the Tanami Rd, is a conduit for artists around the area and features bright acrylic dot-style works as well as lithographs and glass works. Phone first, before leaving the highway.

Bidyadanga Community Art Centre (p208) South of Broome, this intriguing centre brings together both desert and coastal influences in WA's largest remote community.

Nagula Jarndu Women's Resource Centre (p212) Don't miss the incredible printed fabrics at this Broome women's centre.

Marnin Studio (p227) Famous for their carved boab-nuts, the women at this Fitzroy Crossing studio also hand-print paper and silk scarves.

For more information, look up www.desertriversea.com.au and download the *Kimberley Aboriginal Art Trail* map, or find it in a visitor centre.

If time's short, wander through the Short St Gallery **Bungalow** (p212) in Hopton St Broome for a sample of the different Kimberley styles.

Gulliver's Tavern PUB
(☑08-9168 1666; www.facebook.com/gulliverstavernkununurra; 196 Cottontree Ave; burgers $12.50, mains $20-36; ⊙noon-10pm) The town's main boozer has a shady beer garden and live music from Friday to Sunday. The pub-grub dinners (6pm to 8pm) are hit-or-miss, though the lunch burgers (served till 2pm) continually perform.

🛍 Shopping

Bush Camp Surplus SPORTS & OUTDOORS
(☑08-9168 1476; www.facebook.com/bushcampsurplus; cnr Papuana St & Konkerberry Dr; ⊙8.30am-5pm Mon-Fri, to noon Sat) The biggest range of camping gear between Broome and Darwin.

Artlandish ART
(☑08-9168 1881; www.artlandish.com; cnr Papuana St & Konkerberry Dr; ⊙9am-4pm Mon-Fri, to 1pm Sat) Stunning collection of Kimberley ochres and Western Desert acrylics to suit all price ranges.

Kununurra Markets MARKET
(White Gum Park; ⊙8am-noon Sat dry season; 🐾) Your typical friendly arts, crafts and bric-a-brac moshfest in the park next to the visitor centre (p232).

ℹ Information

Visitor Centre (☎1800 586 868; www.
visitkununurra.com; Coolibah Dr; ⊙8.30am-
4.30pm Apr-Sep, shorter hours Oct-Mar) Can help
find accommodation, tours and seasonal work.

Parks & Wildlife Office (DPAW; ☎08-9168
4200; www.dpaw.wa.gov.au; Lot 248, Ivanhoe
Rd; ⊙8am-4.30pm Mon-Fri) For park permits
and publications.

ℹ Getting There & Away

Airnorth (TL; ☎1800 627 474; www.airnorth.
com.au) flies to Broome and Darwin daily, and
to Perth on Saturdays. **Virgin Australia** (VA;
☎13 67 89; www.virginaustralia.com.au) has
four flights a week to Perth.

WORTH A TRIP

LAKE ARGYLE

Enormous Lake Argyle, where barren
red ridges plunge spectacularly into
the deep blue water of the dammed
Ord River, is Australia's second-largest
reservoir. Holding the equivalent of 18
Sydney Harbours, it provides Kununurra
with year-round irrigation, and important wildlife habitats for migratory
waterbirds, freshwater crocodiles and
isolated marsupial colonies.

Lake Argyle Cruises (☎08-9168 7687;
www.lakeargylecruises.com; adult/child
morning $80/40, lunch $125/70, sunset
$95/60; 🖐) Popular sunset cruises take
in the lake's highlights. Book ahead as
under-subscribed trips are often can-
celled.

Argyle Homestead (☎08-9167
8088; Lake Argyle Rd; adult/child/family
$4/2.50/10; ⊙8am-4pm Apr-Sep; P)
Relocated when the waters rose, this
former home of the famous Durack
pastoral family is now a museum.

Lake Argyle Village (☎08-9168 7777;
www.lakeargyle.com; Lake Argyle Rd; un-
powered/powered sites $35/45, cabins from
$259; P❄@🛜🏊🐾) Superbly located
high above the lake, Lake Argyle Village
offers grassy camp sites, a variety of
cabins, and hearty meals from its licensed bistro. Don't miss a swim in the
stunning infinity pool.
  Helicopter flights over the lake and
onto the Bungle Bungles start at $125.

Greyhound (☎1300 473 946; www.greyhound.
com.au) buses stop at the **BP Roadhouse**
(☎08-9169 1188; 5 Messmate Way; ⊙24hr)
and leave Sunday to Friday for Broome ($165,
13 hours) via Halls Creek ($104, four hours),
Fitzroy Crossing ($121, 8½ hours) and Derby
($141, 10 hours). Buses for Darwin ($145, 12½
hours) via Katherine ($108, 7½ hours) leave
Tuesday to Sunday.

Avis (☎08-9168 1999), **Budget** (☎08-9168
2033) and **Thrifty** (☎1800 626 515) all have
offices at the airport. **Ordco** (Weaber Plains Rd;
⊙24hr) is a local co-op selling the cheapest
diesel in Kununurra.

Purnululu National Park & Bungle Bungle Range

The bizarre, ancient, eroded sandstone
domes of the Unesco World Heritage Purnululu National Park (p232) will take your
breath away. Known colloquially as the
'**Bungle Bungles**', these remote rocky ranges are recognised as the finest example of
cone karst sandstone in the world.

The park is a microcosm of fauna and
flora and several easy walks lead out of the
baking sun into cool, shady palm-fringed
gorges. Sunsets here are sublime. Facilities
in the park are refreshingly minimal and visitors must be totally self-sufficient. Temperatures can be extreme. Rangers are in attend-
ance during the high season when the small
visitor centre (p234) opens. There are two
large, basic bush camping grounds at either
end of the park.

Access is by a rough, unsealed, flood-
prone 4WD-only track from the Great
Northern Highway north of Halls Creek, or
by air on a package tour from Kununurra or
Warmun.

⊙ Sights & Activities

★**Purnululu National Park** NATIONAL PARK
(per car $12; ⊙Apr-Nov; P🖐) Looking like a
packet of half-melted Jaffas, World Heritage
Purnululu is home to the incredible ochre
and black striped 'beehive' domes of the
Bungle Bungle Range.

The distinctive rounded rock towers
are made of sandstone and conglomerates
moulded by rainfall over millions of years.
Their stripes are the result of oxidised iron
compounds and algae. To the local Kidja
people, *purnululu* means sandstone, with
Bungle Bungle possibly a corruption of 'bundle bundle', a common grass.

Purnululu National Park

Over 3000 sq km of ancient country contains a wide array of wildlife, including over 130 bird species. Rangers are based here from April to November and the park is closed outside this time.

You'll need a high-clearance 4WD for the 52km twisting, rough road from the highway to the visitor centre (p234) near Three Ways junction; allow 2½ hours. There are five deep creek crossings, and the turn-off is 53km south of Warmun. Kurrajong (p233) and Walardi (p233) camps have fresh water and toilets. Book camp sites online via www.parkstay.dpaw.wa.gov.au.

Kungkalanayi Lookout VIEWPOINT
(P ⚲) Sunsets and sunrises are spectacular from this hill near Three Ways.

Piccaninny Gorge GORGE
A 30km return trek (two to three days) from the southern car park to a remote and pristine gorge best suited for experienced hikers. There are plenty of opportunities for further exploration in the upper gorge. Take plenty of water, and go early in the season. You must register at the visitor centre (p234) first.

Echidna Chasm GORGE
(P ⚲) Look for tiny bats high on the walls above this palm-fringed, extremely narrow gorge in the northern park. The entrance is fringed by *Livistona* palms. Allow one hour for the 2km return walk.

Cathedral Gorge GORGE
(P ⚲) Aptly named, this immense and inspiring circular cavern is an easy 2km (return) stroll from the southern car park.

Whip Snake Gorge GORGE
Leave early for this energetic half-day outing (10km return, three hours) from the southern car park to a shady gorge filled with ferns, figs and brittle gums. There's a small terminal pool.

Bungle Bungle Expeditions SCENIC FLIGHTS
(☏ 08-9169 1995; www.bunglebungleexpeditions. com.au; 1-day bus tour $315, helicopter tour from $295) Bus and helicopter tours of the Bungles from the Mabel Downs (p234) caravan park, near the highway.

☞ Tours

Bungle Bungle Guided Tours WALKING
(☏ 1800 899 029; www.bunglebungleguidedtours. com.au; Bellburn Airstrip, Purnululu) Indigenous-run half-day walking tours to Cathedral Gorge (p233) and Echidna Chasm (p233) and a full-day helicopter ride/hike ($799) to Piccaninny Gorge (p233). Tours depart from the park airstrip at Bellburn, and can be linked up with scenic flights from Kununurra, Warmun and Halls Creek.

🛏 Sleeping

Kurrajong Campsite CAMPGROUND $
(sites per person $12; ⊙ Apr-Nov; P) In the northern end of Purnululu National Park (p232), there are dusty camp sites with water, toilets and the odd picnic table, and thankfully no generators.

Walardi Campsite CAMPGROUND $
(sites per person $12; ⊙ Apr-Nov; P) Fresh water, toilets and some generator-free areas in the southern park.

Mabel Downs   CAMPGROUND **$**
(Bungle Bungle Caravan Park; ☑08-9169 1995; www.bunglebunglecaravanpark.com.au; tent/powered sites $35/50, safari tents with/without bathroom $250/150; ☺Apr-Sep; ☎) Situated just 1km from the highway, outside Purnululu National Park (p232), so don't expect much privacy. Tents are jammed between helicopters and ridiculously long trailers. Breakfast and dinner ($35) are available, and for those without wheels, a Bungle Bungle Expeditions (p233) bus day tour will set you back $315.

❶ Information

Visitor Centre (☑08-9168 7300; ☺8am-noon & 1-4pm Apr-Sep) Pay for your permit and grab a map. If closed, use the honesty envelopes.

❶ Getting There & Away

If you haven't got a high-clearance 4WD, consider taking a tour instead. You can fly in from Kununurra, Warmun and Halls Creek.

Wyndham

POP 900

A gold-rush town that has fallen on leaner times, Wyndham is scenically nestled between rugged hills and **Cambridge Gulf**, some 100km northwest of Kununurra. Sunsets are superb from the spectacular **Five Rivers Lookout** (☐☐☐) on Mt Bastion (325m) overlooking the King, Pentecost, Durack, Forrest and Ord Rivers entering Cambridge Gulf.

A giant 20m croc greets visitors entering town. The historic port precinct is 5km further and contains a small **museum** (☑08-9161 1857; Old Courthouse, Port Precinct; ☺10am-3pm daily dry season; ☐) and pioneer graveyard.

Parry Lagoons
Nature Reserve   NATURE RESERVE
(☐☐) This beautiful Ramsar-listed wetland, 25km from Wyndham, teems in the Wet with migratory birds arriving from as far away as Siberia. There's a bird hide and boardwalk at **Marlgu Billabong** and an excellent view from **Telegraph Hill**. Nearby Parry Creek Farm (p234) has a small camping ground and raised rooms overlooking a billabong, perfect for birdwatching.

★Parry Creek Farm   FARMSTAY **$**
(☑08-9161 1139; www.parrycreekfarm.com.au; Parry Creek Rd; unpowered/powered sites $30/35, r $125, cabin $230; ☺dry season; ☐☐☐) Surrounded by Parry Lagoons Nature Reserve (p234), 25km from Wyndham, this tranquil farm with grassy camp sites attracts hordes of wildlife. Comfy rooms and air-con cabins are connected by a raised boardwalk overlooking a billabong for easy bird spotting. The licensed cafe (open April to September) serves excellent baked barramundi, woodfired pizzas and other gourmet delights. Ring ahead.

★Rusty Shed   CAFE **$**
(☑08-9161 2427; www.facebook.com/therustyshedcafe; O'Donnell St, Port Precinct; mains $7-17; ☺8am-3pm Mon-Fri year-round, Sat & Sun dry season; ☐) ✆ This local favourite has great coffee and juices, sophisticated breakfasts and delicious cakes and pastries. Also opens for Sunday night roasts during the Dry, and randomly on other nights when there are guest musicians.

Greyhound (p232) drops passengers 56km away at the Victoria Hwy junction; you'll need to arrange a pick-up prior to arrival. There's no taxi service in Wyndham.

Understand West Coast Australia

West Coast Australia Today

Welcome to a city, state and economy in flux, where the mining-led confidence and growth of the last decade has been replaced with the need for a more diversified economy. Perth's infrastructural boost, including new public spaces, transport hubs and a riverfront stadium, is approaching spectacular completion, but challenges still lie ahead as Western Australia continues to build an economy less dependent on getting stuff out of the ground and selling it.

Best on Film

Gallipoli (1981) Young men from rural WA enlist to fight as Anzac soldiers in the ill-fated Gallipoli campaign.

Rabbit-Proof Fence (2002) Three Aboriginal girls trek through the WA desert to be reunited with their families.

Tracks (2013) Recreating Robyn Davidson's epic 1975 journey by foot from Alice Springs to the Indian Ocean.

Goldstone (2016) Indigenous land rights and the machinations of the mining industry combine in this compelling outback blend of film noir and Western.

Best in Print

Cloudstreet (Tim Winton; 1991) A chronicle of post-WWII working-class families sharing a house in Perth.

Sand (John Kinsella and Robert Drewe; 2010) Poetry and prose exploring the role of sand in the Australian psyche.

That Deadman Dance (Kim Scott; 2011) Novel exploring the 19th-century interactions between settlers, whalers and the Indigenous Noongar people of Albany.

Island Home (Tim Winton; 2015) This self-described 'landscape memoir' explores the relationship WA novelist Tim Winton has with the bold terrain and seascapes of his home state.

Perth's Extreme Makeover Continues (With Caveats)

In Western Australia's state capital, major construction and infrastructure projects are now approaching completion. Linking the central business district to the Swan River, the Elizabeth Quay development will enliven Perth with new restaurants, international hotels – an overdue initiative in a city recently lacking accommodation options – and a transport hub combining buses, trains and ferries.

Along the Swan River, the new 60,000-seat Perth Stadium is set to drive the development of East Perth when it opens for the 2018 AFL season, and the nearby Riverside area is another mega-project approaching completion with restaurant and retail precincts and apartments for 7000 residents. In the CBD, the heritage State Buildings now house excellent new restaurants and a world-leading luxury hotel, and the City Link project incorporating an underground bus station and the pedestrian plaza of Yagan Sq is uniting central Perth with Northbridge. The gentrification of Northbridge itself also continues apace with new hotels joining cool laneway bars and a more diverse dining scene.

Yet balancing all this industry and energy is the slowdown of Western Australia's mining sector, which has definitely cooled Perth's economy. The state's budget deficit increased to an all-time high in 2016, while real-estate prices in the city fell by 8%. After almost nine years of government by the right-leaning Liberal Party, the economic over-extension of Perth's extreme makeover became a key issue in the Western Australian state elections in March 2017,and the left-leaning Labor Party won in a landslide.

Caught Out by a One-Trick-Pony Economy

Further north in the mining towns of the Pilbara, the real-estate slowdown has been even more severe. Following the completion of major construction projects, including a $54 billion petroleum plant, and the collapse of resource prices (between 2013–14 and 2015–16 international iron ore prices fell by 58%), house prices in towns like Port Hedland have fallen by up to 47%. Homes that were renting for $3000 a week a few years ago now go for $400 – if the owners can find tenants at all – and mine workers have been forced to return to Perth to look for work, or head back to New Zealand or Ireland as job opportunities diminish.

Western Australia's resources industry is still hugely important – on some nights the busy docks at Port Hedland export over 1.5 million tonnes of iron ore to China, making it the busiest bulk export port on the planet. But the boom times fuelled by a growing Chinese economy exporting consumer goods to the world have slowed, and this has been exacerbated by the need for additional infrastructural investment in mining areas. More than ever, Perth and Western Australia need to further broaden what has been a myopic and one-trick-pony economy across recent years.

The Need to Look Northeast

While the mega-economies of Asia have impacted on Western Australia, it's these same countries – including China, India, Indonesia and Japan – that can provide alternative sources of income for the state. Perth's proximity to Asia means it is seen as a safe and affordable haven for many migrants – providing a potential boost to the city's flagging apartment market – and low-cost airlines linking WA to Singapore, Bali and Kuala Lumpur mean the artisan food producers and vineyards of Margaret River are as popular with visitors from Mumbai and Malaysia as they are with travellers from Adelaide or Auckland.

Flights from Singapore to Perth take around five hours, and a weekend visit taking in the Swan Valley, Fremantle and Rottnest Island is a popular option around Chinese New Year and other Asian holidays. The announcement of direct flights from Perth to London on Qantas from March 2018 – a backside-numbing long haul of 17 hours – also promises to increase visitor numbers from the UK and Europe.

The economies of Asia are also vital to Western Australian agribusiness, and there is potential for the state to become a high-margin gourmet food basket for China or Japan. Margaret River wines, Cervantes lobsters or Manjimup truffles could all be the export stars of the next decade. With savvy marketing, Perth's edge-of-the-continent location can become a key selling point for WA exporters.

POPULATION: **2.71 MILLION**

AREA: **2,529,875 SQ KM**

GDP: **$2.49 BILLION**

GDP GROWTH: **2.5%**

UNEMPLOYMENT: **6.25%**

if Perth were 100 people

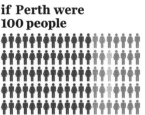

65 would be born in Australia
11 would be born in the UK
3 would be born in New Zealand
21 would be born elsewhere

belief systems
(% of population)

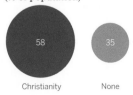

population per sq km

History

Western Australia's history is one of hardship, boom, bust, and boom again. Humans had already been in occupation 40,000 years before Dutchman Dirk Hartog sighted the shores of WA in 1616. The British later settled Perth in 1829, sparking conflict with its Noongar inhabitants. WA first boomed with the 1880s discovery of gold, then suffered through wars and depression, before the nickel boom of the 1960s. The state's prosperity and its immense mineral wealth remain inextricably linked as it moves forward into the 21st century.

First Arrivals

People first arrived on the northern shores of Australia at least 40,000 years ago. As they began building shelters, cooking food and telling each other tales, they left behind signs of their activities. They left layers of carbon – the residue of their ancient fires – deep in the soil. Piles of shells and fish bones mark the places where these people hunted and ate. And on rock walls across WA they left paintings and etchings, some thousands of years old, which tell their stories of the Dreaming, that spiritual dimension where the earth and its people were created and the law was laid down.

Contrary to popular belief, these Aboriginal people, especially those who lived in the north, were not entirely isolated from the rest of the world. Until 6000 years ago, they were able to travel and trade across a bridge of land that connected Australia to New Guinea. Even after white occupation, the Aboriginal people of the northern coasts regularly hosted Macassan fishermen from Sulawesi, with whom they traded and socialised.

When European sailors first stumbled on the coast of 'Terra Australis', the entire continent was occupied by hundreds of Aboriginal groups, living in their own territories and maintaining their own distinctive languages and traditions. The fertile Swan Valley around Perth, for example, is the customary homeland of about a dozen groups of Noongar people, each speaking a distinctive dialect.

TIMELINE	40,000 BC	4000 BC	1616
	First humans arrive on the shores of Australia.	Aboriginal communities from northwestern Australia trade and interact with Macassan fishermen from Sulawesi.	Dutch explorer Dirk Hartog lands on an island in Shark Bay, marking his visit with a pewter plate on which he inscribed a record of his visit.

The prehistory of Australia is filled with tantalising mysteries. In the Kimberley, scholars and amateur sleuths are fascinated by the so-called Bradshaw paintings. These enigmatic and mystical stick figures are thousands of years old. Because they look nothing like the artwork of any other Aboriginal group, the identity of the culture that created them is the subject of fierce debate.

Meanwhile there are historians who claim the Aboriginal peoples' first contact with the wider world occurred when a Chinese admiral, Zheng He, visited Australia in the 15th century. Others say that Portuguese navigators mapped the continent in the 16th century.

Early Dutch Exploration

Most authorities believe that the first man to travel any great distance to see Aboriginal Australia was a Dutchman named Willem Janszoon. In 1606 he sailed the speedy little ship *Duyfken* out of the Dutch settlement at Batavia (modern Jakarta) to scout for the Dutch East India Company, and found Cape York (the pointy bit at the top of Australia), which he thought was an extension of New Guinea.

Ten years later, another Dutch ship, the *Eendracht,* rode the mighty Atlantic trade winds, bound for the 'spice islands' of modern Indonesia. But the captain, Dirk Hartog, misjudged his position, and stumbled onto the island (near Gladstone) that now bears his name. Hartog inscribed the details of his visit onto a pewter plate and nailed it to a post. In 1697, the island was visited by a second Dutch explorer, named Willem de Vlamingh, who swapped Hartog's plate for one of his own.

Other Dutch mariners were not so lucky. Several ships were wrecked on the uncharted western coast of the Aboriginal continent. The most infamous of these is the *Batavia*. After the ship foundered in the waters off modern Geraldton in 1629, the captain, Francis Pelsaert, sailed a boat to the Dutch East India Company's base at Batavia. While his back was turned, some crewmen unleashed a nightmare of debauchery, rape and murder on the men, women and children who had been on the ship. When Pelsaert returned with a rescue vessel, he executed the murderers, sparing only two youths whom he marooned on the beach of the continent they knew as New Holland. Some experts believe the legacy of these boys can be found in the sandy hair and the Dutch-sounding words of some local Aboriginal peoples. The remains of the *Batavia* and other wrecks are now displayed at the Western Australian Museum in Geraldton and in the Fremantle Shipwreck Galleries, where you can also see de Vlamingh's battered old plate.

The Dutch were businessmen, scouring the world for commodities. Nothing they saw on the dry coasts of this so-called 'New Holland'

Today Western Australia, the largest state in the country, is also the most sparsely populated, being home to just over 10% of the population.

1629	1644	1697	1826
Debauchery, rape and murder break out while the *Batavia* is shipwrecked at the Houtman Abrolhos Islands. All crew but two are subsequently executed at senior merchant Francisco Pelsaert's behest.	Dutchman Abel Tasman charts the western and southern coasts of Australia.	Willem de Vlamingh replaces Hartog's plate with his own.	The British army establishes a military post in Albany, on the southern coast.

convinced them that the land or its native people offered any promise of profit. When another Dutchman named Abel Tasman charted the western and southern coasts of Australia in 1644, he was mapping not a commercial opportunity but a maritime hazard.

The British Claim the West Coast

Today the dominant version of Australian history is written as though Sydney is the only wellspring of Australia's identity. But when you live in Western Australia, history looks very different. In Sydney, white history traditionally begins with Captain James Cook's epic voyage of 1770, in which he mapped the east coast. But Cook creates little excitement in Albany, Perth or Geraldton – places he never saw.

Cook's voyage revealed that the eastern coastline was fertile, and he was particularly taken with the diversity of plant life at the place he called 'Botany Bay'. Acting on Cook's discovery, the British government decided to establish a convict colony there. The result was the settlement of Sydney in 1788 – out of which grew the great sheep industry of Australia.

By the early 19th century, it was clear that the Dutch had no inclination to settle WA. Meanwhile, the British were growing alarmed by the activities of the French in the region. So on Christmas Day 1826, the British army warned them off by establishing a lonely military outpost at Albany, on the strategically important southwestern tip of the country.

The Founding of Perth

The founding of Perth is most famously depicted in George Pitt Morison's painting The Foundation of Perth (1829). it is often erroneously credited as an authentic record of the ceremony rather than a historical reconstruction.

The challenge to Aboriginal supremacy in the west began in 1829, when a boatload of free immigrants arrived with all their possessions in the territory of the Noongar people. This group was led by Captain James Stirling – a swashbuckling and entrepreneurial naval officer – who had investigated the coastal region two years earlier. Stirling had convinced British authorities to appoint him governor of the new settlement, and promptly declared all the surrounding Aboriginal lands to be the property of King George IV. Such was the foundation of Perth.

Stirling's glowing reports had fired the ambitions of English adventurers and investors, and by the end of the year, 25 ships had reached the colony's port at Fremantle. Unlike their predecessors in Sydney, these settlers were determined to build their fortunes without calling on government assistance and without the shame of using convict labour.

1829	1829	1834	1840-41
Led by Captain James Stirling, a boatload of free immigrants land in the territory of the Noongar people.	Governor Stirling declares all surrounding Aboriginal lands to be the property of King George IV. Perth is founded.	The Battle of Pinjarra occurs after Stirling leads a punitive expedition against the Noongar. It is thought that 25 Aboriginal people are shot, with Stirling's camp suffering one fatality.	An Aboriginal man called Wylie and explorer Edward Eyre make a staggering journey across the Nullarbor Plain to Albany.

Frontier Conflict

As a cluster of shops, houses and hotels rose on the banks of the Swan River, settlers established sheep and cattle runs in the surrounding country. This led to conflict with Aboriginal people, following a pattern that was tragically common throughout the Australian colonies. The Aboriginal people speared sheep and cattle – sometimes for food, sometimes as an act of defiance. In the reprisals that resulted, people on both sides were killed, and by 1832 it was clear that Aboriginal people were organising a violent resistance. Governor Stirling declared that he would retaliate with such 'acts of decisive severity as will appal them as people for a time and reduce their tribe to weakness'.

In October 1834 Stirling showed he was a man of his word. He led a punitive expedition against the Noongar, who were under the leadership of the warrior Calyute. In the Battle of Pinjarra, the governor's forces shot, according to one report, around 25 people and suffered one fatality themselves. This display of official terror had the desired effect. The Noongar ended their resistance and the violence of the frontier moved further out.

The Deployment on Convicts

Aboriginal resistance was not the only threat to the survival of this most isolated outpost of the British Empire. The arid countryside, the loneliness and the cost of transport also took their toll. When tough men of capital could make a fortune in the east, there were few good reasons to struggle against the frustrations of the west, and most of the early settlers left. Two decades on, there were just 5000 Europeans holding out on the western edge of the continent. Some of the capitalists who had stayed began to rethink their aversion to using cheap prison labour.

In 1850 – just as the practice of sending British convicts to eastern Australia ended – shiploads of male convicts started to arrive in Fremantle harbour.

Built by convicts, the Fremantle Arts Centre was once a lunatic asylum and then a poorhouse, or 'women's home'. Today this Gothic building is a thriving arts centre, which is well worth a visit.

Exploration & Gold

Meanwhile, several explorers undertook journeys into the remote Aboriginal territories, drawn in by dreams of mighty rivers and rolling plains of grass 'further out'. Their thirsty ordeals mostly ended in disappointment. But the pastoralists did expand through much of the southwestern corner of WA, while others took up runs on the rivers of the northwest and in the Kimberley.

1850	1860s	1880s–90s	1890
Shiploads of male convicts start to arrive in Fremantle. They go on to build key historical buildings such as Fremantle prison, Government House and Perth Town Hall.	With no democracy, a network of city merchants and squatters exercises control over the colony.	Gold changes everything. The first discoveries are in the Kimberley and the Pilbara, followed by massive finds in Coolgardie and Kalgoorlie.	The state's first trade unions are formed by three men. Unions exert a substantial influence for the following century.

Perhaps the most staggering journey of exploration was undertaken by an Aboriginal man called Wylie and the explorer Edward Eyre, who travelled from South Australia, across the vast, dry Nullarbor Plain, to Albany.

By the 1880s, the entire European population of this sleepy western third of Australia was not much more than 40,000 people. In the absence of democracy, a network of city merchants and large squatters exercised political and economic control over the colony.

The great agent of change was gold. The first discoveries were made in the 1880s in the Kimberley and the Pilbara, followed by huge finds in the 1890s at Coolgardie and Kalgoorlie, in hot, dry country 600km inland from Perth. So many people were lured by the promise of gold that the population of the colony doubled and redoubled in a single decade. But the easy gold was soon exhausted, and most independent prospectors gave way to mining companies who had the capital to sink deep shafts. Soon the miners were working not for nuggets of gold but for wages. Toiling in hot, dangerous conditions, these men banded together to form trade unions, which remained a potent force in the life of WA throughout the following century.

The Great Pipeline to Kalgoorlie

The year 1890 also saw the introduction of representative government, a full generation after democracy had arrived in the east. The first elected premier was a tough, capable bushman named John Forrest, who borrowed courageously in order to finance vast public works to encourage immigrants and private investors. He was blessed with the services of a brilliant civil engineer, CY O'Connor. O'Connor oversaw the improvement of the Fremantle harbour, and built and ran the state's rail system. But O'Connor's greatest feat was the construction of a system of steam-powered pumping stations along a mighty pipeline to drive water uphill, from Mundaring Weir near Perth to the thirsty goldfields around distant Kalgoorlie.

By the time Forrest opened the pipeline, O'Connor was dead. His political enemies had defamed him in the press and in parliament, falsely accusing him of incompetence and corruption. On 10 March 1902, O'Connor rode into the surf near Fremantle and shot himself. Today, the site of his anguish is commemorated by a haunting statue of him on horseback, which rises out of the waves at South Beach.

Ironically, just as the water began to flow, the mining industry went into decline. But the 'Golden Pipeline' continues to supply water to the mining city of Kalgoorlie, where gold is once again being mined, on a

Kim Scott's *Benang* (1999), which won the Miles Franklin Award in 2000, is a confronting but rewarding read about the assimilation policies of the 20th century and the devastating effect they had on Aboriginal Australia.

1890	1893	1901	1902
Representative government is formed. Bushman John Forrest is the first elected premier.	Inception of the Education Act, which allows white parents to bar Aboriginal children from schools. What follows is a policy of removal of 'half-caste' children from their parents.	Western Australia and the other colonies are federated to form the nation of Australia.	Following false accusations of incompetence and corruption, CY O'Connor, engineer of the great pipeline from Perth to Kalgoorlie, takes his own life at a Fremantle beach.

Herculean-scale unimaginable a century ago. Today you can visit the No 1 Pump Station at Mundaring Weir and follow the Golden Pipeline Heritage Trail as a motorist from Perth to Kalgoorlie, where you can visit the rather astonishing Super Pit.

The Stolen Generations

At the turn of the century, the lives of many Aboriginal people became more wretched. The colony's 1893 Education Act empowered the parents of white schoolchildren to bar any Aboriginal child from attending their school, and it was not long before Aboriginal children were completely excluded from state-run classrooms. The following decade, the government embarked on a policy of removing so-called 'half-caste' children from their parents, placing them with white families or in government institutions. The objective of the policy was explicit. Full-blood Aboriginal people were to be segregated, in the belief that they were doomed to extinction, while half-caste children were expected to marry whites, thereby breeding Aboriginal people out of existence. These policies inflicted great suffering and sorrow on the many Aboriginal peoples who were recognised in the 1990s as 'the stolen generations'.

Wars & the Depression

On 1 January 1901, WA and the other colonies federated to form the nation of Australia. This was not a declaration of independence. This new Australia was a dominion within the British Empire. It was as citizens of the empire that thousands of Australian men volunteered to fight in the Australian Imperial Force when WWI broke out in 1914. They fought in Turkey, Sinai and in Europe – notably on the Somme. More than 200,000 of them were killed or wounded over the terrible four years of the war. Today, in cities and towns across the state you will see war memorials that commemorate their service.

Though mining, for the time being, had ceased to be an economic force, farmers were developing the lucrative Western Australian wheat belt, which they cultivated with the horse-drawn stump-jump plough, one of the icons of Australian frontier farming. At the same time, a growing demand for wool and beef and the expansion of dairy farming added to the state's economic growth.

Nevertheless, many people were struggling to earn a living – especially those ex-soldiers who were unable to shake off the horrors they had endured in the trenches. In 1929, the lives of these 'battlers' grew even more miserable when the cold winds of the Great Depression blew through

Largely set in WA, *Gallipoli* (1981, directed by Peter Weir, screenplay by David Williamson) is an iconic Australian film about WWI, exploring naivety, social pressure to enlist and, ultimately, the utter futility of the Gallipoli campaign.

1914	1933	1939	1963
Over 200,000 Australians are killed or wounded in WWI.	Two-thirds of the voting population votes to secede from the rest of the country. Although never enacted, secession remains topical.	WWII begins. Several towns in WA's north, including Broome, are bombed during the war. Fremantle is turned into an Allied naval base, and a US submarine-refuelling base is established at Exmouth.	Development of the gargantuan Ord River Irrigation Scheme to fertilise the desert.

the towns and farms of the state. So alienated did Western Australians feel from the centres of power and politics in the east that, in 1933, two-thirds of them voted to secede from the rest of Australia. Although the decision was never enacted, it expressed a profound sense of isolation from the east that is still a major factor in the culture and attitudes of the state today.

In 1939, Australians were once again fighting a war alongside the British, this time against Hitler in WWII. But the military situation changed radically in December 1941 when the Japanese bombed the American fleet at Hawaii's Pearl Harbor. The Japanese swept through Southeast Asia and, within weeks, were threatening Australia. Over the next two years they bombed several towns in the north of the state, including Broome, which was almost abandoned.

It was not the British but the Americans who came to Australia's aid. As thousands of Australian soldiers were taken prisoner and suffered in the torturous Japanese prisoner-of-war camps, Western Australians opened their arms to US servicemen. Fremantle was transformed into an Allied naval base for operations in the Indian Ocean, while a US submarine-refuelling base was established at Exmouth. In New Guinea and the Pacific, Americans and Australians fought together until the tide of war eventually turned in their favour.

Once bankrupt and convicted of corporate fraud, Alan Bond's wealth was estimated at $265 million by *Business Review Weekly* in 2008.

Postwar Prosperity

When WWII ended, the story of modern WA began to unfold. Under the banner of 'postwar reconstruction', the federal government set about transforming Australia with a policy of assisted immigration, designed to populate Australia more densely as a defence against the 'hordes' of Asia. Many members of this new workforce found jobs in the mines, where men and machines turned over thousands of tonnes of earth in search of the precious lode. On city stock exchanges, the names of such Western Australian mines as Tom Price, Mt Newman and Goldsworthy became symbols of development, modernisation and wealth. Now, rather than being a wasteland that history had forgotten, the west was becoming synonymous with ambition, and a new spirit of capitalist pioneering. As union membership flourished, labour and capital entered into a pact to turn the country to profit. In the Kimberley, the government built the gigantic Ord River Irrigation Scheme, which boasted that it could bring fertility to the desert – and which convinced many Western Australians that engineering and not the environment contained the secret of life.

1967	1970	1979	1980s
Australia's Indigenous people are recognised as Australian citizens and granted the right to vote.	The *Indian Pacific* train completes its first transcontinental journey from Sydney to Perth.	The *Skylab* space station crashes in the state's remote southeastern sector. Remnants are now at the Esperance Museum.	The state becomes known as WA Inc, a reference to its image as a giant corporation intent on speculation and profit.

WESTERN AUSTRALIA IN BLACK & WHITE

Like other Indigenous Australians in the rest of the country, the 70,000 or so who live in WA are the state's most disadvantaged group. Many live in deplorable conditions; outbreaks of preventable diseases are common, and infant-mortality rates are higher than in many developing countries. Indigenous employment in the resources sector is slowly increasing, but the mining boom has not alleviated Indigenous social and economic disadvantage to any large degree.

In 1993, the federal government recognised that Aboriginal people with an ongoing association with their traditional lands were the rightful owners, unless those lands had been sold to someone else.

Despite this recognition, the issue of racial relations in WA remains a problematic one, and racial intolerance is still evident in many parts of the state.

There was so much country it hardly seemed to matter that salt was starting to poison the wheat belt or that mines scoured the land. In 1952 the British exploded their first nuclear bomb on the state's Monte Bello Islands. And when opponents of the test alleged that nuclear clouds were drifting over Australia, the government scoffed. The land was big – and anyway, it needed a strong, nuclear-armed ally for protection in the Cold War world.

This spirit of reckless capitalism reached its climax in the 1980s when the state became known as 'WA Inc' – a reference to the state as a giant corporation in which government, business and unions had lost sight of any value other than speculation and profit. The embodiment of this brash spirit was an English migrant named Alan Bond, who became so rich he could buy anything he pleased. In 1983 he funded a sleek new racing yacht called *Australia II* in its challenge for the millionaire's yachting prize, the America's Cup. Equipped with a secret – and now legendary – winged keel, the boat became the first non-American yacht to win the race. It seemed as though everyone in Australia was cheering on the day Bond held aloft the shining silver trophy.

But in the 1990s, legal authorities began to investigate the dealings of Alan Bond, and of many other players in WA Inc. Bond found himself in court and spent four years in jail after pleading guilty to Australia's biggest corporate fraud.

When *Australia II* won the America's Cup in 1983, Australian Prime Minister Bob Hawke opined, 'Any boss who sacks a worker for not turning up today is a bum.'

1983	1987	1990s	1990s
'Bondie' (Alan Bond) funds the racing yacht *Australia II*, which wins the America's Cup with its secret winged keel. Bond is later jailed for corporate fraud.	Sleepy Fremantle is transformed for Australia's first defence of the America's Cup. Australia loses 5-0 to the United States.	Aboriginal rock art, featuring distinctive stick-like images, is found in the Kimberley. Known as the Bradshaw paintings, these could be among the earliest figurative paintings ever executed.	The stolen generations are formally recognised.

The State Today

Throughout the early 21st century, WA's mining boom made the state one of the most dynamic parts of the country. The populations of Perth and key mining areas such as the Pilbara grew faster than those of east-coast Australia; of the state's total population of 2.55 million, many were born overseas. There are substantial South African and British communities in Perth, and many New Zealanders and Irish immigrants are working in the mining and resources sector.

From late 2014, however, signs became evident that the vital Chinese economy fuelling the mining boom was definitely slowing down, causing a weakening in the Australian currency, lessening employment opportunities and reducing the stock-market value of the resources sector. As well, the construction phase of WA's resources industry was largely complete, with roads, ports and railways all in place to better accommodate industry and exports.

With the weakening of the Australian dollar, some relief emerged for the growing tourism sector, and a general easing of salaries in the resources sector eased the pressure for those Perth and WA residents not earning a mine-worker's salary.

Going ahead, WA is still firmly focused on the benefits of the resources sector, but agricultural exports to nearby mega-Asian economies such as China, Indonesia and Vietnam are also growing in importance.

The chill winds blowing through Australia's economy from early 2015 cannot be ignored, but WA's energy and resilience will continue to be vital drivers for the nation's eventual economic re-emergence and strengthening.

Opening in March 2018 for the beginning of the AFL season, the new Perth Stadium will drive the further development of the riverside area of East Perth.

1995	1998	2000s	From 2016
The Fremantle Dockers join the Australian Football League.	One of Australia's most infamous trade union battles is waged in Fremantle between the Maritime Union and the Patrick Corporation (a stevedore company).	Economic growth due to the mining boom, albeit with a reduction in vital Chinese demand from late 2014.	Major Perth urban projects including Elizabeth Quay, Perth Stadium and City Link are completed.

Local Produce & Wineries

Regional produce and local wines are highlights of Western Australia (WA), and leisurely, outdoor eating is best experienced in the vineyard restaurants of the Margaret River, the Porongurups, Denmark and the Swan Valley. Select spots up north – Geraldton, Kalbarri, Carnarvon, Kununurra and Broome – include a few local gems. For the best of WA's excellent craft beer scene, focus on Fremantle, the Swan Valley and Margaret River.

Regional Produce

Regional produce includes marron (small freshwater crayfish unique to the southwest), crayfish (rock lobster, from up north), McHenry Hohnen beef (Margaret River) and barramundi (the Kimberley). Much of WA's best produce is also available at supermarkets and delicatessens. Look out for Browne's iced coffee and yoghurts, Harvey Fresh products – especially its fresh orange juice – and excellent chilli mussels.

Perth's leading chefs celebrate the region's produce by showcasing Manjimup truffles, Mt Barker chicken and Shark Bay scallops. Top-end spots in the central city include Restaurant Amusé (p73), Wildflower (p71) and Balthazar (p72), while Mt Lawley has Must Winebar (p74) and St Michael 6003 (p74). Excellent midrange cafes and restaurants include Brika (p72) and Bivouac Canteen & Bar (p73) in Northbridge, Duende (p75) and Sayers (p74) in Leederville, and Mrs S (p73) and Beaufort Local (p74) in Mt Lawley. In Fremantle, Bread in Common (p91) and Manuka Woodfire Kitchen (p92) are both very good. Regional dining highlights include the Studio Bistro (p135) near Yallingup, Pepper & Salt (p152) in Denmark, and Piari & Co (p129) in Dunsborough.

Across the state you can easily pay too much for pathetic pasta or a boring burger, and unfortunately lax service and attention to detail are often prevalent both in Perth and regional WA.

The best value can usually be found at the top end, and then budget spots such as farmers markets, Northbridge's Asian eateries, and food halls in central Perth's shopping malls.

Then There's Beer

WA's leading working-class beers are Emu Bitter (EB) and Swan Draught. They're both pretty bland, so focus instead on exploring the craft-beer scene. In Fremantle and the southwest in particular, local microbreweries abound, and the Swan Valley is also a top spot.

In Fremantle, visit the Norfolk Hotel (p93) and the Monk (p93) for blackboards full of ever-changing brews. Freo also has the iconic Little Creatures (p94), now owned by a multinational company but still tasting great with its hoppy Pale Ale.

In the Swan Valley, the best craft breweries are Homestead (p111) at Mandoon Estate, Feral Brewing Company (p111) and Mash (p111). Mash also has locations in Bunbury and Rockingham.

Eating Out

Tipping is not required in WA.

BYO – bringing your own beer or wine to the restaurant – is a widely accepted and budget-friendly practice.

Wine for Dudes (p130) has excellent wine tours led by a winemaker. Around the Great Southern, hook up with Denmark Wine Lovers Tour (p151).

Local Produce & Wineries

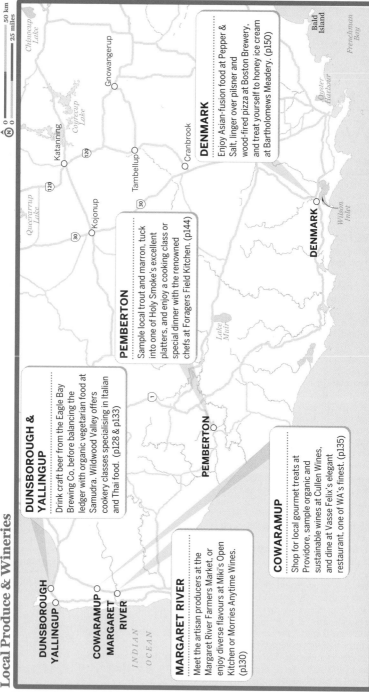

0   50 km
0   25 miles

DUNSBOROUGH & YALLINGUP

Drink craft beer from the Eagle Bay Brewing Co. before balancing the ledger with organic vegetarian food at Samudra. Wildwood Valley offers cookery classes specialising in Italian and Thai food. (p128 & p133)

PEMBERTON

Sample local trout and marron, tuck into one of Holy Smoke's excellent platters, and enjoy a cooking class or special dinner with the renowned chefs at Foragers Field Kitchen. (p144)

DENMARK

Enjoy Asian-fusion food at Pepper & Salt, linger over pilsner and wood-fired pizza at Boston Brewery, and treat yourself to honey ice cream at Bartholomews Meadery. (p150)

MARGARET RIVER

Meet the artisan producers at the Margaret River Farmers Market, or enjoy diverse flavours at Miki's Open Kitchen or Morries Anytime Wines. (p130)

COWARAMUP

Shop for local gourmet treats at Providore, sample organic and sustainable wines at Cullen Wines, and dine at Vasse Felix's elegant restaurant, one of WA's finest. (p135)

Continuing south, the Margaret River region is a definite craft-beer hot spot, and a guided tour with Margaret River Brewery Tours (p130) will get you to the best of the breweries. Denmark's Boston Brewery (p152) and Pemberton's Jarrah Jacks (p146) are both worth visiting, and good beers and ciders are crafted at the Cidery (p143) in Bridgetown.

Up north, the only craft brewery you'll find is Matso's (p216) in Broome. EB and Swan are surprisingly difficult to find, and east-coast beers such as Carlton, XXXX and Tooheys dominate the mainstream market.

Australian beer has a higher alcohol content than British or American beer. Standard beer is around 5% alcohol (midstrength is around 3.5%, light 2% to 3%).

Wine & the Cellar Door

Wine is a big deal in WA, with the focus firmly on the quality end of the market. The Margaret River region produces only 3% of Australia's grapes but accounts for over 20% of the country's premium wines.

The first wineries were established in the southwest in the 1960s, and Vasse Felix was a notable early player. Because the southwest has always focused on low-yield, quality output, it wasn't as influenced by the over-supply problems that beset the Australian wine industry in 2005 and 2006. Fortuitous combinations of rain and warm weather also produced consistently excellent Margaret River vintages from 2007 to 2013.

Aside from Margaret River, other key wine areas are the Swan Valley, the Great Southern (Frankland, the Porongurups, Denmark, Mt Barker), Pemberton, and the Peel and Geographe regions. These all uphold WA's reputation as a world-class wine producer.

Margaret River

WA's best wineries are in Margaret River, 250km (3½ hours' drive) south-west of Perth. The climate is defined by cooling ocean breezes, producing Margaret River's distinctively elegant and rich wines.

Margaret River also produces many blends of semillon and sauvignon blanc grapes. These very popular fruity wines are not Margaret River's very best, but they are often the most affordable. Cape Mentelle, Cullen Wines and Lenton Brae all make good examples. Cullen Wines is also renowned for its organic and sustainable approach to wine making.

Smaller cellar doors to explore around Margaret River include the following:

Ashbrook (p136) A friendly family-owned operation.

Thompson Estate (p136) With a spectacular award-winning tasting room.

Stella Bella (p141) Excellent wines and wonderfully-designed labels.

Stormflower Vineyard (p136) Organic with highly regarded cabernet shiraz.

In central Perth, Lalla Rookh (p76) is a classy wine bar with an excellent selection of Western Australian wines.

Best Margaret River Winery Restaurants

Rustico at Hay Shed Hill (p135)

Knee Deep in Margaret River (p136)

Leeuwin Estate (p141)

Vasse Felix (p136)

Wills Domain (p135)

LOCAL PRODUCE & WINERIES WINE & THE CELLAR DOOR

MARGARET RIVER'S FOUNDING FIVE

Five top wineries compose the cornerstone of Margaret River.

Cape Mentelle Makes consistently excellent cabernet sauvignon as well as a wonderful example of sauvignon blanc semillon.

Cullen Wines (p136) Still in the family, producing superb chardonnay and excellent cabernet merlot while adhering to sustainable wine-making principles.

Leeuwin Estate (p141) Stylish cellar door, a highly regarded restaurant, and responsible for putting chardonnay on the map in Australia with its Art Series.

Moss Wood Makes a heady semillon, a notable cabernet sauvignon and a surprising pinot noir.

Vasse Felix (p136) Must-see winery with a renowned restaurant.

Swan Valley

The Swan Valley may once have aspired to take on mighty Margaret River, but now the region's true merit lies in its proximity to Perth and its small clutch of winery-restaurants – not the wines per se. It's hotter than down south, so leisurely outdoor-dining opportunities are better. You can also travel from Perth along the Swan River to the Sandalford Winery (p110).

Houghton (☑08-9274 9540; www.houghton-wines.com.au; Dale Rd, Middle Swan; ☺10am-5pm) is the area's best winery, and the Houghton Classic White, a blend of white-wine grapes that drinks like a mix of tropical, zesty fruits, is the Swan Valley's most ubiquitous wine. Others of note include Lamont's (p110) and Sandalford. Best for lunch are RiverBank Estate (p110) and Lamont's (tapas only).

Peel & Geographe Regions

Because the Peel region starts about 70km south of Perth, it's often hot, dry and rugged. Much like the Swan Valley, wine here is not generally considered to be of great significance. **Millbrook Winery** (☑08-9525 5796; www.millbrookwinery.com.au; Old Chestnut Lane; ☺10am-5pm Wed-Sun), relatively close to Perth, is excellent for lunch, with a verandah right beside the vines.

Further south, in the slightly cooler Geographe region, are wineries of varying quality. Many people come to visit Capel Vale (p126). This winery has a 30-year history of wine-making excellence, particularly with chardonnay, shiraz and, more recently, merlot.

Great Southern & Pemberton

The Great Southern region will never challenge Margaret River's pre-eminence among wine-touring regions – Margaret River is so spectacularly beautiful – but it nevertheless produces good-quality wines. Wine tourism here is not as developed, and that can be a good thing. Shiraz, cabernet sauvignon, riesling and sauvignon blanc do especially well.

The region stretches from the southeast town of Frankland, further southeast to Albany, and then west again to Denmark. Mt Barker, in the middle, is 350km southeast of Perth. The Great Southern's wines are full of flavour and power, and have a sense of elegance – try the peppery shirazes.

In Frankland, **Alkoomi** (Map p153; www.alkoomiwines.com.au; 225 Stirling Tce; ☺11am-5pm Mon-Sat) is still a family-run business, and produces great cabernet sauvignon and riesling. Ferngrove produces an honest chardonnay, an excellent shiraz and a brilliant cabernet sauvignon–shiraz blend called 'the Stirlings'. Frankland Estate is one of the key wineries that has helped revitalise riesling.

There are more wineries southwest of Frankland, in Mt Barker, and among the nearby Porongurup range. Riesling and shiraz are consistently great performers here; also try the lean, long-flavoured cabernet sauvignon. Two of the best are Forest Hill (p152) – try its cabernet sauvignon – and Plantagenet Wines (p158), the area's best winery.

Further south, in Denmark and Albany, are some of Australia's most esteemed wine names. Howard Park (p152), the area's standout, has superb cabernet sauvignon, riesling and chardonnay. West Cape Howe (p158) is a straightforward winery that's excellent value, while Wignall's Wines is noted for its pinot noir.

Travelling east of Margaret River in the direction of the Great Southern wine region, you'll hit the Pemberton–Manjimup area (280km due south of Perth). Pemberton is a beautiful, undulating area, home to forests of the area's famous karri trees, and its cool-ish climate produces cooler wine styles – pinot noir, merlot and chardonnay, in particular.

Organic & Sustainable

City Farm Market
(p71)

Margaret River
Farmers Market
(p137)

Little Concept
(p93)

Cullen Wines
(p136)

Raw Kitchen
(p92)

Best for Vegetarians

Raw Kitchen
(p92)

Little Concept
(p93)

Kakulas Bros
(p71)

Veggie Mama
(p73)

Maleeya's Thai
Cafe (p158)

For information and tasting notes about Western Australian wines, and to shop online for reds and whites, visit www.mrwines.com.

Mining &
the Environment

If you fly into Perth, you'll notice one thing straight away. The fly-in, fly-out 'FIFO' lifestyle is not only ubiquitous but now the norm. Large clutches of workers nonchalantly board their flights to remote mines and oil and gas plants every few hours. Some will be wearing their fluorescent orange or yellow 'high-vis' vests, required attire on site and an understated badge of honour at the airport.

A few years ago, many construction workers were also part of this airborne ebb and flow, but now that massive infrastructure projects are largely completed in WA's north, this movement mainly comprises mining workers. Contraction of the vital Chinese economy throughout 2014 has slowed Australia's exports of iron ore considerably, causing the Aussie dollar to devalue and the Australian economy to weaken, but mining is still the biggest game in town out west.

Teens just out of school have been bypassing the traditional employment rite of passage of an apprenticeship to earn annual incomes topping six figures. Irish and New Zealand workers have flocked to Western Australia to join in the resources-led bonanza, and Perth restaurant owners and wheatbelt farmers have found it hard to lure workers away from the well-paid appeal of the mines.

And against this backdrop of growth and opportunity, tempered by a slowing of Chinese demand for Australia's iron ore, the boom's effect on the environment remains a source of concern for many in Western Australia and across the country.

Life on the Mines

The source of the state's affluence remains outside many travellers' fields of vision. Take the Pilbara gold-mining town of Telfer, for instance, considered the most remote town in Western Australia. Life here is altogether different to that in the leafy western suburbs of Perth. For Telfer is less traditional country town (with main street, two quiet pubs, maybe a community town hall) and more giant mine plus attendant camp, purpose-built for its hundreds of workers.

The 'four weeks on, one week off' fly-in, fly-out schedule on the mines is referred to as the 'divorce roster'.

The Birth of the Mobile Workforce

In an effort to accommodate a workforce that periodically grows and shrinks, Telfer has been dismantled and rebuilt a few times by mining companies over the years. But in the mid-1990s it was discovered that it was cheaper to simply fly the entire workforce in and out rather than continually build and reconstruct permanent accommodation. Under the new plan, those flown in would work for a sustained period of time (say four weeks), then have a week or two off back home – in Perth, over east, in New Zealand, or even in Bali. The company would then be able to draw from a broader, more skilled labour force, and workers would no longer need to contemplate the unattractive lifestyle of living permanently in the middle of nowhere. As this business model was adopted across the state, the FIFO work culture was born.

Setting Up Camp

The fly-in, fly-out (FIFO) lifestyle is perhaps nowhere more apparent than in Karratha, once a sleepy, nondescript town but today harbouring a FIFO population, relatively expensive food and accommodation shortages. The recent slowing of WA's resources sector has now brought Karratha's accommodation prices to a more realistic level, and there's a better sense of community here as a few more families commit to the town long term.

Woodside, a major oil and gas producer, has set up camp here, exploring for gas off the north coast. The pace of expansion has been so speedy, that there wasn't time to build brick-and-tile homes for the workers. And so today in Karratha, bolted onto the original small town centre, are a number of suburbs composed of 'dongas' – makeshift, moveable, one-man accommodation units. A typical donga in Gap Ridge, the main suburb, has a single bed, a TV, a shower and a toilet carved into a shipping-container-like box-home. Meals are taken in the 'wet mess', much like a mess hall.

Karratha locals have for some time been voicing concerns that an entire FIFO population parties in their town without regard for the community. Places like Gap Ridge are home to an almost entirely young, moneyed, male population, and this has created a pattern of influx and change in Karratha that is echoed in other mining towns across the state. Many labourers are away from home and family, and have considerable funds to sink into beer and good times.

Such social shifts have not gone unnoticed by politicians, including former Western Australian premier Colin Barnett. One initiative rolled out since the peak of the boom is 'Royalties for Regions' – putting money back into regional areas such as Karratha, which had not been able to easily build much-needed infrastructure despite the boom. Mobile-phone coverage is now being expanded on the remote highways.

Work Hard, Play Hard

Drinking has long been part of Australian culture, but clocked-off FIFO workers focus particularly keenly on playing hard. Throughout the global financial crisis (or 'GFC' in Australian parlance), letting off steam over a few beers simply continued apace for many. But by late 2014, the Chinese economy had slowed considerably, and falling iron-ore and nickel prices had started to reduce the number of nights out on the town. Jobs had been shed, and share prices for resource companies had fallen. And it is perhaps those who hold the mantra 'work hard, play hard' most closely to their hearts who have been found to be the most vulnerable to shakes in the economy. Many young workers have limited education and have been earning big sums from a young age. For some, the upkeep of their lifestyle (jet skis, cars, houses) has always been contingent on a mining salary that did not waver. Now that the economy has inevitably slowed, some workers are struggling to unearth a Plan B.

You're In or You're Out

Employment of Indigenous Australians within the mining industry is very low. Some argue that training programs for Indigenous Australians – attempts to settle Australia's most disadvantaged into the Western working life – have not proved effective. In 2008 mining magnate

Tim Flannery's *The Future Eaters* is a highly readable overview of evolution in Australasia, covering the last 120 million years of history, with thoughts on how the environment has shaped Australasia's human cultures.

Field Guide to the Birds of Australia is full colour, splendidly detailed, accessible and portable. This endlessly fascinating reference, Graham Pizzey and Frank Knight's claim to fame, is in its 8th edition.

In *The Weather Makers*, Tim Flannery argues lucidly and passionately that there is an immediate need to address the implications of a global change in climate that is damaging all life on earth and endangering our very survival. An accessible read.

Andrew 'Twiggy' Forrest, who Forbes labelled Australia's richest man in 2010, boldly promised support for 50,000 jobs for Indigenous Australians. This government-backed program is also one of the most high-profile attempts by a key mining figure to not only change employment patterns but also speak frankly about the lack of opportunity afforded to Aboriginal communities across the state. Just how the 50,000 jobs will be effectively taken up in the long term is yet to be determined, and that will be the tricky bit. By late 2012, four years after the program was developed, some 10,000 positions had been taken up.

In 2014, Andrew Forrest also released *Creating Parity,* an Australian government-sponsored review of Indigenous jobs and training. From September 2014, public submissions were invited on the report's recommendations, but some ideas – such as a cashless 'Healthy Welfare Card' promoted to aid family budgeting and minimise access to drugs and alcohol – came under criticism from Indigenous and welfare rights advocacy groups.

It is now more widely acknowledged that the gap between the resource-boom-driven 'haves' and 'have-nots' is real and ever increasing, with signs of economic strain creeping up the social strata. The tension between income and cost of living – strongly driven by the high cost of housing – has become so tight that some middle-class workers employed on good salaries struggle to pay the rent. Foreign financial investment is gargantuan, and it will likely be here for some years to come. But patterns of recent job losses are causing many to wonder aloud if the good times have indeed passed.

Keep your eyes peeled for the banded anteater, also known as the numbat. Tiny, light-footed and incredibly shy, the numbat is a solitary creature who will venture outside its neatly delineated territory only to find a mate. Singular dietary requirement: termites.

Recent Environmental Flashpoints

James Price Point

James Price Point is an expanse of wilderness along the Kimberley coast 60km north of Broome. A multinational consortium and the WA state government was proposing a liquefied natural gas (LNG) station here – the biggest in the world. In 2013, eight years after first proposing the development, Woodside Petroleum Ltd announced that the refineries were not economically viable, which was a significant victory for environmental groups seeking to protect the largely pristine Kimberley coastline.

Aside from its dinosaur fossils, the proposed area is a playground for dolphins, dugongs and breeding bilbies. Humpback whales breed and calve along the coastline, and the rainforest backing the coast harbours a multitude of plant species. Not least, this is traditional Aboriginal land. Woodside negotiating a native title deed this size would have marked a historic achievement.

James Price Point had become a leading symbol of tensions between the growing financial fortunes of the state and the less easily quantified value of an untouched landscape. Not only were business interests, traditional land owners, politicians and environmentalists in fierce disagreement with each other, but divisions *within* these groups continue to run deep despite the amendment of the project to utilise floating offshore LNG rigs. For locals in nearby Broome, 'whose side you're on' is often common knowledge, and this lack of anonymity is a further source of strain.

Following lobbying by the Wilderness Society and environmental-impact studies, the Supreme Court of Western Australia overruled the Western Australian Environment Minister and the Western Australian Environmental Protection Authority to block the proposed Browse LNG plant at James Price Point

For detailed directions on where and how to surround yourself with wildflowers, see the Wildflower Society of Western Australia's website (www.wildflower-societywa.org.au).

Elsewhere on the Land

WA's environmental flashpoints are by no means limited to the extended controversy surrounding proposed onshore LPG processing plants at James Price Point. Other controversial sites slated for mining include the Burrup Peninsula in the Dampier Archipelago, which is the location of many petroglyphs (rock art), archaeological wonders thought to date from the last ice age. Although disruption to the works began in the 1960s, in 2007 Woodside Petroleum Ltd had several petroglyphs gingerly removed and fenced off in a separate area to better facilitate development. Some argue that the works are not discrete: that the disruption of one petroglyph compromises the entire site. Elsewhere in the state, uranium mines are under consideration.

Meanwhile, ground water has been utilised freely for decades; alternative water sources, using desalination plants, have been in place for some time. Old-growth forests, with their 1000-year-old karri trees, were logged until the 1990s; today scientists cite lowered rainfall in the southwest as the result of deforestation.

And, much like other major cities in Australia, Perth is subject to suburban sprawl. Because the mining boom has driven much property development, the city now tails out across 100km, densely studded with so-called affordable housing. The environmental effects of the lifestyle out here are not immediately apparent, but may nevertheless prove significant. Many housing estates are divorced from public-transport routes, so people must always drive for their litre of milk, and the roads are becoming increasingly congested. Many have long been calling for more high-density housing in and near the city of Perth.

Boomtown 2050, by landscape architect Richard Weller, is a nicely packaged book about how a rapidly growing town like Perth could be developed – sustainably.

Balancing Economy & Environment

Going ahead, the balancing act between the economy and environmental issues remains at the very heart of Western Australian society and politics, and the stakes have never been higher. Now that the Chinese economy's appetite for iron ore has eased, developers and the Western Australian government will be even more focused on tapping other rich veins of WA's resources sector. Inevitably, there will be more conflict between industrial interests and environmental advocates. For many Western Australians, the benefits of a prosperous resources economy has provided them with access to a rewarding and cosmopolitan lifestyle.

The boom has spawned mega-rich mining magnates whose influence extends well beyond resources into politics and the media, and they are eyeing further wilderness areas as sites for the development of new mines and gas plants, with all the costs and benefits they entail.

The Western Australian – and therefore Australia's – resources boom may be slowing slightly, but the ongoing tension between economic growth and environmental protection will continue to define Australia's most sprawling state for the foreseeable future.

Mt Augustus (1106m), on the central west coast, is the largest rock in the world, twice the size and three times as old as Uluru in the Northern Territory.

How It All Began

Really, mining is old news – this is a frontier land founded on mining money. Although in the 1800s Western Australia was quietly focused on acquiring more modest fortunes from wheat, meat and wool, in 1892 gold was discovered in Coolgardie, and in 1893 it was uncovered again in Kalgoorlie. And so the economic transformation began. Today, gold mining is still going strong, albeit with incrementally diminishing returns. In Kalgoorlie you can visit the Super Pit, an open-pit gold

NINGALOO'S CLOSED SCRAPE

Some locals still sport 'Save Ningaloo' bumper stickers on their cars. No one seems to pay much attention to the faded stickers these days, but they're a reminder of one of the most high-profile and fiercely contested environmental campaigns WA has seen. 'Save Ningaloo', with its thousands of protesters, successfully blocked development of a massive marina resort (slated for 2003) on a loggerhead-turtle nesting ground. Comprising 280km of coral reef, and visited by species such as manta rays, whale sharks, dugongs, humpback whales and turtles, Ningaloo is one of the last healthy major reef systems in the world.

The area did nevertheless remain a site of interest for property developers and the resources sector, and in late 2012 BHP Billiton submitted a proposal to the state government to explore for liquefied natural gas some 5km from Ningaloo's perimeter.

This proposal was rejected and now BHP Billiton have joined with Australia's CSIRO (Commonwealth Scientific and Industrial Research Organisation) in a five-year marine research partnership.

mine the size of 35 football fields sunk 360m into the ground. Copper, nickel, oil and gas are also steady sources of income for the state, with uranium mining (slated for Wiluna, in the midwest) a current aspiration.

But iron ore is today's multi-billion-dollar blockbuster industry. Karara mine in the midwest, for example, sits on just under $100 billion worth of iron ore. All this magnetite dug up out of the ground, later to become iron ore, is expected to generate $3 billion per year in export revenue for the next 30 years. Most of it will go to China, but the demand for it in recent years has been slowing, sending a chill through the entire Australian economy.

Of course, foreign investment remains big business. And while such major investment has now been criticised for exposing the state to the capricious fortunes of the Chinese economy, the boom would never have occurred without it. For an iron-ore mine, for example, about $1 billion must be available up front just to develop the extraction machinery. These biscuits are just too big for the Australian economy alone.

Head to Ningaloo Reef from around April to June to swim alongside whales sharks that are many metres long and remarkably docile.

MINING & THE ENVIRONMENT HOW IT ALL BEGAN

Indigenous Art in Western Australia

Experiencing the indigenous art of Western Australia (WA) creates an indelible link for travellers to this land of red dirt and desert expanses. Ancient rock art echoes across the centuries, traditional designs and motifs inspire modern artists, and Indigenous tour operators inform with stories of spirituality, bush tucker and 'country'.

Indigenous Art

Rock Art

Some Aboriginal rock paintings are believed to date back between 18,000 and 60,000 years and provide a record of changing environments and lifestyles over the millennia. For the local Indigenous people, rock-art sites are a major source of traditional knowledge – they are historical archives in place of a written form.

The earliest hand or grass prints were followed by a naturalistic style, with large outlines of people or animals filled in with colour. Then came the dynamic style, in which motion was often depicted (a dotted line, for example, to show a spear's path through the air). In this era the first mythological beings appeared, with human bodies and animal heads. Following this were simple human silhouettes, and then the more recent X-ray style, displaying the internal organs and bones of animals.

Art of the Kimberley

The art of the Kimberley is perhaps best known for its images of the Wandjina, a group of ancestral beings who came from the sky and sea and were associated with fertility. They controlled the elements and were responsible for the formation of the country's natural features.

Wandjina images are found painted on rock as well as on more recent contemporary media; some of the rock images are more than 7m long. They generally appear in human form, with large black eyes, a nose but no mouth, a halo around the head (representative of both hair and clouds) and a black oval shape on the chest.

WHERE TO SEE ROCK ART

➡ Mulka's Cave (p107), near Wave Rock and Hyden.

➡ Burrup Peninsula, Pilbara with Ngurrangga Tours (p198).

➡ Mitchell Plateau in the Kimberley, especially Mitchell Falls (p227) and Munurru Campground (p227).

➡ Mt Elizabeth Station (p12) on the Gibb River Road.

➡ Some of the Wandjina and Gwion Gwion images hidden across the Kimberley are accessible from some stations on the Gibb River Road.

BEST NORTHERN WA GALLERIES

→ Short Street Gallery, Broome (p211)

→ Mowanjum Art & Culture Centre, Gibb River Road (p224)

→ Waringarri Aboriginal Arts Centre, Kununurra (p228)

→ Artlandish, Kununurra (p231)

→ East Pilbara Art Centre, Newman (☏08-9175 1020; www.martumili.com.au; Newman Dr; ☺10am-4pm Mon-Fri)

→ Spinifex Hill Studios, Port Hedland (p200)

Each Wandjina traditionally has its own custodian family, and to ensure good relations between the Wandjina and the people, the images have to be retouched annually.

Another significant painting style found in the Kimberley is that of the Gwion Gwion figures (also named the Bradshaw images after the first non-Indigenous person who saw them). The Gwion Gwion figures are generally small and seem to depict ethereal beings engaged in ceremony or dance. It is believed that they pre-date the Wandjina paintings, though little is known of their significance or meaning.

Western Desert Painting

Western Desert painting, also known as dot painting, is probably the most well known of Indigenous painting styles. It partly evolved from 'ground paintings', which formed the centrepiece of dances and songs. These were made from pulped plant material, with designs made on the ground. While dot paintings may look random and abstract, they depict Dreaming stories and can be read in many ways, including as aerial landscape maps. Many paintings feature the tracks of birds, animals and humans, often identifying the land's ancestral beings. Subjects may be depicted by the imprint they leave in the sand – a simple arc depicts a person (as that is the print left by someone sitting cross-legged), a coolamon (wooden carrying dish) is shown by an oval shape, a digging stick by a single line, and a campfire by a circle. Men or women are identified by the objects associated with them: digging sticks and coolamons for women, spears and boomerangs for men. Concentric circles usually depict Dreaming sites, or places where ancestors paused in their journeys.

The Western Desert Mob is a coalition of artists cooperatives of the Ngaanyatjarra lands of Western Australia. Mediums include *punu*, the traditional art of woodcarving.

While these symbols are widely used, their meaning in each painting is known only by the artist and the people closely associated with them – either by clan or by the Dreaming – since different clans apply different interpretations to each painting. In this way sacred stories can be publicly portrayed, as the deeper meaning is not revealed to uninitiated viewers.

Buying Indigenous Art Ethically

By buying authentic items you are supporting Indigenous culture and helping to ensure that traditional and contemporary expertise and designs continue to be of economic and cultural benefit to Indigenous individuals and communities. Unfortunately, some of the so-called Indigenous art sold as souvenirs is ripped off – it features designs illegally taken from Indigenous people or it's just plain fake – and sometimes made overseas by underpaid workers. Artworks should have a

BEST INDIGENOUS CITY GALLERIES

➡ **Art Gallery of Western Australia, Perth** (p53)

➡ **Indigenart, Perth** (p81)

➡ **Japingka, Fremantle** (p94)

certificate of authenticity. Note that haggling is not part of Aboriginal culture.

It's best to buy art either directly from the communities that have art collectives, or from galleries and outlets that are owned and operated, or supported, by Indigenous communities. You can then be sure that the items are genuine and that the money you spend goes to the right people. However, some Indigenous artists continue to be paid small sums for their work, only to find it being sold for much higher prices in commercial galleries in cities.

To negate this, it's vital to do some research. The Australian Commercial Galleries Association (www.acga.com.au) lists galleries considered to observe ethical practices.

Survival Guide

Directory A–Z

Accommodation

Accommodation in Western Australia (WA) ranges from campgrounds to high-end hotels. Perth's accommodation is generally more expensive, although Margaret River, Broome, the Coral Coast and Pilbara mining towns come very close.

Over summer (December to February) and around school and public holidays, prices are at their highest. Outside these times discounts and lower walk-in rates can be found. One exception is the far north, where the wet season (November to March) is the low season and prices can drop by as much as 50%. Listed prices include all state and federal taxes.

Accommodation in the Pilbara can be hard to find, due to the fly-in, fly-out (FIFO) mining phenomenon. Camping is often the best option.

B&Bs

Bed and breakfast (B&B) options range from rooms in heritage buildings to a bedroom in a family home. A full cooked breakfast is not the norm. Tariffs for couples are typically in the $150-to-$250 range but can be much higher for exclusive properties.

Booking Services

For online information:

➡ www.australianbedand-breakfast.com.au
➡ www.babs.com.au
➡ www.ozbedandbreakfast.com

Camping & Holiday Parks

For many travellers, touring with a tent or campervan is the consummate WA experience. In the outback and up north you often won't even need a tent as you can use a swag or rent a cabin, Check with visitor centres before heading out to confirm locations of free roadside stops. Many stops have been phased out immediately north of Perth but are more frequent further away from the city.

Designated camp sites in national parks cost $10/2.20 per adult/child with no or basic facilities. Sites with showers (including unpow-ered caravan sites) cost $10/2.20. You'll also need to pay entrance fees ($12 per car) for many national parks, but only when you enter the park. If you're exploring several parks, pick up a four-week national-park holiday pass ($44). Some national-park camp sites can be booked online, and this is recommended for popular locations like Cape Range National Park from April to October. See https://park-stay.dpaw.wa.gov.au.

At WA's ubiquitous holiday parks, prices are from around $30 to $50 for two people, ranging from unpowered tent sites to powered caravan sites. Many caravan parks are phasing out unpowered sites because they are less profitable. Most holiday parks offer private accommodation, from simple chalets to flash-er motel units, and some also offer hostel accommodation with dorm rooms.

Pick up the free *Caravanning, Camping and Motorhoming in WA* at visitor centres or see www.caravan-wa.com.au.

Dongas

Commonly found in the outback, especially in mining towns, the donga is basically a prefabricated tin room (usually air-conditioned) with a single bed, TV and small fridge.

Farmstays & Station Stays

The Gascoyne and Pilbara areas are popular spots for station stays, and at some you may be asked to pitch in. Accommodation is either in the main homestead (B&B style, with dinner on request) or in adjacent self-contained cottages. Other farms provide budget options in outbuildings or former shearers' quarters. Search for 'Farmstay' online at www.touristradio.com.au.

Hostels

Prices for dorm beds range from $25 to $35, while private rooms range from $70 to $90. Hostel staff can sometimes help in securing seasonal work.

Some hostels – especially in Perth – are popular as short-term accommodation for 'fly-in, fly-out' (FIFO) workers, but this also changes the traditional travellers' vibe.

A Youth Hostel Association (www.yha.com.au) or Hostelling International (www.hihostels.com) annual membership ($25) gives a 10% discount at participating hostels. Sign up online or at the first YHA you stay in.

VIP Backpackers (www.vipbackpackers.com) also offers discounts in participating WA hostels. For $47 you'll receive a 12-month membership, with discounts on accommodation and some transport, tours and activities. Join online or at VIP hostels.

Pubs, Hotels & Motels

Full-service hotels are rare outside Perth, and coastal properties tend to be resort-style, with standalone cottages or apartments. Rates vary widely, but there are benefits in booking early directly with the properties, or last minute on accommodation-booking websites.

In rural areas book ahead, as motels are used by government workers and tour groups.

You can sometimes rent a single room at a country pub for not much more than a hostel dorm. If you're a light sleeper, never book a room above the bar.

Some pubs also have separate motel-style accommodation.

Rental Accommodation

The ubiquitous holiday flat resembles a motel unit but has cooking, and often laundry, facilities. They're often rented on a weekly basis, and nightly prices are higher for shorter stays. For listings of holiday homes, see www.stayz.com.au.

Self-contained accommodations, many of which have full kitchens, are a good option for saving money by not eating out.

In cities a good alternative is an apartment, especially in Perth and around Fremantle, and Airbnb has been enthusiastically adopted in Western Australia.

Customs Regulations

For comprehensive information, contact the Australian Customs Service.

On arrival, declare all goods of animal or plant origin, as it's vital to protect Australia's unique environment and agricultural industries. If you fail to declare quarantine items on arrival, you risk an on-the-spot fine of over $200 or even prosecution and imprisonment. For more information contact the Australian Department of Agriculture (www.agriculture.gov.au/biosecurity).

Duty-free allowances:

➜ Alcohol – 2.25L

➜ Cigarettes – 50

➜ Other goods – up to $900 value; or items for personal use that you will be taking with you when you leave.

Discount Cards

The most common card for discounts on accommodation, transport and some attractions in WA is the International Student Identity Card (www.isic.org), issued to full-time students aged 12 years and over. See the International Student Travel Confederation (www.istc.org).

The ISTC also has an International Youth Travel Card (IYTC or Go25), issued to people between 12 and 26 years of age who are not full-time students. Benefits are equivalent to the ISIC.

Electricity

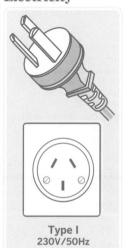

Type I
230V/50Hz

PRACTICALITIES

➺ **Newspapers** Key newspapers are the *West Australian* (www.west.com.au) or the *Australian* (www.theaustralian.com.au), a national broadsheet, from Monday to Saturday, and the *Sunday Times* (www.perthnow.com.au) on Sunday.

➺ **TV** networks include the commercial-free ABC, multicultural SBS, and commercial TV stations Seven, Nine and Ten.

➺ **Radio** Tune in to the ABC on the radio – pick a program and frequency from www.abc.net.au/radio.

➺ **DVDs** sold in Australia can be watched on players accepting region 4 DVDs (the same as Mexico, South America, Central America, New Zealand, the Pacific and the Caribbean). The USA and Canada are region 1 countries, and Europe and Japan are region 2.

➺ **Weights & Measures** The metric system is used.

➺ **Smoking** Banned on public transport and planes, in cars carrying children, between the flags at patrolled beaches, within 10m of a playground and in government buildings. It's also banned within bars and clubs but permitted in some alfresco or courtyard areas.

Embassies & Consulates

The principal diplomatic representations to Australia are in Canberra, but many countries are represented in Perth by consular staff.

Remember that while in Australia you are bound by Australian laws. Your embassy will not be sympathetic if you end up in jail after committing a crime locally, even if such actions are legal in your own country.

Canadian Consulate (☑08-9322 7930; www.canadainternational.gc.ca; 3rd fl, 267 St Georges Tce)

Dutch Consulate (☑08-9486 1579; http://australia.nlembassy.org; 1139 Hay St)

German Consulate (☑08-9321 2926; www.canberra.diplo.de; 1113 Hay St; ☺9am-noon Mon-Fri)

Irish Consulate (☑08-6557 5802; www.consulateofirelandwa.com.au; 1/100 Terrace Rd, East Perth; ☺by appointment 10.30am-2pm Mon-Fri)

New Zealand Consulate (☑08-9364 1700; info@nzconsulateperth.com; 1 Sleat Rd, Applecross; ☺8am-5pm Mon-Fri)

UK Consulate (☑08-9224 4700; www.british-consulate.org; Level 12, 251 Adelaide Tce; ☺9.30am-1pm & 2-3.30pm Mon-Fri)

USA Consulate (☑08-6144-5100; http://perth.usconsulate.gov; 4th fl, 16 St Georges Tce; ☺8.30am-4.30pm)

Gay & Lesbian Travellers

In general Australians are open-minded about homosexuality, and in WA gay and lesbian people are protected by anti-discrimination legislation and share an equal age of consent with heterosexuals (16 years).

Perth has the state's only gay and lesbian venues and its small scene is centred around Northbridge. It's very unlikely you'll experience any real problems, although the further away from the main centres, the more likely you are to experience overt homophobia.

Useful resources:

➺ **Visit Gay Australia** (www.galta.com.au) Lists WA members offering accommodation and tours.

➺ **Q Pages** (www.qpages.com.au) Gay and lesbian business directory and what's-on listings.

➺ **Living Proud** (Map p62; ☑08-9486 9855, counselling 1800 184 527; www.livingproud.org.au; 2 Delhi St, City West Lotteries House) Information and counselling line.

Health

Australia is a healthy country for travellers. Malaria and yellow fever are unknown, cholera and typhoid are unheard of, and animal diseases such as rabies and foot-and-mouth disease have yet to be recorded. The standard of hospitals and health care is high.

Few travellers should experience anything worse than an upset stomach or a bad hangover.

Before You Go

Pack medications in their original, clearly labelled, containers. A signed and dated letter from your physician describing your medical conditions and medications, including generic names, is also a good idea. If carrying syringes or needles, be sure to have a physician's letter documenting their medical necessity.

HEALTH INSURANCE

If your health insurance doesn't cover you for medical expenses abroad, consider getting extra insurance – check www.lonelyplanet.com for more information. Find out in advance if your insurance plan will make payments directly to providers or reimburse you later for overseas health expenditures.

Availability & Cost of Health Care

Health insurance is essential for all travellers. While health care in Australia is of a high standard and not overly expensive by international standards, considerable costs can build up and repatriation is extremely expensive.

Australia's health-care system is a mixture of privately run medical clinics and hospitals alongside a government-funded system of public hospitals. The Medicare system covers Australian residents for some health-care costs. Visitors from countries with which Australia has a reciprocal health-care agreement (New Zealand, the UK, the Netherlands, Sweden, Finland, Norway, Italy, Malta, Ireland, Slovenia and Belgium) are eligible for benefits to the extent specified under the Medicare program. If you are from one of these countries, check the details before departure. In general the agreements provide for any episode of ill health that requires prompt medical attention. For further details see www.humanservices.gov.au and search for 'reciprocal'.

Over-the-counter medications are widely available at pharmacies. These include painkillers, antihistamines for allergies and skin-care products.

Some medications readily available over the counter in other countries are only available in Australia by prescription. These include the oral contraceptive pill, most medications for asthma and all antibiotics. If you take medication on a regular basis, bring an adequate supply and ensure you know the generic name, as brand names may differ.

Infectious Diseases

BAT LYSSAVIRUS

This disease is related to rabies and some deaths have

VACCINATIONS

No vaccinations are needed. Proof of yellow-fever vaccination is required from travellers entering Australia within six days of having stayed overnight or longer in a yellow-fever–infected country. For a full list of these countries see the websites of the World Health Organization (www.who.int/wer) or the Centers for Disease Control & Prevention (www.cdc.gov/travel).

---

occurred after bites. The risk is greatest for animal handlers and vets. Rabies vaccine is effective, but the risk to travellers is very low.

DENGUE FEVER

Also known as 'breakbone fever', because of the severe muscular pains that accompany the fever, this viral disease is spread by a species of mosquito that feeds primarily during the day. Most people recover in a few days, but more severe forms of the disease can occur, particularly in residents who are exposed to another strain of the virus (there are four types) in a subsequent season.

GIARDIASIS

Giardiasis is widespread in the waterways around Australia. Drinking untreated water from streams and lakes is not recommended. Water filters, and boiling or treating water with iodine, are effective in preventing the disease. Symptoms consist of intermittent bad-smelling diarrhoea, abdominal bloating and wind. Effective treatment is available (tinidazole or metronidazole).

MENINGOCCAL DISEASE

This disease occurs worldwide and is a risk with prolonged, dormitory-style accommodation. A vaccine exists for some types of this disease, namely meningococcal A, C, Y and W. No vaccine is presently available for the viral type of meningitis.

ROSS RIVER FEVER

The Ross River virus is widespread throughout Australia and is spread by mosquitoes

---

living in marshy areas. In addition to fever the disease causes headache, joint and muscular pains and a rash, before resolving after five to seven days.

SEXUALLY TRANSMITTED DISEASES

STDs occur at rates similar to those in most other Western countries. Always use a condom with any new sexual partner. Condoms are readily available in chemists and through vending machines in many public places, including toilets.

VIRAL ENCEPHALITIS

Also known as the Murray Valley encephalitis virus, this is spread by mosquitoes and is most common in northern Australia, especially during the wet season (November to April). This potentially serious disease is normally accompanied by headache, muscle pains and light sensitivity. Residual neurological damage can occur and no specific treatment is available. However, the risk to most travellers is low.

Insurance

Sign up for a travel-insurance policy covering theft, loss and medical problems.

Some policies exclude designated 'dangerous activities' such as scuba diving, parasailing or even bushwalking. Ensure your policy fully covers you for activities of your choice. Check you're covered for ambulances and emergency medical evacuations by air.

Third-party personal-injury insurance (p274) is included in vehicle registration cost, and comprehensive insurance is usually included when hiring a vehicle, though consider reducing your excess to offset costs in the event of an accident.

Worldwide travel insurance is available at www. lonelyplanet.com/bookings.

Internet Access

Internet cafes have virtually vanished across Australia with the growth of smartphones and other internet-enabled mobile devices. Many backpacker hostels and public libraries offer wi-fi connections. In smaller towns visit Community Resource Centres. The cost ranges from around $5 an hour in Perth to $10 an hour in locations that are more remote.

The best bets for free wi-fi connections are public libraries and cafes. Wi-fi is becoming almost ubiquitous in accommodation; it's sometimes free in hostels but is often charged for in caravan parks and hotels.

Legal Matters

Police have the power to stop your car and see your licence (you're required to carry it), check your vehicle for road-worthiness and compel you to take a breath test for alcohol.

First-time offenders in possession of small amounts of illegal drugs are likely to receive a fine rather than go to jail, but a conviction may affect your visa status. If you remain in Australia after your visa expires, you will officially be classified as an 'overstayer' and could face detention and expulsion, and be prevented from returning to Australia for a period of up to three years.

Maps

Tourist-information offices usually have serviceable town maps. For more detailed information, the Royal Automobile Club of WA (www.rac.com.au) has road maps available (including downloadable route maps). UBD publishes a handy *South West & Great Southern* book.

Hema Maps (www.hemamaps. com.au) Best for the north, especially the dirt roads. The website has a wealth of planning information and specialists apps and GPS navigation systems can be purchased.

Landgate (www.landgate.wa.gov. au) State-wide maps as well as topographical maps for bushwalking.

Money

All prices are given in Australian dollars, unless otherwise stated.

ATMs & Eftpos

Bank branches with 24-hour ATMs can be found statewide. In the smallest towns there's usually an ATM in the local pub. Most ATMs accept cards from other banks and are linked to international networks.

Credit & Debit Cards

Visa and MasterCard are widely accepted and a credit card is essential (in lieu of a large deposit) for car hire. With debit cards, any card connected to the international banking network (Cirrus, Maestro, Plus and Eurocard) will work. Diners Club and Amex are not as widely accepted.

Currency

The Australian dollar is made up of 100 cents; there are 5¢, 10¢, 20¢, 50¢, $1 and $2 coins, and $5, $10, $20, $50 and $100 notes.

Cash amounts equal to or in excess of the equivalent of A$10,000 (in any currency) must be declared on arrival or departure in Australia.

Changing foreign currency or travellers cheques is usually no problem at banks throughout WA.

Tipping

Tipping is not required in WA, but around 10 to 15% is appropriate if you feel service in a restaurant has been exemplary. Many cafes have a tip jar on the counter for loose change and this is usually shared between all the staff.

TAP WATER & OTHER WATER SOURCES

Tap water is mainly safe to drink in WA, but a few small towns do have bore water, which will need to be sterilised before drinking. Ask it you're not sure. Increasing numbers of streams, rivers and lakes, however, are being contaminated by bugs that cause diarrhoea, making water purification essential. The simplest way to purify water is to boil it thoroughly. Consider purchasing a water filter; it's very important when buying a filter to read the specifications, so that you know exactly what it removes from the water and what it doesn't. Simple filtering will not remove all dangerous organisms, so if you cannot boil water it should be treated chemically. Chlorine tablets will kill many pathogens, but not some parasites, such as giardia and amoebic cysts. Iodine is more effective in purifying water and is available in tablet form. Follow the directions carefully and remember that too much iodine can be harmful.

Photography

Purchase memory cards and batteries in larger cities and towns, as they're cheaper than in remote areas. Most photo labs have self-service machines from which you can make your own prints and burn CDs and DVDs.

Post

Mail services are generally efficient, and main cities and towns all have centrally located post offices. In smaller centres, postal services may be offered by bookshops or information centres.

Public Holidays

New Year's Day 1 January

Australia Day 26 January

Labour Day First Monday in March

Easter (Good Friday and Easter Monday) March/April

Anzac Day 25 April

Foundation Day First Monday in June

Queen's Birthday Last Monday in September

Christmas Day 25 December

Boxing Day 26 December

Safe Travel

Environmental Hazards

HEAT EXHAUSTION & HEATSTROKE

Heat exhaustion occurs when fluid intake does not keep up with fluid loss. Symptoms include dizziness, fainting, fatigue, nausea or vomiting. On observation the skin is usually pale, cool and clammy. Treatment consists of rest in a cool, shady place and fluid replacement with water or diluted sports drinks.

Heatstroke is a severe form of heat illness that

occurs after fluid depletion or extreme heat challenge from heavy exercise. This is a true medical emergency: heating of the brain leads to disorientation, hallucinations and seizures. Prevention is by maintaining an adequate fluid intake to ensure the continued passage of clear and copious urine, especially during physical exertion.

HYPOTHERMIA

Hypothermia is a significant risk, especially during the winter months in southern parts of Australia. Early signs include the inability to perform fine movements (such as doing up buttons), shivering and a bad case of the 'umbles' (fumbles, mumbles, grumbles, stumbles). The key elements of treatment include changing the environment to one where heat loss is minimised, changing out of any wet clothing, adding dry clothes with windproof and waterproof layers, adding insulation and providing fuel (water and carbohydrate) to allow shivering, which builds the internal temperature. In severe hypothermia, shivering actually stops – this is a medical emergency requiring rapid evacuation in addition to the above measures.

Animal Hazards

Australia is home to some seriously dangerous creatures. On land there are poisonous snakes and spiders, while the sea harbours deadly box jellyfish and white pointer sharks. The saltwater crocodile spans both environments.

In reality you're unlikely to see these creatures in the wild, much less be attacked by one. Far more likely is a hangover after a big night, or getting sunburnt after not wearing sunscreen.

BOX JELLYFISH & OTHER MARINE DANGERS

There have been fatal encounters between swimmers and box jellyfish on the northern coast. Also known as the sea wasp or 'stinger', they have venomous tentacles that can grow up to 3m long. You can be stung any time, but from November to March you should stay out of the water unless you're wearing a 'stinger suit' (available from sporting shops).

If you are stung, first aid consists of washing the skin with vinegar to prevent further discharge of remaining stinging cells, followed by rapid transfer to a hospital; antivenin is widely available.

Marine spikes from sea urchins, stonefish, scorpion fish, catfish and stingrays can cause severe local pain. If this occurs, immediately immerse the affected area in water that's as hot as can be tolerated. Keep topping up with hot water until the pain subsides and medical care can be reached. The stonefish is found only in tropical Australia; antivenin is available.

CROCODILES

In northwest WA, saltwater crocodiles can be a real danger. They live around the coast, and are also found in estuaries, creeks and rivers, sometimes a long way inland. Observe safety signs or ask locals whether an inviting waterhole or river is croc-free before plunging in. The last fatality in WA caused by a saltwater crocodile was in 1987, and attacks occurred in 2006, 2012, 2015 and 2016.

INSECTS

For four to six months of the year you'll have to cope with flies and mosquitoes. Flies are more prevalent in the outback, where a humble fly net is effective. Repellents may also deter them.

Mosquitos are a problem in summer, especially near wetlands in tropical areas, and some species are carriers of viral infections. Keep your arms and legs covered after sunset and use repellent.

The biting midge (sandfly) lives in WA's northern coastal areas. Locals often appear immune, but it's almost a rite of passage for those heading north to be covered in bites. Cover up at dusk.

Ticks and leeches are also common. For protection, wear loose-fitting clothing with long sleeves. Apply 30% DEET on exposed skin, repeated every three to four hours, and impregnate clothing with permethrin.

SHARKS

From 2011 to 2016, there were nine fatal shark attacks in WA, and most involved surfers at more remote beaches. Around popular coastal and city beaches, shark-spotting methods include nets, spotter planes, jet skis and surf lifesavers. Almost 900 sharks, including 220 great whites, are also monitored by a government program.

In early 2014, a three-month trial using baited lines was launched around Perth and southwest beaches, but while 68 sharks were caught and shot, none were great whites. Following protests from environmental and animal-rights groups, the catch-and-kill policy was discontinued after the trial. However, the WA Fisheries Department has the authority to trap and kill individual sharks deemed to be a risk to public safety.

SNAKES

There are many venomous snakes in the Australian bush, the most common being the brown and tiger snakes. Unless you're interfering with one, or accidentally stand on it, it's extremely unlikely you'll be bitten.

Australian snakes have a reputation that is justified in terms of the potency of their venom, but unjustified in terms of the actual risk to travellers and locals. They are endowed with only small fangs, making it easy to prevent bites to the lower limbs (where 80% of bites occur) by wearing protective clothing (such as gaiters) around the ankles when bushwalking.

The bite marks are small and preventing the spread of toxic venom can be achieved by applying pressure to the wound and immobilising the area with a splint or sling before seeking medical attention. Application of an elastic bandage (you can improvise with a T-shirt) wrapped firmly, but not tightly that circulation is cut off, around the entire limb – along with immobilisation – is a life-saving first-aid measure.

SPIDERS

The redback is the most common poisonous spider in WA. It's small and black with a distinctive red stripe on its body. Bites cause increasing pain at the site followed by profuse sweating and generalised symptoms. First aid includes application of ice or cold packs to the bite and transfer to hospital. White-tailed (brown recluse) spider bites may cause an ulcer that is very difficult to heal. Clean the wound thoroughly and seek medical assistance.

Hospitals have antivenin on hand for all common snake and spider bites, but it helps to know which type you've been bitten by.

Other Hazards
BUSHFIRES

Bushfires are a regular occurrence in WA, so in hot, dry and windy weather, be extremely careful with any naked flame. Even cigarette butts thrown out of car windows can start fires. On a total-fire-ban day it's forbidden even to use a camping stove in the open.

Bushwalkers should seek local advice before setting out. When a total fire ban is in place, delay your trip until the weather improves. If you're out in the bush and you see smoke, even a long distance away, take heed – bushfires

GST REFUNDS

The goods and services tax (GST) is a flat 10% tax on all goods and services with the exception of basic food items (milk, bread, fruits and vegetables etc). By law the tax is included in the quoted or shelf price of goods, so all prices we list are GST inclusive.

If you purchase goods with a minimum value of $300 from any one supplier (on the same invoice) no more than 60 days before you leave Australia, you are entitled under the Tourist Refund Scheme (TRS) to a refund of any GST paid. The scheme only applies to goods you take with you as hand luggage or wear on the plane or ship when leaving. You can collect your refund at the airport up to 30 minutes before departure. At Perth Airport, the refund counter is just after passport control. Using a recently launched app speeds up the process. For more information, contact the Australian Customs Service.

move fast and change direction with the wind. Go to the nearest open space, downhill if possible. A forested ridge is the most dangerous place to be during a bushfire.

CRIME
Western Australia is a relatively safe place to visit, but you should still take reasonable precautions. Don't leave hotel rooms or cars unlocked, and don't leave valuables unattended and visible in cars.

In recent years there has been a spate of glassings (stabbings with broken glass) at Perth venues. If you see trouble brewing, it's best to walk away. Take due caution on the streets after dark, especially around hot spots such as Northbridge where many venues enforce lockouts after midnight – that is, if you're not inside the venue before a certain time, you will not be able to gain entry.

There have also been reports of drinks spiked with drugs in Perth pubs and clubs. Authorities advise women to refuse drinks offered by strangers in bars and to drink bottled alcohol rather than that in a glass.

DRIVING
Australian drivers are generally a courteous bunch, but rural 'petrolheads', inner-city speedsters and drink drivers can pose risks. Open-road dangers can include wildlife, such as kangaroos (mainly at dusk and dawn); fatigue, caused by travelling long distances without the necessary breaks; and excessive speed. Driving on dirt roads can also be tricky for the uninitiated.

OUTBACK TRAVEL
If you're keen to explore outback WA, it's important not to embark on your trip without careful planning and preparation. Travellers regularly encounter difficulties in the harsh outback conditions far from potential assistance, and trips occasionally prove fatal.

A BIT OF PERSPECTIVE
Despite the recent increase in fatal shark attacks in WA, statistically it's still very unlikely that visitors will be attacked. Blue-ringed octopus deaths are even rarer – only two in the last century – and there's only ever been one confirmed death from a cone shell. Jellyfish kill about two people annually, but you're still 100 times more likely to drown.

On land, snakes kill one or two people per year (about the same as bee stings, or less than one-thousandth of those killed on the roads). There hasn't been a recorded death from a tick bite for over 50 years, nor from spider bites in the last 20.

SWIMMING
Popular beaches are patrolled by surf life-savers and flags mark out patrolled areas. Even so, WA's surf beaches can be dangerous places to swim in if you aren't used to the often heavy surf. Undertows (or 'rips') are the main problem. If you find yourself being carried out by a rip, just keep afloat; don't panic or try to swim against the rip, which will exhaust you. In most cases the current will stop within a couple of hundred metres of the shore and you can then swim parallel to the shore for a short way to get out of the rip and swim back to land.

On the south coast, freak 'king waves' from the Southern Ocean can sometimes break on the shore with little or no warning, dragging people out to sea. In populated areas there are warning signs; in other areas be extremely careful.

People have been paralysed by diving into waves in shallow water and hitting a sandbar; check the depth of the water before you leap.

Telephone
➤ The two main telecommunications companies are Telstra (www.telstra.com.au) and Optus (www.optus.com.au).

➤ Mobile (cell) services are provided by Telstra, Optus, Vodafone (www.vodafone.com.au) and Virgin (www.virginmobile.com.au).

➤ Local calls from private land lines cost 15¢ to 30¢, while local calls from public phones cost 50¢; both allow for unlimited talk time. Calls to mobile phones attract higher rates and are timed.

➤ All of WA shares a single area code (08), but once you call outside the immediate area, it may be classed as a long-distance call.

➤ PIN-protected phonecards can be used with any public or private phone. Some public phones also accept credit cards.

Mobile Phones
➤ Australia's mobile networks service more than 90% of the population but leave vast tracts of the country uncovered, including much of inland WA.

➤ Perth and larger centres get good reception, but service in other areas can be haphazard or non-existent.

➤ Telstra has the best coverage, especially in the more remote north, but if you're sticking to the southwest and northern tourist areas, coverage is largely similar, so shop around for a good deal from the four mobile operators.

➤ Australia's mobile network is compatible with most European phones, but generally not with the US or Japanese systems. The main service providers offer prepaid SIMs.

Phone Codes

☑**0011** International calling prefix (the equivalent of 00 in most other countries).

☑**61** Country code for Australia.

☑**08** Area code for all of WA. If calling from overseas, drop the initial zero.

☑**04** All numbers starting with 04 (such as 0410, 0412) are mobile phone numbers. If calling from overseas, drop the initial zero.

☑**190** Usually recorded information calls, charged at anything from 35¢ to $5 or more per minute (more from mobiles and public phones).

☑**1800** Toll-free numbers; can be called free of charge from anywhere in the country, though they may not be accessible from certain areas or from mobile phones.

☑**1800-REVERSE (738 3773) or** ☑**12 550** Dial to make a reverse-charge (collect) call from any public or private phone.

☑**13 or 1300** Charged at the rate of a local call. The numbers can usually be dialled Australia-wide, but may be applicable only to a specific state or STD district.

Note: Telephone numbers beginning with ☑1800, ☑13 or ☑1300 cannot be dialled from outside Australia.

Tourist Information

For general statewide information, try the **WA Visitor Centre in Perth** (Map p58; ☑1800 812 808, 08-9483 1111; www.bestofwa. com.au; 55 William St; ◷9am-5.30pm Mon-Fri, 9.30am-4.30pm Sat, 11am-4.30pm Sun). Tourism Western Australia (www.westernaustralia.com) or the Department of Parks & Wildlife (https://parks.dpaw. wa.gov.au).

Around WA, tourist offices with friendly staff (often volunteers) provide local knowledge, including info on road conditions.

Travellers with Disabilities

Disability awareness in WA is excellent. Legislation requires that new accommodation meet accessibility standards, and discrimination by tourism operators is illegal. Many of the state's key attractions provide access for those with limited mobility and an increasing number are addressing the needs of visitors with visual or aural impairments. Contact attractions in advance to confirm the facilities.

Useful resources:

Lonely Planet Download the free Accessible Travel guide from http://lptravel.to/AccessibleTravel.

National Information Communication & Awareness Network (Nican; ☑1300 655 535, 02 6241 1220; www.nican.com. au) Australia-wide directory providing information on access, accommodation, sports and recreational activities, transport and specialist tour operators

National Public Toilet Map (www.toiletmap.gov.au) Lists more than 14,000 public toilets around Australia, including those with wheelchair access.

People with Disabilities WA (www.pwdwa.org) Website detailing WA's major disability service providers.

Tourism WA (www.westernaustralia.com) Website highlighting all accessible listings (accommodation, restaurants, tours etc).

VisAbility (☑08-9311 8202, 1800 847 466; www.visability. com.au) Support for people living with blindness and vision impairment.

WA Deaf Society (☑08-9441 2677, TTY 08-9441 2655; www. wadeaf.org.au)

Visas

All visitors to Australia need a visa – only New Zealand nationals are exempt, and even they receive a 'special category' visa on arrival. Visa application forms are available from Australian diplomatic missions overseas, travel agents or the website of the Department of Immigration and Border Protection (www. border.gov.au). All visitors require a visa, although New Zealanders receive one on arrival. Residents of Canada, the US, many European countries and some Asian countries can apply online.

eVisitor

Many European passport holders are eligible for an eVisitor visa, which is free and allows visitors to stay in Australia for up to three months. eVisitors must be applied for online and they are electronically stored and linked to individual passport numbers, so no stamp in your passport is required. It's advisable to apply at least 14 days prior to the proposed date of travel to Australia. Applications are made on the Department of Immigration and Border Protection website (www.border.gov.au).

Electronic Travel Authority (ETA)

Passport holders from eight countries that aren't part of the eVisitor scheme – Brunei, Canada, Hong Kong, Japan, Malaysia, Singapore, South Korea and the USA – can apply for either a visitor or business ETA. ETAs are valid for 12 months, and allow stays of up to three months on each visit. Apply online at www.border.gov.au.

Tourist Visas

Short-term tourist visas have largely been replaced by the eVisitor and ETA. However, if you are from a country not covered by either, or you want to stay longer than three months, you'll need to apply for a visa. Tourist visas cost from $135 and allow single or multiple entry for stays of three, six or 12 months and are valid for use within 12 months of issue.

Visa Extensions

If you want to stay in Australia for longer than your visa al-

RESPONSIBLE INDIGENOUS TRAVEL

There are a range of protocols for visiting Indigenous lands, but it's always courteous to make contact prior to your visit. In many cases you must acquire a **permit** (DAA; ☑1300 651 077; www.daa.wa.gov.au; 151 Royal St, East Perth) to enter, so check with local Indigenous Land Councils and police stations before visiting.

Some Indigenous sites are registered under heritage legislation and have conditions attached, or may only be visited with permission from their traditional custodians or in their company. Don't touch artworks, as the skin's natural oils can cause deterioration. Dust also causes problems – move thoughtfully at rock-art sites and leave your vehicle some distance away. Respect the wishes of Indigenous custodians by reading signs carefully, keeping to dedicated camping areas and staying on marked tracks. Remember that rock art and engravings are manifestations of sacred beliefs and laws.

When interacting with Indigenous Australians, you'll generally find them polite and willing to share their culture with you – but it must be on their terms. Show respect for privacy and remember that your time constraints and priorities may not always be shared. In some areas, English is not a first language, but in others many people speak English fluently. Body language and etiquette often vary: the terms 'thank you', or 'hello' and 'goodbye', may not be used in some areas, or direct eye contact may be avoided. So take note of local practices: take them as they come and follow the cues. Some Aboriginal communities are 'dry'. There may be rules relating to the purchase and consumption of alcohol, or it may be forbidden altogether.

---

lows, you'll need to apply for a new visa (usually a tourist visa 676) through the Department of Immigration and Border Protection at www. border.gov.au. Apply at least two or three weeks before your visa expires.

Work & Holiday Visas (462)

Nationals from 16 countries including Argentina, Chile, China, Indonesia, Malaysia, Poland, Slovenia, Spain, Thailand, Turkey, Uruguay and the USA between the ages of 18 and 30 can apply for a work and holiday visa prior to entry to Australia. It allows the holder to enter Australia within three months of issue, stay for up to 12 months, leave and re-enter Australia any number of times within that 12 months, undertake temporary employment to supplement a trip, and study for up to four months.

Working Holiday Maker (WHM) Visas (417)

Young visitors (those aged 18 to 30) from Belgium, Canada, Cyprus, Denmark, Estonia, Finland, France,

Germany, Hong Kong, Ireland, Italy, Japan, Korea, Malta, the Netherlands, Norway, Sweden, Taiwan and the UK are eligible for a WHM visa, allowing visits of up to one year for casual employment.

The emphasis of this visa is on casual and not full-time employment, so you're only supposed to work for any one employer for a maximum of six months. A first WHM visa must be obtained prior to entry to Australia and can be applied for at Australian diplomatic missions abroad or online (www.border.gov. au). You can't change to a WHM visa once you're in Australia, so apply up to 12 months before your departure to Australia.

Volunteering

Lonely Planet's *Volunteer: A Traveller's Guide to Making a Difference Around the World* provides useful information about volunteering.

Online resources:

Go Volunteer (www.govolunteer. com.au) National website listing volunteer opportunities.

i-to-i (www.i-to-i.com) Conservation-based volunteer holidays in Australia.

Responsible Travel (www. responsibletravel.com) Volunteer travel opportunities.

Transitions Abroad (www. transitionsabroad.com) Listings of volunteer opportunities.

Volunteering Australia (www. volunteeringaustralia.org) Support, advice and volunteer training.

Useful organisations:

Conservation Volunteers Australia (CVA; ☑1800 032 501, 03-5330 2600; www. conservationvolunteers.com. au) A nonprofit organisation focusing on practical conservation projects such as tree planting, walking-track construction, and flora and fauna surveys. Most projects are either for a weekend or a week, and all food, transport and accommodation is supplied in return for a contribution to help cover costs.

Department of Parks & Wildlife (https://dpaw.wa.gov.au) Current and future opportunities at national parks all over WA. Online, click on the Get Involved tab and then Volunteering Opportunities. Opportunities vary enormously, from turtle tagging at Ningaloo Marine Park to feral-animal control at Shark Bay. Working with the dolphins at Monkey Mia is a popular option (contact: monkeymiavolunteers@westnet. com.au). Those concerned with the welfare of dolphins should be aware that swimming with dolphins in the wild is considered by some to be disruptive to the habitat and behaviour of the animals.

Willing Workers on Organic Farms (www.wwoof.com.au) WWOOFing is where you do a few hours of work each day on a farm in return for bed and board. Most hosts are concerned to some extent with alternative lifestyles, and have a minimum stay of two nights. Join online for $70. You'll get a membership number and a booklet listing participating enterprises ($5 overseas postage).

Earthwatch Institute (✆03-9016 7590; www.earthwatch. org) Offers volunteer 'expeditions' focusing on conservation and wildlife.

STA (www.statravel.com.au) Volunteer holiday opportunities in Australia – click on 'Planning' on their website then the volunteering link.

Women Travellers

WA is generally a safe place for women travellers, although the usual sensible precautions apply. Avoid walking alone late at night in major cities and towns, and always keep enough money aside for a taxi home. The same applies to outback and rural towns with unlit, semi-deserted streets between you and your temporary home. Lone women should be wary of staying in basic pub accommodation unless it appears safe and well managed.

Lone hitching is risky for everyone, but women especially should consider taking a male companion.

Work

If you come to Australia on a tourist visa then you're not allowed to work for pay – working for approved volunteer organisations in exchange for board is OK. If you're caught breaching your visa conditions, you can be expelled from the country and banned for up to three years. Those travellers who wish to work while in the country should investigate the Work & Holiday (p269) and Working Holiday Maker (p269) visas.

Seasonal Work

WA is experiencing a labour shortage and a wealth of opportunities exist for travellers (both Australian and foreign) for paid work year-round.

In Perth, plenty of temporary work is available in tourism and hospitality, administration, IT, nursing, childcare, factories and labouring. Outside Perth, travellers can easily get jobs in tourism and hospitality, plus a variety of seasonal work. Some places have specialised needs; in Broome, for example, there is lucrative work in pearling, on farms and boats.

INDUSTRY	TIME	REGION
grapes	Feb-Mar	Denmark, Margaret River, Mt Barker, Manjimup
apples/pears	Feb-Apr	Donnybrook, Manjimup
prawn trawlers	Mar-Jun	Carnarvon
bananas	Apr-Dec	Kununurra
bananas	year-round	Carnarvon
veggies	May-Nov	Kununurra, Carnarvon
tourism	May-Dec	Kununurra
flowers	Sep-Nov	Midlands
lobsters	Nov-May	Esperance

Information

Backpacker accommodation, magazines and newspapers are good resources for local work opportunities.

Useful websites:

Australian Jobsearch (www. jobsearch.gov.au) Government site offering a job database.

Career One (www.careerone. com.au) General employment site; good for metropolitan areas.

Department of Human Services (www.humanservices.gov. au) The Australian government employment service has information and advice on looking for work, training and assistance.

Gumtree (www.gumtree.com. au) Great classified site with jobs, accommodation and items for sale.

Harvest Trail (https://jobsearch. gov.au/harvest) Specialised recruitment search for the agricultural industry, including a 'crop list' detailing what you can pick and pack, when and where.

Jobfinder (www.jobfinder.com. au) Online job listings.

Job Shop (www.thejobshop. com.au) WA-based recruitment agency specialising in jobs for WA as well as the Northern Territory.

Adzuna (www.adzuna.com.au) Website for general employment; good for metropolitan areas.

Seek (www.seek.com.au) General employment site, good for metropolitan areas.

Travellers at Work (www.taw. com.au) Excellent site for working travellers in Australia.

Transport

GETTING THERE & AWAY

Unless you're coming by land from other states in Australia, chances are you'll be touching down in Perth. And, as you'll be told at some point no doubt, the capital of Western Australia (WA) is actually closer to Jakarta than Sydney.

Flights, tours and rail tickets can be booked online at www.lonelyplanet.com/bookings.

Entering the Country

Global instability has resulted in increased security in Australian airports, in both domestic and international terminals. Customs procedures may be a little more time-consuming but are still straightforward.

Air

Perth Airport (☑08-9478 8888; www.perthairport.com. au) The Connect Shuttle runs every 50 minutes to five convenient and central locations in Perth ($15). A taxi is about $40 to $45 to central Perth and $60 to $70 to Fremantle. Buses run every 10 to 30 minutes to the city, hourly after 7pm; journey time is 44 minutes.

If you're coming to Australia from Europe, Asia or Africa you'll find it quicker to fly directly to Perth Airport, rather than via the east coast cities. If you do fly to the east coast first, there are frequent connecting flights to Perth from major cities. Port Hedland and Broome both welcome interstate flights, and there are weekend flights between Port Hedland and Bali.

Airlines Flying to/from WA

Air Asia (D7;☑1300 760 330; www.airasia.com) Budget flights from Kuala Lumpur and Denpasar (Bali).

Air Mauritius (MK;☑1800 247 628; www.airmauritius. com) Flies from Mauritius.

Air New Zealand (NZ;☑13 24 76; www.airnewzealand.com. au) Flies from Auckland year round and from Christchurch from December to April.

Cathay Pacific (CX;☑13 17 47; www.cathaypacific.com) Flies from Hong Kong.

China Southern Airlines (CZ;☑1300 889 628; www.csair.com/en) To/from Guangzhou.

Emirates (EK;☑1300 303 777; www.emirates.com) Flies from Dubai.

Etihad (EY;☑1300 532 215; www.etihad.com) Flights from Abu Dhabi.

CLIMATE CHANGE & TRAVEL

Every form of transport that relies on carbon-based fuel generates CO_2, the main cause of human-induced climate change. Modern travel is dependent on aeroplanes, which might use less fuel per kilometre per person than most cars but travel much greater distances. The altitude at which aircraft emit gases (including CO_2) and particles also contributes to their climate change impact. Many websites offer 'carbon calculators' that allow people to estimate the carbon emissions generated by their journey and, for those who wish to do so, to offset the impact of the greenhouse gases emitted with contributions to portfolios of climate-friendly initiatives throughout the world. Lonely Planet offsets the carbon footprint of all staff and author travel.

Garuda Indonesia (GA; ☑08-9214 5101; www.garu-da-indonesia.com) Flies from Denpasar and Jakarta.

Jetstar (JQ; ☑13 15 38; www.jetstar.com) Runs cheapies from Sydney, Melbourne, Cairns, Adelaide and the Gold Coast. International routes include Singapore and Denpasar.

Malaysia Airlines (MH; ☑13 26 27, 08-9263 7043; www.malaysiaairlines.com) Flies from Kuala Lumpur.

Qantas (QF; ☑13 13 13; www.qantas.com.au) In-state flights from Perth to Kalgoorlie, Exmouth, Karratha, Paraburdoo, Newman, Port Hedland and Broome. Interstate flights from Darwin, Cairns, Sydney, Melbourne, Brisbane, Adelaide, Alice Springs and Canberra, and internationally to Auckland.

Singapore Airlines (SQ; ☑13 10 11; www.singaporeair.com.au) Flies from Singapore.

Thai Airways International (TG; ☑1300 651 960; www.thaiairways.com) Flies from Bangkok.

Virgin Australia (VA; ☑13 67 89; www.virginaustralia.com) Links Perth to Geraldton, Port Hedland, Broome, Karratha and Kalgoorlie. Interstate flights link Perth to Sydney, Melbourne, Darwin, Adelaide and Brisbane.

Land

The nearest state capital to Perth is Adelaide, 2560km away by the shortest road route. To Melbourne it's at least 3280km, Darwin is around 4040km and Sydney is 3940km. Despite the vast distances, sealed roads cross the Nullarbor Plain from the eastern states to Perth, and then up the Indian Ocean coast and through the Kimberley to Darwin.

Bus

The only interstate bus is the daily **Greyhound** (☑1300 473 946; www.greyhound.com.au) service between Darwin and Broome (from $263, 26

hours), via Kununurra, Fitzroy Crossing and Derby.

Car, Motorcycle & Bicycle

Driving to Perth from any other state is a *very* long journey, but it's a great way to see the country. Be aware that there are strict quarantine restrictions on fruit and vegetables when crossing the border into WA.

People looking for travelling companions for driving to WA from Sydney, Melbourne, Adelaide or Darwin frequently leave notices in backpacker hostels, or you can look for car-sharing options online:

➡ www.coseats.com

➡ www.gumtree.com.au

➡ www.shareyourride.net/carpool/Australia

Hitching

Hitching is never entirely safe – we don't recommend it. Hitching to or from WA across the Nullarbor is definitely not advisable, as waits of several days are not uncommon.

Train

The only interstate rail link is the famous *Indian Pacific*, run by **Great Southern Rail** (☑1800 703 357; www.greatsouthernrail.com.au), which travels 4352km to Perth from Kalgoorlie (10 hours), Adelaide (two days), Broken Hill (2¼ days) and Sydney (three days). From Port Augusta to Kalgoorlie the seemingly endless crossing of the virtually uninhabited centre takes well over 24 hours, including the 'long straight' on the Nullarbor – at 478km this is the longest straight stretch of train line in the world. You can take 'whistle-stop' tours of some towns on the way.

Flexible one-way adult fares for the full journey start from $1669. Substantial discounts are available off the seat-only price for backpackers, students, children and pensioners, and

advance purchase at least six months before travel secures the best prices for sleeper cabins. Across December to January, cheaper low-season fares are often available.

Cars can be transported between Perth and Sydney, Melbourne and Adelaide – a good alternative to driving across the Nullarbor Plain in both directions. Note that service is usually around 25% cheaper *from* Perth, than *to* Perth.

Sea

The only way to reach WA by sea is on a scheduled cruise liner docking at Fremantle.

GETTING AROUND

Air

Airlines Flying Within WA

Airlines that offer internal WA flights include the following:

Airnorth (☑1800 627 474; www.airnorth.com.au)

Alliance Airlines (☑1300 780 970; www.allianceairlines.com.au)

Qantas (QF; ☑13 13 13; www.qantas.com.au)

Rex (ZL; ☑13 17 13; www.rex.com.au)

Skippers Aviation (☑1300 729 924; www.skippers.com.au)

Virgin Australia (VA; ☑13 67 89; www.virginaustralia.com)

Bicycle

Bicycle helmets are compulsory in WA, as are white front lights and red rear lights for riding at night.

If you're coming specifically to cycle, bring your own bike. Check with your airline for costs. Within WA you can load your bike onto a bus to skip the boring bits of the country. Book ahead so that you and your bike can travel on the same vehicle.

Suffering dehydration is a very real risk in WA and can be life-threatening. It can get very hot in summer, so take things slowly until you're used to the heat. A prudent plan is to start riding every day at sunrise, relax in the shade – bring your own shelter – during the heat of the day and then ride a few more hours in the afternoon. Always wear a hat and plenty of sunscreen, and drink *lots* of water.

Outback travel needs to be planned thoroughly, with the availability of drinking water the main concern. Those isolated water sources (bores, tanks, creeks) shown on your map may be dry or undrinkable, so you can't always depend on them. Also, don't count on getting water from private mine sites as many are closed to the public. Bring necessary spare parts and bike-repair knowledge. Check with locals (start at the visitor centres) if you're heading into remote areas, and always let someone know where you're headed before setting off.

Useful contacts for information on touring around WA, including suggested routes, road conditions and cycling maps:

Cycle Touring Association of WA (www.ctawa.asn.au)

Bicycle Transportation Alliance (☑0400 047 349; www.btawa.org.au)

Bus

WA's bus network could hardly be called comprehensive, but it offers access to substantially more destinations than the railways. All long-distance buses are modern and well-equipped, with air-con, toilets and films. Bus companies offering services within WA include the following:

Greyhound (☑1300 473 946; www.greyhound.com.au)

Integrity Coach Lines (☑1800 226 339; www.integritycoachlines.com.au)

South West Coach Lines (☑08-9261 7600; www.southwestcoachlines.com.au)

Transwa (☑1300 662 205; www.transwa.wa.gov.au).

Car & Motorcycle

Providing the freedom to explore off the beaten track, travelling with your own vehicle is the best transport option in WA. With several people travelling together, costs can be contained, and if you don't have major mechanical problems, there are many benefits.

The climate is good for motorcycles for much of the year, and many small trails into the bush lead to perfect camping spots. Bringing your own motorcycle into Australia requires valid registration in the country of origin and a Carnet de Passages en Douanes (CPD), allowing the holder to import their vehicle without paying customs duty or taxes. Apply to the motoring organisation/association in your home country. You'll also need a rider's licence and a helmet. A fuel range of 350km will cover fuel stops up the centre and on Hwy 1 around the continent. The long, open roads are really made for large-capacity machines above 750cc.

The **Royal Automobile Club of Western Australia** (RAC; ☑13 17 03; www.rac.com.au) has useful advice on state-wide motoring, including road safety, local regulations and buying/selling a car. It also offers car insurance to members, and membership can secure discounts on car rentals and motel accommodation.

Also popular are car-share sites, especially for securing a lift to Broome, Perth, Denmark and Darwin. See www.coseats.com, www.gumtree.com.au and www.shareyourride.net/carpool/Australia.

Driving Licences

You can use your home country's driving licence in WA for up to three months, as long as it carries your photo for identification and is in English. Alternatively, arrange an International Driving Permit (IDP) from your home country's automobile association and carry it along with your licence.

Fuel

Fuel (predominantly unleaded and diesel) is available from service stations. Liquefied petroleum gas (LPG) is not always stocked at more remote roadhouses – if your car runs on gas, it's safer to have dual fuel capacity.

Prices vary wildly in WA, even between stations in Perth. For up-to-date fuel prices, visit the government fuel-watch website (www.fuelwatch.wa.gov.au).

Distances between fill-ups can be vast in the outback, but there are only a handful of tracks where you'll require a long-range fuel tank or need to use jerry cans. However, if you are doing some back-road explorations, always calculate your fuel consumption, plan accordingly and carry a spare jerry can or two. Keep in mind that most small-town service stations are only open from 6am to 7pm and roadhouses aren't always open 24 hours. On main roads there'll be a small town or roadhouse roughly every 150km to 200km.

Always carry two spare tyres and at least 20L of water.

Hire

Competition between car-rental companies in Australia is fierce, so rates vary and special deals come and go. The main thing to remember when assessing your options is distance – if you want to travel widely, you need to weigh up the price difference between an unlimited-kilometres deal and one that offers a set number of kilometres free with a fee per kilometre over that set number.

Local firms are always cheaper than the big operators – sometimes half the price – but cheap car hire often comes with restrictions on how far you can take the vehicle away from the rental centre.

Some, but not all, car-rental companies offer one-way hires, so research this option before you arrive. It's worth investigating and combining with an internal flight if you're travelling to somewhere like Exmouth, Broome or Esperance. A significant premium is usually charged. There are sometimes good deals for taking a car or campervan from, say, Broome back to Perth, but you'll need to contact local rental companies closer to the time of rental.

You must be at least 21 years old to hire from most firms – if you're under 25, you may only be able to hire a small car or have to pay a surcharge. A credit card will be essential.

Renting a 4WD enables you to safely tackle routes off the beaten track and get out to more remote natural wonders. Note that many 'normal' rental cars aren't allowed off main roads, so always check insurance conditions carefully, especially the excess, as they can be onerous. Even for a 4WD, the insurance offered by most companies does not cover damage caused when travelling 'off-road', which basically means anything that is not a maintained bitumen or dirt road.

Avis (☎13 63 33; www.avis. com.au; 46 Hill St) Branches at the airport and in the CBD.

Bayswater Car Rental (☎08-9325 1000; www.

bayswatercarrental.com.au; 160 Adelaide Tce) Local company with four branches in Perth and Fremantle.

Britz Rentals (☎1800 331 454; www.britz.com.au) Hires fully equipped 4WDs fitted out as campervans, popular on the roads of northern WA. Britz has offices in all the state capitals, as well as Perth and Broome, so one-way rentals are possible.

Budget (☎1300 362 848; www.budget.com.au; 960 Hay St) Branches at the airport and CBD.

Campabout Oz (☎08-9301 2765; www.campaboutoz.com. au) Campervans, 4WDs and motorbikes.

Hertz (☎13 30 39; www.hertz. com.au) Branches in the CBD and at the airport.

Thrifty (☎1300 367 227; www.thrifty.com.au) Branches at the airport and in the CBD.

Insurance

In Australia, third-party personal-injury insurance is always included in the vehicle registration cost. This ensures that every registered vehicle carries at least minimum insurance. You'd be wise to extend that minimum to at least third-party property insurance as well – minor collisions with other vehicles can be surprisingly expensive.

If you're bringing your own car from within Australia, take out the most comprehensive roadside assistance plan you can. It's not a matter of if your car will break down, but when. Having the top cover will offset your recovery costs considerably.

For hire cars, establish exactly what your liability is in the event of an accident. Rather than risk paying out thousands of dollars if you do have an accident, you can take out your own comprehensive insurance on the car, or (the usual option) pay an additional daily amount to the rental company for an 'insurance excess reduction' policy. This brings

4WD DRIVING TIPS

We don't need to see more 4WDs on tow trucks; the victims of a dirt-road roll over, a poorly judged river crossing, or coming to grief when meeting the native fauna on the road. Here are some tips to help keep you from riding up front in a tow truck:

➡ Before heading off-road, check the road conditions at www.mainroads.wa.gov.au.

➡ Recheck road conditions at each visitor centre you come across – they can change quickly.

➡ Let people know where you're going, what route you're taking and how long you'll be gone.

➡ Don't drive at night: it's safer to stop in the mid-afternoon to avoid wildlife.

➡ Avoid sudden changes in direction – 4WDs have a much higher centre of gravity than cars.

➡ On sand tracks, reduce tyre pressure to 140kpa (20psi) and don't forget to re-inflate your tyres once you're back on the tarmac.

➡ When driving on corrugated tracks, note that while there is a 'sweet spot' speed where you feel the corrugations less, it's often too fast to negotiate a corner – and roll overs often happen because of this.

➡ When crossing rivers and creeks, always walk across first to check the depth – unless you're in saltwater crocodile territory, of course!

the amount of excess you must pay in the event of an accident down from between $2000 and $5000 to a few hundred dollars. However, check your travel insurance policy as well as any insurance you have through your credit card before forking out the cash to reduce your excess, as excess reduction may already be covered by a policy you already have. Alternatively, companies such as Tripcover and RAC offer excess-reduction policies that often cost much less than those offered by car-hire companies.

Be aware that if you're travelling on dirt roads, you may not be covered by insurance. Because of potential accidents with wildlife, some insurance policies may preclude driving after dusk. Also, most companies won't cover the cost of damage to glass (including the windscreen) or tyres. Always read the small print.

Purchase

If you're planning a stay of several months that involves lots of driving, buying a second-hand car will be much cheaper than renting. But remember that reliability is all-important. Breaking down in the outback is very inconvenient (and potentially dangerous) – the nearest mechanic can be a very expensive tow-truck ride away!

You'll probably get any car cheaper by buying privately through the newspaper (try Saturday's *West Australian*) rather than through a car dealer. Buying through a dealer can include a guarantee, but this is not much use if you're buying a car in Perth for a trip to Broome. Online, see www.carpoint.com.au and www.drive.com.au to buy a car.

There are local regulations to comply with when buying or selling a car. In WA a vehicle has to have a compulsory safety check and obtain a road-worthiness certificate (RWC) before it can be reg-

istered in the new owner's name – usually the seller will indicate whether the car already has a RWC. Stamp duty has to be paid when you buy a car; as this is based on the purchase price, it's not unknown for the buyer and the seller to agree privately to understate the price.

To avoid buying a lemon, you might consider forking out some extra money for a vehicle appraisal before purchase. The **RAC** (RAC; ☑13 17 03; www.rac.com.au) offers this kind of check in Perth and other large WA centres, and also offers extensive advice on buying and selling cars on its website.

The beginning of winter (June) is a good time to start looking for a used motorbike. Local newspapers and the bike-related press have classified advertisement sections.

Fremantle has a number of secondhand-car yards, including a cluster in North Fremantle on the Stirling Hwy, while in Perth there's the **Traveller's Auto Barn** (☑1800 674 374; www.travellers-autobarn.com.au; 16 Adrian St, Welshpool). See the website for directions from the city or the airport. It also hires out cars and campervans.

Road Conditions

WA is not criss-crossed by multi-lane highways; there's not enough traffic and the distances are too great to justify them. All the main routes are well surfaced and have two lanes, but not far off the beaten track you'll find yourself on unsealed roads. Anybody seeing the state in reasonable detail can expect some dirt-road travelling. A 2WD car can cope with the major ones, but for serious exploration, plan on a 4WD.

Driving on unsealed roads requires special care – a car will perform differently when braking and turning on dirt. Under no circumstances exceed 80km/h on dirt roads; if you go faster you won't have

enough time to respond to a sharp turn, stock on the road, or an unmarked gate or cattle grid. Take it easy and take time to see the sights.

It's important to note that when it rains, some roads flood. Flooding is a real problem up north because of cyclonic storms. Exercise extreme caution at wet times, especially at the frequent yellow 'Floodway' signs. If you come to a stretch of water and you're not sure of the depth or what could lie beneath it, pull up at the side of the road and walk through it (excluding known saltwater-crocodile areas, such as the Pentecost River crossing on the Gibb River Rd!). Even on major highways, if it has been raining, you can sometimes be driving through water 30cm or more deep for hundreds of metres at a time.

Mainroads (☑13 81 38; www.mainroads.wa.gov.au) provides statewide road-condition reports, updated daily (and more frequently if necessary).

Road Hazards

Travelling by car within WA means sometimes having to pass road trains. These articulated trucks and their loads (consisting of two or more trailers) can be up to 53.5m long, 2.5m wide and travel at around 100km/h. Overtaking them is tricky – once you commit to passing there's no going back. Exercise caution and pick your time, but don't get timid mid-manoeuvre. Also, remember that it is much harder for the truck driver to control their giant-sized vehicle than it is for you to control your car.

WA's enormous distances can lead to dangerous levels of driver fatigue. Stop and rest every two hours or so – do some exercise, change drivers or have a coffee. The major routes have rest areas and many roadhouses offer free coffee for drivers; ask the RAC for maps that indicate rest stops.

Cattle, emus and kangaroos are common hazards on country roads, and a collision is likely to kill the animal and cause serious damage to your vehicle. Kangaroos are most active around dawn and dusk, and they travel in groups. If possible, plan your travel to avoid these times of the day. If you see a roo hopping across the road in front of you, slow right down – its friends are probably just behind it.

It's important to keep a safe distance behind the vehicle in front, in case it hits an animal or has to slow down suddenly. If an animal runs out in front of you, brake if you can, but don't swerve unless it is safe to do so. You're likely to come out of a collision with an emu better than a collision with a tree or another vehicle.

Road Rules

Driving in WA holds few surprises, other than those that hop out in front of your vehicle. Cars are driven on the left-hand side of the road (as in the rest of Australia). An important road rule is 'give way to the right' – if an intersection is unmarked, you must give way to vehicles entering the intersection from your right.

The speed limit in urban areas is generally 60km/h, unless signposted otherwise. The state speed limit is 110km/h, applicable to all roads in non-built-up areas, unless otherwise indicated. The police have radar speed traps and speed cameras, often in carefully concealed locations.

Oncoming drivers who flash their lights at you may be giving you a warning of a speed camera ahead – or they may be telling you that your headlights are not on. It's polite to wave back if someone does this. Don't get caught flashing your lights yourself, as it's illegal.

Seat belts are compulsory, and not using them incurs a fine. Children must be strapped into an approved safety seat. Talking on a handheld mobile phone while driving is illegal.

Drink-driving is a serious problem in WA, especially in country areas, and random breath tests are used to reduce the road toll. If you're caught driving with a blood-alcohol level of more than 0.05%, expect a hefty fine, a court appearance and the loss of your licence.

Local Transport

Perth has an efficient, fully integrated public-transport system called **Transperth** (☑13 62 13; www.transperth. wa.gov.au) covering public buses, trains and ferries in a large area that reaches south to include Fremantle, Rockingham and Mandurah. Larger regional centres, including Bunbury, Busselton and Albany, have limited local bus services.

Taxis are available in most of the larger towns.

Tours

The **WA Visitor Centre** (Map p58; ☑1800 812 808, 08-9483 1111; www. bestofwa.com.au; 55 William St; ⊘9am-5.30pm Mon-Fri, 9.30am-4.30pm Sat, 11am-4.30pm Sun) in Perth has a wide selection of brochures and suggestions for tours all over the state. Prices given are rates per person in twin share; there's usually an extra supplement for single accommodation. Students and YHA members often get a discount.

The hop-on, hop-off bus options are a popular way for travellers to get around in a fun, relaxed atmosphere. Some adventure tours include serious 4WD safaris, taking travellers to places that they simply couldn't get to on their own without large amounts of expensive equipment.

AAT Kings Australian Tours (☑1300 228 456; www. aatkings.com.au) A long-established and professional outfit offering a wide range of fully escorted bus trips and 4WD adventures. Tours in WA range from a six-day Perth to Monkey Mia trip to an 11-day Untamed Kimberley adventure.

Adventure Tours (☑1300 654 604; www.adventuretours. com.au) WA trips up to 14 days, often with a focus on adventure and Indigenous culture. Accommodation may include hostels and camping, and tour options include Perth to Broome ($1795, 10 days).

Flying Sandgroper (☑0438 913 713; www.flyingsandgroper. com.au) From April to October, this company can get you out exploring the northwest, including Ningaloo and Karijini National Park. A no-frills two-day tour of Karijini is $385; six days exploring Karijini and Ningaloo is $1535.

Outback Spirit (☑1800 688 222; www.outbackspirittours. com.au) Luxury all-terrain explorations including a Western Wildflowers Discovery tour ($7395, 156 days) and Pilbara, Karijini and Ningaloo Reef ($6795, 10 days).

Red Earth Safaris (☑1800 827 879; www.redearthsafaris. com.au) Operates a six-day Perth to Exmouth minibus tour ($785) with a two-day return trip ($200). Also available is a five-day trip from Perth to Monkey Mia ($635).

Train

The state's internal rail network, operated by **Transwa** (☑1300 662 205; www. transwa.wa.gov.au), is limited to the *Prospector* (Perth to Kalgoorlie), the *AvonLink* (Perth to Northam) and the *Australind* (Perth to Bunbury). Transperth's local train network reaches as far south as Mandurah.

Behind the Scenes

SEND US YOUR FEEDBACK

We love to hear from travellers – your comments keep us on our toes and help make our books better. Our well-travelled team reads every word on what you loved or loathed about this book. Although we cannot reply individually to your submissions, we always guarantee that your feedback goes straight to the appropriate authors, in time for the next edition. Each person who sends us information is thanked in the next edition – the most useful submissions are rewarded with a selection of digital PDF chapters.

Visit **lonelyplanet.com/contact** to submit your updates and suggestions or to ask for help. Our award-winning website also features inspirational travel stories, news and discussions.

Note: We may edit, reproduce and incorporate your comments in Lonely Planet products such as guidebooks, websites and digital products, so let us know if you don't want your comments reproduced or your name acknowledged. For a copy of our privacy policy visit lonelyplanet.com/privacy.

WRITER THANKS

Brett Atkinson

Thanks to Tourism WA and visitor information centres and Parks and Wildlife offices throughout the state. Cheers to WA's talented craft brewers for refreshment on the road, and special thanks to Tasmin Waby at Lonely Planet for another opportunity to explore my spectacular neighbour. Thanks also to my fellow authors, Carolyn and Steve, and the industrious in-house editors and cartographers. Final thanks to Carol for helping me devour the excellent Hippocampus gin and Temper Temper chocolate when I got home.

Carolyn Bain

Covering such vast distances and calling to check on some astoundingly beautiful coastline was a joy – my thanks to Tasmin Waby for the commission, and to fellow WA scribes Brett Atkinson and Steve Waters for sharing info. In the west, sincere thanks to all those who guided me to find ancient rocks, manta rays, deserted beaches and breathtaking aerial panoramas, and to those who shared a beer, a chat, travel tips and recommendations.

Steve Waters

Thanks to Trace & Heath, Brodie, Abbie, Meika & Kaeghan for midnight arrivals, James, Toby, John, Sam, Lauren, Dana & the rest of MC for gorge love, Di for making us a cuppa during the grand final, Unruly Ted for getting that trivia question, Roz & Megan for caretaking and especially Hamish & Kaz for sharing all those sunsets and sunrises and drowning out the dust, heat and corrugations with grace, good humour and lashings of ginger Matsos.

ACKNOWLEDGEMENTS

Climate map data adapted from Peel MC, Finlayson BL & McMahon TA (2007) 'Updated World Map of the Köppen-Geiger Climate Classification', *Hydrology and Earth System Sciences*, 11, 163344.

Cover photograph: Cable Beach/Ulrich Hollmann/ Getty

THIS BOOK

This 9th edition of Lonely Planet's *West Coast Australia* guidebook was researched and written by Brett Atkinson, Carolyn Bain and Steve Waters. The previous edition was researched and written by Brett Atkinson, Kate Armstrong and Steve Waters. This guidebook was produced by the following:

Destination Editor
Tasmin Waby

Product Editors Will Allen, Shona Gray, Tracy Whitmey

Senior Cartographer
Julie Sheridan

Book Designer Lauren Egan

Assisting Editors Sarah Bailey, Michelle Bennett, Katie Connolly, Victoria Harrison,

Charlotte Orr, Saralinda Turner, Simon Williamson

Assisting Cartographers
Alison Lyall, Diana Von Holdt

Cover Researcher
Campbell McKenzie

Thanks to Sasha Drew, Richard Gill, Indra Kilfoyle, Anne Mason, Graham Newman, Helmut Novak, Wibowo Rusli, Ellie Simpson

Index

Map Legend

Sights

- Beach
- Bird Sanctuary
- Buddhist
- Castle/Palace
- Christian
- Confucian
- Hindu
- Islamic
- Jain
- Jewish
- Monument
- Museum/Gallery/Historic Building
- Ruin
- Shinto
- Sikh
- Taoist
- Winery/Vineyard
- Zoo/Wildlife Sanctuary
- Other Sight

Activities, Courses & Tours

- Bodysurfing
- Diving
- Canoeing/Kayaking
- Course/Tour
- Sento Hot Baths/Onsen
- Skiing
- Snorkelling
- Surfing
- Swimming/Pool
- Walking
- Windsurfing
- Other Activity

Sleeping

- Sleeping
- Camping

Eating

- Eating

Drinking & Nightlife

- Drinking & Nightlife
- Cafe

Entertainment

- Entertainment

Shopping

- Shopping

Information

- Bank
- Embassy/Consulate
- Hospital/Medical
- Internet
- Police
- Post Office
- Telephone
- Toilet
- Tourist Information
- Other Information

Geographic

- Beach
- Gate
- Hut/Shelter
- Lighthouse
- Lookout
- Mountain/Volcano
- Oasis
- Park
- Pass
- Picnic Area
- Waterfall

Population

- Capital (National)
- Capital (State/Province)
- City/Large Town
- Town/Village

Transport

- Airport
- Border crossing
- Bus
- Cable car/Funicular
- Cycling
- Ferry
- Metro station
- Monorail
- Parking
- Petrol station
- Subway station
- Taxi
- Train station/Railway
- Tram
- Underground station
- Other Transport

Note: Not all symbols displayed above appear on the maps in this book

Routes

- Tollway
- Freeway
- Primary
- Secondary
- Tertiary
- Lane
- Unsealed road
- Road under construction
- Plaza/Mall
- Steps
- Tunnel
- Pedestrian overpass
- Walking Tour
- Walking Tour detour
- Path/Walking Trail

Boundaries

- International
- State/Province
- Disputed
- Regional/Suburb
- Marine Park
- Cliff
- Wall

Hydrography

- River, Creek
- Intermittent River
- Canal
- Water
- Dry/Salt/Intermittent Lake
- Reef

Areas

- Airport/Runway
- Beach/Desert
- Cemetery (Christian)
- Cemetery (Other)
- Glacier
- Mudflat
- Park/Forest
- Sight (Building)
- Sportsground
- Swamp/Mangrove

OUR STORY

A beat-up old car, a few dollars in the pocket and a sense of adventure. In 1972 that's all Tony and Maureen Wheeler needed for the trip of a lifetime – across Europe and Asia overland to Australia. It took several months, and at the end – broke but inspired – they sat at their kitchen table writing and stapling together their first travel guide, *Across Asia on the Cheap*. Within a week they'd sold 1500 copies. Lonely Planet was born.

Today, Lonely Planet has offices in Franklin, London, Melbourne, Oakland, Dublin, Beijing and Delhi, with more than 600 staff and writers. We share Tony's belief that 'a great guidebook should do three things: inform, educate and amuse'.

OUR WRITERS

Brett Atkinson

Perth & Fremantle, Around Perth, Margaret River & the Southwest Coast, Southern WA For this edition, Brett uncovered new restaurants, bars and distilleries in Perth and Fremantle, and jumped from beach to forest and back to beach throughout Margaret River and the southwest. In Albany, a poignant highlight was the National Anzac Centre telling the story of brave WWI soldiers. Brett has contributed to Lonely Planet guidebooks spanning Europe, Africa, Asia, the United States and the Pacific, and covered over 60 countries as a food and travel writer. See www.brett-atkinson.net for his latest adventures. Brett also wrote the Plan Your Trip, Understand (other than History) and Survival Guide chapters.

Carolyn Bain

Monkey Mia & the Central West, Ningaloo Coast & the Pilbara A travel writer and editor for 16 years, Carolyn has lived, worked and studied in various corners of the globe, including London, Denmark, St Petersburg and Nantucket. She is regularly drawn north from her base in Melbourne, Australia to cover diverse destinations for Lonely Planet, from dusty outback Australia to luminous Greek islands, by way of Maine's lobster shacks and Slovenia's alpine lakes. The Nordic region stakes a large claim to her heart, with repeated visits to Iceland and Denmark for work and pleasure.

Carolyn writes about travel and food for a range of publishers; see carolynbain.com.au for more.

Steve Waters

Broome & the Kimberley Travel and adventure have always been Steve's life, he couldn't imagine a world without them. He's been using Lonely Planet guidebooks for over 30 years in places as diverse as Iran, Central Asia, Kamchatka, Tuva, the Himalaya, Canada, Patagonia, the Australian Outback, NE Asia, Myanmar and the Sahara. Little wonder then that he finally got a gig with the company he was supporting! He's contributed to Iran, Indonesia and the past 4 editions of Western Australia and come any September you're likely to find him in a remote gorge somewhere in the Kimberley.

Travel gives you a unique view of the world. Patience, acceptance, resourcefulness and flexibility are all lessons well learnt. Plans change, where some people see obstacles, others see possibilities. Go with an open mind. But go!

Contributing Writer

Michael Cathcart Michael teaches history at the Australian Centre, University of Melbourne. He is well known as a broadcaster on ABC Radio National and has presented history programs on ABC TV. Michael wrote the History chapter.

Published by Lonely Planet Global Limited
CRN 554153
9th edition – November 2017
ISBN 978 1 78657 238 7
© Lonely Planet 2017   Photographs © as indicated 2017
10 9 8 7 6 5 4 3 2 1
Printed in China

Although the authors and Lonely Planet have taken all reasonable care in preparing this book, we make no warranty about the accuracy or completeness of its content and, to the maximum extent permitted, disclaim all liability arising from its use.